China's Approach to Energy Security

Shaofeng Chen

China's Approach to Energy Security

An International Comparative Perspective

palgrave
macmillan

Shaofeng Chen
Peking University
Beijing, China

ISBN 978-981-99-3572-7 ISBN 978-981-99-3573-4 (eBook)
https://doi.org/10.1007/978-981-99-3573-4

This Palgrave Macmillan imprint is published by the registered company Springer Nature Singapore Pte Ltd.
The registered company address is: 152 Beach Road, #21-01/04 Gateway East, Singapore 189721, Singapore

To my mother Xiao Fudi, and my father Chen Shitang,
with forever love and gratitude.

Acknowledgments

I dedicate this book to the memory of my mother Fudi Xiao and my father Shitang Chen. Tons of gratitude are owed to them for their unconditional love, education, and support. It is their nurturing and education that furnish me with the spirit of braveness, persistence and hard work. It is their support and encouragement that helps me conquer various obstacles and challenges and prompt me to keep marching forward.

My profound gratitude first and foremost goes to four leading scholars I was fortunate to have as my supervisors—Prof. Kun-Chin Lin, Dr. Kripa Sridharan, Associate Professor Chen An, and Dr. Alan Chong Chia Siong. Not only have they carefully read through my whole work, but also provided me with various support. Their conscientious instructions and insightful suggestions undoubtedly have facilitated my research. It is their instructions, flexibility, and understanding that help me to improve myself in conducting research, and make this seemingly arduous enterprise a very pleasant journey.

My foremost intellectual debt is due to Prof. Wenxiu Liu, Prof. Yongnian Zheng, Prof. Zhengyi Wang and Prof. Xinning Song. Their instructions, like the pirate lamp in the sea, always tell me where I should go and provide me with courage. Their rich knowledge, keen eyesight, work efficiency, and friendship undoubtedly are the direction where I should make my efforts towards.

Hereupon I would like to acknowledge the help from those who generously facilitate my fieldwork. Without the help from them, I am sure the fieldwork would be much more difficult to be accomplished. Among the people I owe a great deal of gratitude to are: Pan Jiang, Nan Jiang, Congwen Qu, Kaiyun Zhang and Weizhen Ye (couple), Sixin Sheng, Wei Jia, Dawei Hu, Ye Tian, Jianjun Zhu, Yu Li and Bo Jiang (couple), Xinchun Wang, Zhongfu Chen, Pengfei Shi, Zhigang Wang, Yishan Xia, Chengtao Sun, Yibo Du, Qinghua Fang, Rongbin Han, Guanghui Zeng, Shengwei Huang, Prof. Youxing Lang, Dongsheng Li.

Likewise, heavy debts of gratitude have also been accumulated to many colleagues at Peking University and East Asian Institute, NUS.

I also appreciate my wife Fei Chen and my son Yange Chen, for the love, support, and happiness they have rendered to me. Both of them are my true blessings in my whole life.

Many people have helped me in many ways with this work. They offered advice, suggestions, and corrections. The views and opinions in this book are nevertheless of the author alone and the responsibility for any shortcomings and errors remains mine.

Introduction

What is China's perception of energy security? How has China dealt with energy security challenges? Why has China taken such an approach? And to what extent does China's approach differ from other countries'? These are the central questions that this book aims to examine.

Energy security, defined as "the availability of energy at all times in various forms, in sufficient quantities, and at affordable prices,"[1] matters not only because reliable access to affordable energy underpins the economic strength of a country, but also because disruptions of energy supplies and fluctuations of energy prices are likely to produce cascading effects on national security, public health and safety, and the ecologic system. Moreover, disruptions in any part of the world can have global consequences. As such, energy security is a high priority for almost every country in the world.

In the case of China, it has to struggle for a balance among three different goals of economic growth, energy security, and environmental protection. The three "Es" sometimes are incompatible with each other. First and foremost, reliable access to affordable energy underpins economic growth, which has constituted the backbone of China's rise

[1] United Nations Development Programme, *World Energy Assessment*, New York: UNDP, 2000. In fact, Scholars are at variance with the definition of energy security. Some advocate that energy security should take account of the demand-side impact on the environment.

and the legitimacy of the ruling party. Second, a reversal of the aggravating environmental pollution implies that China should pay attention not only to the quantity of energy supplies but also to the quality of energy resources, thus entailing a change in China's energy use pattern. Third, for most developing countries including China, environmental protection in most cases is in collision with economic growth. Within China debates arise concerning how to boost China's energy security, and "this debate pits the forces of energy nationalism against pragmatic internationalist voices over what path the country should follow to secure its energy future."[2] Holding different stakes, different ministries, provinces, industries, and enterprises all try to exercise their influence on the policy process. The government has to balance the interests of the energy industry and other industries, tackle market openness and domestic protection, integrate energy conservation and the Chinese residents' affordability, and so on. Therefore, the approach that China has applied to cope with energy insecurity provides a good window to see how the Chinese government delimits boundaries between state and market, what views it holds on to the outside world, what its calculations are, and how the national energy companies (NECs) interact with the government.

Other than the domestic ramifications, "the China factor" has often been put in the spotlight when it comes to issues pertaining to world energy. Currently, China is the world's biggest consumer of energy, iron & steel, and alumina. In 2021, China's total consumption of coal reached nearly 86 exajoules, accounting for 53.6% of the world's total coal consumption.[3] China's energy rise, manifested in its burgeoning demand for energy resources and unchecked environmental pollution, combined with the emergence of its state-owned energy companies as major competitive players in the international energy market, have created a defining impact, internally, on China's foreign policy, and externally, on global energy markets and regional energy geopolitics.[4] Daniel Yergin,

[2] Jean A. Garrison, *China and the Energy Equation in Asia*, Boulder & London: FirstForumPress, 2009, p. 141.

[3] BP, *Statistical Review of World Energy 2022.*

[4] Sascha Müller-Kraenner, "China's and India's Emerging Energy Foreign Policy", (Discussion Paper, Deutsches Institut für Entwicklungspolitik <German Development Institute>, Bonn 2008); Russell Hsiao, "Energy Security the Centerpiece of China's Foreign Policy," *China Brief*, Vol. 8, Iss. 16, Aug. 2008.

a highly respected authority on energy, has highlighted two big new challenges that the world energy system is facing today. Besides cyber-vulnerability, the other challenge pertains to surging energy demands in China, India, and other major emerging markets.[5] It is argued that in energy, China and the United States are now "increasingly joined at the hip, the new E-2 of global energy."[6] As the largest primary energy consumer, oil importer and the second largest oil consumer, China's new role in global energy markets has generated great anxiety, not only for China but also for the rest of the world.[7] How has China fed its appetite for energy resources? What implications will have from China's approach to energy security on the global energy market? Will China's thirst for oil and gas fuel its confrontation with other countries, particularly with those that have territorial disputes? Thus, the Chinese approach to energy security and its ramifications for the world deserves our in-depth studies.

Debates arise with regard to the approach that China has used to deal with energy security challenges. Some contend that China has taken a strategic approach (State-controlled approach, or SCA),[8] whereas their opponents claim that China has followed a market-dominated approach (MDA).[9] It is true that the Chinese petroleum sector has long been under state control, but simultaneously deregulation has been underway.[10] Thus far, more and more market ingredients have been ushered in. In light of the above criteria, the Chinese government seems to turn to both MDA

[5] Daniel Yergin, "New Challenges to Energy Security," *The Journal of the International Energy Agency*, Issue 3, Autumn 2012, p. 8.

[6] Mikkal E. Herberg, "China's Energy Rise: The U.S. and the New Geopolitics of Energy," Special Study, Pacific Council on International Policy, Los Angeles (Apr. 2010).

[7] Daniel Yergin, *The Quest: Energy, Security, and the Remaking of the Modern World* (New York: The Penguin Press, 2011), p. 192.

[8] See Philip Andrews-Speed, Xuanli Liao and Roland Dannreuther, *The Strategic Implications of China's Energy Needs*, London: International Institute for Strategic Studies, 2002.

[9] See Robert A Manning, *The Asian Energy Factor: Myths and Dilemma of Energy Security, and the Pacific Future*. New York: Palgrave, 2000.

[10] Deregulation is the process in which a government removes business barriers for purpose of enhancing market efficiency. Its rationale is that fewer regulations are conducive to improving competitiveness, and thus bring about higher productivity, higher efficiency and lower prices.

and SCA instruments in most energy policies.[11] Tracing Chinese oil policy reform, it is easy to find that the reform presents the attribute of "one step forward, two steps back."[12] As Downs argues, the strife between MDA and SCA features Chinese energy security rhetoric and practice.[13] Both the state and the market are brought into play, and a mix of both state intervention and market operation coexists in the Chinese petroleum sector. Hence, as argued in one of my papers, China has adopted a state-managed marketization approach (SMMA) to deal with its energy security challenges.[14]

This book intends to study how and why China employs a SMMA to cope with energy security, and what its implications are. It is argued that China's approach to energy security in terms of oil and natural gas has largely been dictated by the interplay between the government and the national oil corporations (NOCs), the pivotal policy-maker and the overriding policy enforcer, respectively. Specifically, an MDA or an SCA would be employed respectively when one side's role can be expected and accepted by the other; but if they have different role expectations, a competing paradigm approach would be the policy option.

Methodology

This study adopts case studies. Why case studies? As this study intends to account for the reasons why China takes SMMA to cope with oil security by focusing on the interplay between the central government and the NOCs, it involves the perceptions and considerations of these actors, whose examination apparently calls for detailed data and in-depth analysis.

[11] For instance, crude oil price has been integrated with global market, but refined oil price for a long time was under government control; Maintaining state-ownership, NOCs were allowed to float in foreign exchange markets; Despite some policy constraints, foreign investors have been better treated than Chinese private firms; Both economic and administrative instruments including trade bans have been employed to regulate oil and gas trade; and the Chinese government has engaged in both energy cooperative projects and competitions for oil and gas acquisitions.

[12] Robert A. Manning, 2000, ibid., p. 84.

[13] Erica S. Downs, *China's Energy Security*, PhD dissertation, Princeton University, Publication Number: AAT 3110228, 2004, p. 4.

[14] Shaofeng Chen, "State-Managed Marketization:The Role of the Chinese Statein the Petroleum Industry," *The Copenhagen Journal of Asian Studies*, Vol. 30, No. 2, 2012, pp. 29–60.

Case studies may not be so confident to construct an accurate theory, but they work well in "plausibility probe." "The rich details of case studies allow the analyst to look at more than linear correlations between variables across an entire population, and to look for more complex processes in particular contexts."[15] Second, economic concerns or sociopolitical/security concerns are fundamentally subjective. Such subjectivity can hardly be accurately measured by quantitative figures. Third, the number of cases that have involved the pair of actors and embodied their concerns is not so many, mainly because the energy security problem did not exist in China until 1993, and even after that problem occurred, it did not draw much attention from the central leadership. As a result, the state followed the conventional management way of the planned economy. Closer heed was paid to the problem roughly around the early new millennium. Due to the limited cases available, this study has to rely more on event data, which further entails the use of case studies. Finally, relying on case studies is also because it is quite hard to do systematic surveys in China.[16]

How to select cases? Since Chinese energy policies reside in both internal and external spheres, this study is conducted at two levels—internal and external. Accordingly, I select three domestic-oriented cases, namely, the failure of creating a Ministry of Energy, China's oil policies—China's oil pricing reform and the West-East Gas Pipeline project (WEGP), and three external-oriented cases concerning China's oil diplomacy—China–Japan tussle over a Russian oil pipeline, Sino-Kazakhstan oil pipeline, and CNOOC acquisition battle over Unocal.

Why choose these cases? Cases are selected according to the variation of independent variables of this study,[17] i.e., the central government's role

[15] Christopher H. Achen and Duncan Snidal, "Rational Deterrence Theory and Comparative Case Studies," *World Politics*, Vol. 41, No. 2, Jan. 1989, p. 160.

[16] The difficulties derive from two facts: one is that most policy makings remain the elites' privileged business, and most civilians are excluded from this process (Sometimes some ministries may hold public hearings, but officials may still disregard the opinions voiced). The Chinese high-ranking officials are rather sensitive about surveys, especially those issues related with national security, for fear that they might tread on the bomb zone of "leaking state secret" (*xieluo guojia jimi*) and thus affect their official careers. Therefore, decision-making process remains a black box, and it is very hard to approach the high-ranking officials.

[17] Geddes has discussed the adverse effects of selecting cases on the dependent variable. According to him, studies of cases selected on the dependent variable are useful to "identify plausible causal variables". See Barbara Geddes, *Paradigms and Sand Castles:*

propensity based on its priority of concern about the oil and gas sector: economic efficiency promoter and internal stabilizer, and the NOCs' role propensity: market actor or SPSOU. First, the cases selected are projects/policies after 1993 since China has become a net oil importer, which is the direct and overarching factor leading to the so-called oil security problem. Second, cases last long enough, allowing the independent variables to have undergone certain variations, which lead to distinct dependent variables (MDA, SCA, or state-market condominium). Third, previous literature has set out some factors that influence China's approach to oil security, such as Chinese historical baggage, learning effect, technology level, etc., most of which have relatively kept stable despite some small changes; whereas the major independent variables vary in these cases.

Specifically, I select the case of the Chinese oil pricing reform not only because the price is the soul of the modern economy, affecting all parties concerned, but because both the government and the NOCs have policy propensities driven by different considerations. Choosing the case of failing to establish a Ministry of Energy contributes to understanding the internal tussles among the bureaucratic organizations. The WEGP case is chosen because the Chinese government was involved in this project to a different degree in different stages. This project also exhibited the NOC's strategies to convince the government. The cases of Sino-Japan competition over the Russian oil pipeline and the Sino-Kazakhstan oil pipeline are selected mainly because readers can see clearly how the Chinese government and the NOCs changed their concerns and strategies when facing different constraints from outside. Incorporating the case of CNOOC acquisition over Unocal is primarily because the government took different approaches from the above case. This case also can help us observe how China and its NOCs, strive hard to secure oil concessions overseas, how the Chinese government perceives the global oil market, and what constraints it faces.

Theory Building and Research Design in Comparative Politics, Ann Arbor: The University of Michigan Press, 2003, pp. 89–129.

Time Frame

This study focuses on the years from 1993 to 2022 because of the occurrence of the so-called oil security problem, but this problem has not drawn much attention from the central leadership until the end of the 1990s, when the trend of growing reliance on foreign oil imports became irreversible. The year 1998 became another time threshold in the sense that the industrial restructuring in that year shaped the basic market structure today. For the first time, China had taken the first step by linking domestic oil prices directly with international ones. Such an institutional change directly affects the NOCs' behaviors. In the previous time, most of the time the NOCs stayed in line with state directives despite they might also bargain with the government. Since 1998, they have been more profit-driven and as such, are more liable to running against government policies.

Data Collection

I collected data from both interviews and archives. Interviews were mainly conducted in Beijing, Daqing, Guangzhou, Shanghai, and Hangzhou respectively from November 2004 to March 2005, from November 2005 to February 2006, and June–August 2020. I conducted in-depth interviews with central officials and local provincial officials, oil companies' managers and employees, and scholars. All of my interviewees have either direct working experience or special knowledge pertaining to oil. Each interview lasted an average of one and a half hours, and some informants were interviewed more than once. If allowed, I recorded our conversations. In addition to interviews, I also collected a large number of archival data ranging from official statistics, laws, regulations, and other documents, yearbooks of the NOCs, book and journal articles, statistical data, news reports, and papers from some professional energy websites, and other news agencies. Data mainly focus on Chinese oil and gas, but they also encompass other countries' energy information.

Organization of the Book

The following Chapter 1 develops a theoretical framework for the book. Chapter 2 sets forth what energy security means for China in the views of the government and the NOCs, respectively. Energy security in China is first and foremost the problem of oil and gas supply security from the supply side. Chapters 3–7 aim to analyze how and why China has taken a state-managed marketization approach to deal with energy security. After introducing the major actors and their Janus-faced identities with regard to China's energy security, Chapter 3 sketches out the evolution of China's institutional reform and expounds on the effects of the Chinese institutional layout on its approach. Chapter 4 lays out the major internal-oriented energy policies and measures that China has taken to cope with energy security from both the supply and the demand sides, highlights China's biased preference for the supply-side policies of expanding oil and gas supplies, and lastly, analyzes why they present the SMMA characteristics. This chapter mainly focuses on the internal measures and places the external measures in Chapter 6.

Chapters 5–7 analyze how the major actors interact with each other through case studies. In Chapter 5, I use two domestic-oriented cases to see how the central government and the NOCs interact with each other. The case of the Chinese oil pricing reform also serves the purpose to see how China tries to improve oil security in terms of its oil pricing reform. Chapter 6 sets out how China has conducted oil diplomacy and what its motivations are, how the Chinese government and the NOCs take different considerations and strategies in the process of securing oil and gas abroad. Chapter 7 draws on three cases of the China–Russia oil pipeline, China–Kazahkstan oil pipeline, and the CNOOC acquisition of Unocal to illustrate why and how China uses an SMMA in the NOCs' foreign energy quest.

Chapter 8 has discussed to what extent China's SMMA is distinct from that of the US and India. It could be found that their differences are not that palpable. The following Chapter 9 sums up the effect of the role compatibility model on the SMMA, analyzes the major factors influencing the SMMA, and further elucidates the theoretical ramifications of the triangular relationship among the state, the NOCs, and the market in the globalization era. The Conclusion part concludes this book by making an overall analysis of why China adopts such a SMMA and what the specific mechanisms are.

Contents

Abbreviations

/b	per barrel
/cm	per cubic meter
/t	per ton
APM	Administered Pricing Mechanism
bbl/d	barrels per day
BBOE	Billion Barrels of Oil Equivalent
Bcm	Billion cubic meters
BPCL	Bharat Petroleum Corporation Limited, India
Bt	Billion tons
CBM	Coal Bed Methane
CCP/CPC	Chinese Communist Party/Communist Party of China
CEO	Chief Executive Officer
Chinaoil	China National United Oil Corporation
CIA	Central Intelligence Agency
CICC	China International Capital Corporation
CIM	Coal Industry Ministry, P.R. China
CNOOC	China National Offshore Corporation
CNPC	China National Petroleum Corporation
CPCIF	China Petroleum and Chemical Industry Federation
CSR	Corporate Social Responsibilities
DRCSC	Development Research Center of the State Council, P.R. China
E&P	Exploration and Production
EIA	Energy Information Administration, U.S.
EIM	Electricity Industry Ministry, P.R. China

ERI	Energy Research Institute, National Development and Reform Commission
FCIM	Fuel and Chemical Industry Ministry, P.R. China
FIM	Fuel Industry Ministry, P.R. China
FY	Financial Year
GAIL	Gas Authority of India Limited
GDP	Gross Domestic Product
GHG	Greenhouse Gas
GSPL	Gujarat State Petronet Limited
GW	Gigawatts
HPCL	Hindustan Petroleum Corporation Limited, India
INR	Indian Rupee
IOCs	International Oil Companies
IOCL	Indian Oil Corporation Limited
Kh	Kilowatt-hours
km	Kilometers
Kw	Kilowatts
LNG	Liquefied natural gas
LPG	Liquefied petroleum gas
Mb	Million barrels
Mcm	Million Cubic Meters
MEE	Ministry of Ecology and Environment, P.R. China
MEP	Ministry of Environmental Protection, P.R. China
MHURD	Ministry of House and Urban-Rural Development, P.R. China
MIIT	Ministry of Industry and Information Technology, P.R. China
MLR	Ministry of Land and Resources, P.R. China
MOA	Market-Oriented Approach
MOCs	Multinational Oil Corporations
MoE	Ministry of Energy
MoF	Ministry of Finance, P.R. China
MOFCOM	Ministry of Commerce, P.R. China
MoT	Ministry of Transport, P.R. China
MPNG	Ministry of Petroleum and Natural Gas, India
MST	Ministry of Science and Technology, P.R. China
Mt	Million tons
Mtce	Million tons of standard coal
MWR	Ministry of Water Resources, P.R. China
NBS	National Bureau of Statistics of China
NCCPC	National Congress of Communist Party of China
NDRC	National Development and Reform Commission, P.R. China

NEA	National Energy Administration, P.R. China
NEC	National Energy Committee, P.R. China
NELG	National Energy Leading Group, P.R. China
NOCs	National Oil Corporations
NORO	National Oil Reserve Office, P.R. China
NPC	National People's Congress, P.R. China
ODI	Outbound or Offshore Direct Investment
OIL	Oil India Limited
ONGC	Oil and Natural Gas Corporation, India
OPEC	Organization of Petroleum Exporting Countries
OVL	ONGC Videsh Ltd, India
PBOC	People's Bank of China
PCIM	Petroleum and Chemical Industry Ministry
PIM	Petroleum Industry Ministry
PipeChina	National Oil and Gas Pipeline Network Company
PLA	People's Liberation Army
PRC or P.R. China	People's Republic of China
PSU	Public Sector Undertakings
RGTIL	Reliance Gas Transportation Infrastructure Limited, India
RIL	Reliance Industries Ltd., India
RMB	Renminbi, China's Official Currency
SAFE	State Administration of Foreign Exchange, P.R. China
SASAC	State-owned Assets Supervision and Administration Commission of the State Council, P.R. China
SAWS	State Administration of Work Safety, P.R. China
SBPCI	State Bureau of Petroleum and Chemical Industries
SDA	State-Dominated Approach
SDPC	State Development and Planning Commission, P.R. China
SERC	State Electricity Regulatory Commission, P.R. China
SETC	State Economic and Trade Commission, P.R. China
SEPA	State Environmental Protection Administration, P.R. China
Sinochem	China National Chemicals Import and Export Corporation
Sinopec	China Petrochemical Corporation
SMMA	State-Managed Marketization Approach
SOE	State-Owned Enterprise
SCP	Standing Committee of the Politiburo
SPC	State Planning Commission, P.R. China
SPR	Strategic Petroleum Reserve
SPSOU	State Policy & Social Obligation Undertaker
Tce	Tons of standard coal equivalents
Tcm	Trillion cubic meters

Unipec	China International United Petroleum & Chemical Co., Ltd.
US	United States
WEGP	West-to-East Gas Pipeline project
WTO	World Trade Organization

List of Charts

List of Figures

List of Maps

List of Tables

CHAPTER 1

Debates on China's Approach and the Theoretical Framework

The chapter intends to review the preceding literature concerning China's approach to energy security, introduce the state-managed marketization approach (SMMA), the dependent variable of this book, and set out the theoretical framework to be used to comprehend how and why China has taken this approach to deal with its energy security challenges.

1.1 Debates on China's Approach

Scholars are divided concerning what approach China has taken to deal with energy security. Other than institutionalism and the perspective of hedging, studies on China's approach to energy security have three levels: state-, firm-, and system-level analyses.

1.1.1 State-Level Analysis

The state-level analysis has dominated the study of China's approach to energy security. It stresses that the state is the power center which is active and powerful enough in penetrating society despite some bifurcations: whether the state is a unit with one consolidated national interest (statism) or an entity composed of different parts, each of which holds disaggregated interests (elite theory and bureaucratic politics). Differences also exist with regard to which institution is closest to the power hub.

S. Chen, *China's Approach to Energy Security*,
https://doi.org/10.1007/978-981-99-3573-4_1

Statists hold that the state (represented by state institutions and political elites) per se not only has its own interest distinctive from various social interests but also enjoys certain autonomy.[1] While sublimating its own interest as national interest, the state makes every effort to fulfill it. Thus, state capacity, defined as the state's ability "to penetrate society, regulate social relationships, extract resources, and appropriate or use resources in determined ways,"[2] has become the catchword in statist literature. But later statist accounts acknowledge that the state can hardly distance itself from the society where it is embedded.[3] In the energy arena, the state also plays a dominant role in preserving and promoting energy security within one country. State intervention in enhancing energy security is not an issue of necessity, but a must in the intensely competitive global milieu.

From the viewpoint of China, three distinct views on its approach to oil security have been developed. The most prevalent views revolve around the dichotomized debate between a "strategic" (or "state-controlled") *vs* a "market" approach. As mentioned below, underlying a "strategic" approach is the belief that securing energy is a zero-sum game, so countries should use whatever means in order to acquire more energy resources. As a result, tussles for energy resources may even result in interstate confrontations. In the case of China, Speed et al. argue that the measures that China has taken were characteristic of "strategic" rather than a "market" approach to energy security. Chinese approach was intrinsically "strategic" owing to the following grounds: being desperate to secure oil concessions even irrespective of economic costs,[4] scrambling for

[1] According to Krasner, this approach is based on the assumption that "it is useful to conceive of a state as a set of roles and institutions having peculiar drives, compulsions and aims of their own that are separate and distinct from the interests of any particular societal group." See Stephen D. Krasner, *Defending the National Interest: Raw Materials Investments and U.S. Foreign Policy*, Princeton: Princeton University Press, 1978.

[2] Joel S. Migdal, *Strong Society and Weak State: State-Society Relations and State Capabilities in the Third World*, Princeton: Princeton University Press, 1988, p. 4.

[3] Stephen Bell, "Statist Analysis," in A. Parkin, J. Summers and D. Woodward (eds), *Government, Politics, Power and Policy in Australia*, Melbourne: Longman Cheshire, 1994.

[4] See Philip Andrews-Speed, Xuanli Liao and Roland Dannreuther, *The Strategic Implications of China's Energy Needs*, London: International Institute for Strategic Studies, 2002; Philip Andrews-Speed, "China's Energy Policy and its Contribution to International Stability. Facing China's Rise: Guidelines for an EU Paper," Chaillot Paper

energy resources in the disputed South and East China Sea, and defying the predominant role the United States plays in those energy producing regions and the transportation sea lanes, which would lead to regional or world instability.[5] More broadly, the Chinese government favors

> a hands-on approach to energy security, be it in form of strong government monopoly on indigenous production, on foreign investments and in enhancing relationships with producer countries. This is achieved through political and financial factors, diplomatic relations accompanied by the sale of goods and important investments.[6]

Ryan Opsal asserts that both China and the US have factored energy security into their grand strategies, but China resorts to "a centralized, state-driven, neo-mercantilist approach" while the US relies on "a decentralized, market-driven, neoliberal method."[7] From the perspective of overseas investment, Amineh and Yang contend that such activities by the Chinese NOCs are crucial to the country's energy supply security and part of China's "statist," state-led economic globalization.[8]

The "strategic" approach view falls into line with a much more prevalent thesis of "state capitalism," or what some called "authoritarian capitalism" in accounting for China's economic miracle. Central to "state

No. 94, December 2006; Gal Luft, "U.S., China Are on a Collision Course over Oil," *Los Angeles Times*, 2 February 2004; Gal Luft, "Fueling the Dragon: China's Race into the Oil Market," Institute for the Analysis of Global Security, available at: www.iags.org/china.htm, accessed 21 April 2023; and Peter Hatemi and Andrew Wedeman, "Oil and Conflict in Sino-American Relations," *China Security*, Vol. 3, No. 3, 2007, pp. 95–118.

[5] See Calder, 1998; Mamdouh Salameh, "China, Oil and the Risk of Regional Conflict," *Survival*, Vol. 37, No. 4, Winter 1995–1996, pp. 133–46; Thomas Kane and Lawrence Serewicz, "China's Hunger: The Consequences of Rising Demand for Food and Energy," *Parameters*, Vol. 31, Autumn 2001, pp. 63–75.

[6] François Godement, François Nicolas and Taizp Yakushiji, "An Overview of Options and Challenges," in Godement et al. (eds.), *Asia and Europe: Cooperating for Energy Security, A CAEC Task Force Report*, Paris: Institute Français des Relations Internationals, 2004, pp. 9–28; and Christian Constantin, "Understanding China's Energy Security," *World Political Science Review*, Vol. 3, No. 3, 2007, pp. 1–30.

[7] Ryan Opsal, *American and Chinese Energy Security: A Grand Strategic Approach*, Lexington Books, 2019.

[8] Mehdi P. Amineh and Guang Yang, "China's Geopolitical Economy of Energy Security: A Theoretical and Conceptual Exploration," *African and Asian Studies*, Vol. 17, No. 1–2, February 2018, pp. 9–39.

capitalism" are policies that champion state-owned enterprises (SOEs) and sovereign wealth funds, provide state funding to these clients to help them lock in long-term agreements and use the market to bolster the Chinese government's domestic political positions.[9] They contend that China's way of development, underscoring the overriding role of the state and being skeptical of free markets, was quite special when compared with the market-driven Western economic system. With the rise of China and the "shrinking of Western appeal as a politicoeconomic brand," state capitalism was undermining Western capitalism, resulting in the risk of "the end of the free market" (Bremmer 2010; Halper 2010).

In contrast to the strategic approach, proponents of a "market" approach have emphasized three points: first, it needs to bring market forces into full play in order to address energy security issues. In a free market, competition and transparency help to prevent disruption of oil supply. Second, thanks to interdependence between countries cooperation is entailed to maintain stability in the global oil market. Third, investment in new capacity contributes to expanding the world oil supply. In light of these points, they argue that China followed a market-dominated approach in that China was making efforts to engage in international energy trade, gradually relegate oil pricing power to the market, cooperate with other countries to tap the remote resources and enjoy the public goods of sea lane security provided by the US.[10] In particular, they rebut the assertion that Chinese NOCs' foreign energy quest would deprive other countries of sufficient energy supply and thus aggravate inter-state competition. Instead, China's investments in foreign countries, including in those "problem" states, are conducive to a better-supplied world oil market.[11]

The above-competing paradigms have contributed to our understanding of China's approach to energy security. Their opposite views and angles coincidentally illustrate the complexity of the Chinese economy

[9] Ian Bremmer, *The End of the Free Market: Who Wins the War Between States and Corporations*? New York and London: Penguin Group, 2010.

[10] See Robert A Manning, *The Asian Energy Factor: Myths and Dilemma of Energy Security, and the Pacific Future*, New York: Palgrave, 2000; Las Yergin et al., "Fueling Asia's Recovery," *Foreign Affairs*, March/April, March/April 1998.

[11] Mikkal E. Herberg, statement before the US–China Economic and Security Review Commission, hearing on 'China's Energy Consumption and Opportunities for US–China Cooperation to Address the Effects of China's Energy Use', 14–15 June 2007.

and society. Questionable in the two models, however, is their premise to build their arguments. According to the market-dominated approach, market forces seemed to prevail over state power in running the Chinese energy sector. To some extent this is true, but it may be too early to make such a judgment given that the Chinese state remains to leave a strong hand in this sector. On the contrary, the state-controlled approach presupposes the existence of a monolithic state with super strong capability, which can act at will in both decision-making and policy implementation. Conversely, other actors in the market are merely the puppets of the Chinese government. We doubt such preconditions.

Moreover, just like a group of blind men touching an elephant, their accounts are partial; as a result, they are liable to make either over-optimistic or over-pessimistic conclusions. For instance, Manning argues that energy could contribute to China's economic integration into the world, while Lee saw little possibility of bilateral or multilateral cooperation in the Asian-Pacific region.[12] It is true that the Chinese oil sector has long been under state control, but simultaneously deregulation has been underway.[13] Thus far, more and more market ingredients have been ushered in, particularly into the refinery and distribution chains. Hence, it is hard to conclude which view is correct, as both can find evidence to support their arguments. In light of the above criteria, the Chinese government turns to both MDA and SCA instruments in most energy policies.[14] Tracing Chinese oil policy reform, it is easy to find that the reform presents the attribute of "one step forward, two steps back."[15]

Downs suggests a middle way, holding that the Chinese approach to oil security encompasses the ingredients of both a market approach and

[12] Pak K. Lee, "China's Quest for Oil Security: Oil (Wars) in the Pipeline?" *The Pacific Review*, Vol. 18, No. 2, June 2005, pp. 265–301.

[13] Deregulation is the process in which a government removes business barriers for purpose of enhancing market efficiency. Its rationale is that "fewer regulations will lead to a raised level of competitiveness, therefore higher productivity, more efficiency and lower prices overall."

[14] For instance, crude oil price has been integrated with global market, but refined oil price is under government control; NOCs can be allowed to float in foreign exchange markets; Despite some policy constraints, foreign investors have been better treated than Chinese private firms; Both economic and administrative instruments including trade bans have been employed to regulate oil and gas trade; and the Chinese government has engaged in both energy cooperative projects and competitions for oil and gas acquisitions.

[15] Robert A Manning, 2000, ibid., p. 84.

a state-dominated one. As she argues, the strife between MDA and SCA features Chinese energy security rhetoric and practice.[16] Both the state and the market are brought into play, and a mix of both state regulation and market operations coexists in the Chinese oil sector. She has incisively observed that Chinese oil security rhetoric and practice feature with a struggle between economic liberalism and economic nationalism, and this struggle, in her view, was an option between a pair of dilemmas—the pursuit of self-sufficiency and participation in international trade.[17]

The above research takes a static view to examine China's conception of energy security. As such, it is too early to argue that market forces have gained an upper hand presently, or "strategic thinking" dominates the Chinese approach. Their accounts have oversimplified the evolution of China's energy policy and the underlying changes in the leadership's view on energy security. As Constantin maintains, "[f]ocusing on measures taken by China during the 1990s to draw inferences about the future fails to take into account the profound debate about future path for Chinese development."[18] In view of this, Constantin analyzes the sources of the Chinese government's view on energy security, the evolution of energy policies, and their international impacts, particularly the impacts of the "conservation-minded society"(*jieyue shehui*) and "scientific development concept" (*kexue fazhanguan*) initiated under the fourth generation of leaders. Contrary to Downs' view that Chinese conceptions of energy security are "state-centric, supply-side biased and overwhelmingly focused on oil,"[19] he suggests that a more comprehensive approach should be adopted to take account of all types of energy rather than merely oil when studying China's energy security, and that "supply is far from being the most important aspect of Beijing's energy policy."[20]

Statism can be applied to China as it conforms to the authoritarian nature of its political system. The influence of the one-party state indeed

[16] Erica S. Downs, *China's Energy Security*, PhD dissertation, Princeton University, Publication Number: AAT 3110228, 2004, p. 4.

[17] Erica S. Downs, 2004, ibid.

[18] Christian Constantin, "China's Conception of Energy Security: Sources and International Impacts," *Working Paper* of the Centre of International Relations, University of British Columbia, No. 43, March 2005, p. 6. Available at: http://www.iir.ubc.ca/Papers/Constantin-WP43.pdf, accessed 21 April 2023.

[19] Erica S. Downs, 2004, ibid., p. 6.

[20] Christian Constantin, March 2005, ibid.

can be said to have deeply penetrated society. As Lee argues, "Through its control over the economy, political propaganda and personnel management of cadres, the Leninist state has been able to deny much autonomy for civil society while maintaining its ability to respond to its own needs."[21] It is a convenient way for analysts to treat the Chinese state as a united entity as it can help comprehend the Chinese strategies and the subsequent effects without the need to go into the "black box." In particular, statism works well when it comes to studying China's foreign policy or strategy considering that the right to conduct diplomacy only resides in the central state and at most times the Chinese government tries to speak with one voice. Moreover, by reference to the statist approach, the important role that the Chinese state has played in trying to ensure oil security can be highlighted.

However, there are some problems with statism to account for China's approach to oil security. First of all, statism assumes that the state leadership and bureaucracies are a unity that pursues the alleged national interest. The problem is whose interest it is, and it is a question mark to presuppose that they are a unity. The life-and-death struggle among the CCP's top leaders and conflict among various social groups during the Cultural Revolution smashed the above ideas.[22] China's reform and opening up have further led to the division of interests among different provinces, economic sectors and social groups. Thus, policy-making often calls for bargaining, and sometimes serious conflicts may be overtly disclosed. Second, pertaining to the above, the NOCs in the previous accounts are often treated as merely the arms of state policy, without their own considerations. This cannot hold true even in a period of a highly planned economy.[23] When more market ingredients have been adopted by China, the identity of NOCs as well as their behaviors has changed a lot. Third, critics of the statist theory point out that state autonomy

[21] Hong Yung Lee, "Book Review: Political Reform in Post-Mao China: Democracy and Bureaucracy in a Leninist State," *The Journal of Asian Studies*, Vol. 53, No. 3, 1994.

[22] Kenneth Lieberthal and Michel Oksenberg, *Policy Making in China: Leaders, Structures, and Processes*, Princeton: Princeton University Press, 1988.

[23] Naughton has discussed how the government and Chinese enterprises conducted bargaining over a wide range of topics before and after reform. See Barry Naughton, "Hierarchy and the Bargaining Economy: Government and Enterprise in the Reform Process," in Kenneth Lieberthal and David Lampton (eds.), *Bureaucracy, Politics, and Decision Making in Post-Mao China*, Berkeley, Los Angeles and Oxford: University of California Press, 1992, pp. 245–279.

is not identical with state capacity.[24] Besides, apart from considering the nature of the state, the nature of society should also be examined when measuring state capacity, in view of the possible disjuncture between central policy-making and local policy implementation. Hence, without considering the institutional influence, it is hard to know why China raised the goal of constructing a "conservation-minded society," nor can we learn its possible effect on the transformation of China's approach to energy security. Finally, we cannot open the black box of policy-making by reference to statism. In particular, who are the major actors, and how do they interact with China's pursuit of energy security?

Unlike statism which postulates a unified state with the unitary national interest, the other state-centered theories turn their attention to certain groups. The elite theory was developed as a criticism against pluralism for its neglect of the reality that political power and access to policy processes are unevenly distributed even in democratic countries. Elite theory argued the fewer elite class rules the numerous non-elite class by performing all political functions, monopolizing power, and enjoying the advantages that arise from that power.[25] Thus, researchers should focus on those minority groups of political elites when studying a country's policy-making.

According to bureaucratic politics, official policy is viewed as the outcome of bargaining among competing administrative units rather than societal groups. There are two models developed to understand bureaucratic motives and actions. One is the "organizational process" model, which sets forth the impact of government agencies' behavioral patterns, entrenched cultures or organizational values on final decisions. The other is the "bureaucratic politics" model, which denies the existence of a unitary state interest. Rather, it asserts that each government agency has its own views and interests regarding a policy, and therefore it will try to persuade and win over the others. As Allison argues, the bureaucracy "is not one calculating decisionmaker but is rather a conglomerate of large organizations and political actors."[26]

[24] Susan Hayes Whiting, *The Micro-Foundations of Institutional Change in Reform China: Property Rights and Revenue Extraction in the Rural Industrial Sector*, dissertation for PhD degree in the University of Michigan, 1995, p. 5.

[25] Gaetano Mosca, *The Ruling Class*, translated by Hannah D. Kahn, edited by Arthur Livingston, New York: McGraw Hill, 1939, p. 50.

[26] Graham T. Allison, *Essence of Decision: Explaining the Cuban Missile Crisis*, Glenview (Illinois) and London (England): Scott, Foresman and Company, 1971, p. 3.

Combining the use of elite theory and bureaucratic politics, Lieberthal and Oksenberg systematically analyzed the energy policy-making process in China. Contrary to the traditional authoritarian image, they first found the fragmented structure of authority. Due to that kind of fragmentation, there is no cohesive and consistent national energy policy, and a subtle and complex consensus building both horizontally and vertically is often required in the policy process in China.[27] Therefore, the "fragmented authoritarianism" model has defied the statist assumptions that the state is a unitary entity, and highlighted the importance of Chinese political institutions in influencing economic policy process.

Countering against the "fragmented authoritarianism" model, Taylor Monique developed a "bureaucratic authoritarianism" model, arguing for China's state-led approach to energy security. The new model underscores the decisive role of bureaucratic officials in the petroleum sector, and China's state capacity in the strategic sectors, including oil, has been reinforced, rather than being undermined in recent years.[28]

Elite theory could help identify the key figures who facilitate energy policy formation, but the problems are: who comprises the elites regarding oil? And how does the power of those elites arise? The bureaucratic theory could identify the dynamics and inertia in the policy process, but sometimes it is difficult to distinguish the agency's interest and the personal interest of its leaders. Also, this theory seems to underestimate the personal role of political leaders and the impact of individual goals and ideas in the policy process.

1.1.2 Firm-Level Analysis

In their analyses of the competitiveness of Chinese NOCs vis-à-vis the MOCs, both Zhang and Mai found that the NOCs still have a long way to go to compete with the global oil firms. According to Zhang, the problem of where the headquarters are still exists despite the apparent

[27] Kenneth Lieberthal and Michel Oksenberg, *Bureaucratic Politics and Chinese Energy Development*, Washington, DC: U.S. Department of Commerce, International Trade Administration, 1986.

[28] Monique Taylor, *The Chinese State, Oil and Energy Security*, Basingstoke: Palgrave Macmillan, 2014; Monique Taylor, "Fuelling China's Rise: Building Oil State Capacity," *China: An International Journal*, Vol. 16, No, 1, February 2018.

progress that has been made.[29] Mai found that the Chinese NOCs are weaker than their multinational rivals, but they have current and potential competitive advantages such as monopoly status, cost advantage in labor, and so forth.[30]

Both insightfully perceive that the key to China's oil security is closely associated with the competence of the NOCs because they are the major agents and policy implementers. Although the competitiveness of the NOCs is an important variable for China's oil security, it does not mean that the stronger the NOCs are, the higher China's oil security. Hypothetically this stands true in the Chinese government's mind, but this thesis argues that it depends on how to define oil security and from whose perspective, and at most it is merely a necessary condition.

1.1.3 System-Level Analysis[31]

Both state- and firm-level analyses are fundamentally domestic-oriented, excluding foreign influences when analyzing the policy process. Yet in the globalization era, the state is not insulated from outside influences. Economically, every aspect of the economy, ranging from raw materials and labor to finance and distribution, is interdependent across the globe.[32] Politically, while the domestic situation within one state will affect the stability of the international system, the latter in turn has a substantial impact on that state. Gourevitch highlights the international impact on domestic structures and interest group preferences, such as specific decisions, regime type, and coalition patterns.[33] The two-level

[29] Jin Zhang, *Catch-up and Competitiveness in China*, London and New York: RoutledgeCurzon, 2004.

[30] Yinhua Mai, *Can the New Chinese Oil Giants Compete After China's WTO Entry?* Singapore: East Asia Institute (EAI), National University of Singapore, EAI Working Paper No. 74, 8 May 2001.

[31] Hereupon I use "system" to refer to all foreign influences, not necessarily to the international system.

[32] Martin Carnoy, et al., *The New World Economy in the Information Age: Reflections on Our Changing World*, Pennsylvania: The Pennsylvania State University Press, 1993.

[33] Peter Gourevitch, "The Second Image Reversed: The International Sources of Domestic Politics," *International Organization*, 1978, Vol. 32, No. 4, pp. 881–911.

game model developed by Putnam is a laudable effort to combine international factors and domestic political economy to spell out a country's policy outcome.[34]

Scholars making system-level analyses usually stand from the outsider's stance to look at China's approach to oil security, specifically to see the impact of China's pursuit of oil security on the world, with the US in particular. Dannreuther argues against the claim that China's painstaking efforts for oil and gas would exacerbate competition for energy supply, so as to lead to an arms race or confrontation.[35] Lee rightly observes that "China tends to view its oil security through the prism of American-Japanese containment of China." Based on realist logic, he averred that China's quest for oil security entangled relations with other countries, and rendered energy cooperation very remote, but the results China received were at best mixed.[36] Unlike Lee, Lieberthal and Herberg take a slightly different view and have perceived two possibilities of China's efforts with the US: cooperation or conflict, but they hold a more sanguine view about the future, coinciding with Constantin's prediction that "cooperation is the most likely path that will result from China's energy policy."[37]

The system-level analysis can help understand those international factors that affect domestic policy-making, as well as China's interaction with other nations. However, their analysis only took a uni-dimensional perspective except for Lee, but Lee considered the outside influence more from a power politics perspective, without allowing for interstate interdependence and the attributes of the global energy market. That is to say, most of them only set out China's influence on the world without considering the outside influence including globalization on China. As a result, they could hardly interpret how and why China's conceptions of oil security have arisen, and why China took a state-managed marketization approach. Also, the system-centered approach tends to neglect domestic variables. Therefore, it needs to combine with other approaches to analyze China's energy policy-making.

[34] Robert Putnam, "Diplomacy and Domestic Politics: The Logic of Two Level Games," *International Organization*, Vol. 42, No. 3, Summer 1988, pp. 427–460.

[35] Roland Dannreuther, "Asian Security and China's Energy Needs," *International Relations of the Asia-Pacific*, Vol. 3, 2003, pp. 197–219.

[36] Pak K. Lee, June 2005, ibid.

[37] Christian Constantin, March 2005, ibid., p. 40.

1.1.4 Hedging

Unsatisfied with such a simplistic dichotomy of a "strategic" *vs* a "market" approach, Øystein Tunsjø and Brock Tessman & Wojtek Wolfe have offered a third type of explanation by drawing on "hedging" to explain China's approach, respectively. Tunsjø maintains that China has developed sophisticated hedging strategies to insure against risks in the international petroleum market. Hedging was defined "as a strategy to deal with current risks in order to prevent future threats" (p. 36). By marrying security of supply (government concern) with profit (energy companies' commercial initiatives), China's energy security, in his view, could be "insured," not necessarily be "secured." Compared with traditional strategies of diversification, he is of the belief that "hedging strategies incorporate more scope for limiting and managing risk." While his preceding paper only focuses on the external dimension of China's rising reliance on oil imports,[38] his book has comprehensively analyzed China's domestic, global, and maritime petroleum strategies and policies.[39]

Tessman & Wolfe used the case of Chinese energy security strategy as a case study to verify a strategic hedging framework, which they developed as a structural theory of interstate competition. Apparently, China's approach to energy security is not their ultimate research goal or focus. Akin to the "strategic" approach, they highlighted the competition side in Sino–US relations in the case study, which is biased.

By virtue of the concept of hedging, Tunsjø has developed a new framework, trying to encompass both the "strategic" and "market" approaches, thus offering a better explanation of China's energy policy. While his account succeeds in showing how China has used this strategy to minimize or manage risks, it also raises a number of questions. First, the assumption on which his analysis is based seems questionable. He assumes that the Chinese government's central concern is energy security while the NOCs care more about profit. As will be discussed, energy security is at most one important, but not necessarily the central goal for Beijing. On many occasions, energy security has to be subject to other objectives. While seeking profit maximization most times, the NOCs, led by their

[38] Øystein Tunsjø, "Hedging Against Oil Dependency: New Perspectives on China's Energy Security Policy," International Relations, Vol. 24, No. 1, 2010, pp. 25–45.

[39] Øystein Tunsjø, *Security and Profit in China's Energy Policy: Hedging Against Risk* (Contemporary Asia in the World), Columbia University Press, 2013.

management, also pursue other goals for their career. Second, underlying his analysis is a statist logic that holds that "the hedging strategies form part of a "grand plan" which has been drawn up in a coordinated way at the highest level of government(or the Party)," which does not comply with the "muddling through" nature of the actual policy decision-making in China.[40] Third, as a latecomer to international oil markets, Chinese NOCs' entry into those so-called pariah states such as Iran, Sudan, and Venezuela, was not driven by a hedging strategy but was a compelled choice because they could hardly compete with the IOCs and because the latter was reluctant or unable to invest in those countries.[41]

1.1.5 Historical Institutionalism

The state-, firm-, and system-level analyses tend to treat the individual and/or organizational interests as given, without considering the impact of institutions. Historical institutionalists do not deny that political actors follow the rational choice logic of acting rationally to maximize their interests, but they argue we should not halt at that; more importantly, a historically based analysis is needed to learn "what they are trying to maximize and why they emphasize certain goals over others."[42] They believe that the state and societal institutions can shape the interests of the political actors, construct and constrain their strategies and goals, and structure their power relations. Institution, defined by Peter Hall, includes "the formal rules, compliance procedures, and standard operating practices that structure the relationship between individuals in various units of the polity and economy."[43] It is said that once an

[40] Philip Andrews-Speed, book review on Øystein Tunsjø, *Security and Profit in China's Energy Policy: Hedging against Risk* (New York: Columbia University Press, 2013), *The China Quarterly*, Vol. 218, June 2014, pp. 553–555.

[41] Janet Xuanli Liao, book review on Øystein Tunsjø, *Security and Profit in China's Energy Policy: Hedging Against Risk* (New York: Columbia University Press, 2013), *The China Journal*, No. 73, January 2015, pp. 284–286.

[42] Kathleen Thelen and Sven Steinmo, "Historical Institutionalism in Comparative Politics," in Sven Steinmo, Kathleen Thelen, and Frank Longstreth (eds.), *Structuring Politics: Historical Institutionalism in Comparative Analysis*, Cambridge and New York: Cambridge University Press, 1992, p. 9.

[43] Peter Hall, *Governing Economy: The Politics of State Intervention in Britain and France*, New York: Oxford University Press, 1986, p. 19. On surface, Hall's definition has no much difference from rational choice institutionalism. For example, North defines it

institution or a policy takes shape, it will engender an effect of "path dependency," an inertial tendency or a continuing influence persisting into the future.[44] The vestige of decades of planning the economy is set to affect current economic reform and practice in China. For instance, despite the Chinese government's use of a "disembeddedness" strategy to transform the NOCs, previous social relations persist and are used by local agents to confound its attempt.[45] Feng Lu identifies two institutional factors that make it impossible for the SOEs to automatically respond to marketization, albeit the absence of effective managerial control over the production process, and the evolution of SOE into a self-serving organization under the command economy.[46]

Indeed, the dialectic and eclectic nature of historical institutionalism has made it a strong analytic tool to illustrate the persistence of patterns within countries and policy variations across countries.[47] While acknowledging the role of institutions, historical institutionalists admit it is not the sole "cause" of political outcome, and they do not reject other political forces working on that result, including the class structure in Maxism and group dynamics in pluralism.[48] Furthermore, historical institutionalists "have constructed important analytical bridges: between state-centered and society-centered analyses by looking at the institutional arrangements that structure relations between the two,[49] and between grand theories that highlight broad cross-national regulations and narrower accounts

as "any form of constraint that human beings devise to shape human interaction," which includes both formal rules and informal conventions and codes of behavior. Historical institutionalism differs from rational choice institutionalism in the way in which political institutions affect preference formation, political behavior, and the source of institutions. See Douglass C. North, *Institutions, Institutional Change, and Economic Performance*, Cambridge: Cambridge University Press, 1990, p. 4.

[44] Stephen Krasner, "Approach to the State: Alternative Conceptions and Historical Dynamics," *Comparative Politics*, Vol. 16, 1984, pp. 223–246.

[45] "Disembeddedness" is defined as a set of calculated actions aiming to disrupt preexisting embedded relations. See Kun-Chin Lin, "Disembedding Socialist Firms as a Statist Project: Restructuring the Chinese Oil Industry, 1997–2002," *Enterprise & Society*, Vol. 7, No. 1, 2006, pp. 59–97.

[46] Feng Lu, 1999, ibid.

[47] Kathleen Thelen, Sven Steinmo, and Frank Longstreth, 1992, ibid., p. 13.

[48] Kathleen Thelen, Sven Steinmo, and Frank Longstreth, 1992, ibid., p. 3.

[49] Peter J. Katzenstein (ed.), *Between Power and Plenty: Foreign Economic Policies of Advanced Industrial States*, Madison: University of Wisconsin Press, 1978.

of particular national cases, by focusing on intermediate-level variables that illuminate sources of 'variation on a common theme'."[50] However, historical institutionalism appears to face a hard time in explaining and predicting policy and institutional changes,[51] and it presents a tendency towards mechanic and static accounts, which is liable to leave an image of institutional determinisms.[52] In that regard, historical institutionalism manifestly feels at a loss to construe the 1998 oil industrial restructuring in China.

All in all, from the perspective of analysis unit, most previous studies on China's approach to energy security focus either on the Chinese state, adopting the statist approach and presupposing the state organs as a unitary entity, or on the major market actors in the energy industry—the NOCs and MOCs. Except for historical institutionalists, previous literature has not considered the interplay mechanisms in China's energy policy process, but the former can hardly ascertain the institutional dynamism and explain policy changes. Second, in the above statist case, the NOCs were merely treated as government subdivisions, which obediently carry out the government's policies without interest considerations of their own. Finally, from the perspective of research foci and stances, previous literature embarks on their studies either taking an "insider" view—from the perspective of China itself to consider issues related to China or adopting an "outsider" view—mainly expounding the ramifications of China's approach on Western countries, particularly the US. Ironically few of them have considered the influence of the system-centered factors on the Chinese actors' perceptions and behaviors. In view of these drawbacks, this book aims to study how and why China takes an SMMA, treating the NOC as an independent actor and considering its interaction with the state in the petroleum sector, as well as probing into the world's impact on China's approach and vice visa.

The SMMA that China has taken provides readers with a new perspective to understand the state–market relationship in the globalization

[50] Peter Hall, *Governing the Economy*, 1986, ibid.

[51] Krasner has proposed a model of "punctuated equilibrium" to cope with this problem, but his explanation appears to be in tautology. Stephen Krasner, 1984, ibid. For the shortcomings of this explanation, refer to B. Guy Peters, *Institutional Theory in Political Science*, London and New York: Pinter, 1999, pp. 68–71.

[52] Kathleen Thelen and Sven Steinmo, 1992, ibid., p. 16.

world. While Lu suggests that state engagement to promote marketization is a must in China, Lin verifies that state capacity building goes hand in hand with marketization.[53] I suggest that market deregulation and state regulation coexist and mutually shift within the two opposite transitional phases (decentralization before 1998 and recentralization since 1998) in the Chinese oil industry identified by Lin. State capacity is important for initiating reform, but with marketization going on, it is not necessarily compatible with marketization. Thus far state capacity has been undermined not only by local governments but also by the NOCs as well.

Second, I explain China's energy security issue from a new perspective of the government-NOC interplay. Though the Chinese NOCs are nominally subordinate to and separate from the government, they "have considerable power and influence based on their importance to the national economy, their near-monopoly status despite the 1998 reform, and their previous status as government departments or ministries."[54] Philip Andrews-Speed simply portrays the role of NOCs in China without probing into their interaction with other players.[55] Based on the 1998 overhaul, Lin finds that the core subsidies stood together with the state whereas the noncore parts reacted against the state's further reform due to the state's distinct policies towards them.[56] Based on his findings, I further argue that the NOCs have both pro- and anti-liberalization propensities, and even the core subsidies do not merely take orders from the state, whereas the state is not so strong as to escape bargaining from the NOCs. Moreover, besides the coercion underpinning Lin's "strong state" logic and bargaining relationship that previous studies have identified (though for the whole state-owned enterprises, SOEs), I argue the relationship between the state and the NOCs more often resides in reciprocity.

[53] Feng Lu, *State, Market, and Enterprises: The Transformation of Chinese State Industry*, Doctoral dissertation, Columbia University, 1999, UMI No.: 9916899; Kun-Chin Lin, *Corporatizing China: Reinventing State Control for the Market*, PhD dissertation, University of California, Berkeley, Fall 2003.

[54] Philip Andrews-Speed, et al., "The Ongoing Reforms to China's Government and State Sector: The Case of the Energy Sector," *Journal of Contemporary China*, Vol. 23, No. 9, 2000.

[55] Philip Andrews-Speed, Xuanli Liao and Roland Dannreuther, 2002, ibid.

[56] Kun-Chin Lin, 2003, ibid.

Third, the relationship between the state and the SOEs has long arrested attention in academia, but I take a new way to comprehend the state-NOC interplay by reference to a role theory. Since the roles that the state and the NOCs have taken are influenced by the overall social structure, I construe their roles from an institutional angle. In the meantime, I am inclined to perceive economic reform as a role transformation process. In order to improve China's energy security, I stress the importance of role compatibility and transparent role expectancy for each other.

1.2 State-Managed Marketization Approach (SMMA)

The SMMA is defined as a process wherein the state has recourse to a set of mixed means to divert the oil sector from state control to market operation, but in that process, it is up to the state to decide and adjust the extent and scope of market activities. Central to this approach is the Chinese government's intention of pushing forward marketization in the petroleum sector in an orderly and controllable manner.

China's SMMA can be considered as a portfolio, comprising the SCA, competing paradigms approach (CPA), and MDA, which are the three values of the dependent variable. The CPA denotes such a situation where the state and market compete with each other to influence an energy policy decision and or an energy project. Apparently, the party-state assumes a variety of roles in governing China's economy and society, and in some circumstances, some of the roles are conflicting with each other. Hence, the state is concerned about the development and balance of the different roles and has to accommodate the conflicting roles and adjust its key role so as to cater to the complex and changing settings.

Differing from the CPA, the SMMA is a collection of state–market interactive dynamisms, whereas the CPA is in a competing situation or a kind of equilibrium wherein state control intermingles with market forces and none of them has controlled the commanding heights. Also, the SMMA differs both from the SCA, where every business is under stringent state control, and from the MDA, where the market plays a deciding role in running the oil sector. With the SMMA, the state intervenes in the oil market for the purpose of social stability, economic security, and or state asset increment, rather than merely for market efficiency. Theoretically, we may indicate their differences as shown in Chart 1.1.

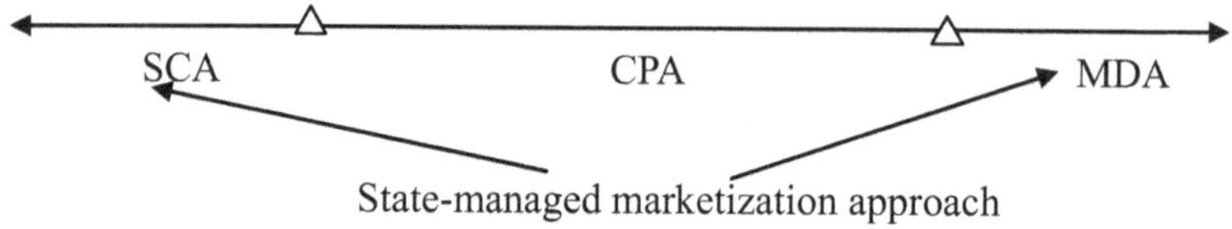

Chart 1.1 Approach to energy security

China's approach reflects gradualism, the overall guiding principle of Chinese reform epitomized by "groping for stones to cross a river" (*mozhe shitou guohe*). It is true that the reform and opening-up in the Chinese oil industry comply with this principle, but should we go no further, we might lose sight of the strategic thinking of the Chinese government, the opportunities and constraints it has confronted, and the ongoing competitions in the Chinese oil market. Neither can we understand why deregulations or re-regulations came about at certain junctures, nor can we tell the future direction of China's approach.

In practice, the SCA dominated the command economy period. After China embarked on economic reform, the MDA eventually ascended in importance and played a more decisive role in the Chinese petroleum sector. To a large extent, China's economic transition implies a drift away from the traditional SCA to the MDA, or the MDA has represented a big torrent. But during the transitional process, the two approaches often take turns. After President Xi Jinping took office, one view holds that the state's power in the economy has even been reinforced.

1.3 Central Hypothesis and Role Compatibility Model

The book will revolve around the following hypothesis: *China's SMMA to energy security has largely been shaped by the interplay between the Chinese government and the NOCs, through a mechanism of "role compatibility."* Besides central state regulators, there are a variety of stakeholders involved in China's energy policy process, but it is the relationship between ministries and state-owned firms such as the national oil corporations that has played an overarching role in affecting policy output.[57] Before expounding this model, I first introduce the roles of the state and the NOCs with regard to energy security.

1.3.1 Roles/Goals of the Chinese State

The Chinese government embraces a host of goals that have a direct bearing on energy policies. Philip Andrews-Speed et al. have highlighted four major objectives of energy policy for policy-makers in China: supply security, economic efficiency, social equity, and environmental protection.[58] This is stimulating, but rather than taking place in a vacuum, energy policy in China has intertwined with and is sometimes even subject to other policy goals. Apparently, the state is undertaking a multitude of roles in governing Chinese society. For instance, it is the owner of energy resources and land within China, central policy maker, key industrial regular, and referee for market actors. While overseeing the development of the petroleum sector, it has to take care of the development of other sectors as well. These roles sometimes are bound to be conflicting with each other. The state has to learn to balance these different roles and the interests of different groups of people and adjust its roles in different milieus. In general, the government per se is not a billiard ball, whose decisions are affected by social influences. When making a policy, the state has to take into account national interest, each party's interest (including interest groups and bureaucratic officials), and other factors. State output is a result of struggles among state organs and with relevant non-state organizations.[59]

Having said that, however, the Chinese government has two major concerns in the petroleum sector: economic concern and sociopolitical/

[57] Michal Meidan (ed.), *Shaping China's Energy Security: The Inside Perspective*, Paris: Asia Centre/Centre etudes Asie, 2007; Lin Kun-Chin, review on the above book, *The China Journal*, No. 62, July 2009, pp. 203–206.

[58] See, Philip Andrews-Speed, *Energy Policy and Regulation in the People's Republic of China*, London: KluwerLaw, 2004, p. 47; Michal Meidan, Philip Andrews-Speed and Ma Xin, "Shaping China's Energy Policy: actors and processes," *Journal of Contemporary China*, Vol. 18, No. 61, 2009, p. 593.

[59] Peter Dauvergene, *Weak and Strong States in Asia-Pacific Societies*, Australia: Allen & Unwin Australia Pty Ltd, 1998, p. 2.

security concern,[60] which sometimes are incompatible. On the one hand, thanks to its "economic concerns," the state has to introduce more market mechanisms into the whole economy including the petroleum and petrochemical sectors and even let the market play a crucial role to decide who wins or loses for the sake of improving economic efficiency.[61] It has to accommodate market forces due to the impact of globalization,[62] its own concerns of ensuring adequate energy supply to meet demand, conserving energy, reducing its fiscal burdens or enriching its own coffers, negotiated obligations with international institutions, and the need to transform people's "public action" (demands for political reform) to "private interest" (economic activities) for the purpose of ruling legitimacy.[63] Moreover, the government is aware that overprotection is not conducive to the growth of the NOCs, as evidenced by its woeful experience in the car industry. That purpose entails market openness, such as lower or no tariff, no quota constriction, fewer or no

[60] This classification is based on the two most fundamental functions of modern states: pursuit of efficiency and equity. It merits noting that 'efficiency' and 'equity' in this study are in light of the Chinese government's understanding rather than the authentic version in economics. In that sense, 'efficiency' is not free market competition but more in the sense of competition under its control; and 'equity' is not complete social fairness but more of maintaining social stability and economic growth.

[61] It is said that successful industrial firms worldwide have some common features: "first, the overwhelming majority are privately owned. ... In addition, competitive firms devote much effort to continuously enhancing efficiency in small and large ways. ..." (See Shahid Yusuf, Kaoru Nabeshima, and Dwight H. Perkins, *Under New Leadership: Privatizing China's State-Owned Enterprises*, The World Bank and Stanford University Press, 2006, pp. 20–21).

[62] Yongnian Zhang, *Globalization and State Transformation in China*, Cambridge: Cambridge University Press, 2004, pp. 29–31.

[63] Albert O. Hirschman, *Shifting Involvements: Private Interests and Public Action*, Princeton, NJ: Princeton University Press, 1982. Considering that market openness benefits the society as consumers have more choices and face lower costs, it is also a way to vent social indignation towards the serious social disparity and oil shortages derived from the NOCs' monopolies. The industrial monopoly problem including the NOCs' monopoly has been widely rebuked in China because that reduces market efficiency, intensifies social inequality, and abuses the monopoly power etc. Such articles can refer to: Zeyuan Yu, "Jingjixuejia Wu Jinglian: Fubai he Longduan shi pinfu xuanshu zhuyin" ("Economist Wu Jinglian: Corruption and Monopoly Are the Primary Factors Leading to Great Income Gap"), *Lianhezaobao*, 27 June 2006, http://www.zaobao.com/gj/zg060627_501.html, accessed 12 November 2006; Lin Cao, "liuyue duikang: fangle zhongnu de longduan hai neng tingli duojiu" ("Confrontation in June: How Long Can the Monopoly Ruffling the Public Survive"), *Zhongguo Qingnian Bao* (China Youth Daily), 30 June 2006.

entry/exit barrier, no policy discrimination, no subsidies, price formed after the complete market competition, hard budget constraint,[64] and more autonomy for oil companies in business operation, profit allocation, pricing and investing decisions, as well as a set of laws and regulations preserving market order.

On the other hand, the state bears "sociopolitical/security concerns" in mind, implying that the central government is concerned about the possible destructive effects on national security, sociopolitical stability and overall economic development resulting from disruption of oil and gas supply and/or price fluctuation. Under such circumstances, the state may wish or even force the NOCs to take social obligations in time of emergency even at the expense of their commercial interests. The government's understanding of energy security "appears to include the expectations that the oil companies will forgo windfall profits when there are price-hikes on the international market."[65] In a 2002 interview, Tian Fengshan, the former Minister of Land and Natural Resources, claimed that oil self-sufficiency would be the optimal state for the sake of security; from an economic angle, due to the higher costs of domestic oil exploration, it would be a sub-optimal choice to import a certain amount of oil. However, in order to enhance China's oil security, Tian recommended increasing domestic oil E&P as the key measure.[66] When perceiving that energy problems may engender chaos, it may recur to instruments of a command economy to prevent and curb the crisis. Moreover, because the NOCs may abuse their monopolizing power, the state also needs to ensure that social interests are not harmed to the extent that may incur social unrest, and that the macro economy would not be destabilized. To some extent, the government is confronting such a paradox of state control and market domination.[67] Hence, it seems unlikely that state

[64] 'Hard budget constraint' denotes that firms assume full responsibility for whatever decision they make, and the government will not bail out the losses they incur.

[65] "Vice-Premier Wu Bangguo inspects Daqing oil field and Daqing Petrochemical plant", August 4, 1999, in *CNPC Yearbook 1999,* pp. 59–60. Cited from Speed et al., 2002, p. 52.

[66] Chuanguang Yu and Xiangxing Shi, "Guotu ziyuanbu buzhang Tian Fengshan: guanzhu shiyou ziyuan anquan," ("Minister of Land and Natural Resources Tian Fengshan: Attention Must Be Paid to Oil Security"), *Jiefangjun Bao* (Liberation Army Daily), 20 July 2002.

[67] Shaofeng Chen, "Marketization and China's Energy Security," *Policy and Society*, Vol. 27, 2009, pp. 249–260.

control would be removed overnight. Sometimes state control may be resumed in those deregulated areas, particularly when a crisis is at hand.

Accordingly, the state's role in terms of energy security can be defined as economic efficiency promoter (EEP), and internal stabilizer. "EEP" denotes that the state regulates oil and gas market with economic means, and ushers in proper market competition into the petroleum sector.[68] It would not force the NOCs to "extinguish fire" even in case of the advent of oil crisis. On the contrary, I define "internal stabilizer" as the role the state plays to prevent and cope with any crisis that may jeopardize sociopolitical stability and economic development with instruments in disregard economic logic, foster the NOCs' growth through various preferential policies such as subsidies, tax redemption, and market protection, and compel the NOCs to accept policies or take social obligations on some occasions. It is worth noting that the state's role as an EEP will not necessarily hurt the interest of the NOCs. The latter may sometimes push the government to act in that way. Also, the government's role as an internal stabilizer may foster or block their profit accruement, depending on specific situations.

1.3.2 Dual-Identities and the Autonomy of the NOCs

CNPC, Sinopc, and CNOOC are the three major NOCs that have almost monopolized the Chinese petroleum market. The NOCs have Janus-face identities: market actor and state policy & social obligation undertaker (SPSOU).[69] On the one hand, they are market actors. Reforming China's SOEs has become the core of China's transition to a market economy, and previous reforms have greatly enhanced SOEs' incentives to pursue their own interests.[70] Particularly, with the advance of the market economy, the

[68] 'Proper market competition' means that the competition introduced would not engender social chaos. It may take the form of endowing more autonomy to the NOCs, allowing private investors into certain policy areas, more flexible pricing practice, and so on.

[69] Both Vernon and Noreng have identified that the SOEs in general have been created with various goals, and thus may need to play different roles. See Raymond Vernon, "Introduction," in Raymond Vernon and Yair Aharoni (eds.), *State-Owned Enterprise in the Western Economies*, London: Croom Helm, 1981; Oystein Noreng, *Oil and Islam: Social and Economic Issues*, New York, Singapore, etc.: Wiley, 1997.

[70] Yingyi Qian, "Enterprise Reform in China: Agency Problems and Political Control," *Economics of Transition*, Vol. 4, No. 2, October 1996, pp. 427–447.

management and employees' welfare is more closely associated with the NOCs' performance. As listed companies, they need to be accountable to shareholders. Acting as market actors, they pursue profit maximization, greater autonomy, and even market monopoly status.[71] Sometimes, they are willing to collaborate with the MOCs in exchange for their capital, technology, and managerial skills. However, it is worth noting that the NOCs' identity as market actors is not equivalent to the one in classical economics. Market actors in classical economics mean that they not only have strong incentives to maximize profits, but also face the threat of insolvency; whereas the NOCs' role as a market actor only denotes that they have profit-maximizing incentives, but do not face such a threat of bankruptcy, which results in the problem of soft budget constraint or "too big to fall" paradox.[72]

On the other hand, as major actors in the Chinese petroleum industry, the NOCs are the principal state policy implementers and are required to shoulder some social obligations, serving China's energy security, helping redistribute income, and preserving social stability. In spite of efforts that have been made to reduce direct government involvement, marketization and corporatization of these NOCs do not mean they merely act as strictly profit-seeking commercial firms.[73] Not only does direct government involvement in SOEs' operations exists,[74] but the SOEs have been burdened with "social responsibilities." As state-owned companies, the NOCs are expected to undertake social responsibilities and serve the

[71] It merits noting that the NOCs are state owned, but their profits had not been shared by the public until June 2006 when Beijing started to levy windfall profit tax over the NOCs, and the resource taxes they pay to the government are much lower than the MOCs to their parent states. While reaping windfall profits, the NOCs still keep pressurizing the government to raise oil and gas prices, which the Chinese public feel indignant about. Hence, compared with other industries, employees in the monopolizing sectors get much higher incomes.

[72] Janos Kornai, "The soft budget constraint," *Kyklos*, Vol. 39, 1986, pp. 3–30. The nature of the "soft-budget constraint" in the context of China's SOEs can also be seen in: Bruce Reynolds (ed.), *Reform in China: Challenges and Choices*, Armonk, NY: M. E. Sharpe, 1987.

[73] Louis Putterman and Xiao-Yuan Dong, "China's State-Owned Enterprises: Their Role, Job Creation, and Efficiency in Long-Term Perspective," *Modern China*, Vol. 26, No. 4, October 2000, pp. 403–447.

[74] Xiaobo Hu, "The State, Enterprises, and Society in Post-Deng China: Impact of the New Round of SOE Reform," *Asian Survey*, Vol. 40, No. 4, July–August 2000, pp. 641–657.

government's strategic, political, and/or socioeconomic interests when necessary. In particular, they are obliged to ensure and help improve China's energy security. Therefore I define the "SPSOU" as the role of the NOCs in implementing state policies at the expense of their commercial interest or acting against market principles.

Nonetheless, in a market milieu where firms and individuals seek utility maximization, assuming the SPSOU role is not without payoffs, such as maintaining monopoly or being endowed with more privileges, state backup for their "go out," direct subsidies, and so forth. Each time assuming that role enhances their bargaining power vis-à-vis the state.[75] It deserves noting that acting as an SPSOU does not necessarily go against the will of the NOCs. The latter sometimes may even volunteer to take that role because of the following factors: The management is eager to enhance their images before the top leaders; The NOCs want to seek government protection because they are less competitive vis-à-vis other market rivalries or because they are reluctant to let others slice the pie; The management have their own selfish interests which would be more likely attained in the name of serving public interests. Distinctions between the NOC's roles as a market actor and SPSOU first and foremost lie in their different goal priorities; namely, a market actor prioritizes profit maximization, while the SPSOU role gives priority to social stability or political considerations.

It is apparent that the NOCs have their own interest considerations that may not be in line with the government's. The "Janus-face" nature implies that their interest preferences are congruent most times given that the state endeavors to shore up the growth of the NOCs, while at other times, their preferences may be contradictory, particularly with the NOCs becoming more market-oriented and the state facing a daunting challenge of preserving social stability and promoting social equities. Nominally the NOCs are part of the economic system, but it is by no means the case

[75] One tricky thing is the complicated identity of the NOCs. It can be said that they are part of the state in the sense that they are ministry- or vice ministry-level work units and their managements are high-ranking officials in the Chinese nomenclatura system. As such, no important energy policy could be made without their involvement. On the other hand, they are not part of the state since the 1998 restructuring explicitly stipulated to separate the NOCs' administrative functions from them. This interlink may affect our analysis to some extent, but I prefer to distinguish the state from the NOCs as the NOCs' and their managements' interests (economic gains and career promotion) highly hinge upon the performance of the enterprises.

that they just follow the government's mandates.[76] As one commentator in the state-run newspaper, *The People's Daily*, candidly pointed out, "It would be easy if the government's decision is consistent with the enterprises' wishes. But in reality, the two are usually inconsistent and even contradictory with each other, making it difficult to integrate them."[77] In an economic vein, this is a typical principal–agent problem prevalent in any type of firm where ownership and management rights are separated.

In the Chinese NOCs, such a divorce is more serious in that it is unclear who is the specific delegate of the state, and there are at least three principal–agent problems[78]: between the state and the headquarters, between the headquarters and their branches, and between managers and team members.[79] As Feng Lu indicates,

> As managers' motivation is greatly bound by the pressure of, and the obligation to, their work forces, the socialist enterprise tends to give higher priority to its internal community's welfare over its contribution to the society (such as profits, goods and services). This is why the behavior of socialist enterprise tended to deviate increasingly from the official goals in the late socialism and the enterprise tends to become self-serving community as soon as the state control is loosened up under liberalization.[80]

[76] Mark Allen Groombridge, *The Politics of Industrial Bargaining: The Restructuring of State-Owned Enterprises in the People's Republic of China, 1978 to 1995*, Doctoral dissertation for Columbia University, 1998, p. 8.

[77] "Clearly Defined Relation Ownership and Management Needed," *Renmin Ribao* (People's Daily), 30 November 1993. Cited from Mark Aleen Groombridge, 1998, ibid.

[78] Simply put it, by rejecting the firm theory in classical neo-economics which assumes unselfishness of business managers and perfect information, the principal-agent theory posits that there is variance in objectives between firm owners and firm managers. The latter possess more information than the former, while the owners need to take costs to know every detail of the managers' operations, thereby agent costs will be engendered, which further affects the performance of the firm. For more information, see A. Alchian and Harold Demsetz, "Production, Information Costs and Economic Organization," *American Economic Review*, Vol. 62, December 1972, pp. 777–795; Joseph E. Stigliz, "Principal and Agent," in Murray Milgate, John Eatwell, and Peter Newman (eds.), *The New Palgrave: A Dictionary of Economics*, London: Macmillan, 1987.

[79] In team production theory, the function of managers resides in the need to monitor the shirking behavior of the team members, and the profit (residuals) is the payoff for implementing this function. See A. Alchian and Harold Demsetz, 1972, ibid.

[80] Feng Lu, *State, Market, and Enterprises: The Transformation of Chinese State Industry*, Doctoral dissertation, Columbia University, 1999, UMI No.: 9916899, p. 5.

Accordingly, the NOCs press the government to provide them with preferential policies, while they may attempt to dodge those policies or regulations unfavorable to them. In other words, domestically, the NOCs are reluctant to lose their monopoly status. Externally, the NOCs actively boost investments abroad because it is conducive to enhancing national energy security and competitiveness.[81]

A related question is whether the NOCs are powerful and independent enough to interact with the Chinese state. The NOCs have evolved into a strong interest group that can deeply influence national energy policy, which will be discussed at length in Chapter 3.

Nonetheless, to admit the autonomy of the NOCs does not mean to reject the interdependent relations, on which their interaction is based. It is true that the NOCs need to approach the central government for special treatment, but the state also falls back on the NOCs. As illustrated above, in the policy process, the NOCs are the major energy policy implementer, policy advisor, energy information providers, and in some sense policy-maker. In the economic arena, the state pins its hope on the large SOEs (including the NOCs) to meet the challenge of globalization and help China lift its international status. Virtually the NOCs are at the same time an important source of central coffers.

Since the government requires the NOCs to sacrifice their commercial interest in order to serve the country's energy security, this in return, provides leeway for the NOCs to influence the government's energy policy-making, and evade adverse regulations or policies. "In general, the domestic political and foreign policy interests of the government, which are critical variables in the conceptualization of energy security, are not part of the same calculus of interests of the oil companies."[82] Therefore, their relations are not simply the patron–client ones.

Some people may suspect the viability of this point as the top management of the NOCs are assigned by the CCP system. This is true, but most NOCs management are part of the "constituents" that hold important ballots in the election of the central leaders. The author does not deny that management of the NOCs may abide by the commands from the above; otherwise, they may face risks of being demoted or even removed.

[81] Erica S. Downs, "The Chinese Energy Security Debate," *The China Quarterly*, Vol. 177, March 2004, p. 25.

[82] Speed et al., 2002, p. 52.

But it is beyond doubt that they impose great influence on the government oil and gas policy-making by taking advantage of their monopoly and expertise. In practice, such cases did take place. As an energy expert from ERI under NDRC, Gao Shixian contends, "as the SOEs, they take the responsibility for maintenance and increment of appreciation of the values of state assets, and then assist the government's macro regulations. Take the strategic petroleum reserve as an example, the oil companies should play a major role."[83] However, the NOCs have their calculations. In October 2002 when other oil importing country raised their SPRs due to the intensified situation in the Middle East, one NOC acted against the current. Not having obeyed the government's mandate to increase oil stocks, it stopped oil stockpiling and was involved in arbitrages by taking advantage of oil price surges. It was estimated that, through this arbitrage, the company made a profit of RMB30 million, whereas its aggregate sales revenue was only RMB37.8 million in that year.[84]

Moreover, the NOCs as strong interest groups have also been borne out by the exposure of a host of corruption cases in the petroleum sector in recent years; in these cases, massive state-owned assets had been stripped away as a result of "transactional losses," denoting that state assets were sold on the cheap rather than at a fair price, either through incompetence, rent-seeking and/or black box operations.[85] Such corruption cases leading to great losses of state-owned assets go against the state interest. For the first time, the Chinese official media *Xinhua Agency*, reconfirmed the existence of an "oil clique" (*shiyou bang*), "secretary clique" (*mishu bang*), and "Shanxi clique" (*Shanxi bang*), and these gangs are a flagrant violation of party disciplines.[86] Some people may

[83] Chen Ting and Chen Jibao, "Shui lai jianguan san da shiyou guatou?" ("Who Will Supervise the Three Oil Oligarchs?"), *21 Shiji Jingji Baodao* (21 Century Economic Report), 30 December 2003. http://www.nanfangdaily.com.cn/southnews/zt/jjtk/xlzg/200312300114.asp, accessed 15 November 2006.

[84] This case is quoted from Chen Ting and Chen Jibao, 30 December 2003, ibid.

[85] For instance, Zhou Yongkang (a former Standing Committee member of the Political Bureau of the CPC Central Committee and former chairman of CNPC), Jiang Jiemin (former head of the SASAC and former chairman of CNPC), Chen Tonghai (former chairman of Sinopec), and five senior executives of CNPC including Wang Yongchun, Li Hualin, Ran Xinquan, Wang Daofu and Wen Qingshan, Luo Weizhong (General Manager of CNOOC Gas & Power Group, a Fully Owned Subsidiary of CNOOC).

[86] Mengda Wu and Hongyi Chen, "Fanfu dadiao de naxie 'tuantuanhuohuo'" (Those "Gangs" Wiped Away by anti corruption), *Xinhua Agency*, 3 January 2015.

claim that their individual behaviors could not represent the NOCs, but the problem is almost all of the corruptionists were in top positions of the NOCs and very influential in the hierarchical closed system. Other than "transactional losses," "systematic loss" (*tizhixing liushi*), referring to assets being poorly managed because of the overall system thanks to poor accountability, perverse incentives, and a lack of competition, maybe more serious but has fallen off the radar.[87]

1.3.3 *Role Compatibility*[88] *and China's Approach to Energy Security*

"Role compatibility" denotes that a certain approach to energy security would be taken when the roles of the state and the NOCs are accepted by each other. Specifically,

- when the state encourages the growth of NOCs and the NOCs also act as market actors, an MDA will be used;
- when the state expects the NOCs to serve social responsibility and the latter are willing to accept this mandate, a SCA will be employed;

In the above two scenarios, the government is willing to follow the role propensity of the NOCs, or vice versa, thus forming an MDA or an SCA;

- but in case of role incompatibility, or if they have different role expectations, the state has to turn to a CPA (see Table 1.1).

[87] Editorial Board of the Economic Observer, "The Hidden Losses of SOEs," *Jingji Guancha Bao* (the Economic Observer), 12 September 2013.

[88] Role theory is mainly used in sociology, psychology and management, but it is also applied in international relations. See, for example, Stephen G. Walker (ed.), *Role Theory and Foreign Policy Analysis*, Durham, NC: Duke University Press, 1987; Carl W. Backman, "Role Theory and International Relations: A Commentary and Extension," *International Studies Quarterly*, Vol. 14, No. 3, September, 1970, pp. 310–319; Alvin Magid, "Methodological Considerations in the Study of African Political and Administrative Behavior: The Case of Role Conflict Analysis," *African Studies Review*, Vol. 13, No. 1, April, 1970, pp. 75–94; Glenn Chafetz; Hillel Abramson and Suzette Grillot, "Role Theory and Foreign Policy: Belarussian and Ukrainian Compliance with the Nuclear Nonproliferation Regime," *Political Psychology*, Vol. 17, No. 4, December, 1996, pp. 727–757.

Table 1.1 "Role Compatibility" model

		Central Government	
		Economic efficiency promoter (EEP)	*Internal stabilizer*
NOC	Market actor	I. MDA	II. CPA
	State policy & social obligation undertaker (SPSOU)	III. CPA	IV. SCA

Having realized the importance of developing firms' capabilities to compete in the market, the state is heading to turn these NOCs into entities responsible for their own balance sheets, though in a piece-meal fashion. For the NOCs, as discussed above, they will act as market actors out of concern of their welfare and accountability to shareholders. However, as Guthrie argues, "neither the firms nor the managers who run them can be viewed simply as rational profit-maximizing economic actors who will pursue power and plenty given the right structural circum-stances."[89] The NOCs have the propensity to act as rent-seekers, because such activities could help retain their monopoly status. In return, they may be willing to act as SPSOU as reciprocity, but their "willingness" may also be due to the state's coercion, or a "tribute" to the state for firm leaders' promotion or exemption from being dismissed, or for stronger bargaining power. Moreover, it goes against their interests if the society falls into unrest due to their non-cooperation in times of oil crisis.[90]

In order to understand the *logic of the role compatibility* argument, it is necessary to know why the result of role compatibility would influence

[89] Doug Guthrie, *Dragon in a Three-Piece Suit: The Emergence of Capitalism in China*, Princeton: Princeton University Press, 1999, p. 6.

[90] My emphasis on the interaction of the state and the NOCs does not deny the influ-ence of other factors on China's SMM, such as impacts of the MOCs, lobbying activities by local governments, historical heritage regarding energy security, ideology, technology level. But none would deny the central government and the NOCs are the decisive powers in Chinese monopolized energy market. Local government has been divested its power pertaining to oil after the 1998 restructuring, and MOCs' access to the market has largely been constricted by a set of protective measures. The impact of the MOCs will be reflected by the perception and response of the state. And for other factors, they are relatively stable, existing before and after China's energy security problem emerge. But highlighting the most important factors can help us find the most fundamental rules.

China's approach to energy security (see Chart 1.2). I argue that both the state and the NOC would judge the other's role expectations before taking any action, and would try to stand in alignment with each other's role expectations either through self-adjustment or through lobbying or bargaining.[91] For the state, if its role is compatible with that of the NOC, policy implementation would be facilitated. In particular, if the state makes a policy that may damage the interest of the NOCs, it has to take account of policy feasibility; For the NOCs, role compatibility with the state means that their privileges would be more assured and that the management would have more opportunities to get promoted.

Of course, it is possible that role incompatibility will occur. In that case, bargaining will be the first choice, but coercion can be an alternative in case no consensus can be reached through negotiation. Under such a circumstance, the risks (policy non-implementation for the state, and punishment risk for the NOCs) would be larger.[92] Therefore, role

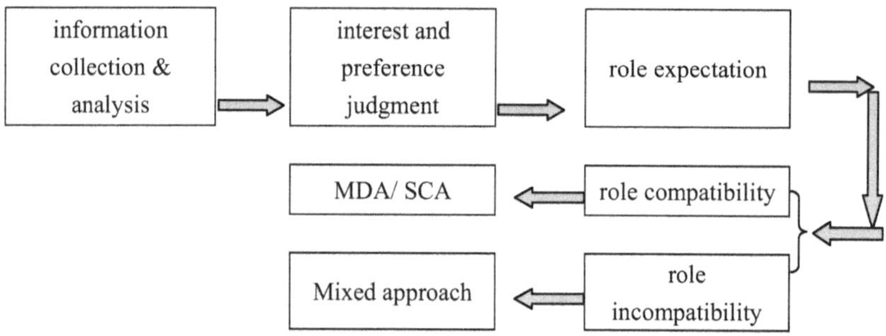

Chart 1.2 Logic of the role compatibility model (*Source* Chart made by the author)

[91] This logic virtually complies with rational expectations theory in economics. The theory argues that on average people's expectations about the future will be accurate because "they form their expectations on a rational basis, using all the information available to them optimally, and learn from their mistakes"; therefore, people can "learn to anticipate government policy changes and act accordingly". See "Economics A-Z," *Economist*, http://www.economist.com/research/Economics/alphabetic.cfm?LETTER=R#RATIONAL%20EXPECTATIONS, accessed 16 November 2006.

[92] In psychology and sociology, "role theory" holds that role conflict can bring about poor role performance and a negative affective state, albeit the so-called "role strain". The existence of role strain hinges upon the individual's perception on whether his self-concepts and role demands are congruent, and role performance is more "effective, proper,

compatibility not only means less or no interest conflict between the state and the NOC but also may help augment their common interests. In contrast, role incompatibility would place them at greater risk. As rational identities, both the state and the NOC favor beneficial opportunities and evade damaging ones.

Then the next question would be: why the interest-based expectancy would lead to different approaches to oil security in China? As mentioned earlier, the state is the policy-maker while the NOCs have a strong influence on this process. When the state is inclined to act as EEP, trying to usher more market mechanisms into the petroleum sector while the NOCs are willing to gain more autonomy to be market actors, acting rationally in light of the central goal of profit maximization, both embrace market mechanisms. As a result, the policy options for them are more likely to form a MDA. By the same token, when the state feels it necessary to act as an internal stabilizer, intervening in the market with economic and/or administrative instruments (including forcing the NOCs) to prevent or resolve any emergency, while the NOCs are also willing to work as SPSOU even at the expense of their commercial interests, the policy options for them are more likely to form an SCA.

Complicated is the following two circumstances under which the state and the NOCs have incongruent role perceptions or expectations in terms of a certain policy or social event, and thus different strategies may be used. First, when the government prefers to act as an internal stabilizer, requiring the NOCs to shoulder some social obligations, the NOCs might try to evade them, which would lead to a situation of bargaining. If bargaining fails, the state may resort to coercion. As a result, the government may either bring out more state control, or market openness, or both, whichever is the most effective option to resolve the crisis. Most of the time, while preferring the use of commanding instruments, the Chinese government tends to encourage market competition so as to

and appropriate" when self-characteristics are congruent with role requirements. (Source: Theodore Sarbin and L. Allen, "Role Theory," in Gardner Lindzey and Elliot Aronson (eds.), *The Handbook of Social Psychology*, Reading, MA: Addison-Wesley Pub. Co, 1968). Hiller and Philliber suggested that "relationships are more stable when role expectations are consistent with self-concepts, while incongruence between self-concepts and role expectations results in stress" (cited from Laurie Chassin, Antonette Zeiss, et al., "Role Perceptions, Self-Role Congruence and Marital Satisfaction in Dual-Worker Couples with Prescholl Children," *Social Psychology Quarterly*, 1985, Vol. 48, No. 4, p. 302).

mitigate social indignation.[93] Thus, a state-market condominium is most likely to be used.

Second, when the government is inclined to be an EEP, pushing the NOCs to the market and not harming their economic interests even in times of some energy emergency (without imposing direct mandates or pressures on the NOCs), whereas the NOCs voluntarily act as a SPSOU, sacrificing their economic interests to serve the public, reciprocity and bargaining would be the major interaction form. That the NOCs would act in that way maybe because they miscalculate the center's spirit, or they figure out that their "bounty" would comply with the center's guidelines or would be appreciated by their superiors, or they have other calculations. More importantly, the NOCs may want to make use of the opportunity to lobby for what they expect from the government. Due to the "sacrifice" the NOCs have made, bargaining may occur when they require certain compensation or lobby for some policy, or block the state's action when it attempts to change some policy not in their favor. When market openness is preferred by the state while the NOCs resist losing their privileges, a state-market condominium will be the most likely arrangement.

The role compatibility model can better set forth how and why China adopts SMMA to cope with energy security because this model has combined the strengths of the state-, firm- and system-level analyses as well as historical institutionalism. First, in recognition of their interest variations, I separate the NOCs from the state and treat them as two interdependent entities, rather than simply regard the NOCs as arms of state policy. Second, after separating the NOCs, I turn to a statism approach by assuming that the other parts of the Chinese state is a complete entity whose paramount objective is to retain the exclusive ruling power, which has been sublimated as national interest.[94] Third, in the process of examining how they interact with each other, the role compatibility model also

[93] Preference of commanding instrument is not only because they are more efficient in the short run, but because these are the means the government has got used to. Social indignation arises mainly because the public believes that crisis like oil shortages resulted from the monopolies of the NOCs and they thus have obligation to serve the public.

[94] Wu argues that in China, "the state is the paramount referent of security on both the domestic and international levels, and regime security is usually considered an element of national security." See Wu Xinbo, "China: Security Practice of a Modernizing and Ascending Power", in Muthiah Alagappa, *Asian Security Practice: Material and Ideational Influences*, Stanford: Stanford University Press, 1998, p. 123.

allows for the institutional and global factors including the impact from the MOCs to see how they shape and influence the role expectations, preferences and strategies of the state and the NOCs. Fourth, this model does not rule out the possibility that the state is not a unified entity and that interest conflicts also exist among the NOCs. In either case, this model claims it would improve the bargaining power of the consolidated side.

It is worth noting that this model has weaknesses as well. One lies in the difficulty in accurately and quantitatively measuring the role expectations and preferences of the parties concerned, as well as the three dependent variables MDA, SCA, and state-market condominium. Measuring the changes in these variables has to rely on qualitative narrations and inductive methods; as a result, bias is inevitable. Second, there are many factors and actors influencing China's approach to energy security, but the role compatibility model takes a simplified view, merely considering the interplay between the state and the NOCs. Consequently, other factors have been left out. It is conceivable that may dismay some. In addition, when the state organs speak in more than one voice, it is hard to conclude which role the state presents to us. My way to deal with the above problems is: first, I try to look at not only what they said, but what they did. Second, in the last case, I will consider whether they have settled their conflicts and how they did that.

1.4 Conclusion

This chapter has defined the dependent variable—the SMMA and set out the theoretical framework. In a nutshell, this book will conduct analyses from three different levels: global, national, and sub-national levels. However, by virtue of the role compatibility model, the focus of this study will be on the interplay between the Chinese government and the NOCs. In the meantime, the book will take account of global factors, discussing the impact of the international energy market on the preferences of the Chinese government and the NOCs in particular.

CHAPTER 2

Energy Security: Perceptions and Realities

This chapterprovides an overview of the Chinese government's perceptions of energy security and the underlying causes that help shape its view. To account for China's approach to energy security, first and foremost is to learn how China perceives energy security, which to a large extent has constituted the basis for its energy policy-making. This perception has not only pertained to the ideologies of the Chinese leadership but also derived from the energy realities that China has confronted. These realities contain a variety of direct and indirect factors, among which indigenous energy endowments and supply–demand equilibrium particularly stand out. Moreover, as the Chinese economy has been more integrated with the world economy and China has become more dependent on energy imports, the global energy market also has profound impact on China's perception of energy security. Hence, with changes in the leadership and the realities, China's perception of energy security has been evolving, rather than staying intact.

Unlike most previous studies that tend to give a static view of China's perceptions of energy security, the author argues that China's perceptions are changing thanks to the changes in leadership, new economic environment, supply–demand equilibrium, technical innovation, China's learning curve, and so forth. In general, the availability, reliability, and affordability of oil and gas are considered the core of China's energy security, and for a long time China's energy security concern tilted towards the supply

S. Chen, *China's Approach to Energy Security*,
https://doi.org/10.1007/978-981-99-3573-4_2

side while ignoring the demand side, but in recent years it is in a more balanced state. While highlighting the major concerns of the Chinese government on energy issues, we will analyze the major objectives of the Chinese government and the NOCs in terms of the oil and gas sector.

The following first reviews previous literature on China's perception of energy security, followed by my rendition of why China deems oil supply security as the core of energy security, the underlying causes shaping its view, and the government's new conceptions. The end of this part will evaluate China's SMMA from the perspective of its perceptions.

2.1 China's Energy Security: A Review

Scholars are at variance with the definition of energy security because of the various dimensions to it,[1] but most scholars tend to embrace a supply-side view, which holds that fundamentally, energy security is a problem of adequate supplies at affordable prices.[2] Or as the United Nations Development Programme (UNDP) defines, "the availability of energy at all times in various forms, in sufficient quantities, and at affordable prices."[3] Apart from availability and affordability, Daniel Yergin emphasizes the way to get energy should not "jeopardize national values and objectives."[4]

However, from the environmental perspective, the supply-based view of energy security is biased since it takes no account of the demand-side impact. Proponents argue that energy, security, and the environment are intimately bound together, and environmental pollution should be minimized to the least extent in every segment of the energy chain from

[1] These dimensions include economic, supply-based, political/security, environmental, technological, social/cultural, and military/security dimensions, but some of them are overlapped. See Peter Hayes and David von Hippel, "Energy Security in Northeast Asia," *Global Asia*, Vol. I, No. I, September 2006.

[2] Fereidun Fesharaki, et al., *Promoting Energy Security in APEC Through Improved International Fuel Market Operations*, Honolulu, Hawaii: Program on Resources: Energy and Minerals, East-West Center, for the APEC Energy Working Group, 1998, p. vii; David A. Deese, "Energy: Economics, Politics, and Security," *International Security*, Vol. 4, No. 3, Winter 1979–1980, pp. 140–153.

[3] United Nations Development Programme, *World Energy Assessment*, New York: UNDP, 2000.

[4] Daniel Yergin, "Energy Security in the 1990s," *Foreign Affairs*, Vol. 67, No. 1, Fall 1988, p. 112.

production to consumption. The IEA advocates policies that coordinate energy security, economic growth, and environmental protection.[5]

What is China's energy security? Overwhelmingly, most Chinese scholars and think tanks believe that oil security is the core of China's energy security. Unanimously, they tend to regard it as a condition in which continuous and stable oil supplies are available to satisfy domestic oil demands in order to ensure national survival, social stability, and economic development.[6] Some scholars stress that the utilization of energy resources should not be a big threat to the ecological environment.[7]

[5] IEA Statement on Sustainable Development, World Summit on Sustainable Development, Johannesburg 26 August–4 September 2002, http://www.iea.org/envissu/johannesburg/sust.htm/, accessed 2 November 2005.

[6] There are a plethora of writings on China's energy security, some of them are just the patchwork of others or convey little useful information. For the supply-side view, see, for example, Lei Wu, *ZhongGuo Shiyou Anquan* (China's Oil Security), Beijing: China Social Sciences Press, 2003; Jun Tan, *Da Bosha: Shiji Shiyou zhi zheng* (Struggle for Oil for Centuries), Beijing: World Knowledge Press, 2004; Wei Li, "Zhongguo Shiyou Anquan de Dongnanya Yinsu" (The Southeast Asia Factor in China's Oil Security), *Dongnanya Zongheng* (Around Southeast Asia), Vol. 10, 2003; Lantao Zhang, "Lun shiyou liyi yu rushihou woguo de shiyou anquan" (On Oil Interest and China's Oil Security After the Entry into WTO), *Guojiguangxi xueyuan xuebao* (Journal of University of International Relations), No. 5, 2002; Fengquan An, Jun'an Liu, Peng Hai, "Shiyou anquan weixi guomai" (Oil Security Maintains the Nation's Pulse), *Zhongguo shihua* (China Petrochemicals), Vol. 7, 2003; Xingshan Zhu and Dadi Zhou, "Ruhe sikao Zhongguo de nengyuan anquan wenti" (How to Think About China's Energy Security Problem), *Guoji Shiyou Jingjixue* (International Petroleum Economics), No. 10, 2002. For the think tanks' views, see, for example, the speech made by Qingtai Chen, Vice President of The Development Research Center of the State Council of the PRC, in Qingtai Chen, "zhongguo guojia nengyuan zhanglue he zhengce" (China National Energy Strategy and Policy), Xin Nengyuan Wang (New Energy), 12 July 2006, http://newenergy.giec.cas.cn/zcfg/200607/t20060712_184070.html, accessed 26 February 2023; National Economic Department, SDPC, "Zhongguo shiyou de jiben shexiang" (Basic Plans for China's Oil Reserve), *Jingji Yanjiu cankao* (Economic Research Reference), 9 January 2002.

[7] Lei Zhang, "Lun Zhongguo nengyuan anquan" (On China's Energy Security), *Zhongguo Shiyou Jingji* (International Petroleum Economics), Vol. 9, No. 3, 2001; Hongtu Zhao, "Huanjing baohu xia de nengyuan anquan" (Energy Security Under Environmental Protection), *Zhongguo shiyou shihua* (China Petroleum and Petrochemics), No. 10, 2002; Yimin Wei, *Zhonguo Nengyuan Baogao: Zhanlue yu Zhengce Yanjiu* (China Energy Report: Studies on Its Strategies and Policies), Beijing: Kexue Chubanshe, 2006; Zhongguo Nengyuan Fazhan Baogao (The Energy Development Report of China), Beijing: Shehui Kexue Wenxian Chubanshe, 2006.

Bo Kong posits that it is important to consider China's actual insecurity and perceived insecurity, and it is the government's perceptions of the insecurity that drives China's energy policy.[8] His interpretation is very comprehensive as it has covered a variety of aspects, but readers may be hard to find the focus of China's conceptions. Downs argues that Chinese conception of energy security is "state-centric, supply-side biased, overwhelmingly focused on oil, and tends to equate security with self-sufficiency."[9] I echo her view as it rightly points out the importance of oil security in China's energy equation and the Chinese leadership's preoccupation with self-sufficiency.[10] However, this type of view is static and uni-dimensional, which does not comply with the evolving nature of Chinese perceptions. Indeed, China regards the availability, reliability, and affordability of oil as the core of its energy security challenges, but the government has a growing concern about environmental pollution and energy conservation. In the following, I first account for why China's view tilts towards the supply side, and then explain its current trend.

[8] Actual insecurity includes cyclical, structural and institutional insecurities, while perceived insecurity comprises of perceived energy availability, reliability and affordability. Bo Kong, *An Anatomy of China's Energy Insecurity and Its Strategies*, PNNL-15529, Pacific Northwest National Laboratory, Prepared for the U.S. Department of Energy under Contract DE-AC05-76RL01830, October 2005, https://www.pnnl.gov/main/publications/external/technical_reports/PNNL-15529.pdf, accessed 26 February 2023.

[9] Erica Downs, "The Chinese Energy Security Debate," *China Quarterly*, No. 177, 2004, pp. 22–23; Eric Downs, China's *Energy Security*, PhD dissertation, Princeton: Princeton University, 2004, p. 6.

[10] Other scholars who hold similar view, i.e., Philip Andrews-Speed, Xuanli Liao and Roland Dannreuther, *The Strategic Implications of China's Energy Needs*, Adelphi Paper, No. 346, New York: International Institute for Strategic Studies, 2002; Pak K. Lee, "China's Quest for Oil Security: Oil (Wars) in the Pipeline?" *The Pacific Review*, Vol. 18, No. 2, June 2005, pp. 265–301; David Zweig and Bi Jianhai, "China's Global Hunt for Energy," *Foreign Affairs*, September/October 2005; Phar Kim Beng and Vic Y. W. Li, "China's Energy Dependence on the Middle East: Boon or Bane for Asian Security?" *The China and Eurasia Forum Quarterly*, Vol. 3, No. 3, November 2005; Amy Myers Jaffe and Steven W. Lewis, "Beijing's Oil Diplomacy," *Survival*, Vol. 44, No. 1, Spring 2002.

2.2 From a Dominating Supply-Side View to a More Balanced View

The Chinese leadership's perceptions of energy security have been evolving, but gaining adequate oil and supply remains a central concern. During the Deng Xiaoping era, Beijing expected to increase oil supply primarily by making full use of the domestic market. In recognition of the strategic importance of energy to the overall economic development,[11] Deng put forward an oil eastward strategy, calling for the whole petroleum industry to focus on oil exploration and development in the east of China.[12] In the initial years after China became a net oil importer, the Jiang Zemin-Li Peng team showed indifference to energy security as they held the fantasy that China could go back to oil self-sufficiency. Largely they pinned their hope on the West of China, a vast area that has been untapped. Also, the long-term low prices of crude oil in the international energy market, which on average was around 15.8$/billion from 1993 to 1998,[13] was another factor contributing to their indifference.

Relatively speaking, the Jiang Zemin-Zhu Rongji administration was more market-oriented and prioritized economic efficiency,[14] as evidenced by the GDP-centered cadre assessment system. In practice, improving energy efficiency was merely a secondary policy option. Also, this administration saw the debut of China's new strategy "two market, two resources," meaning that China would try to meet its demand by utilizing oil and gas resources both at home and abroad. Hence, they started to underscore the importance of oil diplomacy. The "go out" strategy

[11] Deng Xiaoping, "Qian shinian wei hou shinian zuo hao zhunbei" (Formal Ten Years Should Make Good Preparation for the Next Ten Years), *Deng Xiaoping Wenxuan* (Deng Xiaoping Analects), Vol. 3, 14 October 1982, p. 17.

[12] Jinguo Chen, "Chongwen Deng Xiaoping tongzhi dui shiyou gongye fazhan de qinqie guanhuai he zhongyao zhishi" (Reviewing Deng Xiaoping's Cordial Concern About and Important Instructions on the Petroleum Industry), *Zhongguo Shiyou Bao* (China Petroleum), 20 August 2004. http://www.oilnews.com.cn/GB/misc/2004-08/20/content_583529.htm, accessed 8 August 2006.

[13] Calculated according to Dubai oil, the largest volume of crude that China imported from the Middle East. Data source: *BP Statistical Review of World Energy*, June 2004.

[14] Yongnian Zheng, *Globalization and State Transformation in China*, Cambridge: Cambridge University Press, 2004, p. 55.

was initiated to encourage domestic firms to venture abroad in 2000.[15] Much of the oil diplomacy focused on acquiring oil assets and locking up long-term oil and gas supplies. Surmount within that strategy was China's "pan-Asia global energy bridge" blueprint, under which China endeavors to forge itself as the hub linking oil-producing regions in the Middle East, Russia, and Central Asia with other Asian oil-consuming countries.[16] Apparently, this blueprint has not been materialized thus far.

With an aim to redress the public's mounting complaints of rampant official corruption, growing social disparity, and deteriorating environmental pollution in China, the Hu Jintao-Wen Jiabao team put forth a "harmonious society" (*hexie shehui*) guideline to instruct China's development.[17] This guideline differed from Jiang's at least in the following two aspects: firstly, it accentuated sustainable development. The pre-Hu era stuck to the doctrine that "development is of overriding importance" since the launch of China's reform, whereas the Hu-Wen administration stressed that "development must be scientific," denoting that economic growth could not sacrifice the environment and merely pursue high output. Secondly, the Hu-Wen administration for the first time incorporated environmental pollution and energy use inefficiency into the cadre assessment system.[18] Environmental protection has been stressed more than ever before and even written into some official documents and regulations.[19] The Hu-Wen administration set targets in 2009, aiming to reduce the intensity of carbon dioxide emissions per unit of GDP in

[15] Hongjiang Wang, "Zhongguo guanzhu shiyou anquan" (China Pays Attention to Oil Security), Beijing: Zhongguo Hongguan Jingji Xinxi wang (China Macroeconomic Information Web), 26 April 2001, http://www.macrochina.com.cn/zhzt/000044/002/20010426002822.shtml, accessed 20 August 2006.

[16] *Diyi Caijing Shibao* (First Financial Times), "Zhongguo Bushu Yaou Dalu Shiyou Anquan Zhanlue" (China Laid Out Eurasian Continent Oil Security Strategy), 16 December 2004.

[17] The Sixth Plenary Session of the 16th Central Committee of the Communist Party of China adopted the "Resolution on Major Issues Regarding the Building of a Harmonious Socialist Society" on 11 October 2006. See "Resolution on harmonious society published," *China Daily*, 19 October 2006. http://www.chinadaily.com.cn/china/2006-10/19/content_711520.htm, accessed 26 February 2023.

[18] It still needs time to see whether the incorporation of energy use efficiency and environmental pollution can be effective to check local government's impulse to pollute the environment and consume more energy.

[19] Both the *Eleventh Five-Year Plan* in 2006 and the draft of *China's Medium- and Long-term Energy Development Programme (2004–2020)* in 2004 have emphasized the

2020 by 40–45% compared with the level of 2005 and produce 15% of its energy from non-fossil fuels by 2020.[20] In practice, China reduced its energy intensity by 19% during the 11th five-year plan period (2006–2010). In China's 12th Five-Year Plan (2011–2015), targets have been set to cut the energy intensity and carbon intensity per unit of GDP by 2015 by 16% and 17%, respectively.[21] However, despite their efforts, it remained a far cry from the goal of curbing social inequality and environmental pollution under the Hu-Wen administration. This is also why their successors have to make more painstaking efforts.

The Xi Jinping-Li Keqiang Administration has largely followed their predecessor's energy route of balancing the goals of ensuring China's energy supplies and of conserving energy and protecting the environment. To some extent, the Xi-Li Administration has attached more importance, on the supply side, to the development of renewables, and on the demand side, to energy conservation and environmental protection through technical upgrading and institutional reform. This can be verified by the Chinese government's strong commitment that China will strive hard to have carbon dioxide emissions peak before 2030 and to achieve carbon neutrality before 2060. In order to achieve the above goals, the government has mapped out corresponding strategies and roadmaps. According to the white paper published by the Chinese government in December 2020, China has adopted a new strategy featuring Four Reforms and One Cooperation. Four Reforms refer to improving the energy consumption structure by containing unnecessary consumption, building a more diversified energy supply structure, improving energy technologies to upgrade the industry, and optimizing the energy system for faster growth of the energy sector. One Cooperation denotes cooperation with other countries to promote clean and low-carbon energy based on the principle of

importance of this point and highlighted to prohibit developing any energy project that may seriously damage the environment. See the following.

[20] Hu raised these targets in his speech in the United Nations in 2009. See "Hu Jintao's Speech on Climate Change," *New York Times*, 22 September 2009.

[21] "Carbon Conundrum: A Look at China's Targets," *China Dialogue*, 3 November 2011. https://www.chinadialogue.net/blog/4156-Carbon-conundrum-a-look-at-China-s-targets/en, accessed 21 August 2006.

equality and mutual benefit.[22] Compared with the Hu-Wen team, the Xi-Li administration is determined to let the market play a bigger role in dealing with China's energy security, according to their commitment to streamline the administrative and regulatory systems of the energy sector, reform energy pricing mechanisms and give more space to private enterprises. Hence, they take much account of energy use efficiency and renewable energy development in China, a governing approach that gives more credit to the demand-side view of energy security.

In retrospect, we can find the following features of China's perception of energy security. First of all, energy supply remains an important concern for the Chinese government not only because China's energy demand keeps surging, but also because energy supply directly affects China's economic growth. While emphasis has been laid on diversifying energy import sources, the government has particularly underscored the importance of promoting the development of renewable energy under Xi-Li Administration. Second, central to China's concern about energy supply is the problem of oil and gas availability, reliability, and affordability, which will be further illustrated in the following. In particular, the Russia–Ukraine conflict has further intensified the Chinese government's concern about its energy supply security. Third, equal importance has been attached to energy use efficiency, energy conservation, and environment protection, and in fact, the latter's role has become more prominent, particularly, since Xi's presidency. Fourth, as evidenced by the Belt and Road Initiative, China is more inclined to conducting international cooperation to ensure its energy security. In order to satisfy China's surging appetite, China underscores the importance of "using two legs to walk"—while speeding up E&P within China, the Chinese government has encouraged the NOCs to actively search oil and gas abroad and diversify their import sources.

China's proclivity to the supply-side view arises from a host of factors. Embracing the supply-side view of energy security in the Jiang era was large because many leaders at that time had close liaisons with the NOCs since they used to work in the energy sector.[23] By contrast, the Hu-Wen generation might support market reform, but they keep cautious

[22] The State Council Information Office of the People's Republic of China, *Xin Shidai de Zhongguo Nengyuan Fazhan Baipishu* (The White Paper on Energy in China's New Era), December 2020.

[23] Willy Wo-Lap Lam, *The Era of Jiang Zemin*, Singapore: Prentice Hall, 1999, p. 94.

about that partly due to their experience with the distress in the poor rural regions.[24] Hence, Jiang's experience in studying abroad and Zhu's educational background in economics may help nurture their market orientation, whereas Hu and Wen's long-term working experience in the grassroots may contribute to their concerns about social equity. When it comes to the Xi's era, the rise of China has become a more salient phenomenon, which has resulted in two effects. On the one hand, the growing number of the middle class not only brings about surging demand for energy resources, but also calls for better air quality, which is compatible with the trendy move of heading towards decarbonization in the international community. The latter has further made it a necessity for China to improve its energy consumption structure and energy conservation. On the other hand, one of the most drastic changes during this period may be the reconfiguration of Sino-US relations. Deemed a strategic competitor and suppressed by the US politically and economically, China has grave concerns about its energy supplies from abroad and has to take a rainy day.

The Chinese government's view of energy security has largely been affected by its unease in the global energy market, as well as its strategic concerns. In the eyes of many Chinese, full energy security is almost a synonym of self-sufficiency, and regard reliance on the international market as a vulnerability to risks. The obsession to self-sufficiency, on the one hand, results from China's harrowing experiences when China had to rely on foreign countries. For instance, the Sino-Soviet split and subsequent withdrawal of Soviet advisers from China's oil sector in the 1950s, damaged numerous large-scale projects and resulted in serious energy supply shortages when the supply of more than 50% of its refined oil was disrupted.[25]

On the other hand, China's view of energy security also derives from its uneasiness about the international oil market. First, the international oil market is unfair in that most developed energy spot and futures markets are scattered in developed countries. They have written the rules and possessed much richer experience concerning the oil and gas business in

[24] Joseph Fewsmith, "Generational Transition in China," *The Washington Quarterly*, Vol. 25, No. 4, 2002, pp. 23–35.

[25] Erica S. Downs, *China's Quest for Energy Security*, RAND Document No.: MR-1244-AF, 2000, http://www.rand.org/publications/MR/MR1244/, p. 11, accessed 26 February 2023.

the market. Particularly, most easily extractable oil reserves in the world have been either inaccessible to foreign investors or seized by multinational oil corporations (MOCs). Second, in view of such unfairness, the Chinese government thinks of it as perilous to its energy security. It is apparent that international oil prices are not purely decided by market mechanisms; rather, in its eyes, there exist three "invisible hands," namely, the market, US governments, and hedge funds. China holds a suspicion that the West could manipulate market prices and draw upon price fluctuations to undermine China's economy.[26] By the same token, concerns also exist that the uncontrollable hedge funds might incur oil price volatilities in order to capitalize on them. Due to the strong influence of the US in the Middle East and Central Asia, China is afraid that its access to foreign oil might be denied by the US.[27] Moreover, the underdeveloped strategic petroleum reserves and oil future markets in China have further intensified its qualms.

The Chinese government's perception of energy security, to a large extent, has been influenced by the NOCs, whose conception of energy security fundamentally is supply-side dominated. As Hayes and Hippel argue, the supply-based view is widely accepted largely because "it marches the supply-oriented engineering cultures of major utilities and energy supply corporations, whether public or private."[28] Their real perception might be extrapolated from their management's public speeches. On and off, they would pledge to fulfill their economic, political, and social obligations in China. At the same time, they often highlight the need to expand oil and gas production as the overarching measure to tackle China's energy security problems.[29] Sometimes, the NOCs also stress the need to carry out more overseas acquisitions and

[26] Xinxin Li, "Zhongguo Nengyuan Anquan de Bage Shijiao" ("China's Energy Security as Viewed from Eight Perspectives"), *Liaowang* (Outlook), No. 13, 31 March 2003, pp. 39–41.

[27] Xuanren Qin, "Guoji da huanjing ji daguo nengyuan waijiao yunchou" (The International Environment and the Energy Diplomatic Strategies of the Big Powers), *Guoji shiyou jingji* (International Petroleum Economics), Vol. 12, No. 1, 2004, p. 36.

[28] Hayes, Peter and David von Hippel, "Energy Security in Northeast Asia," *Global Asia*, Vol. 1, No. 1, September 2006, p. 92.

[29] See, for example, Jiang Jieming (the then vice President of CNPC), "CNPC Has Fulfilled Three Obligations to Ensure Energy Security," *Xinhua*, 1 March 2005, http://www.oilnews.com.cn/GB/misc/2005-03/11/content_607576.htm, accessed 21

transport the oil and gas produced abroad back home.[30] It is evident that expanding oil and gas supplies contributes to filling their coffers. Moreover, the NOCs tend to depict a bleak global oil market where latecomers could hardly compete with the prevailing MOCs. By so doing, they can win more state support for their ambitious strategy of going abroad; on the other hand, they would be less blamed for the possible losses incurred.

2.3 Underprovision of Indigenous Oil and Gas: China's Energy Insecurity in Reality

China's supply-side view of energy security particularly refers to the oil and gas availability, affordability, and reliability problems. Its preoccupation with the supply-side view first and foremost springs from the country's inadequate oil and gas supplies to meet domestic demands, whereas its appetite is still growing, which leads to an increasing reliance on foreign oil and gas imports. Going further, this surging appetite originates from many factors. Particularly striking among them is the nation-wide GDP worship and the skyrocketing car ownership in China. In the eyes of Beijing, China's oil supplies in effect are vulnerable to some risks, which among other things, are particularly in the sense of oil diversification, price fluctuation, and transportation. The following will explain these problems in terms of major energy consumption, production, imports and China's major concerns.

On the one hand, China's energy security problem does not spring from the imbalance between aggregate primary energy supply and demand, both of which increased 3.48 and 4.48 times respectively during 1990–2022. In fact, China has a very high degree of energy self-sufficiency. The self-sufficiency rate stayed above 90% from 1990 to 2003. Of course, China's primary energy demand started to exceed domestic supply after 1993 and the gap seems to be widening, implying

February 2007; Li Yuyang, "Three Oil Companies Promised to Take Social Responsibilities," *Jingji Ribao* (Economic Daily), 10 January 2007, http://www.sasac.gov.cn/2007rdzt/2007rdzt_0001/200701100142.htm, accessed 21 February 2007.

[30] An interview with Wang Zhongan, General Manager of the Department of Strategic Planning, CNOOC, see "CNOOC ltd. Ensures China's Energy Security Through Foreign Acquisition," *Shijie Jingliren Zhoukang* (World Entrepreneur Weekly), 26 February 2004, http://www1.cei.gov.cn/energy/doc/NYgsml/200409022438.htm, accessed 21 February 2007.

that China has to import more foreign energy resources in the future (see Chart 2.1). On the other hand, it is not the coal insufficiency problem either. As shown in Chart 2.2, coal has long dominated China's total energy consumption mix with approximately 70% on average. Nonetheless, China can basically fulfill self-sufficiency as coal is substantially rich although it needs to import some coal to meet domestic demands (see Chart 2.3). In fact, China has become a net coal importer since 2011, and it even surpassed Japan to become the largest coal importer in 2011, which is another reason why Beijing is so concerned with energy supply.

In terms of energy consumption composition, the leading energy source is coal, followed by oil, and natural gas had played a marginal role in China's energy equation for a long time. Chart 2.2 indicates that China's energy use mix has witnessed some changes after China's reform and opening-up thanks to the government's efforts to rationalize its energy consumption structure. Coal remains the primary energy source in China's energy consumption equation. Its share in China's energy consumption mix tends to go down, but its domestic production and aggregate consumption remain very tremendous (see Chart 2.3). Oil's role was enhanced slightly in the early 2000s, but fell down and leveled off at about 19% in recent years. However, oil's aggregate consumption

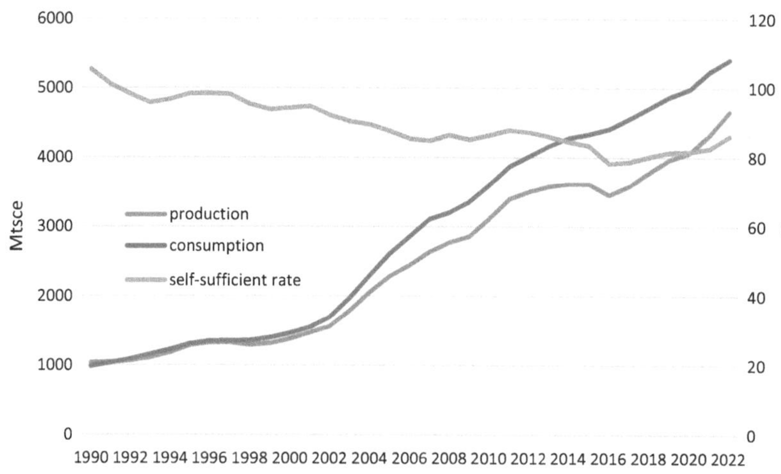

Chart 2.1 China's primary energy production and consumption (*Source* National Bureau of Statistics of China, *China Statistical Yearbook*, various years)

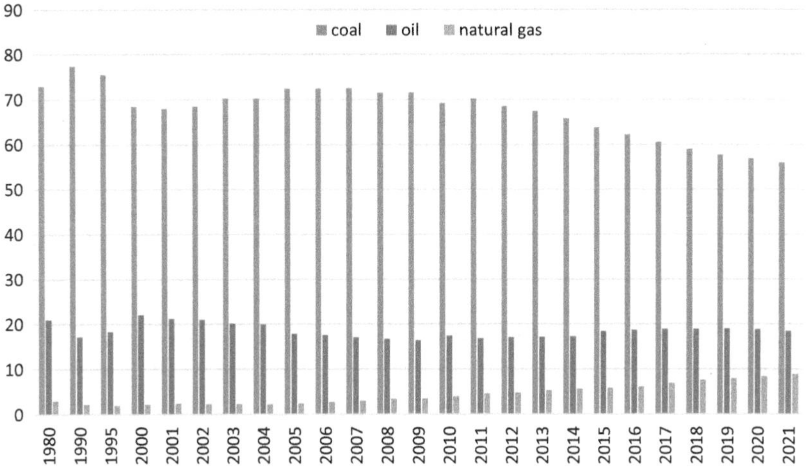

Chart 2.2 China's energy use composition (*Source* National Bureau of Statistics of China, *China Statistical Yearbook*, various years)

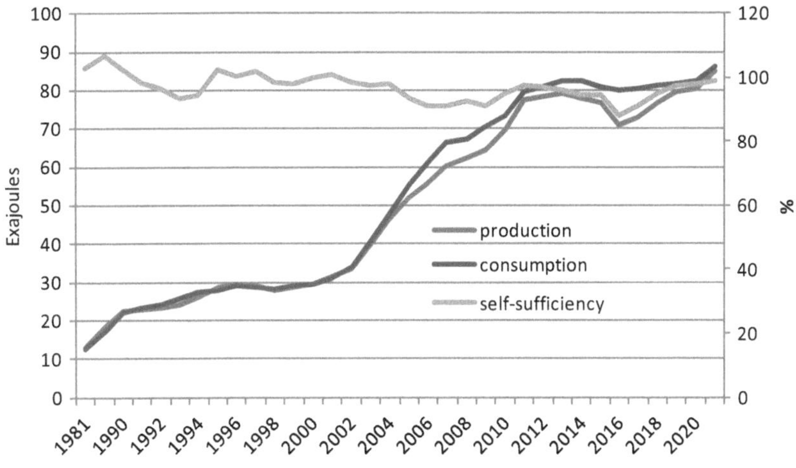

Chart 2.3 China's coal production and consumption (*Source* BP, *Statistical Review of World Energy*, 2022)

keeps rising. As a result, China's oil consumption growth accounted for half of the world's oil consumption growth in 2011.[31] Natural gas's role is looming larger in recent years, with a share of more than six percent since 2016 in China's energy mix (see Chart 2.2).

Domestic oil production can hardly meet China's voracious appetite, thus leading to the oil security problem. First, although domestic output has been on the rise, such an increase cannot catch up with domestic consumption. As Chart 2.4 shows, between 1993 and 2021, domestic oil production went up by 38.1%, peaking in 2015 at a level of 215 Mt, whereas domestic consumption skyrocketed 413.9%, far faster than the former. The constant decline of the self-sufficiency ratio, defined as the proportion of domestic production in gross oil consumed, from 127.4 to 27.7% between 1980 and 2021, indicates that China becomes more and more dependent on foreign oil imports (see Chart 2.4). Thus, with the rapid growth of the Chinese economy and the slim potential to boost domestic oil production, China has to rely more on foreign imports.

Second, the petroleum prospect that China confronts in the future is not so sanguine either. China's dependence on foreign crude oil imports

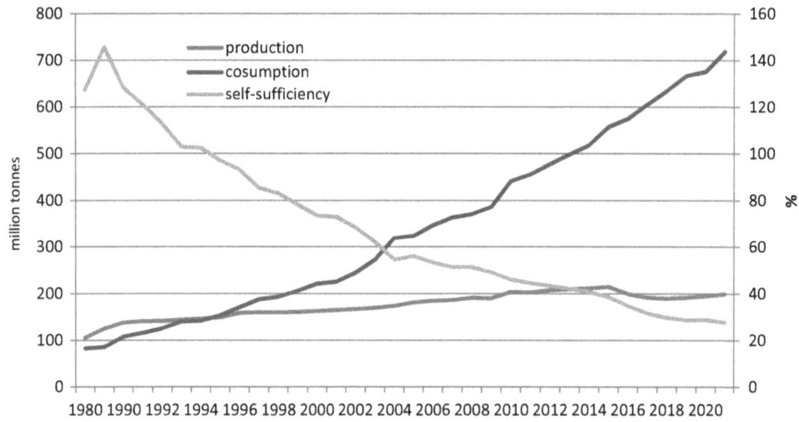

Chart 2.4 China's oil production and consumption (*Source* BP, *Statistical Review of World Energy*, 2022)

[31] US Energy Information Administration, "Country Analysis: China," http://www.eia.gov/countries/cab.cfm?fips=CH, accessed 28 October 2013.

came up to 73.6% in 2020 and slightly decreased to 72% in the following 2021 due to the Covid-19 pandemic.[32] Some projections show that almost 80% of China's total demand would have to depend on oil imports by 2030.[33]

Third, China will be more constrained by domestic supply–demand imbalance owing to the limited indigenous endowment and the growing trend of oil consumption. On the one hand, the domestic endowment of oil is not enough for sustainable development. Over 70% of indigenous crude oil in China is produced in nine large oilfields, among which the Daqing oil field has already come down from its peak of 50 Mt ten years ago to 40 Mt in 2011, whereas other oilfields like Huabei, Zhongyuan, Liaohe, Shengli and Dagang, developed in the 1980s, will soon face cutbacks in production.[34] According to BP, with one percent of world-proven oil reserves, China's R/P ratio was merely 11.4, which means that at the production rate of 2012, the proven reserves of oil can only last 11.4 years.[35] On the other hand, China's appetite for oil is projected to surge when it comes to the following factors.

First, China's per capita oil consumption is much lower than that of most other countries. The per capita oil consumption in China is tantamount to about one-ninth and one-fifth of the U.S. and Japan, respectively.[36] Along with an expanding number of middle class, the "world factory" status and the underway industrialization and urbanization are set to spur oil consumption in great measure, implying that there is a long way to go before China can reach the peak of oil consumption.

[32] Zheng Xin, "China's Oil Dependence on Imports Sees Drop," The State Council of P.R. China, 24 February 2022, https://english.www.gov.cn/news/topnews/202202/24/content_WS6216e221c6d09c94e48a569e.html, accessed 19 March 2023.

[33] See BP: *BP Energy Outlook 2030*, January 2013; Qiang Wang, Shuyu Li, and Rongrong Li, "China's Dependency on Foreign Oil Will Exceed 80% by 2030: Developing a Novel NMGM-ARIMA to Forecast China's Foreign Oil Dependence from Two Dimensions," *Energy*, Vol. 163, November 2018, pp. 151–167.

[34] Qianzhan wang (Forward Business Information), "2020 nian Zhongguo shiyou duiwai yicundu jiang da 70%" (China's Rate of Dependence on Foreign Oil Would Hit 70%), 5 April 2012. http://www.qianzhan.com/indynews/detail/214/20120405-f716dff12e4d1479.html, accessed 1 November 2013.

[35] BP, *Statistical Review of World Energy*, 2013.

[36] CIA World Factbook—Data are accurate as of 1 January 1 2012.

Second, the changing oil consumption pattern indicates that domestic demand for oil will accelerate due to the surging demand from the transport sector, which by far has become the largest consumer of diesel and gasoline. Chart 2.5 shows the transport, storage, and postal sector has seen a galloping rise of 265 and 189% in gasoline and diesel consumption respectively between 2000 and 2020.[37] This trend will persist because the swelling transport sector characterized by soaring private car ownership calls for more oil consumption. The number of private vehicles skyrocketed from 0.82 million in 1990 to 278.73 million in 2022 (see Chart 2.6) although in recent years the number of electric vehicles is growing. China has also become the largest market for cars. Annual sales are expected to rise from 19 m in 2012 to 31 m in 2020.[38]

Third, the institutional factors have contributed to the surge in oil consumption. China's economic growth has spurred strong demands for energy resources, but the reform in the oil sector is too slow. So far, the market has still been monopolized by the NOCs, which seek to expand

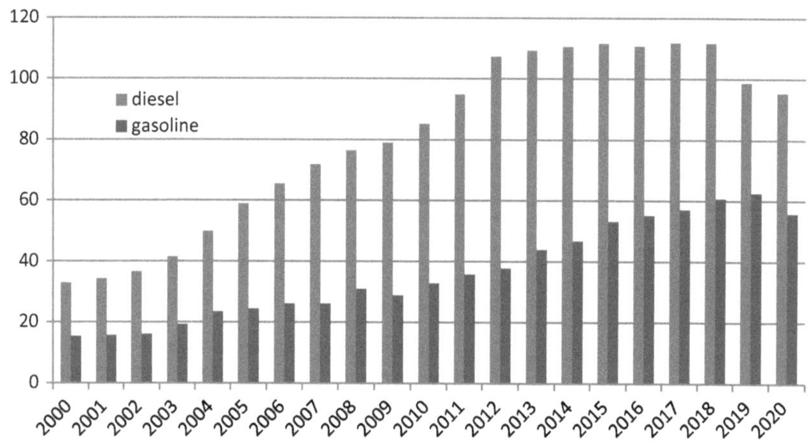

Chart 2.5 Oil consumption by the transport, storage and postal sector (Mt) (*Source* National Bureau of Statistics of China, *China Statistical Yearbook*, various years)

[37] The National Bureau of Statistics of China combines the three sectors in statistics, but transport is apparently the dominant user.

[38] *The Economist*, "The Future of Cars: Gloom and Boom," 20 April 2013.

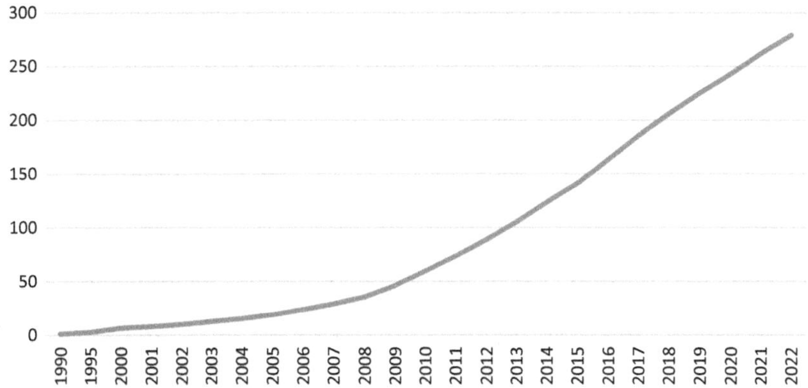

Chart 2.6 Possession of private vehicles (million) (*Source* National Bureau of Statistics of China, *China Statistical Yearbook*, various years)

oil supply and consumption. The state still employs an approach with command-economy characteristics, such as setting oil prices, imposing import quotas, selecting market participants, and so on. As a result, "hesitant and incomplete reform in the energy sector has prevented it from boosting domestic energy output and distribution fast enough to meet growing demand."[39] What makes things worse is that local governments have strong incentives to speed up economic growth thanks to the GDP-centered cadre assessment system.

Fourth, China's energy use efficiency is much lower than the world average, which leaves much room for further improvement. But in the short run, China will still follow such an inefficient route to keep the economy on the fast track.[40]

Fifth, to be related, environmental concern has been set as an important vector in the policy-making agenda. Considering that the primary pollution source stems from coal combustion, efforts have been made to substitute coal with other types of energy resources, and natural gas is

[39] IEA, *China's Worldwide Quest for Energy Security*, Paris: IEA, 2000, p. 14.

[40] Problems and countermeasures regarding China's energy efficiency will be discussed in the next part.

a preferred option while oil is an alternative. For instance, many factories used diesel to generate electricity during the electricity shortages in Zhejiang from 2003 to 2004.

Meanwhile, there are some factors that may help curb the future growth of oil consumption. For instance, these factors include but are not limited to China's moderate economic growth, fast deployment of renewables and electric vehicles, technical upgrading and wider use of artificial intelligence (AI), its effort to improve energy conservation, and energy use efficiency, oil price spikes, and so on. These factors may provide an avenue to retard the surging oil consumption.

Therefore, while some factors such as high oil prices and efforts to improve energy efficiency may slightly retard Chinese oil consumption, there exist stronger incentives driving China's oil demand up to higher levels. Its oil demand is set to go up, but domestic production cannot satisfy it, and neither can domestic oil reserves sustain future demands. Oil availability is and will continue to be a serious problem for China, leading China to be more dependent on foreign imports.

When it comes to natural gas, its share in the gross energy consumption mix during 1993–2021 rose from 1.8 to 8.9% (see Chart 2.2), and the total consumption in 2021 reached 333.99 billion cubic meters (Bcm), 17.6 times that in 1993 (see Chart 2.7). IEA's projection for China's demand for gas in the new policies scenario in 2015 is nearly 301 bcm, rising to 502 bcm in 2035, 11% of China's energy mix.[41] Before 2007, indigenous natural gas output could guarantee domestic consumption. However, China started importing natural gas in 2005. To cut greenhouse gas emissions and clean the environment, together with the government's rigorous support for the use of natural gas, the gap between domestic supply and demand is bound to enlarge. Most organizations project that China's imports of natural gas will dramatically mount up in the future. According to IEA, the imports would reach 212 Bcm by 2035, constituting 42% of total natural gas consumption.[42] Hence, like oil, natural gas availability is also a serious problem.

In sum, the *availability* problem, or the growing gap between domestic oil and gas supply and demand has forced China to become

[41] IEA, *World Energy Outlook*, 2011, pp. 158–159.

[42] Calculated by the author according to IEA figures from IEA, *World Energy Outlook 2011*, pp. 159–165.

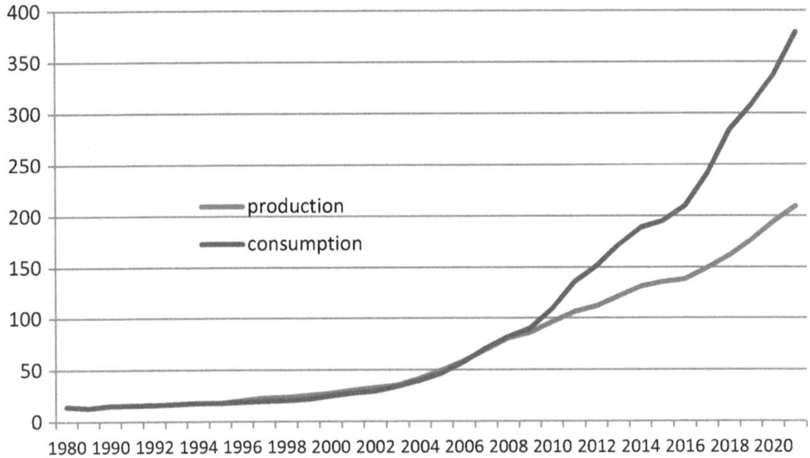

Chart 2.7 China's natural gas production and consumption (Bcm) (*Source* BP, *Statistical Review of World Energy*, 2022)

more dependent on foreign resources, but the Chinese government deems it "too risky" to simply rely on imports because of its unease of the international energy market, thus generating the *oil reliability and affordability problems*. Specifically, the reliability problem consists of two aspects: On one hand, the sources of imports are not so diversified. In particular, China is highly reliant on the Middle East, a region plagued by long-term instability. Among the imported oil in 2012, about 41% came from the Middle East. This rate is lower than 75% of Japan but much higher than 20% of the US in the same year.[43]

On the other hand, oil transportation is vulnerable to great risks since more than 80% of China's oil imports need to pass through the Malacca Strait, and more than 90% of its imported oil has to rely on foreign oil tankers.[44] Besides concerns about terrorism and piracy, Beijing holds misgivings about the US's powerful influence in the region. Because

[43] Calculated according to the data from BP, *Statistical Review of World Energy*, 2013.

[44] Chunlian Li, "Chao jiucheng shiyou jinkou yunshu yilai guowai, Zhongshiyou zi jian daxing youlun pouju" (Over 90% Oil Imports Transportation Needs to Rely on Foreign Oil Cargos, CNPC Builds Large Tankers to Address the Issue), *Zhengquan Ribao* (Securities Daily), 23 October 2012.

China has no powerful naval power to safeguard its oil shipment, it concerns that its sea lane transportation might be interdicted by rival forces.

The *affordability* problem primarily arises from oil price fluctuations. In view of the high costs that China has to pay and the adverse impact on the economy thanks to oil price volatilities, some Chinese officials hold that price risk is one of the vulnerabilities or even the central risk.[45] In Beijing's view, oil price volatilities may arise from geopolitical events, war, speculation of hedge funds, manipulation of some governments, natural disasters, regional instability, and so on. Thus, with deepening reliance on imports, China has to face oil reliability and affordability problems.

However, the growing energy constraints cannot be resolved merely by way of expanding oil and gas supplies. After all, world resources are limited. The serious environmental pollution stemming from tremendous hydrocarbon energy use has compelled China to reflect upon energy security from the demand side.

2.4 Conclusion

The SMMA can be reflected in China's perceptions of energy security. First, despite the centrality of a supply-side view of energy security, the demand-side view has gained new momentum in China, paying more attention to energy saving and environmental protection. For that purpose, it is willing to let the market play a more decisive role, such as getting the oil prices right, open petroleum upstream to private investments, natural gas pricing more market-oriented, and so on. Second, despite some uneasiness, China has a growing trust on the international

[45] These officials include Huai Chen, a high official of the Development Research Center of the State Council (DRC) and some members of the National Congress. See Huai Chen, "Jiage reng shi Zhongguo shiyou anquan zuida fengxian" (Price Risk Is the Central Risk of China's Oil Security), *Beijing Chenbao* (Beijing Morning), 12 October 2002; Yu Fei and Meng Na, "Meiyi zhanzheng yinyun yinfa Zhongguo shiyou anquan huati" (US-Iraq War Eliciting the Topic of China's Oil Security), *Xinhua*, 7 March 2003, http://news.xinhuanet.com/fortune/2003-03/07/content_764778.htm, accessed 25 August 2006; Tang Yongbing, "shiyou qihuo – shichanghua bixian de biran xuanze" (Petroleum Futures—The Necessary Choice of Avoiding Risks for Marketization], *Jingji Ribao* (Economic Daily), 14 November 2003.

energy market. While forging closer ties with oil-exporting countries, it is also more collaborative with other oil-consuming states.

In the meantime, China deems it necessary to leave a strong hand over the energy sector for the sake of China's energy security. State control and/or state support has been justified by its obsession to self-sufficiency, green-hand experience in handling the volatile international oil market, and the lack of prowess of the NOCs vis-à-vis the MOCs. This is set to create some kind of paradox between state control and market forces.

CHAPTER 3

SMMA in the Lens of Institutional Reform

What impact does China's institutional layout have on its approach to energy security? This is the central question this chapter aims to explore. It is argued that China's structure of authority over the energy sector fits in with what Kenneth Lieberthal calls "fragmented authoritarianism." "Authoritarianism" is in the sense that relevant decision-making power rests in the central government whereas nongovernmental organizations and individuals have few channels to be engaged in this process; at the same time, policy-making and implementation are "fragmented" both by the different ministries/bureaucrats and by the NOCs. In particular, compared with the numerous consumption-end consumers, the supply-end NOCs have a much stronger influence on the national energy policy process, while the dispersive institutional power distribution contributes to China's energy policy inconsistency, which in turn has left many loopholes for the NOCs to exert their influence. That being said, two emerging trends deserve noting. One is power devolution from the center to local governments; the other is marketization, due to which government intervention has been reduced.

There are two levels of institutional layout that can affect China's energy security. One is the administration level, on which a variety of government agencies have different missions pertaining to energy administration. The "fragmented authoritarian" nature has often resulted in inter-ministerial tussles and disjointed policy-making. Any major energy

S. Chen, *China's Approach to Energy Security*,
https://doi.org/10.1007/978-981-99-3573-4_3

project or policy initiative has to win the support of many ministerial units that are equal in the Chinese nomenklatura system.[1] The other is the industrial level, on which the unbalanced market structure has endowed some market actors, specifically the NOCs with more prowesses to influence the government policy process, which has been elaborated in the preceding Chapter 1.

The following part first introduces China's institutional reform related to governance over the petroleum sector and sketches out the contours of China's energy governance structure. The second part illustrates the impact on the SMMA brought about by a failure in creating a Ministry of Energy (MoE). At last, the author evaluates the problems in China's oil and gas policy-making process resulting from China's institutional layouts.

3.1 Institutional Reform and Present Administrative Framework

Political institutions can influence the creation of the environment, the perception, and interpretation of policy-makers and thus policy-making, and have an important impact upon political stability.[2] For a country like China undergoing a transition from a planned economy to a market-oriented economy, there are many factors influencing the reform process as well as the formulation of energy policies, such as China's reliance on the foreign energy market, the legacy of the planned economy, the ambitions and ideology of the government and the robustness of state institutions. Yet, due to the opacity and complexity of China's policy-making process, it is intrinsically a hard nut to crack to unveil the black box.[3]

Rosenbaum and Ikenberry spelled out how the US political system shapes its response to the energy problem.[4] Rosenbaum argued that

[1] Lieberthal, 1992; Lieberthal and Oksenberg, 1988.

[2] Jianrong Huang, *The Applicability of Policy-Making Theories in Post-Mao China*, Brookfield, WI, USA: Ashgate, 1999.

[3] Philip Andrews Speed, Xuanli Liao and Roland Dannreuther, 2002, ibid., p. 46.

[4] G. John Ikenberry, *Reasons of State: Oil Politics and the Capacities of American Government*, Ithaca: Cornell University Press, 1988.

energy policy-making is made within constraints imposed by the character of energy resources and by the nature of the political institutions and actors involved.[5] The importance of institutional structure in China's reform process has also been stressed. "A consensus is emerging that the nature of a nation's institutions is critical to the progress and success of the reform process."[6] In the case of China's petroleum sectors, administration power primarily rests at the central level, whereas the ministry or vice-ministry-level NOCs are the overarching industrial actors. The important axes of power consist of the ministries, state companies, and other major government agencies.[7] Once these institutions have gained power, they will try to expand their influence over the oil and natural gas sectors.

3.1.1 Central Government

As shown in Chart 3.1, by August 2022 China has restructured its energy administrative institutions for several times. After the PRC was established, the petroleum sector was under the administration of the General Bureau of Petroleum Administration which was subordinate to the Fuel Industry Ministry (FIM). In the next fifteen years starting from July 1955, there was a special Petroleum Industry Ministry (PIM) overseeing the petroleum sector. This power was taken over by the Fuel and Chemical Industry Ministry (FCIM) in June 1970 and then to the PCIM in February 1975. The PIM was restored in 1978 to supervise the petroleum sector but was replaced in 1988 by the Ministry of Energy (MoE). It was the first attempt of the Chinese government to conduct unified management of the whole energy industry, but due to opposition from the NOCs, the MoE could only govern the two sectors of coal and electricity in practice, and even so its policies could hardly be well implemented because, in its subordinate enterprises, there was no clear line between the functions of the government and enterprises. In 1993, the MoE was disbanded. After its removal, the administration work had been left to the

[5] Walter A. Rosenbaum, *Energy, Politics, and Public Policy*, Washington, DC: Congressional Quarterly Press, 1981.

[6] Philip Andrews Speed, *Energy Policy and Regulation in the People's Republic of China*, The Hague, London, and New York: Kluwer Law International, 2004, p. 48.

[7] Kenneth Lieberthal, *Governing China: From Revolution Through Reform*, New York: W.W. Norton, 1995, pp. 292–313.

three NOCs (CNOOC, Sinopec, and CNPC). To corporatize the three NOCs, the government set up a State Bureau of Petroleum and Chemical Industries (SBPCI) in 1998 to take over the administrative power of the Ministry of Chemical Industry and the three NOCs. Three years later, the SBPCI was canceled, and restructured into the China Petroleum and Chemical Industry Association, responsible for the coordination of the industry. Since then, there is no special energy ministry to manage the energy sector and the petroleum sector has come under multifarious administrations, resulting in a situation where "not the state but different departments are in place" (*bujian guojia, zhi jian bumen*),[8] Energy policies have been fragmented by different institutions, which in turn leaves loopholes for the NOCs and local governments to take advantage.

The dispersed administrative functions among different ministries and commissions, along with their distinct sector interests, are set to bring about different views and policy conflicts on some issues, such as oil and gas market openness, reliance on foreign oil trade, and fuel tax. This is also one important reason why the Chinese energy policies sometimes are inconsistent and even conflicting, as discussed in Chapter 4. The following will portray the major administrative actors pertaining to oil and gas governance in China.

Some scholars introduced China's energy administrative layout, but they incorporated different institutions into their analyses.[9] For instance, in her paper Downs included the Ministry of Foreign Affairs (MFA), the military, the media, academics, and some research institutes. The MFA may show up only in the case of helping NOCs go abroad. And the military only holds sway when an issue relates to China's national security or territorial integrity. Underlying its claim for preserving China's sea lane security is the PLA's intention to lobby for more budgets from the government.[10] Therefore, in most cases especially in terms of

[8] Xiangde Qiu, "Nengyuan Gaige Bianzouqu" (Energy Reform Variations), *Huanqiu Qiyejia (Global Entrepreneurs)*, 22 April 2009.

[9] See Michal Meidan, Philip Andrews-Speed & Ma Xin, "Shaping China's Energy Policy: Actors and Processes," *Journal of Contemporary China*, 18(61), September 2009, pp. 591–616; Erica S. Downs, 2004, ibid., pp. 60–80; Erica S. Downs, "The Chinese Energy Security Debate," *The China Quarterly*, March 2004, Vol. 177, pp. 24–29; Philip Andrews Speed, Xuanli Liao, and Roland Dannreuther, 2002, ibid, pp. 46–53; Asia Research Center, *China: Energy Policy and Natural Gas Use*. Asia Research Center, Murdoch University, Western Australia, 2001, pp. 11–13.

[10] Discussion with Nan Li, a PLA research expert at East Asia Institute, April 2007.

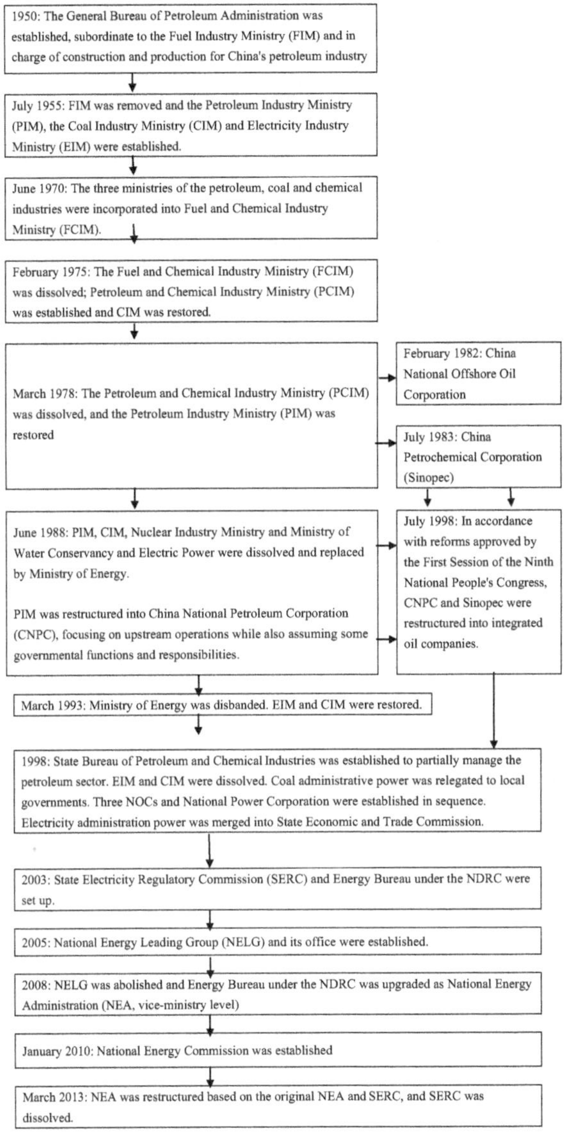

Chart 3.1 History of China's petroleum industry (*Source* Made by the author)

domestic-oriented energy policies, both play a minor role. As far as the media,[11] academics, and research institutes are concerned, overwhelmingly it depends on the leadership to decide whether, when, and how to adopt their views. There is no formal channel for them to engage in policy-making.[12] Hence, the roles of these actors will not be discussed here. This chapter mainly focuses on the key actors in this process: the top national leadership, major government organs concerned, the NOCs, provincial governments, and foreign forces represented by the MOCs.

The top leadership in China resides in the Politburo, the Standing Committee of the State Council, the Secretariat of the CPC, senior military commanders, and provincial leaders.[13] In particular, the supreme power vests in the Standing Committee of the Politburo (SCP), which used to be composed of 5–9 members but is now of 7 members. In general, any Chinese grand strategy including the energy security strategy must be approved by the top leadership first before taking shape. And any giant project calling for huge investments must be noted and endorsed by at least one SCP member,[14] such as the west-to-east gas pipeline project and the Three Gorges project. It is the top leadership that plays the decisive role in defining the framework of China's foreign and domestic strategies as stated above.

As the highest executive organ of state power and the highest organ of state administration, the State Council is responsible for dealing with such affairs as China's internal politics, diplomacy, national defense, finance, economy, culture, and education. As such, it has the authority to formulate China's energy policy and strategy, oversee energy policy implementation, and even override any energy regulation by its ministries or local governments. In recent years, however, the State Council has

[11] One point merits noting is that, as far as the author knows, not all the media in China are just the mouthpiece of the Chinese government. Some of them can often make reports disclosing the unfair or corrupted cases related with government agencies or the SOEs. This is especially the case in the economic arena. The typical "defectors" include: *Finance, China Economic Times, 21 Century Economic Report, Nanfang Daily*, etc.

[12] Barry Naughton, "China's Economic Think Tanks: Their Changing Role in the 1990s'." *China Quarterly*, Vol. 33, 2002, pp. 625–635.

[13] Kenneth Lieberthal and Michel Oksenberg, *Policy Making in China: Leaders, Structures, and Processes*, Princeton, NJ: Princeton University Press, 1988, pp. 35–41.

[14] "The Influence of Asia on Oil Price Fluctuations," *Alexander's Oil and Gas Connections: News and Trends: S and SE Asia*, Vol. 6, Nos. 15, 14 August 2001.

decided to take a series of measures to significantly reduce and decentralize administrative approval items and truly delegate power to the market in the hope to stimulate the vitality of economic and social development and let the market play a more decisive role. Though vested with such immense authority, the State Council often has to balance different vested interests in its policy-making.

In order to have better coordination among different ministries in formulating energy strategies and development planning, the Chinese government set up a National Energy Commission (NEC) in 2010. The NEC is an overarching super-ministry agency responsible for working out national energy development plans, addressing significant issues concerning energy security and energy development, and coordinating major programs of domestic energy development and international cooperation. Headed by Premier Li Keqiang (it used to be former Premier Wen Jiabao), the body is composed of 22 members from other agencies. Most notably, the Chief of the General Staff Department of the PLA, ministers of NDRC, State Security, MLR, Ministry of Finance (MoF), MoC, MFA, MEP, MWR, SASAC, MST, MoT, etc., is on board. "The inclusion of senior intelligence, foreign affairs and military figures in the commission is perhaps the clearest indication that Beijing is elevating energy policy to the level of a national security concern."[15] Reform over the energy sector often involves a plethora of powerful stakeholders, so the creation of the NEC should be conducive to devising more coordinated national energy policies and breaking the obstructions from various entrenched interests.

Under the State Council, the important axes of bureaucratic power concerning energy governance include a multitude of ministries (see Chart 3.2), among which the NDRC/National Energy Administration (NEA), Ministry of Commerce (MOFCOM), the State-owned Assets Supervision and Administration Commission (SASAC), Ministry of Land and Resources (MLR) are designated to become the major government apparatus directly in charge of the administrative work of China's energy industry.

The NDRC, the former NDPC, is the leading institution taking charge of the administrative work of China's energy-related matters. Historically it was the key institution for administering the Chinese economy. Though

[15] Peter Yuan Cai, "China's New National Energy Commission," *East Asia Forum*, 12 March 2010, https://www.eastasiaforum.org/2010/03/12/chinas-new-national-energy-commission/, accessed 22 April 2023.

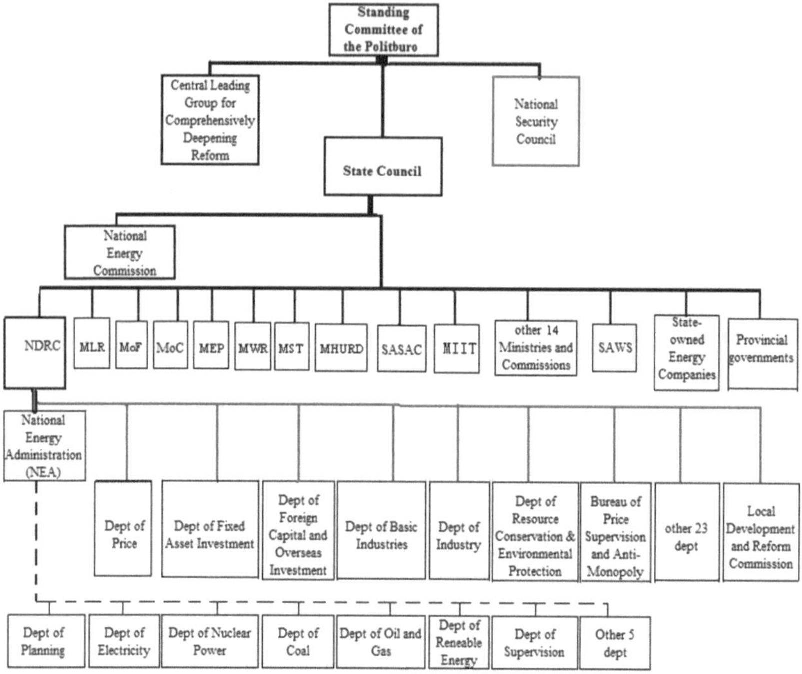

Chart 3.2 China's energy policy-making body (*Source* Drawn out by the author on 20 October 2019)

the NDRC is playing a less influential role in the whole economy, it still predominates over energy prices, foreign investments, energy development plans, and so forth. First of all, the NDRC has been empowered to administer the macro level of economic and social development issues, to organize, implement, oversee, and coordinate the work related to national strategies and policies including energy, long- and medium-term energy plans, import and export plans, comprehensive economic and social development, economic restructuring, energy conservation, and so on. Second, in terms of refined oil prices, it is up to the NDRC to decide when and how to adjust in light of international oil price changes. Likewise, fixing natural gas prices has long been in the hands of the NDRC on the basis of operation costs, transmission costs, and other costs. Third, the NDRC is also tasked to promote the strategy of sustainable development, undertake comprehensive coordination of energy saving and emission reduction, organize the formulation and coordinate the implementation of plans and policy measures for recycling economy, national energy and resource conservation, and comprehensive utilization, organize the formulation of key strategies, plans, and policies in addressing climate change, and take the lead with related ministries in attending international negotiations of climate change. Fourth, the NDRC is in charge of planning key projects and the layout of productive forces, making arrangements for state funding for construction, as well as organizing and managing the work of special inspectors for key projects. In addition, it is also in charge of the construction, management, and law compilation of the strategic petroleum reserves. Fifth, as far as Chinese firms' outbound FDI is concerned, those investments involving "sensitive" countries or regions or industries are subject to NDRC's approval. In a word, the NDRC has great influence on China's economic and social development, whose impact is comprehensive and profound covering not only China's economic efficiency but also social equality.[16]

To endorse the general principle formulated at the Third Plenum of the Eighteenth Central Committee that the market should be allowed to play a decisive role in China's economy, the party state decided to reduce government intervention in the economy. Part and parcel of the scheme is to slash the power of the NDRC at least in the following two aspects: the power in fixing prices of refined oil products and of natural gas, which will be left to the market; examining and approving big projects, which will be relegated to local governments.

The National Energy Administration (NEA) whose predecessor was the Energy Bureau under the NDRC has been promoted as a vice-ministry level agency in China's 2008 super-ministry reform even though it remains under NDRC. The new organization has incorporated all the functions of the previous National Energy Leading Group (NELG), most of the energy-related functions of the NDRC, and the nuclear power management of the previous Commission of Science, Technology, and Industry for National Defense (COSTIND). In the 2010 government reshuffling, China's SERC has been merged into the NEA. After these reforms, the NEA's major functions are to work out and organize the implementation of national energy development strategy, planning

[16] Based on "Main Functions of the NDRC," http://en.ndrc.gov.cn/mfndrc/default.htm, accessed 12 January 2014.

and policies, do research on and put forward energy reform proposals, and carry out energy supervision and administration. Other than that, the NEA has been authorized to represent the Chinese government in carrying out international energy cooperation and negotiating and signing agreements with foreign energy departments and international organizations. Moreover, the NEA is tasked to manage China's strategic petroleum reserves.

The NEA has been authorized to carry out supervision and administration over the energy sector, but it still lacks both the authority and resources necessary for its task notwithstanding the upgrading and expansion of power. According to Zhang Guobao, former head of the NEA, none of the five certificates required to operate a coal mine were issued by the NEA. The NEA is in charge of assessing the qualification of an operator in nuclear power plants, but it is up to the National Nuclear Safety Bureau to issue the certificate.[17] As a result of the fragmented nature of China's system for managing its energy policy, the NEA is facing a lot of constraints in fulfilling its aims of pricing reform, institutional reform, and so forth.

The MLR is acting as the owner of land, minerals, forests, grasslands, wetlands, water, oceans, and other natural resource assets, taking charge of all land and space uses, and handling issues related to the utilization of natural resources including land, mineral reserves, and marine resources. It is within its power purview of drafting laws, and laying down and implement policies, regulations, technical standards, specifications, and methods for the management, protection, and rational utilization of natural resources. It also undertakes the responsibility to engage in geological surveys, monitor and administer mineral reserve E&P. Therefore, any domestic and foreign companies must get approval from the MLR if they want to carry out oil and gas exploration, exploitation and production in China.[18]

The Ministry of Ecology and Environment's (MEE) predecessor was the Ministry of Environmental Protection (MEP), which was built upon the upgrading of the State Environmental Protection Administration in 2008. Compared with the MEP, the MEE has been endowed with more

[17] Peter Yuan Cai, "China's new National Energy Commission," *East Asia Forum*, 12 March 2010.

[18] Based on http://www.mlr.gov.cn, accessed 12 January 2014.

authority. While fully incorporating the power of the MEP, it has integrated the scattered ecological and environmental protection powers and responsibilities from other ministries, such as the NDRC's responsibilities for combating climate change and reducing emissions, the MLR's responsibilities for the supervision and prevention of groundwater pollution, the Ministry of Water Resources' responsibilities for the preparation of water function zoning, the management of sewage outfalls, and the water environment protection of river basins, and so on. Hence, the MEE is no longer merely a toothless tiger. At present, its major functions cover establishing and improving the basic system of the ecological environment, taking charge of overall coordination, supervision, and management of the prevention and control of environmental pollution, emission reduction, and nuclear and radiation safety, organizing the assessment of environmental quality, monitoring natural resource development and utilization, guiding, coordinating and supervising ecological protection and restoration work.

The MOFCOM has been established in 2003 with the merger of part of the functions of the State Economic and Trade Commission (SETC) and the Ministry of Foreign Trade and Economic Cooperation. In general, the MOFCOM specializes in dealing with matters related with market circulation and market order, taking charge of domestic and international trade and international economic cooperation. It also has the responsibilities of helping draft economic plans and strategies, but primarily of standardizing market operation and circulation order, and improving the market system. Hence, it is within the MOFCOM's administrative purview to regulate the energy downstream market and the oil companies' foreign investment activities. Since 2004 the MOFCOM, along with the MFA and NDRC,[19] has published a *Countries and Industries for Overseas Investment Guidance Catalogue* to assist domestic firms to venture abroad.

The fundamental role of the SASAC is to delegate the state to perform the investor's responsibilities so as to supervise "the preservation and increment of the value of state-owned assets," and to help set up modern enterprise system in SOEs.[20] Accordingly, in addition to drawing up

[19] The NDRC was involved starting in 2007.

[20] SASAC, "Main Functions and Responsibilities of SASAC," See http://en.sasac.gov.cn/2018/07/17/c_9258.htm, accessed 19 August 2022.

laws or regulations concerning SOEs management, the SASAC has been authorized to dispatch supervisory panels, appoint and/or dismiss top executives of the SOEs, and establish a corporate executive selection system. The aim of this organization is to change the previous situation where each ministry performed their divided ownership and subsequently, management of assets, business affairs, and employees were separated.[21] Thus far, 98 central SOEs significant for the national economy and the people's livelihood including the four NOCs are under the supervision of the SASAC.[22]

The Ministry of Finance is responsible for preparing and implementing China's annual budget and foreign exchange quotas allocated to support Chinese companies' FDI, fiscal and taxation policies, laws and regulations concerning Chinese businesses abroad, managing state-owned capital gains and central finance used to bolster enterprises, and supervise the finance of central firms. It also sends Chinese delegates to participate in foreign-related tax and international tariff negotiations, and the signing of foreign-related taxation agreements.

Chinese firms have to apply to the SAFE under the central bank (People's Bank of China) for their foreign exchange. The PBOC has been empowered to hold and manage the state's foreign exchange and gold reserves, make payment and settlement rules in collaboration with relevant departments, monitor money-laundering related types of suspicious fund movement, and participate in international financial activities at the capacity of the central bank. Under the central bank, the SAFE is responsible for promulgating regulatory measures governing foreign exchange transactions under the current account, supervising and monitoring foreign exchange transactions under the capital account, including inward and outward remittance and payments, and providing the PBOC with propositions and references for the formulation of exchange rate policy.

[21] Renmin Wang (People Daily Online), "Zhengfu jigou gaige: huantang you huanyao" ("Governmental Organization Reform: Change both Format and Substance"), 18 March 2003. http://www.people.com.cn/GB/guandian/183/6103/6104/20030318/946373.html, accessed 12 January 2014.

[22] The number of central SOEs has been reduced from the original 196 at the time when SASAC was established. See SASAC, "Directory of Central SOEs", http://en.sasac.gov.cn/sasacdirectory.html, assessed 17 August 2022.

Other ministries also play a role in their professional areas. For instance, the newly created Ministry of Emergency Management is responsible for organizing the preparation of national emergency response plans, planning and guiding all regions and departments to respond to emergencies, establishing a disaster reporting system, guiding the prevention and control of fires, floods and droughts, geological disasters, etc., coordinating the construction of emergency response forces and material reserves, and unifying them during disaster relief. It is in charge of the supervision and management of oil exploration and safety production. The Ministry of Water Resources (MWR) is relevant when a water infrastructure project or a project entailing substantial water use or affecting water quality is to be conducted. The Ministry of Housing and Urban–Rural Development (MHURD) is responsible for drawing up national standards of construction, planning urban and rural development, and guiding construction activities, all of which have a direct impact on energy efficiency and energy conservation. The Ministry of Industry and Information Technology (MIIT) is responsible for drawing up China's industrial planning, policies and standards, energy conservation, and comprehensive use of resources in the secondary industry and IT industry.

As an Industrial self-discipline management organization, the China Petroleum and Chemical Industry Federation (CPCIF) is not an administrative organ, but it has still played an important role in the policy process related to oil and natural gas. Specifically, the CPCIF holds duties to establish a statistical survey system, carry out industrial statistical surveys, and be responsible for the collection, analysis, research, and release of statistical information on the development of the petroleum and chemical industry. It also provides opinions and suggestions on relevant industrial policies and legislation to the government, participates in the formulation of industry plans, and conducts preliminary demonstrations of major investment and development, technological transformation, and technology introduction projects in the industry. Moreover, the CPCIF is responsible to strengthen industry self-discipline, standardize industry behavior, maintain fair market competition, and carry out domestic and foreign economic and technological exchanges and cooperation, and so on.

3.1.2 Local Governments

As to the local governments, fundamentally they have been marginalized in the formulation of China's oil and natural gas policies.[23] For instance, local governments were endowed with the power of importing refined oil products in 1993, but in 1994, their import right was abolished. The central government only allowed some trading companies to enjoy such a privilege although with time passing by, government control tends to be loosened.

However, local governments do play a very important role in affecting the implementation of oil and gas policies. In current China's political milieu, the overarching objective of provincial governments is largely dependent on local party secretaries and local governors whose fundamental interest is to get promoted or retain their posts, both of which are preconditioned that social and economic development in their jurisdictions could keep the momentums.[24] In terms of energy issues, "the provinces often have interests that diverge from those of the central government" in that the former barely cares about developing local energy industry whereas the state need to keep it in mind of trying to construct an integrated domestic market.[25] Thus, bargaining may proceed throughout the implementation process and local governments have much discretion for distortion or non-enforcement of policies.[26] And the central government is particularly liable to be influenced by those provinces adjacent to foreign states, such as Xinjiang, Inner Mongolia, and Heilongjiang as they would argue that "energy linkages would ameliorate such security concerns,"[27] that is, trading with neighboring countries would alleviate the threats from minority resistance as well as foreign infiltration.

[23] Philip Andrews Speed, 2004, ibid., p. 50.

[24] The author appreciates Professor Zheng Yongnian for this point.

[25] Asia Research Centre, 2001, ibid.

[26] D. M. Lampton, "A Plum for a Peach: Bargaining, Interest, and Bureaucratic Politics in China," in Lieberthal, Kenneth. and Lampton, D. M (eds), *Bureaucracy, Politics, and Decision Making in Post-Mao China*, Berkeley, CA: University of California Press, 1992, pp. 35–58.

[27] Speed et al., 2002, ibid., p. 53.

Furthermore, there is a very complex resource-dependency between the NOCs and the local political economy. Because all the oil and gas-related activities concerning E&P, refining, and distribution are associated with the jurisdiction of local governments and definitely have a strong impact on the local economy and ecology, local governments have every reason to strive for more autonomy, in particular with regard to disposing of the resources in their regions, to trading with foreigners and to setting tax policies. In the optimum scenario, they can receive sufficient oil and gas resources to feed up the local economy, and create more job opportunities and substantial revenues from oil and gas resources, if possible. Even the 1998 revamp cannot fully cut off the relationship between the NOCs and local governments. When local governments were forced to reduce their shareholding role in the NOCs,[28] they may "resort to predatory behaviors or developing 'recombinant property' forms as a hedging mechanism," such as charging for taking over education and healthcare provisions, over-taxing, imposing stricter labor, health, and safety codes, and so on.[29]

3.1.3 Institutional Window to Watch SMMA

The change of government organs' power boundaries is an appropriate observation window to gauge how the SMMA has evolved, and NDRC, as an influential authority since 1952 when its predecessor, the State Planning Commission was established, has typified this regard. We can take the NDRC's extensive power over China's outbound or offshore direct investment (ODI) as a case.[30] This change has showcased the tendency of the government's dwindling role in controlling ODIs.

[28] Local governments are shareholders of the NOCs, though they are not dominant shareholder.

[29] Kun-Chin Lin and Chen Shaofeng, "The Local Government in Corporate Restructuring: Case Studies in Fractured Bargaining Relations," *Journal of Current Chinese Affairs*, Vol. 42, No. 4, pp. 171–198.

[30] According to Chinese laws, if a domestic enterprise conducts overseas direct investment or M&A transactions, it needs to obtain: (1) NDRC's approval or filing of overseas investment projects; (2) Ministry of Commerce's approval or filing; (3) State Administration of Foreign Exchange's approval of foreign exchange registration and remittance.

Historically, China's ODI regulatory regime was extremely rigid due to its tight foreign exchange control. With growing ODIs by Chinese enterprises, NDRC enacted *Interim Administrative Measures for Approving Investment Projects* on 9 October 2004 (2004 Catalogue). This Catalogue stipulated that any natural resources-related projects of US$30 million or larger (US$10 million or more for non-resources-related projects) were subject to the approval of the NDRC. Approval was required by the local counterpart of NDRC for those projects less than the threshold amount unless the projects were undertaken by central SOEs, which only required a recordation filing with NDRC. The prolonged procedures had made it very cumbersome and time-consuming and often put Chinese investors at a disadvantage, particularly in a competitive bidding process or auction sale.

In the *Notice on Delegating the Power to Approve Outbound Investment Projects* issued by the NDRC on 14 February 2011, only those resource projects and transport infrastructure projects of US$300 million or more, as well as other projects of US$100 million or more, were required to get approval from the NDRC, while the approval authority for projects less than the above categories was delegated to its provincial bureaus. Apparently, the threshold amount for NDRC approval had been ten times increased. Starting in 2012, the government took measures to streamline outbound investment approval procedures in several pilot regions such as Beijing, Shanghai, Jiangsu, Zhejiang, Shandong, and Sichuan.

On December 2, 2013, the State Council released the *Circular Concerning the Catalogue of Investment Projects Subject to Governmental Approvals* (2013 Version) (Guo-Fa [2013] No. 47) (the "2013 Catalogue"). It has superseded the previous 2004 Catalogue from the date of its release and significantly reduced the approval requirements. Prominent among the changes is the phase-out of the decades-old approval system under US$1 billion, which will be replaced by a recordation filing for such projects, except for projects involving designated "sensitive regions" (i.e., Taiwan, countries without diplomatic relations with China, subject to sanctions, and or engaged in ongoing wars or turmoil) or "sensitive industries" (such as telecommunications services, large-scale land development, backbone electric grids and networks, cross-border water resource development, and utilization, etc.). Only investments of US$1 billion or more or those involving "sensitive" countries or regions or industries are subject to NDRC's approval. Any ODI project of less than US$300 million is only required to complete the recordation filing with their provincial authorities.

In the latest "Administrative Measures for the Overseas Investment of Enterprises" (Order No. 11 of the NDRC) promulgated in March 2018, the government has abolished the way of using the number of capital to be invested as a threshold and simply considers what countries and what industries the ODI will be invested. Only those projects to be invested in sensitive countries and regions and sensitive industries are required to be approved by the NDRC. Otherwise, they just need to complete the recordation filing.[31]

In tandem with China's market reform, its administrative institutions have also undergone great changes. These changes, as part and parcel of Chinese marketization efforts, generally aim to enhance efficiency, transparency, and pro-business. They have shown that the Chinese government has striven hard to create a regulatory framework catering to the needs of the modern market economy. Of course, the growing marketization trends have not fundamentally changed the nature of the Chinese economy under state control. The direction is correct, but problems also remain.

3.2 Industrial Actors and Restructuring

As shown in Chart 3.3, the oil and gas industry was divided among various companies. It was dominated by CNPC, Sinopec, CNOOC, Sinochem, and local companies in the 1980s. December 1996 saw another player—the Star Petroleum Limited Corp., which was entitled to carry out both onshore and upstream business. Meanwhile, the Petroleum Industry Ministry was removed in September 1988, and so was the Ministry of Energy in March 1992. Consequently, these companies assumed administrative functions. Hence, before the 1998 overhaul, CNPC only focused on oil and gas E&P and transportation, and Sinopec

[31] Sensitive countries and regions refer to: (1) Countries and regions with which China has not established diplomatic relations; (2) Countries and regions where wars and civil strife occur; (3) Countries and regions that need to restrict investment by enterprises in accordance with international treaties and agreements concluded or acceded to by China; (4) Other sensitive countries and regions. Sensitive industries refer to: Development and production of weapons and equipment; development and utilization of cross-border water resources; news media; and industries that need to be restricted according to Chinese laws and regulations and relevant regulatory policies.

barely concentrated on oil refinery and petrochemical manufacturing. In their fields, there were other actors competing with them, whereas neither of them engaged in the distribution business including domestic marketing and foreign trade.

The 1998 restructure has fundamentally shaped today's petroleum and petrochemical structure in China. After the 1998 reform, both CNPC and Sinopec not only have been entitled to embark on a series of oil and gas businesses but also successfully excluded many other actors from this industry except CNOOC and Sinochem which keeps untouched.[32] The

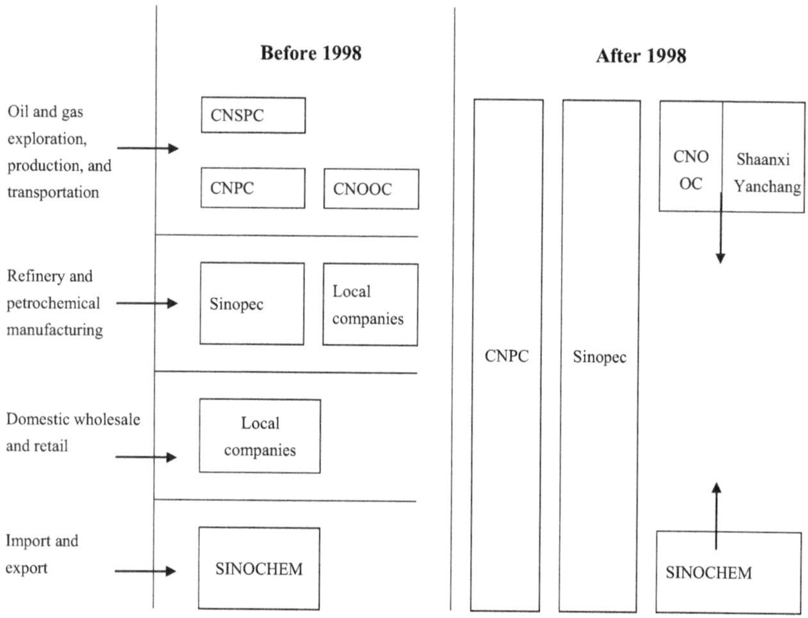

Chart 3.3 The 1998 Overhaul of the petroleum industry in China (*Source* Modified after Mai, Yinhua, *Can the New Chinese Oil Giants Compete after China's WTO Entry*? National University of Singapore, East Asia Institute [EAI], EAI Working Paper No. 74, 8 May 2001)

[32] Sinochem has still been authorized only to do oil and gas import and export business. Unlike other three giants, it is not a vertically integrated corporation.

two oil giants are undertaking their businesses in China on the basis of the geographic divisions set in 1998 revamp.

There were many factors motivating the Chinese government to restructure the oil industry in 1998.[33] Apart from the intention to straight out the chaotic situation in the then oil market, Beijing might have the following considerations: to follow suit of the Western countries which endorse the merges of their globally competitive oil and gas giants, to avoid the possible scenario that domestic NOCs being edged out of the global market in the future, and to help erect some Chinese giants so as ultimately to construct China as a rising power. As the then vice Premier Wu Bangguo said, "Our nation's position in the international economic order will be to a large extent determined by the position of our nation's large enterprises and groups."[34]

Thus far there are three types of industrial actors in the Chinese oil and gas industry. The first type is the NOCs, mainly CNPC, Sinopec, CNOOC, and Sinochem, which are monopolizing the Chinese oil and gas market at present. But with China's accession to WTO, more actors are allowed into the oil and gas market. The second type of actor is a domestic nongovernmental business that has long been discriminated against by Chinese policy. And foreign forces represented by the MOCs are the third type of player in China's oil and gas sector. Thus far the NOCs have monopolized China's oil and gas market, but the role of the other two types of actors especially that of the MOCs is looming larger.

3.2.1 National Oil Corporations

As discussed in Chapter 1, the NOCs have Janus-face identities in nature. The ability of the NOCs to influence the government's oil and gas

[33] Lin has expounded the three conditions to launch such a large-scale industrial reform, "expected gains from further decentralization; financial strength of the central treasury vs. the local state; and demonstration of feasible organizational options" (p. 88). And he further explained why 1998 was the appropriate time to initiate the overhaul. According to him, obstacles against reform were reduced to a large extent due to the structural change from an economy of shortage to one of surplus in 1996 and oil price distortions which led to further interest division among different parties concerned. And this division provided opportunities for the central state to create a new reform coalition. Whereas the new trends in domestic capital market increased the central government's expectation of returns from corporate restructure. See Kun-Chin Lin, 2003, ibid., pp. 77–115.

[34] Wu Bangguo, then-Vice Premier, August 1998.

policy-making depends on many factors, particularly their preferences and their status in the Chinese economy. Hence, the following will start to introduce their evolutions and preferences.

CNPC is the largest monopolist in China's oil and gas industry, the largest producer and supplier of crude oil, and a major supplier of refined products and petrochemicals in China. As indicated by itself, "CNPC's history exemplifies the development of China's entire petroleum industry,"[35] which exactly spells out its close relations with the government. Established on the basis of the former Petroleum Industry Ministry in September 1988 (see Chart 3.1), CNPC's major business at that time was in the upstream. In the meantime, it also undertook some governmental functions. In July 1998, CNPC was restructured into an integrated oil company, covering upstream and downstream activities, domestic and foreign trade. Only until then did it nominally lose the administrative functions. CNPC listed its shareholder subsidiary, PetroChina in the Hong Kong and New York stock exchanges in April 2000. CNPC commenced to gear up its efforts to "go abroad" in the early 1990s and has been the Chinese flagship in this regard. As the largest monopolist in Chinese upstream, CNPC strongly opposes the massive opening of the domestic upstream market, but it is a powerful proponent of introducing oil and gas from Russia and Central Asia to China because these resources could help rejuvenate the Daqing Oilfield, its largest subsidiary.

China Petrochemical Corporation (Sinopec) was established in July 1983, engaging mainly in petroleum refining and processing, and the marketing of oil and gas-related raw materials. Incorporated in July 1998 on the basis of the former China Petrochemical Corporation, Sinopec Corp. thus far is the largest refinery and petrochemical manufacturer and the second largest oil and gas producer in China. In 2001, Sinopec Corp. drew out its best assets to form Sinopec and listed it in the Hong Kong, New York, and London stock exchanges. According to the 1998 restructuring, Sinopec Corp's major businesses concentrate on the South and East of China, the most populated areas in China, but the crude oil produced by itself is far below its refining and processing capacities; hence, it has to purchase large amounts of crude either from CNPC and

[35] CNPC webpage: http://www.cnpc.com.cn/english/gsgk/lsyds.htm, accessed 12 January 2014.

CNOOC or from overseas, which on the contrary, exerts great pressure on it when oil prices stay in long-term high levels. Additionally, the openness of China's downstream market will inevitably impose sharp percussions upon it. Compared with CNPC and CNOOC, it seems that Sinopec Corp. is not so well-off. In order to combat such a bad situation, the company, on one hand, grumbles about its status and especially lower prices of domestic finished oil; on the other hand, it also endeavors to 'go out' in recent years.

CNOOC was created in 1982 in order to cater to the requirement of cooperation with foreign investors. Opening this sector to foreigners was largely motivated by the urgent need for foreign capital and technologies. Foreign investors are allowed to engage in Chinese offshore businesses on the condition of cooperation with the CNOOC.[36] CNOOC thus was endowed with the exclusive power to carry out offshore oil and gas exploration and production and cooperate with foreign investors offshore as the delegate of a Chinese economic entity. Since then, CNOOC has long been exposed to foreign managerial skills and know-how. When its Chinese counterparts were still governed under a highly planned system, CNOOC began a flexible managerial regime, pursuing economic efficiency, and adopting a manager responsibility system. To back its development, Beijing also provides preferential policies such as tax curtailment or exemption, and preferential treatment to earn foreign exchanges. The long-time collaborations have forged CNOOC as an independent operator in some fields since 1999. And from 2001, it has floated in the New York and Hong Kong stock exchanges and carried out several overseas acquisitions.

Sinochem was established in 1950 whose predecessor is China National Chemicals Import & Export Corporation. Originally it monopolized the international trading sector of China's oil and chemical products, and it has survived the 1998 overhaul, but CNPC and Sinopec have also gained trading rights since then. In recent years, Sinochem has expanded its

[36] Some people also opposed the open-up policy. They contended that this policy was amount to "betrayal of our own resources," "lose of sovereignty," or "getting more kicks than halfpence" (de buchang shi). It was the leaders of the Ministry of Energy headed by Kang Shi'en who spared no efforts to do a lot of investigation and lobbying work, and finally received wide support from the leadership. This is another case that illustrates the importance of some VIP in certain circumstances. See Wen, Wen, Houwen et al., *Bainian Shiyou: 1878–2000* (Hundred Year's Oil: 1878–2000), Beijing: Dangdai Zhongguo chubanshe (Contemporary China Press), 2002, p. 310.

business in oil and gas E&P and refinery. More striking is its expansion overseas since it was authorized to invest in foreign upstream businesses. In November 2004 the company made a bid for a South Korean oil refinery, marking its first step toward refinery business. In 2006 it gained the right to develop a gas field in the United Arab Emirates.[37]

Hence, from their establishment till the present, the four NOCs have very close liaisons with the government and have long been enjoying a preferential status in China's energy industry. Both have left chances and laid an economic basis for the NOCs to strongly influence the government, which is to be discussed in the following section.

Yet in recent years in order to boost their ability to protect China's energy security, the government has started to inject more competition among the NOCs by allowing them to conduct mixed business or break up the geographic restrictions. Besides the aforementioned Sinochem case, other NOCs are striving hard to break into others' "demesnes." For instance, since 2000 both CNPC and Sinopec have been authorized to carry out oil E&P in East China Sea and South China Sea, which used to be the monopolized business of CNOOC. Facing their competition, CNOOC also intrudes into their areas. In May 2003, it managed to get the oil import rights, the exclusive prerogative of the other three NOCs before. Its E&P business in the CNPC-controlled Changqing oilfield and its ambition to build China's largest refinery in Guangdong province indicates that CNOOC has planned to forge itself into a more comprehensive entity with an integrated oil business.

3.2.2 Multinational Oil Companies

Confronting the same rivalries, both domestic private firms and MOCs are eager to break the monopoly apart to emulate each other on the same level playing field. In this regard, they are partners. However, both are competing opponents as well in that either side attempts to enlarge their market shares in China.

The MOCs are booming forces in the Chinese energy market by virtue of their sophisticated know-how, ripe expertise, substantial capital, long-year marketing experience, and advanced managerial skills. These

[37] *Gulf Oil and Gas*, "Sinochem Signed Contract to Explore UAQ Gas Field," 31 March 2006, http://www.gulfoilandgas.com/webpro1/MAIN/Mainnews.asp?id=2773, accessed 22 April 2023.

advantages are the very strengths that the Chinese NOCs thirst for, which then provides opportunities for the MOCs to squeeze into the Chinese market by playing their trump cards. For this reason, the MOCs and the NOCs are both partners and rivalries.

The MOCs investing in China have a clear-cut objective of capturing more market shares and eventually contending for the dominant position in the Chinese energy market. They have sped up their investing activities at a faster pace, with a larger scale and within a wider spectrum in recent years. Thus far, almost all the large transnational petroleum and petrochemical companies in the list of *Fortune* 500 have embarked on businesses in China, and the total foreign investments in petroleum and petrochemicals captured 4-5 billion dollars in 2003, twice that amount in 2002.[38] The MOCs' business in China is turning from joint venture and cooperative companies to holding and sole-funded companies, from upstream to mid- and down-stream, and even into petroleum storage and logistics.[39] Chart 3.4 shows the investment activities of the large MOCs. We may consider the MOCs' role in the Chinese market according to the up-, mid- and down-stream areas.

The upstream market (oil and gas E&P) is the earliest field open to foreign investors. The major oilfields available to foreign entry primarily concentrate on offshore and West China such as Tarim Oilfield. CNOOC has exemplified cooperation with foreign counterparts in this field. As of 1 May 2005, CNOOC had signed 167 petroleum contracts and agreements with 72 foreign oil companies from 19 countries and regions. The total acreage of the 27 contracts and agreements under execution is about 120,000 square km and 20 oil and gas fields have been constructed.[40] Chinese accession into the WTO has excluded the onshore upstream from fully opening to foreign investors, which implies that it is up to the Chinese side to decide whether and how to open the onshore oil and

[38] *Jingji Cankao Bao* (*Economic Information Daily*) "Shiyou Shihua: Rushi sannian touzi zhuti duoyuanhua chubu xingcheng" (Petroleum and Petrochemical: Diversified Investing Actors Initially Taken Shape after Three Years' WTO Entry), 7 December 2004, http://www.china.org.cn/chinese/EC-c/722950.htm, accessed 16 August 2006.

[39] Jianping Liu and Zhu, He, "Characteristics and Trend of Investment in China by Multinational Petroleum and Petrochemical Companies in Recent Years," *International Petroleum Economics*, Vol. 11, No. 9, 2003; Shi Pu, "Three New Trends of the MOCs' Businesses in China," *Sinopec Monthly*, June 2005.

[40] CNOOC, "Offshore Contracts under Execution," September 2005, http://www.cnooc.com.cn/defaulten.asp, accessed 21 August 2006.

Company	Current Investment		Predicted Investment in the next 5 Years
Exxon Mobil	–	Full entry into the up-, mid- and down-stream fields, owning 36 petroleum stations	4
Shell	2	Full entry into the up-, mid- and down-stream fields, owning 18 firms and over 500 petroleum stations, with 1600 employees	3
BP	4.5	Full entry into the up-, mid- and down-stream fields, owning more than 20 firms and about 1000 petroleum stations, with over 3000 employees	3
Total Fina Elf	0.7	Full entry into the up-, mid- and down-stream fields, owning 30 exclusively foreign-funded firms and joint ventures, with more than 3000 employees, and plan to set up 200 petroleum stations in China within the next 7 years	0.5-0.6
BASF	4	owning 10 exclusively foreign-funded firms and 9 joint ventures, as well as 8 offices in China, with more than 3000 employees	–
DuPont	0.7	3 branch companies, 22 foreign-funded firms and joint ventures, with about 3500 employees in China	–
Bayer	3.1	18 firms and 14 manufacturing plants	3.1
Dow	0.5	5 offices, 10 producing bases, with 1.6 billion dollars annual sales revenues	–

Chart 3.4 Multinational oil companies' investments in China (*Source*: Liu Jianping and Zhu He, "New Characteristics Analysis of Multinational Petroleum and Petrochemical Companies' Investment in China since Her WTO Entry," International Petroleum Economics, Vol. 13, No. 5, May 2005) (Unit: billion dollars)

gas E&P business in the future. Yet confined by the capital and know-how constraints, Beijing will maintain the open-up policy in this sphere though it is on a case-by-case basis.

The MOCs have also stepped into the midstream of the refinery and processing industry. So far the following projects have been endorsed by the Chinese government: Exxon Mobil and Saudi Aramco's engagement in the Fujian Integrated Refining and Ethylene Joint Venture project in cooperation with Sinopec; the program of expanding the refinery capacity of Guangzhou Petrochemical Company undertaken by Exxon Mobil along with Sinopec; and the refinery project undertaken by CNOOC in collaboration with Shell. Beijing's permission of foreign entry into this field is mainly out of consideration to help China promote the refining capacity because most refineries in China are of small scale, and they have low capacity to produce high-quality petroleum products and process high-sulfur-content crude. The MOCs intend to take this opportunity to capture more market shares and to forge an internal integrated market so as to distribute oil in China at lower costs.

In the downstream sector of oil distribution, the MOCs have exhibited their strengths in the coastal regions and they appear to be more aggressive in the future. China's entry into the WTO requires it to open the retail and the wholesale business of petroleum products to foreign investments in December 2004 and December 2006 respectively. As a matter of fact, before 2004, Exxon Mobil, Shell and BP have already gained the licenses to run petroleum stations in some coastal regions as an exchange for supporting the three NOCs' overseas floating through purchasing part of their stocks.[41] With China's gradual openness of the downstream sector, the MOCs are diverting their business focus from E&P to oil refinery, processing, and downstream distribution.[42]

To strive for more market shares, the MOCs have taken the following measures: first, to comply with the Chinese government's policy prescription that petroleum product wholesaling firms must own a petroleum depot of at least 4000 cubic meters (Cm),[43] they cooperate with the Chinese side to establish petroleum depots in China. For instance, BP-China has established a Nansha Oil Depot and Oil Jetty near Zhujiang River since 2004.[44]Second, foreign-owned petroleum stations are mushrooming in coastal China. As early as 1985 and 1987 Shell set up two

[41] Liu Jianping and Zhu He, *International Petroleum Economics*, Vol. 11, No. 9, 2003, ibid.

[42] Pu, Shi, June 2005, ibid.

[43] "Temporary Measures on the Administration over the Refined Oil Market," *MC Mandate No. 23 in 2004*, 2 December 2004, http://news.xinhuanet.com/zhengfu/2004-12/10/content_2316763.htm, accessed 21 August 2006. This mandate begins to take effect from 1 January 2005.

[44] BP-China and Guangzhou Development Industry (Holdings) Co., Ltd. co-funded to establish Nansha Oil Depot and 80,000 tons Oil Jetty near Zhujiang River from 2004. This Depot could store 360 thousand Cm finished oil of various types, and the Jetty is the largest as well as the most advanced one in China. It was reported that Exxon Mobile is also stepping up the construction of its own oil jetty in China.

petroleum stations in Shenzhen Economic Special Zone. Since then, the number of petroleum stations owned by the MOCs in China has been increasing (see Chart 3.4). BP, Exxon Mobil, Shell, and Total Fina Elf S.A. have reportedly been approved to set up 3600 petroleum stations in collaboration with CNPC or Sinopec in Guangdong, Jiangsu, Zhejiang, Fujian, and north of China.[45] It is straightforward that the completion of these petroleum stations will contribute to their acquisition of the petroleum product market in China. In addition, the MOCs are doing the distribution businesses on lubricant, bitumen, fuel oil, and jet fuel, etc. While holding an absolute advantage over the high-end market of lubricants, they have already dominated China's petroleum additive market.[46]

Therefore, the MOCs' role in China's oil and gas market is inevitably looming larger and in some fields, they even play a dominant part. This has two implications: On one hand, the MOCs' turning stronger implies the relative ebb of the NOCs in the Chinese oil and gas industry, which denotes that state policy implementation through the NOCs might be affected. On the other, as the MOCs prioritize maximizing profits, they have neither will nor obligation to serve China's energy security, which implies that the government's political or strategic thinking can hardly be implemented through them.

3.2.3 Domestic Private Firms

The constant policy discrimination has retarded the development of domestic private firms in the oil and gas industry. They have been deprived of the right to conduct oil E&P in China as yet. Since 1998 they have had no right to distribute petroleum products unless they affiliate CNPC or Sinopec. In doing so, each must pay annual dues of

[45] Xinzhen Lan, "2006 nian waizi neng zhan Zhongguo chengpinyou shichan duoda fen'e" ("What Proportion will Foreign Investment Occupy China's Refined Oil Market after 2006?") *Beijing Zhoubao* (*Beijing Weekly*), 27 April 2005. http://www.china.org.cn/chinese/zhuanti/qkjc/849078.htm, accessed 12 September 2006.

[46] Liu Jianping and Zhu He, *International Petroleum Economics*, Vol. 11, No. 9, 2003, ibid.

RMB35 thousand to them.[47] Only after China entered WTO, the government began slightly loosening its strict policies against them. The MC gave green light to over 20 domestic private companies to do petroleum product wholesale business in October 2003.[48] It was reported that the government would take more initiatives to bolster the development of private firms in the oil and gas sector. In November 2004, Premier Wen Jiabao made a verdict that the government should reform the petroleum administrative regulations as soon as possible.[49] Xu Dingming, director of the Energy Bureau of NDRC, claimed that companies in the energy sector in China will not all be labeled with state ownership, implying that companies of various ownership will be equal before state policies.[50] Virtually, private firms are more flexible, more alert to market changes, and easier to be accepted by foreign countries.

However, the development of private firms is still constrained by the following factors. First, the characteristics of "three highs" in the oil and gas sector: high tech, high input, and high risk, along with the fierce competition from the NOCs and MOCs, may curb their entry into China's oil and gas sector and their further growth. Second, the policy discrimination against them has not been removed thus far, which places the late incomers at a disadvantageous position in future competition. In fact, the policy discrimination that domestic private firms confront is even more serious than that of foreign companies in China. Simply take the income tax as an example, the nominal income tax that foreign companies face is 15 percent and the actual one is 11 percent, whereas domestic firms (including NOCs and private firms[51]) need to pay 33% and 23%,

[47] *Zhongguo gongshang shibao* (*China Business Times*), "Minying you qi qidai 'huayuquan', zongli pishi maotou zhi zhi shiyou jutou" ("Private Oil Firms Expect Having a Say, Premier's Verdict Points to Oil Giant"), 15 December 2004. http://www.china.org.cn/chinese/2004/Dec/729617.htm, accessed 12 September 2006.

[48] *Zhongguo jingyingbao* (*China Business*), 27 October 2003.

[49] *China Business Times*, 15 December 2004. ibid.

[50] *Beijing Chenbao* (*Beijing Morning Post*), "Fagaiwei nengyuanju juzhang toulu: shiyou chanye jiang xiang minqi kaifang" ("Director of Energy Bureau of NDRC Disclose: Oil Industry to be open to Private Firms"), 29 November 2004. http://www.china.org.cn/chinese/EC-c/715979.htm, accessed 12 September 2006.

[51] Here is the comparison between domestic and foreign companies, but in terms of the national treatment comparison between the SOEs and domestic private firms, the former obviously enjoy preferential treatments in a variety of fields such as policy, capital, import and export, market entry and so on, whereas domestic private firms do not.

respectively.[52] Third, compared with the NOCs, private firms have much fewer chances to acquire loans from state banks. Therefore, they also need to conquer the capital constraint.

3.3 Impact of China's Institutional Layout on the SMMA

From the above, it can be found that China's administration of the oil and gas industry presents two characteristics. One is that the ministries and commissions concerned are both policy makers and regulatory bodies. Although there is no universal rule on whether a merger or a separation of policy-making/planning and regulatory power is more optimal, the long-term trend should be separated. From China's preceding practices, the merger of both powers is liable to leading the government more willing to pursue other goals at the expense of economic efficiency. For instance, in order to expand employment, local government may protect local firms from competition.[53] Some people may say that in the electricity sector, China used to set up a regulatory body, SERC, but it did not help improve management and conduct forward-looking planning for the power sector. Yet this criticism is unfair because the SERC did not enjoy the key regulatory power over electricity prices and investments, two indispensable instruments resting in the hands of the NDRC.

The other is that the administrative power, being dispersed among different ministries, remains fragmented. The financial power lies in the MoF; license for land use and oil and gas E&P power is up to the MLR; oil and gas imports & exports and domestic market distribution are in the hands of the MOFCOM; day-to-day business operations are under the supervision of the SASAC. Though the NDRC appears in the dominant supervision position, it mainly takes responsibility for mid- and

[52] Mo Chen, "Zhongwai qiye guomin daiyu chabie jiujing zai nali" ("What is on earth the Difference of the National Treatment between Domestic and Foreign Firms"), *Zhongguo jingji shibao* (*China Economic Times*), 26 January 2005. http://www.ce.cn/new_hgjj/hgplun/more/200501/26/t20050126_2948665.shtml, accessed 12 September 2006.

[53] Miaohan Su, "Nengyuan jianguan jigou de quanli bianjie wenti yanjiu" (Studies on the power boundaries of energy regulatory bodies), *Ecological Civilization and Environmental Resource Law—Collection of Papers of the Annual Meeting of the Environmental Resource Law*, 2009. http://cpfd.cnki.com.cn/Article/CPFDTOTAL-FXHJ200908001233.htm, accessed 20 January 2014.

long-term energy plans, macro energy policies, price setting, and so on. As the NDRC is hierarchically equal to other Chinese commissions, it is conceivable that the NDRC faces various difficulties to coordinate their work on energy. Even within the NDRC, energy administration has been divided.[54]

Such a dispersed institutional layout has brought about several consequences. Fengying Chen, Director of Institute of World Economic Studies, China Institutes of Contemporary International Relations, is of the belief that the overarching risk for China's energy security at the present stage arises not from external threat, but from internal multi-faceted governance, imperfect institutional system and market disorder.[55] First, the consensus-driven decision-making process in which "different ministries, agencies and interest groups all having to 'sign off' on reforms" often requires an enormous amount of discussion and bargaining, and makes policymakers prefer to choose a path of least resistance, with measures that do not face strong resistance from vested interests. However, once no compromise can be made, they will end in a deadlock.[56] Tricky is that even the top national leaders like Hu Jingtao must seek consensus in the name of collective leadership.[57] Consequently, it is

[54] For instance, The Energy Bureau takes the major responsibility to examine and approve energy projects, as well as to lay out energy strategies and policies; The Department of Pricing sets the prices of oil, gas, electricity etc.; The Department of Resources is in charge of the development and comprehensive utilization of minerals, while the Economic Operation Bureau is responsible for the coordination among industries such as energy and transportation, management of electricity demands, and the finished oil market construction; In the meantime, some energy investment projects must get through the Department of Investment; The management of the downstream refining plants is under Department of Industry; The Economic and Trade Department plans the export and import volumes; and energy transportation is in the hands of the Department of Transportation.

[55] Xinmin Li and Li Wang, "Zujian nengyuanbu tiaojian yijing jiben chenshu" (The conditions for setting up a MoE are basically available), *Jingji Cankao Bao* (*Economic Information Daily*), 29 January 2008. http://jjckb.xinhuanet.com/cjxw/2008-01/29/content_83612.htm, accessed 2 February 2014.

[56] Linda Jakobson and Dean Knox, "New Foreign Policy Actors in China," SIPRI (Stockholm International Peace Research Institute) Policy Paper 26, September 2010. http://books.sipri.org/files/PP/SIPRIPP26.pdf, accessed 19 January 2014.

[57] Linda Jakobson and Dean Knox, ibid. Of course, this may be changing with the consolidating of power by the present Xi Jinping, who will take the helm of both the NSC and the Central Leading Group for Comprehensively Deepening Reform.

set to result in an exorbitant cost for coordination, and thus a lack of coordination of Chinese energy policies. Such inconsistency will be discussed in Chapter 5. By the same token, there was no ad hoc department to take into account the across-the-board development of the oil and gas industry. No ministry is willing and can be committed to working out and enforcing a coherent strategy conducive to China's energy development in the long run. As a result, it is hard for the Chinese government to map out any energy strategy or systematic energy policy to deal with energy security problems too.

Second, the dispersed administrative power has whittled the government's regulatory and supervisory capacity over the energy sector, particularly the SOEs. Previous experience seems to show that the central ministries have placed their regulatory emphasis on market access, license, price, and investment, whereas much less attention has been paid to those regulatory issues like environmental protection, work safety, anti-monopoly, abusing market power, and so on.[58] In other words, the government's regulations have underscored ex ante examination and approval, but often slackened ex post supervision. While this kind of pattern has reflected the impact of the legacy of the command economy, it is also a result of the lack of a unified regulatory body on the top. The dispersed nature means that different ministries have differing foci; meanwhile, they have different authority and resources in hand in the Chinese hierarchical system. For instance, the regulatory capacity of NDRC apparently outweighs that of the MEP, which was not a ministry but merely an organization directly under the State Council before 2008. When China used to be self-sufficient in energy, the above regulatory pattern might have had a less significant impact, but the transformation into an importing country and its surging demand for energy resources obviously have posed a daunting challenge for Beijing. Continuously following the old regulating path is bound to cause a lot of problems. Thus far, excess regulation, misplaced regulation, and absence of regulation all exist in the oil and gas sectors in China. The lack of regulation on the environment and safety is one important factor leading to a large number of incidents in China's petroleum and petrochemical industry. In 2011

[58] Philip Andrews-Speed, "Nengyuan Jianguan de Tiaozhan" (Challenges for Energy Regulation), *Huangqiu Qiyejia* (Global Entrepreneur), No. 4, 2006.

this figure was 179, with 149 deaths, 1234 injuries, and 5 missing.[59] In 2012 the number of incidents attracting media attention reached 218, causing 103 deaths, 910 injuries, and 13 missing.[60] Despite the government's strict control, illegal mining activities in the sectors of coal, power generation, and even oil could hardly be stopped.

Third, the dispersed administrative power has left a loophole for energy companies to take advantage. Other than the problem in energy policymaking, strict implementation of national energy policies, which needs to rely on local governments and the NOCs, poses another challenge as the latter have their own interest concerns which may not be consistent with the central government's, as mentioned in other chapters.

Finally, more worrisome, to preserve their power and concurrent vested interests, the ministries often are reluctant to change the status quo of the power structure, particularly when their power might be impaired or deprived. This can be verified by the prolonged delay in setting up a Ministry of Energy (MoE) or a government organization that could serve as an overall regulatory agency covering management of the sectors of oil, gas, electricity, coal, and nuclear power.

The current Xi-Li administration has dedicated itself to further reforms. Deeply knowing where the shoe pinches like the wearer, they have shown great courage to break the predicament described by a very widespread sentence in China: "The decrees cannot get out of Zhongnanhai (the headquarter location of China's power center)." Prominent at the Third Plenum of the Eighteenth Central Committee held in November 2013 is China's decision of creating a Central Leading Group for Comprehensively Deepening Reform and a National Security Council (NSC). As China's reform has come to a crucial abyssal zone and is not merely confined to economic system reform, but it has also involved political, social, cultural, and ecological reforms, China is in urgent need of a top-level design. The Group has been established to undertake a host of overall reform management tasks, including managing the planning and implementation of comprehensive reforms, overall coordination, and advancement of the reforms, and overall economic planning.

[59] Yuewei Feng, "2011, Anquan shigu weihe biaosheng" (Why Incidents skyrocketed in 2011?), Zhonggu*o Shiyou Shihua* (China Petroleum and Petrochemical), No. 3, 2012.

[60] Yuewei Feng, "2012, Anquan shigu yijiu biaosheng" (Incidents continued to rise in 2012), Zhonggu*o Shiyou Shihua* (China Petroleum and Petrochemical), No. 2, 2013.

Likewise, the purpose of the NSC is to coordinate different government organs at the highest level in response to major emergency crises which pose threats to China's security. China is entangled with much more complicated security challenges coming not only from traditional military security and territorial separatism but also from non-traditional security including energy and ecological security. As no single ministry could effectively deal with these security threats, ensuring China's security also calls for a top-level design, and the NSC is expected to be able to safeguard China's national security by enhancing overall planning and coordination of various departments.

In order to accomplish their goals and eliminate various oppositions against reform from interest groups in the system, President Xi Jinping himself is at the helm of the Group and the NSC. Apparently, energy security is part of the security package and has a profound impact on other components of the security concept pertaining to the NSC. At the same time, deepening reform in the energy sector, which has lacked far behind reform in other sectors, is an integral part of China's overall reform. In both regards, the two newly established organs should be conducive to overcoming the drawbacks originating from the absence of a MoE. However, it remains unclear to what extent they could deepen reform in the energy sector and better serve China's energy security. Indeed unlike the NELG they have the necessary authority and resources, but apparently energy security is not on the top agenda of the NSC. Unless there is any emergency crisis of energy security, the NSC might not take heed of the energy issue, let alone map out a coherent and systematic strategy for enhancing China's energy security. Although reform in the energy sector is an important component in China's overall economic reform, it is doubtful that China would have the will to treat the state-owned energy companies as ordinary firms and push them to the market. Thus far the mainstream view in the minds of the Chinese leadership seems to regard energy, particularly oil and gas, as a special sector that calls for a strong hand of the state.

3.4 Creating a Ministry of Energy?

Calls from think tanks and energy experts for establishing an MoE appear whenever Beijing plans to launch a government overhaul. As early as 2000, the China Institute of International Studies, a think tank affiliated with the MFA, made such a proposal.[61] In its report entitled *Developing China's Natural Gas Market: The Energy Policy Challenges*, the IEA also recommended that China establish a central government agency to take charge of the energy sectors.[62] Proponents posit that establishing an MoE is necessitated due to first and foremost the need of coping with new situations of energy supply–demand that China is facing, the need of industrial development, and international cooperation.[63] Akin to the communication sector, energy is the same important fundamental industrial sector, but there is a special Ministry of Communication overseeing the former (aviation, railway and transportation), which used to be governed by three individual government bodies, whereas there is no such administrative agency in the energy sector. Of course, there are some voices against the setup of an MoE given that the energy industry is so complex and each individual sector is so independent,[64] or that an MoE may turn into a mere figurehead or be captured by the SOEs,[65] but support for building an MoE seems to be mainstream. The government apparently has come to realize the regulatory problems originated from dispersed ministries. Every time when reshuffling the government, Beijing has indeed done some repairing work, but thus far, the MoE or a similar organization remains on paper. In 2005, the government set up a National Energy Leading Group (NELG) as the coordination body. This group itself was not a standing organization, but its standing office was affiliated with the NDRC, which means the NDRC had much influence on its routine work and agenda setting. In 2008 the Chinese government disbanded the NELG and set up a National Energy Committee (NEC) in 2010. In March 2013, the National Energy Administration has been established, integrating the responsibilities of the previous National

[61] Ming Zheng and Fujun Chu, "Nengyuanbu huzhiyuchu?" (The MoE was ready to come out?), Zhongg*uo Shiyou Shihua* (China Petroleum and Petrochemical), No. 1, January 2005.

[62] IEA, *Developing China's Natural Gas Market: The Energy Policy Challenges*, OECD Publishing, 2002.

[63] Xinmin Li and Li Wang, 29 Jan. 2008, ibid.

[64] Dai Chen, "Bu chenli Nengyuanbu de daoli: zhege hangye feichang fuza" (The reason why not establish a MoE: The energy industry is extremely complex), *Diyi Caijing Ribao* (*China Business News*), 13 March 2008.

[65] Xinmin Li and Li Wang, 29 Jan. 2008, ibid.

Energy Administration and the State Electricity Regulatory Commission. As the most prominent organization that directly involves in daily energy affairs administration, the new National Energy Administration is still under the management of the National Development and Reform Commission. But thus far a MoE that most experts advocate was still an illusion. China decided to set up NELG and the NEC simply because the NEA is incompetent in accomplishing its goals of well managing and planning China's energy sector thanks to the understaffed problem, its relatively lower ranking, and the lack of necessary authority and resources.

Headed by the premier and composed of a number of top officials, both the NELG and the NEC aim to enhance coordination in policy-making and enforcement among different ministries. However, both are merely deliberative and coordinating organs without administrative power. They may be conducive to partially resolving the problem of lack of coordination, but it is doubtful that they could settle it in view of the following facts: Each member of the committee has economic and political interests in their departments; each member is so overwhelmed with their work that they would have time to reflect upon the strategy. In light of their performance in the past years, we may reasonably be skeptical of their effectiveness in accomplishing their aims. One typical case is the failure of resolving collisions between China's coal and electricity sectors, resulting in a dysfunctional mechanism of coal-electricity price linkage which has often caused power shortage.

As a Chinese reporter asserts, "the failure to establish a MoE was not because it is of no necessity, but because it is the outcome of the struggle among each interest group."[66] One of the hurdles came from those government authorities governing market entry, examination and approval of projects, price formulation and so on like the NDRC, which was concerned that its regulatory power in price and investment might be stripped when establishing a MoE.[67]

[66] Zhong, Qiu, 2004, ibid.

[67] As a strong governmental organ, NDRC enjoys a spate of administrative powers as illustrated above. With China's entry into the WTO, the NDRC has been impaired with the requirement of less administrative intervention in the economy. The grow-up of the market power has also complicated the governance over the economy and to some extent, weakened the state power particularly represented by the NDRC. Hence the establishment of Ministry of Energy would inevitably further weaken its power.

Another obstacle derived from the opposition of the state-owned energy companies, which do not want to have another "superior boss" and a strong supervisor. According to Zhou Dadi, the former director of the Energy Research Institute of NDRC, while these companies themselves still possess some administrative functions (for instance, CNPC and Sinopec have enjoyed the monopoly of import and export of crude oil), they also can directly approach top leaders like the premier for help when they come across some big issues (for example, the two state-owned grid corporations, five largest power generation companies, Shenhua Group, etc. all have ways to get the help from central leaders on many issues. Once an MoE was established, their above privileges might be lost.[68] When the government was brewing the government reforms in 2003, many people had expected recreating an MoE to handle the impending energy security problem. However, "the leadership appears to fall prey to the interests of the state energy enterprises and the NDRC."[69] The NOCs hold misgivings that a new MoE would inevitably strengthen its monitoring power, impair their influence upon energy policy-making, and might add more burdens to them. Moreover, it might introduce more market ingredients to the oil and gas industry, thus further whittling their monopolies.

Of course, in the context of today's China, even if an MoE could be established, it was still likely that the newly established agency could surmount the barriers from different ministries and the NOCs, better design and coordinate China's energy strategies and policies, and facilitate energy policy implementation given that it might lack the capacity and resources for such a job.

Authoritarian as it is, the Chinese state in some respects is not that strong. It could be fragmented not only by the ministries but also by the big SOEs, as this case has spelled out. Such a fragmented state is bound to affect the quality of state "management."

[68] Xinmin Li and Li Wang, 29 Jan. 2008, ibid.

[69] Philip Andrews-Speed, *Energy Policy and Regulation in the People's Republic of China*, The Hague/London/New York: Kluwer Law International, 2004, p. 56.

3.5 Conclusion

The dispersive regulatory layout has thus adversely affected the quality of the SMMA. On the one hand, the power of the different ministries may be used to enhance their department interests rather than the state interests. On the other hand, reluctant to relinquish their administrative power, the ministries concerned are a major force against the reduction of government intervention, thus delaying the process of marketization. Although China is embracing market economy as a goal for its fundamental economic system, a variety of administrative examinations and approvals remain in place and a lot of them are de facto the legacies of the command economy, indicating that the government still has a strong hand in economic activities. As the renowned Chinese economist Daokui Li said, one of the three types of interest groups is some central ministries and commissions. They get accustomed to administrative examinations and approvals and are addicted to power, thus forming a hindrance against reform.[70]

The dispersed administrative authority is bound to make some policies uncoordinated. The author does not deny the tussles and disputes among these administrative agencies, which also exist in other countries, but I prefer to treat the governmental organs and the top leadership as a unity, or the representative of the state, which is a statist approach applied by other scholars.[71] My argument is mainly because it is hard for outsiders to learn their struggles, and more importantly, because any formal energy strategy or policy is the result of negotiations, bargainings and consensus building, and the final outcome should represent the formal stance of the Chinese government. The role of the state is mainly a referee, coordinator and final policy maker. To say this does not mean that the governmental organs possess unlimited power and can press other social actors to do anything.

In China's cases, things become more complicated because the NOCs also intertwine with the policymakers, thereby engendering such a

[70] Hexun, "Li Daokui: sanda liyi jituan chezhou jingji zhidu bianqian" (Daokui Li: Three interest groups encumbered China's economic system reform), 11 Jan. 2014, http://news.hexun.com/2014-01-11/161348300.html, accessed 6 February 2014.

[71] Studies using the 'statist' approach can refer to Stephen D. Krasner, *Defending the National Interest: Raw Materials Investments and U.S. Foreign Policy*, Princeton, NJ: Princeton University Press, 1978.

problem of "regulators being regulated."[72] Nevertheless, the government organs, representing the state, assume the responsibility to preserve and enlarge national interests by ensuring that the state's overall domestic and foreign strategies can be effectively implemented. Particularly, they normally ponder over a policy in light of the priorities and interests in the following descending sequence: survival and regeneration of the CPC, social and political stability, economic development, integrity and unity of the country, notably the reunification of Taiwan, regional influence, and international status.[73] With an eye to the significance of oil and gas to economic growth, social stability, and national security, it is no wonder that the oil and gas policies have been incorporated into domestic and foreign strategies. Hence, an SMMA does not necessarily mean that the state can well manage the energy industry and thus enhance China's energy security.

[72] That is to say, they engage in policy-making, but at the same time, they are also regulated, which easily leads to unfair rules in market competition.

[73] Philip Andrews-Speed, Xuanli Liao and Roland Dannreuther, *The Strategic Implications of China's Energy Needs*, London: International Institute for Strategic Studies, 2002, p. 48.

CHAPTER 4

Energy Policies from the Angle of the SMMA

This chapter aims to set out how an SMMA has been drawn upon in China's general energy policies with oil and natural gas in particular. From an evolutional perspective, the Chinese government's policy inclination is moving from supply-side measures to a more comprehensive way of trying to balance between the supply-side and demand-led measures. Dissecting China's overall energy policies, it is liable to find that China is a fast learner in incorporating a variety of policy tools commonly adopted by other oil-importing countries to quench their energy thirst. However, underlying the supply-side measures is the central role of the NOCs, with the backup of the Chinese government in meeting China's surging oil and gas demand. Viewing the demand-led policies, we can find that China still prefers a top-down approach to meet its ambitious targets, but has made a dent in the involvement of the society.

To ensure its energy security, China has come up with a strategy of "developing two resources (both domestic and international resources) and making full use of two markets (both domestic and international markets)." This slogan rebukes such a view that China is repellent to the use of international energy market. According to this strategy, China's measures to cope with energy security problems can be classified as

S. Chen, *China's Approach to Energy Security*,
https://doi.org/10.1007/978-981-99-3573-4_4

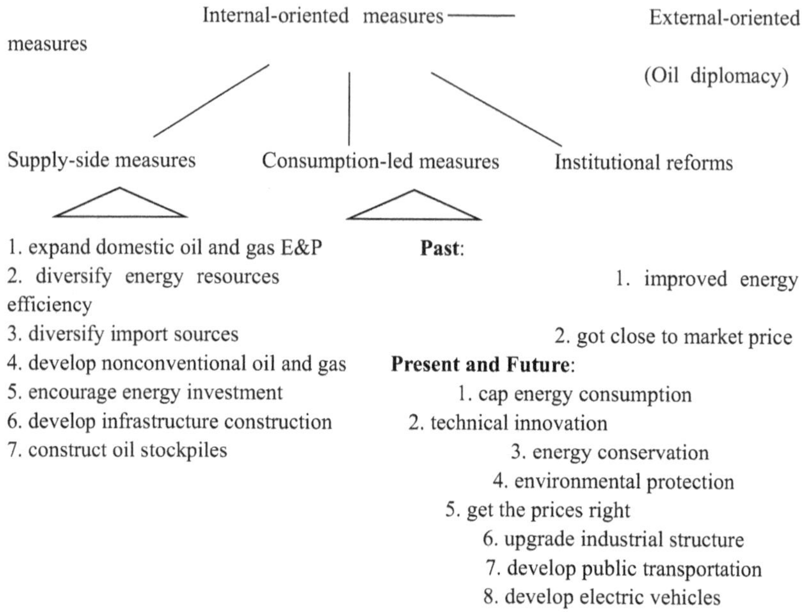

Chart 4.1 Major measures adopted by China (*Source* Chart made by the author)

internal-oriented and external-oriented measures (See Chart 4.1). This chapter primarily focuses on the internal-oriented policies.[1]

4.1 Supply-Side Measures

Initially when China turned into a net oil importer in 1993, China's approach to energy security has been overwhelmingly focused on the supply-side measures which aimed to increase oil and gas supplies rather than the demand-led measures that targeted to bring down domestic oil and gas consumptions.

China has laid down a comprehensive oil development strategy as follows: "Stabilizing existing oil industries in Eastern China, developing

[1] Discussions of institutional reforms and the external measures ("oil diplomacy") can refer to Chapters 3 and 6 respectively.

new ones in Western China, giving equal priority to both oil and gas, and using a strong domestic oil industry as a base to exploit overseas resources" (*wending dongbu, fazhan xibu, youqi bingju, lizu guonei, kaituo guoji*). The strategy obviously shows that the Chinese government has a strong desire to reduce its import dependence and thereby ensure a high degree of self-sufficiency, as well as their propensity to the supply-side measures. This has also been reflected in its 12th Five-Year Plan, in which the government expects that domestic primary energy production will be increased by 4.3%. In view of the difficulties in expanding domestic crude oil production, this augmented volume will mainly come from non-fossil fuels, natural gas, and coal, while ideally oil production can be stabilized (see Table 4.2). Specifically, the principal supply-side measures encompass the following aspects:

First, to try to stabilize domestic crude oil production and expand domestic natural gas E&P. According to a report by the Institute of Resources and Environmental Policy, Development Research Center of the State Council, by 2030, the annual domestic crude oil output will be maintained for more than 200 Mt, and the natural gas output will be about 280 Bcm.[2] The slogan of "stabilizing existing oil industries in Eastern China" was raised largely because most oilfields in the east, which contribute a large part to China's domestic production (around 2/3), have entered their aging stage.[3] Take Daqing Oilfield (the largest oilfield in China, and the world's fourth largest one) as an example, its crude oil output used to account for more than 40% of China's total crude oil since it started to operate in 1960.[4] Shengli Oilfield, the second largest one in China, also contributed about 20% of crude oil in the past five decades.[5] However, after decades of exploitation, most oilfields in

[2] Guowuyuan Fazhan Yanjiu Zhongxin Ziyuan yu Huanjing Zhengce Yanjiusuo (Institute of Resources and Environmental Policy, Development Research Center of the State Council) ed., *Zhongguo Nengyuan Geming Jinzhan Baogao* (Progress Report of China Energy Revolution (2020)), Beijing: *Shiyou Gongye Chubanshe* (Petroleum Industry Press), 2020, p. 33.

[3] Weibing Dong, "Zhongguo Dongbu lao youtian kaifa de shijian tansuo yu qushi" (Probe of developing old oilfields in the east of China and its enlightment), *Kuaiji zhi you* (Friends of Accounting), No. 1, 2001.

[4] *People's Daily*, 14 January 2003.

[5] Yusi Li, "Shengli Youtian 50 nian chanyou zhan quanguo 1/5, 'shierwu' wen chan 2700 wandun" (Crude oil output from Shengli Oilfield accounted for 1/5 in China for 50 years, maintaining an output of 27 Mt during the Twelfth periods), *Zhongguo Jingji*

the east have entered their senile stage, with characteristics of high water cuts and diminishing returns. As shown in Table 4.1, the three largest oilfields in China, which usually account for 40% of crude oil production in China, have peaked in the 1990s. During 1975–2003, Daqing's annual output of crude oil kept exceeding 50 Mt, but after 2003, its output started to decline and stabilized at a level of over 40 Mt.[6] It was said that among every cubic liquid extracted in Daqing oilfields, only 10% was oil and the rest was water.[7] As a result, the crown of the largest oilfield that Daqing used to enjoy has been taken away by Changqing Oilfield since 2012. In 2021, Daqing Oilfield completed domestic and international oil and gas production of 43.2 Mt, among which, the domestic crude oil output was merely 30 Mt, and natural gas hit 5017.96 million cubic meters.[8] According to the *CNPC Annual Report in 2003*, the six oilfields in Eastern China such as Daqing, Shengli, and Liaohe produced 75.68Mt in 2003, which was 1.37Mt less than that of the previous year.[9] Thus, oilfields in the east can hardly continue the predominant role they used to play to feed the majority of oil resources for China's surging demands if there are no large oilfields to be discovered in the future.[10]

wang (China Economic Net), 16 June 2011, http://www.ce.cn/cysc/ny/shiyou/201106/10/t20110610_20989809.shtml, accessed 9 November 2013.

[6] Yumin Zhang, "Daqing Youtian shixian yuanyou siqian wandun shinian wenchan" (Daqing Oilfield Produced 40 Mt with ten-year stabilized production), *Heilongjiang Daily*, 5 January 2013.

[7] Changjie Liu and Xinyu Gou, "Daqing zhaodao xin youtian" ("New oilfields have been found in Daqing"), *Jingji guancha* (*Economic Observer*), 27 October 2006, http://www.eobserver.com.cn/jjgcb/yaowen/2006/10/27/24115.html, accessed 9 November 2013.

[8] *Heilongjiang Ribao* (Heilongjiang Daily), "Daqing Youtian 2021 nian wancheng youqi changliang dangliang 4322.6069 wandun" (Daqing Oilfield Completed 43.226069 million tons of oil and gas equivalent in 2021), 3 January 2022.

[9] Although this may be because of the action that CNPC voluntarily planned to reduce Daqing's crude output in 2003, it contrarily illustrates its concerns of the unsustainability of high crude yields. Data source see: CNPC, *CNPC Annual Report in 2003*. http://www.cnpc.com.cn/jyzk/gsnb2003/10_19.pdf, accessed 9 November 2013.

[10] Recently, it was reported that Daqing has found 0.8–1BT of proved oil reserves in Halar Basin, which will be able to produce some million tons of oil per annum, and 100 BCM of natural gas reserves in Xujiawei. If it is verified, the new oil and gas discoveries can help alleviate China's oil and gas constraint in a great measure, but they cannot reverse the trend of growing reliance on foreign oil and gas imports. News see: Changjie Liu and Xinyu Gou, 27 October 2006, ibid.

Table 4.1 Basic information of the three largest oilfields in China

Oilfield name	*Time of discovery*	*Accumulated proved oil reserves (100 Mt)*	*Accumulated crude oil output (100 Mt)*	*Annual peak crude oil output (Mt) and time*	*Average recovery ratio (%)*
Daqing	1959	60	20	56 (1997)	50
Shengli	1961	48.24	9.36	33.55 (1991)	28.9
Liaohe	1970	25.87	3.54	15.52 (1995)	22.6

Source Based on Weibing Dong, "Zhongguo Dongbu lao youtian kaifa de shijian tansuo yu qushi" (Probe of developing old oilfields in the east of China and its enlightenment), *Kuaiji zhi you* (Friends of Accounting), No. 1, 2001

Confronting such an austere situation, the government has to readjust its strategy to make up for the decline in the east. One way is to direct major efforts to offshore areas and Western China, where the major hopes that China pins in according to former Premier Li Peng.[11] Other ways include substituting oil with gas and other energy types and stepping up efforts to acquire more oil assets abroad.

Chinese leadership tends to hold an optimistic view of China's potential to expand domestic production, in that vast regions of territory with Western China in particular are awaiting further exploration. Put in a broader context, the endeavor to develop oil in the West is in accordance with the national strategy of Western China development (*xibu dakaifa*), which aims to promote the development in the western regions and curtail the regional gap with the east. The major oil fields such as Tarim, Turpan-Hami, and Junggar that China hopes for substantial oil exploitation locate in Xinjiang. In 1997, four major oil-bearing areas with reserves exceeding 100MT were proven in Xinjiang.[12] According to CNPC, Xinjiang will be the largest gas production region too, with a discovery of 10 trillion cubic meters (Tcm) of gas reserves, which accounts for one-fourth of the total in China and thus has been the largest gas

[11] "Li Peng Zongli Lun Zhongguo Shiyou Gongye Fazhan" ("Premier Li Peng talks about the development of China's oil industry"), *Liaowang (Outlook)*, No. 41, 13 October 1997, pp. 4–5.

[12] "Xinjiang oilfields increase production," *China Daily*, 22 January 1998.

Table 4.2 Energy and climate targets by the 12th Five-Year Plan for energy development

Category	*Index*	*Unit*	*2010*	*2015*	*Annual or cumulative growth rate*	*Binding or forecast*
Energy consumption and efficiency	Total primary energy use	100 Mtce	32.5	40	4.3%	Forecast
	Increase of non-fossil fuel usage in primary energy consumption	%	8.6	11.4	[2.8]	Binding
	Total electricity use	trillion Kh	4.2	6.15	8.0%	Forecast
	Decrease in energy consumption per unit of GDP	Tce/10 thousand yuan	0.81	0.68	[−16%]	Binding
	Standard coal use for thermal power	gram/kh	333	323	−0.6%	Forecast
	Comprehensive line loss rate of electric grid	%	6.5	6.3	[−0.2]	Forecast
Energy production and supply	Domestic primary energy production	billion Tce	2.97	3.66	4.3%	Forecast
	Coal production	Bt	3.24	4.1	4.8%	Forecast
	Crude oil production	Bt	0.2	0.2	0	Forecast
	Natural gas production	Bcm	94.8	156.5	10.5%	Forecast
	Non-fossil fuel production	billion Tce	2.8	4.7	10.9%	Forecast
Electricity development	Electricity installed capacity	100 million Kh	9.7	14.9	9.0%	Forecast
	Among which: coal-fired electricity	100 million Kh	6.6	9.6	7.8%	Forecast
	Hydro power	100 million Kh	2.2	2.9	5.7%	Forecast

Category	*Index*	*Unit*	*2010*	*2015*	*Annual or cumulative growth rate*	*Binding or forecast*
	Nuclear power	10 thousand Kh	1082	4000	29.9%	Forecast
	Gas-fired electricity	10 thousand Kh	2642	5600	16.2%	Forecast
	Wind power	10 thousand Kh	3100	10,000	26.4%	Forecast
	Solar power	10 thousand Kh	86	2100	89.5%	Forecast
Ecological environment protection	decrease in CO_2 emissions per unit of GDP				(−17%)	Binding
	coefficient of sulfur dioxide (SO_2) emissions in coal power	gram/Kh	2.9	1.5	−12.4%	Binding
	coefficient of Nitrous Oxides emissions in coal power	gram/kh	3.4	1.5	−15.1%	Binding
Improving the people's livelihood	Residential electricity use per capita	Kh	380	620	10.3%	Forecast
	No. of green energy demonstration counties		108	200	13.1%	Forecast
	Population access to natural gas	100 million	1.8	2.5	6.8%	Forecast

Note (1) Figures within the parenthesis () are accumulative ones within the five-year plan; (2) GDP is calculated based on constant price in 2010; same are other indexes related with values; (3) Natural gas production include conventional natural gas, coal bed methane, and shale gas; (4) hydropower installed capacity in 2015 includes 30 million kilowatts pumped storage power plant capacity

Source State Council, "12th Five-Year Plan for Energy Development," guofa [2013] No. 2, 1 Jan. 2013

reserve.[13] Based on the resource endowments, Xinjiang is poised to be China's predominant oil and gas base in the future. Indeed, after years of hard work, the importance of the western region is gradually looming larger. As shown in Fig. 4.1, in 2000, there were only three oilfields (Xinjiang, Changqing, and Tarim) being listed into the ten largest, but their crude oil output merely accounted for 14.2% in the total output of the ten largest. By contrast, in 2009, among the ten largest oilfields five (Changqing, Yanchang, Xinjiang, Tahe, Tarim in that order) belong to the western region, and their above proportion rose to 33.8%. If we use oil and natural gas output to rank the oil and gas fields in China, six (Changqing, Tarim, Xinjiang, Xi'nan, Yanchang, Tahe, in that order) stood out from the western part of China among the ten largest, with almost half of the aggregate oil and gas production of the ten (see Fig. 4.2).

To fulfill the goal of stabilizing domestic crude oil production, the Chinese government planned to create five large-scale oil and gas-producing areas (see Table 4.3), which include the Tarim and Junggar Basins, the Liaosong Basin, the Ordos Basin, the Bohai Bay Basin, and the Sichuan Basin, three of which are located in the western region, one

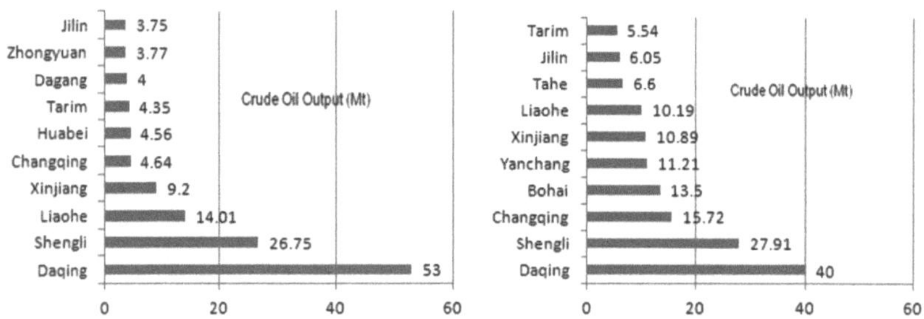

Fig. 4.1 China's ten largest oilfields in **a** 2000. **b** 2009 (*Source* Xiaozong Wang, "09 Nian Zhongguo youqitian yuanyou changliang shi qiang gongbu, Zhongshiyou zhan liuxi" [The ten largest oil and gasfields in terms of crude oil output in 2009 have been publicized, CNPC snatched six], *Zhongguo JIngji Zhoukan* [China Economic Weekly], 10 September 2009)

[13] CNPC, "Xingjiang Is Being Molded into China's Largest Gas Producing Region," 8 December 2004. http://www.cnpc.com.cn/xwygg/1200412080041.htm, accessed 22 August 2006.

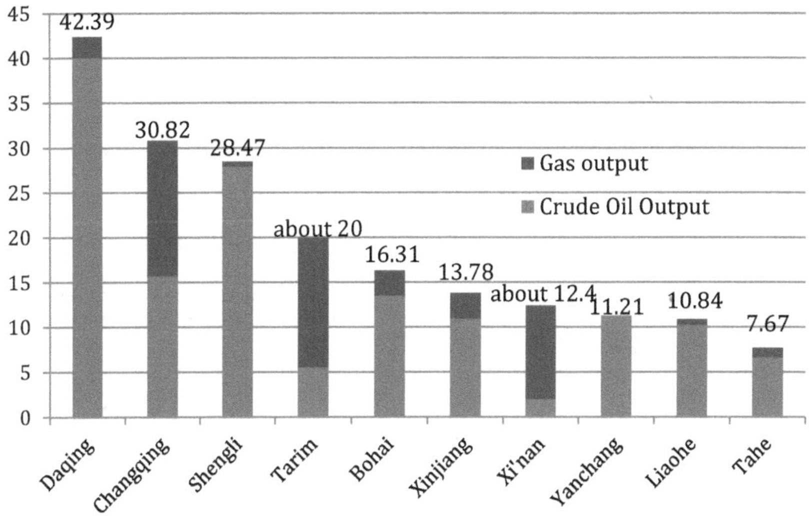

Fig. 4.2 China's ten largest oil- and gas-fields in 2009 (unit: Mtoe/year) (*Source* Ibid.)

in the sea, and the Liaosong Basin is in Northeast China where Daqing is located.

However, thanks to some unfavorable conditions, the western region is confronting some difficulties in constituting the backbone of China's primary oil supplies. First, the natural conditions and geological structure of the western region are formidable, which correspondingly boosts the costs. For instance, Tarim basin[14] sees the most formidable exploration conditions in the world. Temperatures range from − 40c in the winter to 50c in the summer. And the geological structure is miserably detrimental to oil operations. In fact, since 1994 Tarim basin was opened to foreign investments for exploration, but they all (including Esso, Japan National Oil Corp, Agip) quit by 2000 due to disappointing drilling results.[15] In 2006, PetroChina offered 12 blocks in Tarim basin, covering more than

[14] Tarim is the largest onshore basin in the world, covering 560,000 square km—even larger than France.

[15] Tao Wang, "Yingnan'ershang zhengzhan siwang zhi hai—Talimu shiyou kantan kaifa chuqi huiyi" (Meet the difficulties to fight with the death sea—Memory of the initial stage of oil E&P in Tarim Oilfield), *Renmin wang* (People's Daily Online), 3

Table 4.3 Priorities of energy construction

01 Coal development and transformation
Accelerate the construction of coal bases in northern Shaanxi, Huanglong, Shendong, eastern Inner Mongolia, and eastern Ningxia, drive the construction of coal bases in northern, eastern, and central Shanxi, Yunnan, and Guizhou steadily, and start the construction of the Xinjiang coal base. Construct some large coal-fired power bases on the basis of the above coal bases
02 Stabilizing oil output and increasing gas output
Create the 5 large-scale oil and gas-producing areas of the Tarim and Junggar Basins, the Liaosong Basin, the Ordos Basin, the Bohai Bay Basin, and the Sichuan Basin, accelerate the exploration and development of offshore and deepwater oil and gas fields, and strengthen the production and utilization of coal-bed gas in coal mine areas. Increase oil refining capability appropriately
03 Nuclear power
Accelerate the development of nuclear power in coastal provinces, promote nuclear power construction in central provinces steadily, and construct nuclear power projects with a total installed capacity of 40 million kW
04 Renewable energy sources
Construct large-sized hydropower stations in key watersheds, such as those of the Jinsha, Yalong, and Dadu Rivers, and commence the construction of hydropower projects with a total installed capacity of 120 million kW. Construct 6 onshore and 2 coastal and offshore large wind power bases, with an additional installed capacity of over 70 million kW. Construct solar energy power stations with a total installed capacity of over 5 million kW with a focus on Tibet, Inner Mongolia, Gansu, Ningxia, Qinghai, Xinjiang, and Yunnan
05 Oil and gas pipe networks
Construct the China–Kazakhstan crude oil pipeline (Phase 2), the China–Myanmar oil and gas pipeline (domestic section), the Central Asia natural gas pipeline (Phase 2), and the West-to-East Gas Transmission Lines 3 and 4. The total length of oil and gas transmission pipelines attains about 150,000 kilometers. Accelerate the construction of gas storage facilities
06 Power grids
Accelerate the construction of outward power supply projects from large coal power, hydropower, and wind power bases and create some cross-regional power transmission channels using advanced technologies. Complete 330 kV or above power transmission lines of 200,000 kilometers. Carry out trials of intelligent power grid construction, improve substations to intelligent ones, extend the application of intelligent watt-hour meters, and construct electric vehicle charging facilities

Source Xinhua, "China's 12th Five-Year Plan (2011–2015)," chapter 11

11 square km, to foreign investors for bidding, but few had an interest. It is the Chinese companies themselves that have succeeded in finding oil

December 2012. http://gx.people.com.cn/cpc/n/2012/1203/c339646-17807300-10.html, accessed 9 November 2013.

and gas there. The latest official data provided by CNPC indicates that the proved oil reserves there reach eight Bt and gas reserves 10 Tcm.[16] Despite that, oil produced in Xinjiang is not so competitive. "The average onshore oil production or 'lifting' cost in China is $12 per barrel, much higher than the international average of US$8 per barrel. Production costs in Xinjiang are US$10–13 per barrel, while those in the northeast are US$5–7 per barrel, and rising due to declines in output."[17] Second, oil and gas produced in the western region has also been constrained by the transportation problem. To deliver large volumes of oil and gas in the west to consumers in the east of China, thousands of kilometers of pipelines need to be built. Otherwise, it has to go through long-distance transport.

Offshore E&P is another front from which China expects to help stabilize oil production and raise domestic natural gas production. According to the third nation-wide petroleum resource appraisal publicized in 2008, China has 24.6 Bt of oil resources and 16 Tcm of natural gas resources in its offshore waters, each accounting for 23% of China's total petroleum resources and 30% of its total natural gas resources.[18] Having been opened up to foreign investors since the early 1980s, offshore oil has achieved much progress marked not only by increasing annual oil yields but also by the ripe managerial system, higher net profit, and so forth. Thus the offshore has stimulated more interest in the leadership to help alleviate Chinese energy security concerns. Longsheng Jiang, deputy general manager of CNOOC, confidently claimed that in contrast to the gradual depletion of onshore oil, offshore oil has been developed so fast that it will be the principal source of the incremental oil during the 11th Five-Year period.[19] The major promising offshore oil waters lie in the Bohai Bay, Yellow Sea, East China Sea, South China Sea, and the Beibu

[16] CNPC, "Brief introduction of Zhongguo Shiyou Tarim Oilfields Company," April 2013. http://www.cnpc.com.cn/tlmyt/gsgk/tlmjj/, accessed 9 November 2013.

[17] Quoted from Eric Downs, 2004, ibid., p. 92.

[18] Zhongguo Haiyou Xinwen Zhongxin (CNOOC News Center), "Nengyuan gongying: Youqi gongying zongliang fanbei" (Energy supply: Total oil and gas supplies doubled), 10 May 2012. http://www.cnooc.com.cn/data/html/news/2012-05-10/chinese/308129.html, accessed 10 November 2013.

[19] CNOOC, "China's increment of crude oil mainly comes from offshore," 31 March 2004, www.cnooc.com.cn.

Gulf. Huge capitals have been invested for offshore oil exploration, but only until the late 1990s had some large discoveries been identified.

It is certain that offshore oil and natural gas production will play a larger role in China's energy equation, but the prospect that it will replace the central role of onshore production is slim given that it only accounts for a small proportion of China's crude oil and natural gas production. In 2004, 24.72 Mt of crude oil came from offshore waters, an increase of 11% than that in 2003.[20] The offshore oil and natural gas production by CNOOC, the major player responsible for developing offshore oil and gas, for the first time surpassed 50 Mtoe in 2010.[21] By the end of 2021, its crude oil and natural gas output has climbed up to 79.6 Mtoe,[22] and the increment of crude oil accounted for about 80% of the total domestic crude oil increase.[23] During 2012 and 2021, CNOOC's offshore crude oil production increased from 38.57 Mt to 48.64 Mt; Correspondingly, its proportion in China's total crude oil rose from 18.5 to 24.4%. Similarly, CNOOC's offshore natural gas production went up from 11.3 Bcm in 2012 to 19.6 Bcm in 2021, and its proportion in China's total natural gas production dropped from 10.5 to 9.56%.[24]

The above figures illustrate: Offshore oil and natural gas are set to play a larger role in China's energy equation thanks to the rapid growth of offshore oil and gas E&P. Meanwhile, they can hardly fully replace the pivotal role of onshore oil and gas. Not only because provision from offshore will be constrained by its resource base but also because the

[20] CNOOC, www.cnooc.com.cn.

[21] Zhongguo Haiyou Xinwen Zhongxin, 10 May 2012, ibid.

[22] 79.6 Mtoe is roughly equal to 572.9 million barrels of oil equivalent. Data source: CNOOC, *2021 Niandu Baogao* (CNOOC Annual Report in 2021), p. 29.

[23] Xiuying Cao, "2021 nian yuanyou chanliang chao 3000 wandun, Bohai youtian chengwei woguo diyida yuanyou shengchan jidi" (Crude oil production exceeded 30 Mt in 2021, Bohai Oilfield has become China's largest crude oil production base), Keji Ribao (Science and Technology Daily), 9 January 2022. https://www.china-journal.net/news/9785.html, accessed 23 April 2023.

[24] Data in 2012 are from: CNOOC, "What We Do—Upstream," http://en.cnooc.com.cn/data/html/english/channel_118.html, accessed 10 November 2010. Data in 2021 are from: Yanfei Du, "'Santongyou' 2021nian chengjidan: jiada youqi kangtan kaifa, tuijin lvse ditang zhuanxing" ("Three barrels of oil" 2021 report card: increase oil and gas exploration and development to promote green and low-carbon transformation), *Renmin Wang*, 1 April 2022. http://finance.people.com.cn/n1/2022/0401/c1004-32390117.html, accessed 29 August 2022.

exploitation of offshore oil and natural gas has come across some obstacles. Pronounced among them are the territorial disputes over the South China Sea and the East China Sea with neighboring countries. The alleged presence of substantial hydrocarbon resources in these disputed waters has reaffirmed the stance of each claimant state. Drilling in these waters before reaching some kind of consensus is set to complicate China's foreign relations and regional peace, thus making the prospect for a peaceful resolution slimmer. Another obstacle stems from the fact that offshore oil and gas E&P calls for high technology and high investments but faces high risks. Deep sea drilling is indeed a new direction for the future development of the international petroleum industry, but compared with the MOCs, China is merely a beginner in this regard.

Second, diversify the energy consumption structure. The increasing dependence on foreign oil resources has prompted the Chinese government to shift from oil to other types of energy, including coal. Because coal's predominance in China's energy mix has brought about adverse effects on the environment, China has adopted several measures to combat environmental pollution in the process of enhancing its energy security. Table 4.3 has spelled out the priorities of energy construction during the 12th Five-Year Plan (2011–2015).

Prominent in the measures is China's endeavor to expand the use of natural gas, both conventional and nonconventional such as CBM and shale gas. The development of natural gas has long been neglected by the state, resulting in slow progress of natural gas utilization in China. In its energy consumption mix, natural gas only accounted for 5% in 2012, which is far below the world average of 24.1%.[25] According to Jiping Pan, director of the Oil and Gas Strategic Center, National Land and Resource Ministry of China, China has planned to boost the ratio of natural gas in its energy consumption equation to 8% in 2015, 12% in 2020, and 18% in 2030.[26] Moreover, oil price hikes have also stimulated the use of natural gas. Compared with oil whose prices fluctuate very much, natural gas

[25] Ting Zhou, "Nengyuan Jingji guize sheng bian, 'shi'erwu' tianranqi xiaofei bili jiang fanfang" (Energy economic rules changed, the proportion of natural gas consumption will be doubled during "the twelfth five-year" periods), *Zhongguo Zhengquan Bao* (China Securities Times), 3 July 2010.

[26] *Diyi Caijing* (Yicai), "Guotubu Guanyuan: Zhongguo Tianranqi kaifa chuyu zaoqi jieduan, liyong chengdu jin 5%"("MLR official: China's natural gas development is in the early stages, and the utilization rate is only 5%"), 19 June 2013, https://www.yicai.com/news/2792792.html, accessed 23 April 2023.

is a buyers' market with relatively lower and constant prices.[27] In order to achieve the above goals, China has redoubled its efforts to develop unconventional natural gas like Coal Bed Methane (CBM), shale gas, and urban sewage gas, foster the construction of natural gas storage system and let the market play a bigger role in formulating prices of natural gas. In September and October 2013, the government unveiled its policies to shore up the exploration and development of CBM and shale gas. Typical policies include: designating CBM and shale gas as strategic emerging industries, providing subsidies for CBM and shale gas producers, tax reductions or exemptions for producers, and customs tariff exemptions for imported equipment.[28] These policies have indeed greatly boosted China's natural gas production. In 2020, the national natural gas output reached 192.5 Bcm, a year-on-year increase of 9.8%. Among them, the output of coal bed methane was 6.7 Bcm, a year-on-year increase of 13.5%; the output of shale gas exceeded 20 Bcm, a year-on-year increase of 32.6%. Compared with 2015, domestic natural gas production in 2020 increased by 57.9 Bcm, a five-year increase of 43%. During the "13th Five-Year Plan" period, the average annual increase exceeded 10 Bcm, with an average annual increase of 7.4%.[29]

Moreover, besides making efforts to develop indigenous natural gas, China is set to import more gas resources from other countries. In 2020, the import volume of natural gas came to 140.4 Bcm, a year-on-year increase of 3.6%, making China's reliance on natural gas imports continue to grow.[30]

[27] CNOOC, "Fu Chengyi: "Fu Chengyi: Energy Use cannot Over-depend on Oil," 26 April 2004. www.cnooc.com.cn.

[28] On relevant policies, see General Office of the State Council, "Guowuyuan Bangongting Guanyu Jinyibu Jiakuai Meicengqi (meikuang wasi) Choucai Liyong de Yijian"(*"Opinions of the General Office of the State Council on Further Accelerating the Extraction and Utilization of CBM / Coal Mine Gas"*) (国务院办公厅关于进一步加快煤层气(煤矿瓦斯)抽采利用的意见) (Guo Ban Fa [2013] No. 93), 14 September 2013; and National Energy Administration(NEA), "Shale Gas Industry Policy" issued by the NEA, Guojia Nengyuanju Gonggao 2013 nian di 5 hao (国家能源局公告2013年第5号) (NEA Announcement No. 5, 2013) 22 October 2013.

[29] The above figures are quoted from: Department of Petroleum and Natural Gas, National Energy Administration, el al, *Zhongguo Tianranqi Fazhan Baogao* (2021) (China Natural Gas Development Report <2021>), Beijing: Shiyou Gongye Chubanshe (Petroleum Industry Press), 2021.

[30] Ibid.

Nonetheless, large expansion of natural gas has been constrained by the following factors: first and foremost is China's uncompleted natural gas pricing reform, which is bound to affect its wider use. The pricing power has long been in the hands of NDRC, which has taken a cost-plus method to decide both ex-factory price and pipeline transmission price in China. After Xi-Li administration took office, they embarked on natural gas pricing reform. In May 2021, the NDRC issued the "Notice on the Action Plan for Deepening the Reform of the Price Mechanism during the 14th Five-Year Plan," setting a target that by 2025 competitive market prices across the economy, including the gas sector, will be largely market-based.[31]

The "arbitrary low prices" of natural gas were said to retard gas development in China in view that the state-owned energy companies, which possess most reserves, are reluctant to take the risks, while foreign companies are hesitant to invest in China.[32] Another hindrance is that large amounts of capital are entailed to construct the necessary infrastructure. This problem becomes more severe since most gas fields in China locate in remote regions, far from the coastal consumption centers. The third constraint is that competition from other types of energy especially coal may retard the promotion of natural gas. Indeed, given that there is substantial coal in China, consumers could easily choose cheaper coal if they prefer. However, starting from 2012, with the vigorous promotion of energy conservation and emission reduction and air pollution prevention and control policies, the Chinese government has made every endeavor to curtail the use of coal and use natural gas as a type of transit energy before completing energy transition in China. As a result, the proportion of coal in China's total energy consumption has plunged from 70% or so to 56% in 2021. In order to meet the long-term goals of "carbon peak" and "carbon neutrality," the Chinese government has formulated a goal to bring down the proportion of coal in China's energy consumption to around 45% in 2030, and further to below 30% in 2040.[33]

[31] Fagai Jiage [2021] No. 689.

[32] Leslie Hook, "China set to miss targets for shale gasfield development," *Financial Times*, 2 July 2013.

[33] Liding chanye yanjiu wang (Leading Industry Research), "Zai 'tang da feng' 'tang zhonghe' de mubiao xia, meitang xiaofei bizhong 2030 nian jiangzhi 45% zuoyou" (Under

The second step is to make efforts to purify coal before combustion. In the past, majorities of coal were combusted before being purified, thereby resulting in serious environmental pollution. As aforementioned, coal's predominance in the Chinese energy mix will last a very long time. From 2010 to 2020, the proportion of coal in China's primary energy consumption structure dropped from 69.2% to 56.8% but still accounted for more than half. It is predicted that even by 2030, the share of coal consumption will still be around 45% of China's energy mix.[34] In view of coal's indispensability for China's energy security as well as its adverse effect on the environment, China has thus taken measures to purify coal.

In addition, China is also endeavoring to make good use of other types of energy. One choice is nuclear power. Before the eruption of the Fukushima Daiichi nuclear accident in 2011, China was very ambitious to accelerate the development of nuclear power. Acting as a reminder of the possible risks, the Fukushima crisis has reminded China to be more cautious. Since then, the Chinese government had significantly tightened control over adding new nuclear reactors. As a result, the entire nuclear power construction industry has entered a trough. It was not until 2019 that China decided to reopen nuclear power projects, breaking the "zero approval'" status for many years. In 2011, there was only a total generating capacity of 10.8 Gwe from 13 reactors in operation; As of 31 December 2021, there are 53 nuclear power units in operation, and the cumulative power generation of operating nuclear power plants is 407.141 Gwe, accounting for 5.02% of the national cumulative power

the goals of "carbon peak" and "carbon neutrality", the proportion of coal consumption will drop to about 45% in 2030), 30 August 2021, http://www.leadingir.com/hotspot/view/3206.html, accessed 29 August 2022.

[34] Liding chanye yanjiu wang (Leading Industry Research), "Zai 'tang da feng' 'tang zhonghe' de mubiao xia, meitang xiaofei bizhong 2030 nian jiangzhi 45% zuoyou" (Under the goals of "carbon peak" and "carbon neutrality", the proportion of coal consumption will drop to about 45% in 2030), 30 August 2021, http://www.leadingir.com/hotspot/view/3206.html, accessed 29 August 2022.

generation.[35] It is expected that by 2030, China's nuclear power generation will reach 0.9 trillion kilowatts, accounting for 10% of the country's total power generation.[36]

The government also plans to promote the shares of renewable energy, such as hydropower, wind power, solar power, and biomass, in the total primary energy consumption mix. This is also part and parcel of its efforts to meet its core climate pledges—reaching peak carbon by 2030 and carbon neutrality in 2060. To promote the use of renewable energy, on 28 February 2005, China promulgated its first law on renewable energy utilization debuting from 2006 and was revised in December 2009. According to this law, renewable energy users will receive an extra allowance, and power generation units are required to use a certain amount of renewable energy for power generation. The government also worked out a full-amount purchase system, under which the government commits to buying all electricity generated by renewable energy.

The Chinese government has steamed ahead with plans to expand renewable energy capacity in its Five-Year plans. In the latest Fourteenth Five-Year Plan (2021–2025) for Renewable Energy Development, which was released in June 2021, it is expected that the total consumption of renewable energy will reach about 1 billion TCE by 2025. During the "14th Five-Year Plan" period, renewable energy will account for more than 50% of the increase in primary energy consumption. In 2025, the annual power generation from renewable energy will reach about 3.3 trillion KWh, and the increase in renewable energy power generation will account for more than 50% of the increase in electricity consumption in China. In particular, electricity generation from wind power and solar power will be doubled.[37]

[35] Zhongguo Heneng Hangye Xiehui (China Nuclear Energy Association), *Quanguo Hedian Yunxing Qingkuang (2021 nian 1–12 yue)* (National Nuclear Power Operation (January–December 2021)), https://nnsa.mee.gov.cn/ywdt/yjzx/202202/t20220208_968871.html, accessed 31 August 2022.

[36] Zhongguo Hedian Fazhan Zhongxin (China Nuclear Power Development Center) and Guowang Nengyuan Yanjiuyuan (State Grid Energy Research Institute), *Woguo Hedian Fazhan Guihua Yanjiu* (China's Nuclear Power Development Planning Research), 12 December 2019.

[37] NDRC, NEA, MOF, etc., "'Shisiwu' Kezaisheng Nengyuan Fazhan Guihua" (14th Five-Year" Renewable Energy Development Plan), October 2021, https://www.ndrc.gov.cn/xwdt/tzgg/202206/t20220601_1326720.html?code=&state=123, accessed 10 September 2022.

Actions speak louder than words. China has taken the lead in renewable energy. Since the implementation of the Renewable Energy Law on 1 January 2006, the scale of development and utilization of renewable energy in China has been significantly expanded. China's cumulative installed capacity of hydropower, wind power, and photovoltaic power generation ranks first in the world. In 2018, the national renewable energy power generation was 1,867 billion KWh, accounting for 26.7% of the total power generation, an increase of 10.6 percentage points over 2005. Among them, the total installed capacity of non-water renewable energy is 94 times that of 2005, and the power generation is 91 times that of 2005. Renewable energy accounts for about 12.5% of the total primary energy consumption, doubling from 2005.[38] In 2020, China's total renewable energy utilization reached 680 million TCE, accounting for 13.6% of total primary energy consumption.

However, the development of renewable energy industry is still facing some obstacles. First, in China the construction of wind power and solar PV projects has been plagued by "excessive costs" caused by non-technical factors and they often account for 20–30% of the total project construction cost.[39] As the governance of renewable energy affairs has been scattered in a host of governmental agencies, including energy, science and technology, agriculture, forestry, water conservancy, land resources, construction, environmental protection, ocean, meteorology, etc., some of the functions of various departments overlap, resulting in poor coordination and chaotic management. These "non-technical costs" primarily derive from intergovernmental agency tussles and their policy discrepancies. For instance, the inconsistency of land use policies for renewable energy project construction between land and forestry departments has often resulted in project delays or even cancelations. Also, the construction of the financing credit system for wind power and solar PV power generation projects is lagging behind, resulting in high financing costs. The Chinese government's subsidy policies for renewable energy

[38] Hang Xu, "yi fa wei 'duo': Zhutui kezaisheng nengyuan fazhan" (Taking law as the "rudder": boosting the development of renewable energy), *Zhongguo Renda* (China National People's Congress), 21 Jan. 2020, http://www.npc.gov.cn/npc/c30834/202001/e8675d245bae45ada6cdcd10db9f9b89.shtml, accessed 2 September 2022.

[39] Tong Zhu, "Woguo Kezaisheng Nengyuan de Fazhan Jieduan yu Mianlin Tiaozhan" (The Development Stage and Challenges of Renewable Energy in China), *Zhongguo Guoqing Guoli* (China's National Conditions and National Strength) No. 7, 2019.

projects to some extent can help mitigate these "non-technical costs," but with the graduation of the subsidies, the adverse impact of these "non-technical costs" is very likely to loom larger in hindering the development of renewable energy.

Second, thanks to the lagging behind of supporting facilities, the power curtailment of wind and solar power has been very serious. At present, the renewable energy development plan has not been well orchestrated by the power grid construction plan, or both are not well coordinated. Due to the limitation of the regional power grid structure and the lag in the construction of the external transmission channel, massive wind, and solar power generated in those large-scale wind and solar power bases often confronts such a predicament of failing to be delivered to the electric grid and has to be curtailed, causing massive resource wastes. If the disconnection between the construction of renewable energy power stations and the planning of supporting power grids is not improved, the ambitious goal of renewable energy development would hardly be realized.

Third, as the proportion of fluctuating wind power and solar PVs increases to a certain level, flexibility becomes the scarcest resource in the power system and the key to influencing energy transition. However, there are currently obstacles hampering the flexibility of the power system. From a technical point of view, there is a lot of room for improvement in the "flexibility" of each "component" of the power system, such as the scale structure, location, grid structure and connectivity of the regional power grid, and the technical feasibility of real-time load monitoring and adjustment. From the perspective of the market system, the lack of related market systems such as the spot market, the auxiliary service market, and demand-side response leads to the lack of effective market signals and implementation mechanisms for the supply and demand of the power system, which not only leads to the inability to bring the flexibility resources of the existing system into full play but also entails high costs to meet the flexible needs of different sectors[40] (Fig. 4.3).

Third, step up to construct strategic petroleum reserve (SPR) and encourage domestic oil companies to boost commercial reserves in China. Since 1993, there were many debates revolving around the construction of SPR in China, covering the issues like whether China should establish SPR, how to establish it, who should pay for that, how to manage it, and

[40] Tong Zhu, "Woguo Kezaisheng Nengyuan de Fazhan Jieduan yu Mianlin Tiaozhan," 2019.

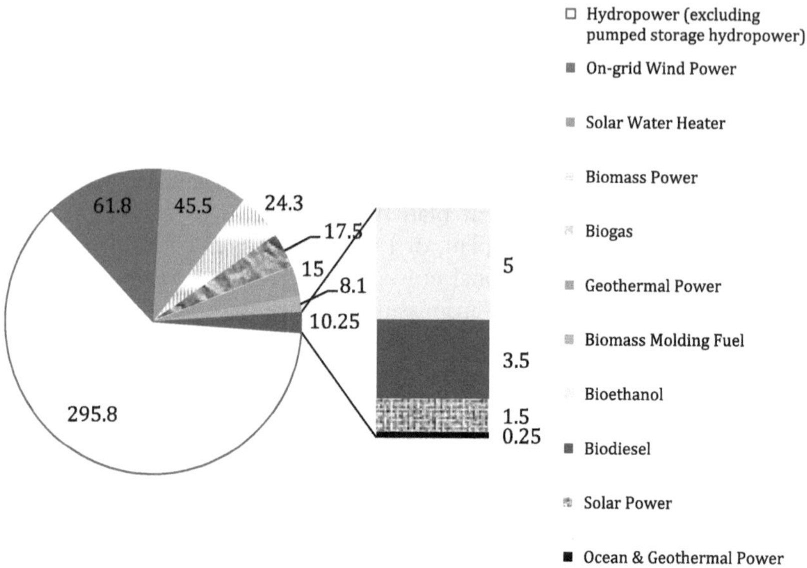

Fig. 4.3 Renewable energy targets by 2015 (million TCE)

so forth.[41] Only until 2003 did the Chinese government draw a formal

[41] Proponents argue that SPR helps to prevent oil supply disruption, check oil price surges, and act as a deterrent force. They also quote the experiences of the U.S. and Japan as the cause to entail the construction of SPR in China. Opponents claim that unlike Japan, China can produce large part of the oil it consumes, and unlike the U.S., China has no adequate financial capability to afford the exorbitant SPR. Moreover, it is not the very time to construct SPR and the small amount of the SPR is nothing to bring world oil price down. See *Zhongguo shiyou shangwu (Oil China)*, "Zhongguo jian zhanlue shiyou chubei, yiqi gongcheng yi zhankai" ("China will establish strategic Petroleum Reserve, the initial project has been unfolded"), 9 June 2005, http://www.oilchina.com/xxzx/xl.jsp?bsm=042A4FC9F.000151F9.751F&db=yw, accessed 30 August 2006; *Zhongguo Wang* (China.org.cn), "Zhongguo jianli zhanlue shiyou chubei tixi weihu guojia shiyou anquan" ("China constructs SPR to preserve national oil security"), September 2004, http://www.china.org.cn/chinese/2004/Sep/668361.htm, accessed 30 August 2006; Webpage of the Consulate General of the People's Republic of China in Houston, "Oil reserve key to energy security," 11 August 2004, http://houston.china-consulate.org/eng/nv/t147043.htm, accessed 30 August 2006; Zhang, Xiaoli, "Shiyou zhanlue chubei li duo haishi bi da" ("Does the SPR have more advantages or disadvantages"), *Guanzhou jingmaowang (Guanzhou economic and trade net)*, 12 July 2004. http://www.gzii.gov.cn/middle2/jjrd/07/72002.htm, accessed 30 August 2006.

decision to establish it. According to its scheme, China has planned to invest RMB100 billion to develop the SPR with a total capacity of 6.8 Mt (around 500 Mb) in three phases in the next 15 years.[42] In the first phase, China originally planned to set up a stockpile of 100 million barrels of crude oil starting from the end of 2005, but due to oil price hikes, China had to postpone its original plan, and only until August 2006 did it start stocking up oil at the Zhenghai base, although at that time, the oil price stayed at 60.6$/b, much higher than the ideal price level—30–40$/b.[43] By the end of 2010, China had filled up the four storage centers with a capacity of 103 mb, all located near big refining centers in the energy-starved coastal regions: Zhenhai in Ningbo, Daishan in Zhejiang, Huangdao in Shangdong, and Dalian in Liaoning.[44] Construction of SPR for the second phase, with a total capacity of 206.9 barrels, has come to an end by the first half of 2012, which involves three cities inland in western China (Lanzhou of Gansu, Dushanzi, and Shanshan of Xinjiang), and the other five in the East and South (Zhanjiang and Huizhou of Guangdong, Jintan of Jiangsu, Jinzhou of Liaonin, and Tianjin), allowing China to fill the facilities from various sources. Figure 4.4 shows the ranking of the capacities of each site in the first two phases, with Tianjin being the largest. The third phase, with a capacity of around 200 m barrels, started to build in early 2013. Daqing of Heilongjiang province and Rizhao of Shangdong province have been chosen as storage sites.[45] Once being completed, China's reserve would contain around 620 m barrels of crude,

[42] Yimin Wei et al., *Zhongguo Nengyuan Baogao (2012): Nengyuan anquan yanjiu (China Energy Report < 2012 > : Energy Security Research)*, Beijing: Kexue Chubanshe (Scientific Press), 2012, p. 129.

[43] Yanzheng Li, "Zhongguo qidong zhanlue shiyou chubei buhui yinfa youjia julue bodong" ("Chinese start of it SPR will not incur drastic oil prices fluctuation"), *Shanghai Zhengquan Bao* (*Shanghai Stock*), 11 October 2006, http://cn.chinagate.cn/economics/2006-10/11/content_2357403.htm, accessed 24 April 2023.

[44] *Zhongguo Shiyou Shangwu* (OilChina), "Zhongguo jian zhanlue shiyou chubei, yiqi gongcheng yi zhankai" ("China will establish strategic Petroleum Reserve, the initial project has been unfolded"), 9 June 2005, http://www.oilchina.com/xxzx/xl.jsp?bsm=042A4FC9F.000151F9.751F&db=yw, accessed 30 August 2006.

[45] Qing He, "Disanqi shiyou chubei kaijian, xuanzhi Heilongjiang Daqing he Shangdong Rizhao" (The third phase of SPR has started, with sites in Daqing and Rizhao), *21 Shiji Jingji Baodao* (21 Century Business Herald), 26 February 2013, p. 18.

higher than the originally planned 500 m barrels,[46] but still lower than the 700-m barrels that the US stores in several caverns.[47] It was estimated that China's SPR reached 85 MT, still lower than Japan's 86 MT and US's 91 MT as of June 2022.[48]

In the meantime, the government has also encouraged the NOCs to expand their commercial reserves, which are not a formal part of

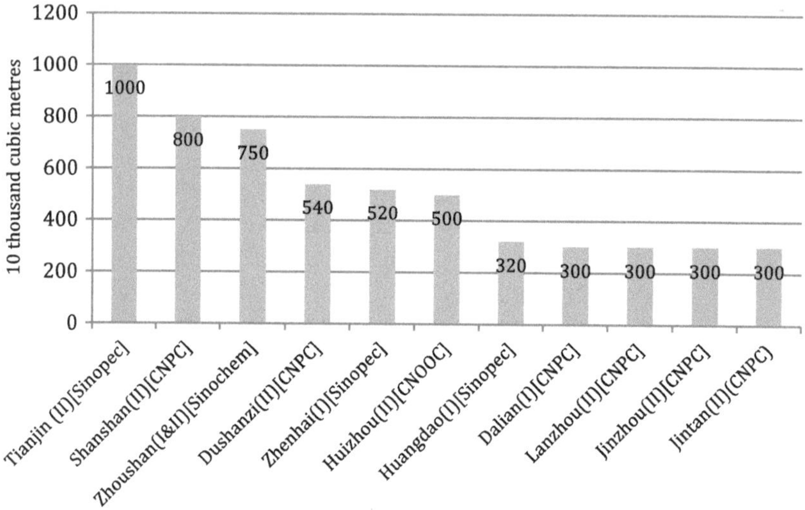

Fig. 4.4 Capacities of the SPR Facilities in China (*Note* () indicate which phase; [] indicates the contractor. *Source Zhongguo Jingji Zhoukan [China Economic Weekly]*, "Jiemi Zhongguo zhanlue shiyou chubei: 2020 nian ti zhi 8500 wandun" [Decipher China's SPR: to be increased to 85 Mt], 18 January 2011)

[46] *Xinhua*, "Zhongjin shangtiao wo zhanlue shiyou chubei guimo yuqi zhi 6.2 yi tong" (CICC raised the scale of China's SPR and expected to reach 620 m barrels), 22 May 2013, http://info.glinfo.com/13/0522/09/86CD0D0F9A0D38F2.html, accessed 3 November 2013.

[47] Javier Blas, "China stops filling strategic oil reserve," *Financial Times*, 23 November 2012.

[48] Xia Shi, "Geguo Shiyou Chubeiliang" (Oil reserves of various countries), *Shang Meiti* (Business Media), 23 June 2022, https://www.163.com/dy/article/HAJ62U9K0531MYZO.html, accessed 15 September 2022.

the emergency response system so far. The distinction between future strategic and commercial storage reserves is not clearly defined yet, and there could be a crossover between some of the facilities. But it is under the government's consideration to impose a minimum stockholding obligation on the industry so as to create a comprehensive National Petroleum Reserve. As shown in Fig. 4.5, the Chinese NOCs are storing both crude oil and refined oil products. In 2010, the commercial storage capacities of crude oil and refined oil products stood at around 310 Mb and 400 Mb, respectively, and crude oil commercial reserves climbed up to 460 Mb in 2012 while oil products commercial reserves are expected to hit 500 Mb in 2015. But data released by the NEA were much more conservative, showing that the capacity of commercial oil reserves merely had 26.5 Mcm (167 Mb) by 2010 in its Report on China's Energy Development for 2011.[49]

Ordering a release from the SPR is decided by the State Council, comprised of the Premier, Vice-Premiers, State councilors, and ministers, while the NDRC, the NEA, and the MoF are jointly responsible for

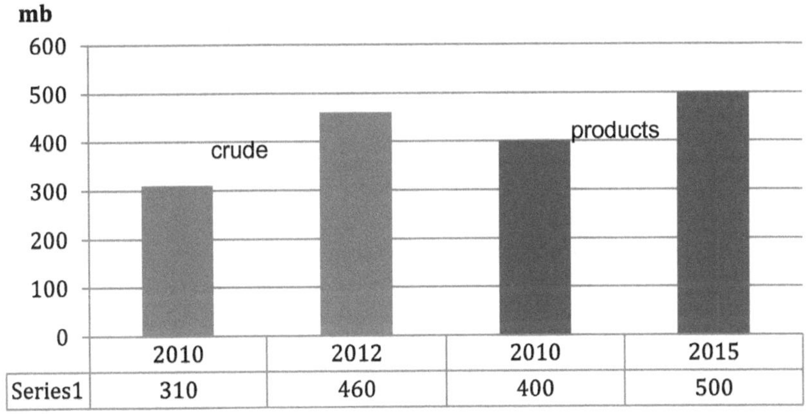

Fig. 4.5 China commercial storage capacity (*Source* CICC Research, quoted from: IEA, "Oil and gas security-emergency response of IEA countries—PR China," 2012)

[49] IEA, "Oil and gas security-emergency response of IEA countries—PR China," 2012.

implementing the orders, and the NOCs serve as contractors for operations of SPR (also see Fig. 4.4).[50] To well manage the oil reserves, the government set up a National Oil Reserve Office (NORO) affiliated with NDRC, which assumes the responsibilities of drafting SPR regulations and laws and administering the operations of SPR. Under the NORO, a National Oil Reserve Center was set up to be responsible for SPR construction and oil procurement. According to Gao Shixian, an energy expert of ERI under NDRC, the principal objective of China's SPR is to prevent oil sanctions, oil transport suspension by major oil exporting countries, or sea lane communication disruption.[51]

To meet its surging oil demand, China is speeding up to expand and upgrade the capacity of domestic oil refineries (For some cases, see Table 4.4). During 1993–2012, China's refining capacity rose from 3.33 Mbbl/d to 11.55 Mbbl/d, while refinery throughputs more than trebled from 2.57 Mbbl/d to 9.37 Mbbl/d.[52] By 2021, the refining capacity in China rose to 910 million tons per year (roughly 18.27 Mbbl/d).[53] Two prominent changes have taken place in this sector in the past years. One change is the processing capability. In the past, many of China's refineries could only process relatively light and sweet crude oils. Such a situation is changing with the NOCs' efforts to build or upgrade facilities that have the capacity of refining a variety of crude slates, including crude oils imported from the Middle East and Latin America that are relatively heavy and sour. The other change is in terms of industrial structure. To encourage economies of scale and energy efficiency, the NDRC issued guidelines in 2011, aiming to eliminate refineries smaller than 40,000 bbl/d by 2013. In the meantime, due to domestic oil pricing regime, refineries, particularly small ones, suffered great losses when international oil prices were soaring. Under the two percussions, dozens of small refineries have been shut down, accounting for about

[50] IEA, "Oil and gas security-emergency response of IEA countries—PR China," 2012.

[51] Jing Wen, "Gao Shixian: jianli shiyou chubei tixi bushi wei pingyi youjia" ("Gao Shixian: the establishment of oil stock system is not for the purpose of curbing oil prices"), Beijing: *Jingji cankao bao* (*Economic Information Daily*), 2 September 2004. http://www.china.org.cn/chinese/OP-c/651226.htm, accessed 30 August 2006.

[52] BP Statistical Review of World Energy 2013.

[53] Zhongshiyou Jingji Jishu Yanjiuyuan (Institute of Economics and Technology, of CNPC), *2021 Nian Guoneiwai Youqi Hangye Fazhan Baogao* (2021 Domestic and Foreign Oil and Gas Industry Development Report), April 2022.

16% of total refinery capacity in recent years.[54] As the two leading companies in China's oil refining sector, Sinopec and CNPC account for 46% and 31% of the capacity, respectively. In 2012, Sinopec possessed about 5 million bbl/d of total oil processing capacity.[55] While foreign oil companies have started to build integrated refineries and petrochemical projects in China, the Chinese NOCs have made overseas investments in refineries in recent years. For instance, the Chinese oil refining industry has witnessed the presence of MOCs and NOCs from Kuwait, Saudi Arabia, Russia, Qatar, and Venezuela. CNPC is seeking investments in refineries and pipelines in African countries, and its listed company, PetroChina completed purchases of Singapore Petroleum Corporation and a portion of Japan's Osaka refinery. Sinopec is acquiring a 37.5% stake in Saudi Arabia's Yanbu refinery.

Other measures include speeding up investments in energy infrastructure constructions. China has invested huge amounts of money to build oil and gas pipelines, gas terminals, electricity grid networks, etc. In recent years, China has accelerated the construction of the strategic transmission channels for northwestern, northeastern, southwestern China, and sea-imported oil and gas, improved the domestic trunk oil and gas pipe network, made unified planning of natural gas import pipelines, LNG receiving stations, and cross-regional trunk gas transmission and distribution networks, and created a gas supply layout in which natural gas, coal-bed gas, and coal-based gas are balanced. By the end of 2021, the total length of oil and gas pipelines in its domestic networks reached approximately 150,000 km in total, including 31,000 km of crude oil pipeline, 30,000 km of oil products pipeline, and 89,000 km of natural gas pipeline.[56] China plans to lay out national oil and gas pipeline networks that will reach 240,000 kilometers by 2025.[57] The trunk pipelines were originally owned and operated by the major NOCs, particularly CNPC and Sinopec. In December 2019, China created the China

[54] EIA, "Country Analysis—China," http://www.eia.gov/countries/cab.cfm?fips=CH, accessed 2 December 2013.

[55] Ibid.

[56] Data from Peng Gao, "2021 Nian Zhongguo Youqi Guandao Jianshe Xin Jinzhan" (New progress in China's oil and gas pipeline construction in 2021), *Guoji Shiyou Jingji* (International Petroleum Economics), No. 3, 2022, pp. 12–19.

[57] NDRC and NEA, *Zhongchangqi Youqi Guanwang Guihua* (The medium and long-term oil and gas pipeline network planning), May 2017.

Table 4.4 Major proposed new refinery projects and upgrades in China

Owner	*Location*	*Capacity*	*Planned start date*	*Notes*
Sinopec	Maoming	200,000	2012 Q4	Upgrade
	Nanjing/ Jinling	110,000	2012	Expansion; Construction
	Caofeidian/ Tianjin	200,000	2013	Construction
	Guangdong/ Zhanjiang	300,000	2015	Construction; developing with Kuwait Petroleum and TOTAL
	Zhenhai/ Zhejiang	300,000	2015	Expansion; Planning
	Lianyungang/ Jiangsu	240,000	2016	Planning; Phase 2 to double capacity
	Fujian	240,000	2018	Expansion with ExxonMobil and Aramco; Preparing EIS
CNPC/ PetroChina	Pengzhou	200,000	2012 Q3	Construction
	Huabei	100,000	2013	Expansion; NDRC approval
	Anning/ Yunnan	260,000	2014	Plans to use oil from Myanmar pipeline; Saudi Aramco to jointly develop
	Guangdong/ Jieyang	400,000	2014	NDRC approval; JV with PDVSA
	Huludao	200,000	2014	Construction
	Qinzhou	200,000	2015	Expansion
	Tianjin	260,000	2015	Feasibility stage; JV with Rosneft
	Changzhou	200,000	2015	Feasibility study
	Chongqing	200,000	2016	Receive oil from China–Myanmar pipeline
	Jiangsu/ Taizhou	400,000	2017	NDRC approval; Environmental approval pending; JV with Qatar and Shell
CNOOC	Huizhou	200,000	2017	Expansion
Sinochem	Quanzhou	240,000	2014	Environmental approval;
	Ningbo	240,000	2020	Pending approval

Sources Global Insight, FACTS Global Energy, PFC Energy, quoted from EIA, "Country Analysis—China," http://www.eia.gov/countries/cab.cfm?fips=CH, accessed 1 December 2013

Oil and Gas Pipeline Network Corporation (PipeChina), responsible for the investment, construction and operation of national oil and gas trunk pipelines and some gas storage and peak shaving facilities. It is expected that such centralized control over these oil and gas pipelines would allow non-state-owned companies to enjoy equal access to these pipelines with NOCs.

So far the following major projects are already in operation: the first West-to-East gas pipeline running from Lunnan in Xinjiang to Shanghai with 4200 km; the Second West–East Gas Pipeline from Horgos in Xinjiang to Hong Kong, with a total length of 8,704 kilometers and a designed annual transportation capacity of 30 billion cubic meters; Lanzhou-Zhengzhou-Changsha oil products pipeline, the longest oil pipeline within China with 2737.8 km; the Lanzhou-Chengdu-Chongqing pipeline; the 1,150-mile Western China crude oil pipeline and the Western China Refined Oil Pipeline, both from Urumqi in Xinjiang to Lanzhou in Gansu, which will connect with other regional spurs to deliver supplies to the coastal regions, as well as accommodate additional oil imports from Kazakhstan; Shan-Jing pipelines, linking the major Ordos basin in the North with Beijing and surrounding areas; the West-to-East electricity transmission grid, and the LNG terminals receiving natural gas imports from Australia and Indonesia in Guangdong and Fujian respectively. In addition, the third West–East Gas Pipeline, running from Horgos of Xinjiang to Fuzhou of Fujian and comprising 7378 km spread over one 5220-km trunkline and eight branches, is under construction. Externally, there are several oil and or gas pipelines linking China with neighboring countries. (1) China–Kazakhstan oil pipeline, China's first transnational oil pipeline, with a total length of 620 miles, connects Atasu in northern Kazakhstan with Alashankou on the Chinese border in Xinjiang. Its current capacity is 200,000 bbl/d, but it is expected to double capacity to 400,000 bbl/d by 2014; (2) Russia's Eastern Siberia-Pacific Ocean Pipeline with a spur to Daqing, which delivers up to 300,000 bbl/d to the Chinese border under a 20-year supply deal; (3) the 1100 km Sino-Myanmar oil and gas pipelines, which will deliver 22 Mt of crude oil and 12 Bcm of natural gas annually to Myanmar and southwest China; (4) Central Asian Gas Pipeline, which spans 1,130 miles and brings natural gas to China from Turkmenistan, Uzbekistan, and Kazakhstan. Linking to the second West–East pipeline at the Chinese border, this pipeline has a capacity of 1.4 Tcf/y, but its capacity is expected to increase.

4.2 Consumption-Led Measures

Other than capping energy use, the consumption-led measures primarily work on energy use efficiency and environmental protection. In order to cope with its energy security challenges, China has to redouble its efforts on the three fronts.

Firstly, China intends to cap its energy use in the future, but its ambition of duplicating the miracle in the first twenty years after its reform may fall apart. During 1980–2000, China succeeded in increasing its energy use at half the pace of economic growth; that is, GDP quadrupled while energy consumption only doubled. This was quite unusual because it contrasts with most developing countries' experience that energy use normally grows faster than GDP, thanks to the development of heavy industry and consumers' transition from non-market fuels such as firewood to market-based fuels such as kerosene and electricity.[58] This phenomenon was primarily ascribed to the SOEs' transition from inefficient operations to more modern and efficient means of production, as well as the faulty Chinese GDP or energy statistics.[59]

In the 16th National Congress of Communist Party of China (16th NCCPC) held in 2002, Beijing formulated the goal that by 2020 the GDP will quadruple that of the year 2000. More ambitiously, it planned to duplicate that successful story again by quadrupling its GDP while only doubling energy consumption from 2000 through 2020.[60] However, such a goal has proved unrealistic. On the one hand, the causes leading to the low consumption of energy during 1980–2000 could hardly repeat again in the following twenty years. On the other hand, as shown in Fig. 4.6, actual energy use already doubled since 2008, much earlier than 2020, and the expanding volume tends to be irreversible. Thus the above goal was set to collapse. As shown in Table 4.2, the 12th Five-Year Plan

[58] Malcolm Shealy and James Dorian, "Growing Chinese energy demand: Is the World in Denial?" CSIS (Center for Strategic and International Studies) Report—A Report of the Energy & National Security Program, October 2007.

[59] Malcolm Shealy and James Dorian, 2007, ibid.

[60] CCTV, former vice premier Zeng Peiyan's speech at global forum Fortune, "Zou kechixu fazhan zhi lu, cujin jingji gongtong fanrong" (Taking a sustainable development way, promote joint economic prosprity), 17 May 2005, http://www.cctv.com/news/financial/inland/20050517/101207.shtml, accessed 20 December 2013. At the 18th National Congress of the CPC, the government set the goal that the GDP and people's per capita income will be doubled by 2020 compared with the level of 2010.

forecasts total primary energy use and total electricity use will be capped at 4 billion Tce and 6.15 trillion Kh, respectively, whereas in 2012 the two figures already hit 3.62 billion Tce and 4.96 trillion Kh, respectively, implying China has to strive harder in order to meet the two targets.

Second, in conjunction with China's economic boom, energy intensity, the ratio of energy used per unit of economic output, has witnessed a sharp decline in the past decades,[61] but it remains much higher than most countries in the world. China's energy efficiency has largely been improved since the onset of economic reform in 1978. As shown in Fig. 4.7, both energy intensity (and oil intensity), the primary energy consumption (or oil consumption) for every unit of GDP, dramatically fell from 13.26 Tsce (or 1.88 tons) for every million dollars of GDP in 1980 to 0.7 Tsce (or 0.09 tons) for every million dollars of GDP in 2012. Apparently, the decline was much sharper during 1978–2002, but since then the rate of decline slowed and energy intensity actually increased in 2003. While oil intensity declined in a continuous manner over the past three decades, energy intensity decline encountered some

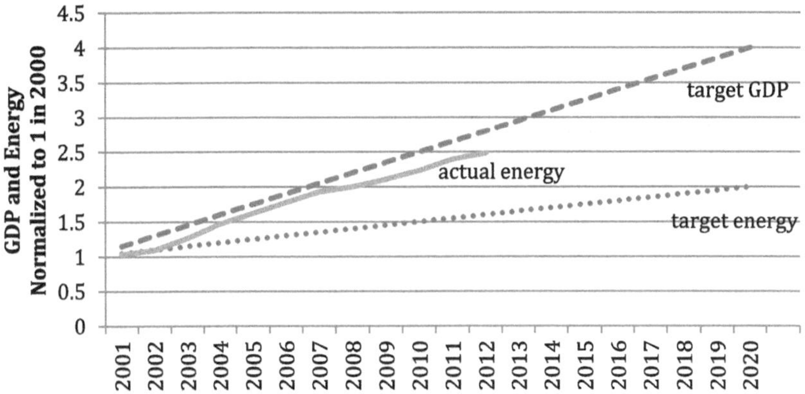

Fig. 4.6 Actual energy use in China is well above target since 2000 (*Source* Based on data from China Statistical Yearbook)

[61] For instance, by 2010, it was reduced by 20 percent compared to 2005 levels. Xinhua News Agency, "China's 'Eleventh Five-Year' emission reduction targets have been completed ahead of schedule," 30 Nov. 2010. http://news.xinhuanet.com/2010-11/30/c_13628755.htm, accessed 20 December 2013.

tumbles in the year 2003 and 2004, in which energy intensity surpassed that in 2002—1.325 Tsce per million dollars, but after that, it resumed the declining trend. Between 2015 and 2018, energy consumption per unit of GDP further dropped from 6.62 Tsce per thousand yuan to 5.7 Tsce per thousand yuan.[62] Moreover, between 1996 and 2000, total energy consumption had fallen by 8%, driven mainly by a 17.4% decline in coal consumption.[63] Scholars are at odds with the underlying reasons of China's energy intensity decline, which is contrary to the experience of other industrial countries. Using logarithmic mean Divisia index techniques to decompose changes in energy intensity in the period 1980–2003, Ma and Stern found that technological change is the dominant contributor to the decline in energy intensity,[64] but many ascribe this drop to the more efficient use of energy by industries.[65] These industries include building materials, chemicals, machinery, ferrous metals, and paper industries, in that order.[66] And the improvement of energy efficiency in industry has primarily resulted from the relative rise of energy prices, R&D expenditures, and enterprise ownership reform, as well as shifts in China's industrial structure.[67] By focusing on four Chinese industries—pulp and paper; cement; iron and steel; and aluminum, the World Bank has identified rising energy costs, followed by China's industrial policies targeting scale economies—for example, "grasping the large, letting go the small"—as significant contributors to the decline in energy intensity in all four industries.[68]

[62] Calculated based on data from National Bureau of Statistics of China.

[63] Karen Fisher Vanden, et al., "What Is Driving China's Decline in Energy Intensity?" *Resource and Energy Economics*, No. 26, 2004, p. 78.

[64] Chunbo Ma and David I. Stern, "China's Changing Energy Intensity Trend:A Decomposition Analysis," Rensselaer Working Papers in Economics No. 0615, December 2006.

[65] See, for example, Jonathan E. Sinton, Mark D. Levine, et al., "Energy Efficiency in China: Accomplishments and challenges," *Energy Policy*. Vol. 26, 1998, No. 11; X. Lin, K.R. Polenske, "Input–output Anatomy of China's Energy Use Changes in the 1980s," *Economic Systems Research*, Vol. 7, No. 1, 1995; R.F. Garbaccio, et al., "Why Has the Energy-Output Ratio Fallen in China?" *Energy* Journal, Vol. 20, No. 3, 1999, pp. 63–91.

[66] Jonathan E. Sinton, et al., 1998, ibid., pp. 812–815.

[67] Karen Fisher Vanden, et al., 2004, ibid., pp. 77–97.

[68] Karen Fisher-Vanden, et al., "Factors Influencing Energy Intensity in Four Chinese Industries," Policy Research Working Paper 6551, The World Bank, July 2013.

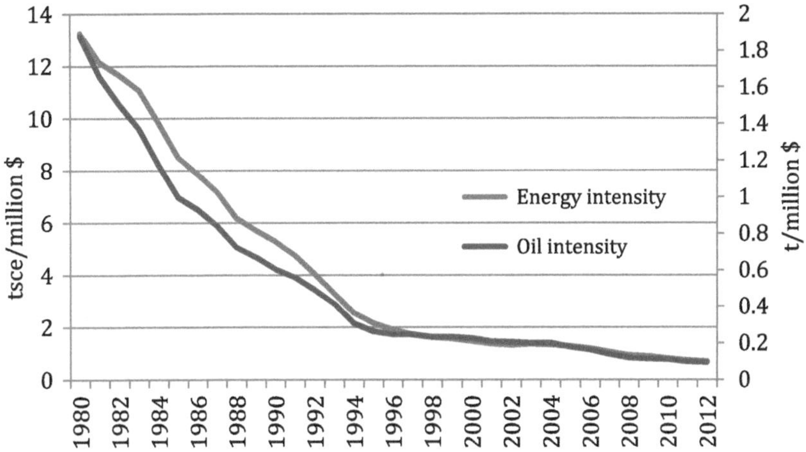

Fig. 4.7 China's energy intensity & oil intensity (*Source* Calculated based on data from National Bureau of Statistics of China, *China Statistical Yearbook*, various years)

Although much progress has been made in the past decades, in 2017, China's energy intensity was still 1.8 times of the world average, 2.5 times of the US and 4.3 times of Japan.[69] Inefficient energy use has aggravated the country's energy constraint given China is set to be reliant on foreign energy imports.

Third, the alarming environmental pollutions have posed an even graver challenge for China. Not only has China stood as world number one in greenhouse gas emissions,[70] but its environmental degradation was staggering. Among the 10 main river basins, around 10.2% of the water was rated as inferior to grade V, the lowest grade among the five classes of water quality standards which can only be applied to agricultural water

[69] *Zhongguo Dianli* (*China Electricity*), "2020 Nian Quanqiu ji Zhongguo Nengyuan Jiegou\Nengyuan Qiangdu Xianzhuang Fenxi ji Yuce" (Analysis and forecast of global and Chinese energy structure and energy intensity in 2020), 26 August 2020, http://www.chinapower.com.cn/zx/jzqb/20200826/28667.html, accessed 19 August 2022.

[70] Some foreign scientists said that China surpassed the US since 2006–2007, but China did not acknowledge that until 2010. See Chris Buckley, "China Says Is World's Top Greenhouse Gas Emitter," *Reuters*, 23 November 2010. http://www.reuters.com/article/2010/11/23/climate-cancun-china-idAFTOE6AM02N20101123, accessed 30 December 2013.

areas and ordinary scenery water areas.[71] According to the MLR, some 50 million mu (8.24 million acres), or 2.5% of China's arable land in 2012 were so contaminated by heavy metals and other pollutants that are unfit for farming.[72] Severe pollution has slashed an average of five and a half years from life expectancy in northern China.[73] The low efficiency and grave environmental pollution problems derived from a host of factors, such as the coal-dominant energy consumption mix, expanding population and urbanization, and low value-added industries to the economy, but to a large extent, it was also a result of the country's discount of the consumption-led measures for a long time in the past.

To counter the environmental challenges, the Chinese government has worked out a plethora of laws and regulations. Simply glancing over the speeches of the Chinese leaders and relevant government regulations, one may jump to the conclusion that "China always puts energy conservation in the first place." Indeed as early as the early 1980s, the Chinese government put forward the development policy of "stressing both development and saving, with priority given to saving." Since then, a number of laws and regulations aiming to improve energy conservation and protect the environment have been released. For instance, China started to put its first Energy Saving law into force on 1 January 1998 and in October 2007 a revised version was promulgated. Its first Environmental Protection Law (for trial implementation) took effect in 1979 and ten years later in December 1989 the formal EPL came into force. Since 1982, the government worked out a number of laws and amendments to counter environmental pollution, such as the Marine Environmental Protection Law, Law on the Prevention and Control of Water Pollution, Law on the

[71] The standards were formulated by the MEP and General Administration of Quality Supervision, Inspection and Quarantine of the PRC in 2002, according to the surface water environmental functions and protected objects. Data cited from: Zhou Shengxian (Minister of MEP), "Towards the New Era of Ecological Civilization—Studying the Important Statement by Comrade Xi Jinping on the Building of Ecological Civilization," Webpage of the MEP, 2 September 2013, http://english.mep.gov.cn/Ministers/Activities/201309/t20130917_260331.htm, accessed 30 December 2013.

[72] James T. Areddy, "Data Illustrate Poor State of China's Soil," *The Wall Street Journal*, 30 December 2013.

[73] Charles Riley, "Air Pollution Cuts Life Expectancy by 5.5 Years in China—Study," *CNN*, 9 July 2013. http://money.cnn.com/2013/07/09/news/china-air-pollution/index.html, accessed 30 December 2013.

Prevention and Control of Air Pollution, Solid Waste Pollution Prevention and Control Law, and so on. Ironically, these laws and regulations have not stalled the deterioration of environmental degradation in China, because most of the time in practice, those laws and regulations had been pushed aside. Considerations of energy efficiency and environmental protection have to subject to economic growth in a milieu where local officials prioritize GDP growth under their jurisdiction.

After Hu-Wen administration came into office, they tried to promote a new approach to development called the "scientific development concept" (*kexue fazhanguan*) that "makes economic and social development people-oriented, comprehensive, balanced and sustainable." Under this doctrine, China would endeavor to ensure sustainable development by boosting production, improving people's lives, and protecting the environment.[74] For the first time, China has set the precedence of energy conservation and improving energy efficiency over its previous emphasis on energy exploitation. In tandem with population control and environmental protection, energy conservation has been exalted to the level of basic national policies in the new era.[75] Former Premier Wen Jiabao had underscored the centerpiece of energy conservation over any other measures for many times. In November 2004 the NDRC enacted the *Plan on Medium- and Long-term Energy Saving*, which set out a three percent target of annual power saving, as well as the blueprint that energy consumption for every RMB10,000 (US$1,210) GDP was expected to decrease by 16% from 2.68 Tce in 2002 to 2.25 Tce in 2010.[76] In its 11th Five-year plan, the government for the first time formulated a

[74] Xinhua, "China Embraces New Scientific Development Concept: Hu," 22 April 2006.

[75] The new *Energy Conservation Law* passed by the Standing Committee of the 10th National People's Congress in October 2007 defines resource conservation as China's basic national policy at the legal level, clearly stipulating: "The state implements the basic national policy of resource conservation, implements the energy development strategy of combining conservation and development, and puts conservation in the first place." See Xinhua News Agency, "Guanzhu 'Jieyue Nengyuan Fa': Jiang Jieyue Ziyuan Queding wei Jiben Guoce" (Pay attention to the Energy Conservation Law: Defining resource conservation as a basic national policy), 28 October 2007, http://www.gov.cn/jrzg/2007-10/28/content_788510.htm, accessed 24 April 2023.

[76] NDRC, "Jieneng zhong changqi zhuanxiang guihua" ("*Plan on Medium- and Long-term Energy Saving*"), Fa Gai Huanzi [2004] No. 2505, 1 May 2004, http://www.nea.gov.cn/2011-08/18/c_131057667.htm, accessed 24 April 2023.

national target of cutting energy intensity by 20% in the five-year period (2006–2010). In the 12th Five-year plan, the Chinese government has set a number of targets pertinent to energy development and climate change. As shown in Table 4.2, the plan requires a cut of energy consumption per unit of GDP and a cut of CO_2 emissions per unit of GDP by 16 and 17%, respectively, compared with 2010 levels, and overall energy efficiency will be raised by 38% by 2015. According to the government's commitment, by 2020 CO_2 emission per unit of GDP will be 40–45% lower than in 2005. In order to meet its energy and climate goals, the Chinese government has ushered in the "dual control" policy, aiming to reduce energy intensity and limit total energy consumption in China. Some local governments directly resorted to power rationing in implementing the dual control policy when local power supply could not meet sudden strong rebound power demand.[77] In reality, China's energy intensity decreased 28.7% from 2011 to 2020,[78] while the CO_2 emissions intensity of GDP went down from 1.22 tCO2 per USD 1000 in 1990 to 0.75 in 2005 and further to 0.46 in 2020, with a 38.7% cut.[79]

To achieve the above goals, the Chinese government has taken a variety of measures. To begin with, it is more willing to let energy prices be formed through market competition although government intervention remains in deciding prices for electricity and natural gas. Energy pundits are of the belief that energy prices are the key to energy conservation. Yet inherent to the gradualism approach to reform is the fact that marketization over the market of factors of production (land, capital, labor, and resource products) is much slower than over the product market.[80] As a result, for a long time, China was hesitant to allow domestic energy

[77] Lara Dong and Xiaonan Feng, "China's 'Dual-Control' Implementation: A Tight Balancing Act Amid the Energy Transition," IHS Markit 26 October 2021, https://ihsmarkit.com/research-analysis/chinas-dualcontrol-implementation-a-tight-balancing-act-amid-t.html, accessed 22 September 2022.

[78] Xinhua News Agency, "Xinhua Headlines: China on Fast Track to Cut Energy Consumption Intensity," 2 November 2021, http://www.news.cn/english/2021-11/02/c_1310286250.htm, accessed 22 September 2022.

[79] IEA, "CO2 emissions intensity of GDP, 1990–2021," 8 March 2022, see https://www.iea.org/data-and-statistics/charts/co2-emissions-intensity-of-gdp-1990-2021, accessed 22 September 2022.

[80] Zhongguo Ti Gai Yanjiuhui Ketizu (Project Team of China Society of Economic Reform), "Tuijin Yaosu shichanghua" (Push forward marketization over factors of production), in *Zhongguo Gaige Luntan yu Zhongguo ti gai yanjiuhui 2005 nian Beijing nianhui*

prices to dance with the international market prices for fear of unbridled inflation rise, loss of competitiveness of made-in-China products, social unaffordability, and/or social unrest. The growing dependence on foreign energy imports, mounting pressure on sustainable development, as well as domestic deepening market reform, have compelled China to eventually relinquish its traditional practice of price control under a command economy. As to be discussed in Chapter 5, the market has played a decisive role in shaping most energy prices except natural gas and electricity, but it is on the government's agenda to further reform gas and power pricing mechanisms.

Second, China began to resort more to the means of resource taxes. It reformed the petroleum taxes by raising the tax rate and changing the levying mode.[81] Before that, China has already increased the tax rate on coal in major coal production provinces.[82] The government also imposed fuel consumption tax since 2008. The NDRC has initiated ten key energy saving projects since May 2005.[83]

Third, industry, building, and transportation are three key energy-intensive industries have particularly been picked up that need to strive hard to promote energy conservation and emission reduction. Taking up more than 70% of China's total energy consumption, the industry holds sway in energy conservation and emission cut. In order to eliminate backward technology, equipment, and products, and develop energy saving and high-value-added products and equipment, the government has drawn up the catalog of advanced and applicable technologies in the

lunwen ji (Collections of Paper of China Economic Reform Forum and Annual Meeting of China Society of Economic Reform*)*, Beijing: China Society of Economic Reform, 2005.

[81] Yin Tong, "Oil resource tax reform takes preliminary shape, use both hands of raising price and tax levying," *Shanghai Zhengquan Xinwen* (*Shanghai Securities News*), 23 May 2005. http://www.oilnews.com.cn/gb/misc/2005-05/23/content_616650.htm, accessed 12 September 2006.

[82] Yan Xiao, "Coal resources tax raised in 8 provinces, limited influence on the performances of coal industry," *Shanghai Zhengquan Xinwen* (*Shanghai Securities News*), 2 June 2005. http://sms.cnstock.com/ssnews/2005-6-2/jryw/t20050602_810780.htm, accessed 12 September 2006.

[83] The ten projects include: oil saving and substitution project, restructuring project of industrial coal-burning boilers, regional thermoelectricity joint production project, utilization of residual heats and residual pressures, energy saving from electricity generation system, optimization of energy system, energy saving in buildings, green lighting project, energy saving in governmental organs, energy saving monitoring, and technologic service construction (NDRC, 30 May 2005, www.sdpc.gov.cn).

fields of energy conservation and emission reduction for key industries such as iron and steel, petrochemicals, non-ferrous metals, and building materials. While establishing a mandatory standards system of quotas for energy consumption per-unit product in key industries, it has undertaken key energy saving projects, including simultaneous generation of heat and power, recycling of industrial by-product gas, construction of enterprise energy-control centers, and fostering of energy saving industries.

In the building sector, the government has formulated the standards for green buildings, actively promoted energy saving renovation of existing buildings, and set quotas for energy consumption by public buildings. It has set up a management system for the life cycles of buildings and exercises strict control over the demolition of buildings. An energy saving plan has been implemented for public institutions, and they are required to establish a supervisory system for energy conservation.

In the transportation sector, China gives priority to public transport and tightens regulations over the auto industry. As shown in Fig. 4.8, transport is the second largest energy-consuming sector, and it keeps a stunningly surging trend. As part of the national strategy to improve people's living standards, in general, China favors more civilians' car ownership.[84] Thus, the number of civil vehicles has increased almost 68 times from 1.78 million in 1980 to 302 million in 2021.[85] Yet, the over-crowded population, frequent traffic jams, deteriorating environment, as well as the impending energy shortage problems all have compelled Beijing to be alert of the car ownership expansion. Thus far, the government still bolsters the expansion of the auto industry, but it prefers developing environmentally benign and energy-efficient vehicles, including electric vehicles. In the meantime, it has taken some precautious measures. Apart from the aforementioned stricter waste emission standards, the government vigorously props up the development of gas- or electric-powered public transportation as a means to mitigate the pressing urban transportation and carbon emission pressures. Considering that Chinese vehicles normally burn 25% more gasoline than cars on European

[84] In fact, China regards the auto industry as a pillar one. To encourage private car purchases, the government formulated *Chinese Auto Industry Policy* in 1994, and provides preferential loans to vehicle buyers. Only this year the Chinese Administration tightened the loan grants to restrain the overheated economy.

[85] National Bureau of Statistics of China, *2022 Yearly Data*. www.stats.gov.cn.

roads,[86] Beijing has relinquished such regulations prohibiting the use of vehicles with low fuel consumption, few emissions, and small engine displacement, either one or all of them.[87] It speeds up the elimination of old automobiles, locomotives, and ships and starts to implement the fuel economy standard of the world's advanced level for automobiles, and popularizes energy saving and environment-friendly vehicles. The government also actively develops intercity rail transportation and rationally encourages green commuting. It has increased the electrification rate in rail transportation and launched energy saving renovations at airports, piers, and railway stations.

Fourth, related to the above, China aims to change the economic growth mode and upgrade its industrial structure. As shown in Fig. 4.8,

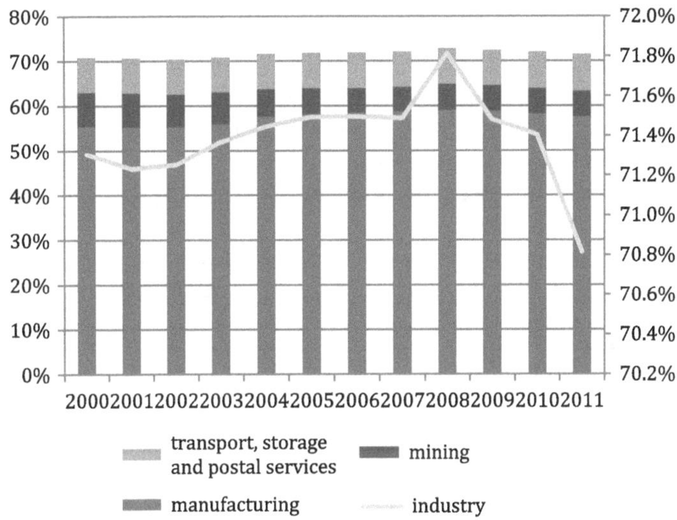

Fig. 4.8 Energy Consumption by Sector (*Source* China Statistical Yearbook, various years)

86 Xie Ye, "Energy-saving a pressing issue," *China Daily*, 9 Dec. 2004. http://www.chinadaily.com.cn/english/doc/2004-12/09/content_398542.htm, accessed 24 April 2023.

87 It seems ridiculous to have such 'protect bad' regulations. The author thinks it was primarily for the sake of protecting the interests of domestic auto industry, since Chinese-grown vehicles are normally of high fuel consumption, and high waste emissions. See NDRC, 25 November 2004, www.ndrc.gov.cn.

during 2000–2011, the proportion of energy consumption by the secondary industries constantly surpassed 71% except in the year 2011, which fell to 70.8%. In particular, the energy-intensive manufacturing sector consumed more than 55% of primary energy resources over the above years. The energy consumption of four major energy-intensive industries—steel, non-ferrous metals, chemicals, and building materials—accounts for 40% of the national total.[88] The energy-intensive sectors have further been intermingled with the problem of excess capacity, which not only results in a glut of relevant products and their sharp decline in prices but also brings about severe environmental pollution and energy wastes. Constrained by the limited energy reserves and environmental sustainability, the current economic growth mode featuring high resource input and high pollution is not sustainable. Thus, the government raises the entry threshold for processing trade, promotes its transformation and upgrading, and more importantly, transforms its energy- and labor-intensive development mode into a capital- and technology-intensive one, upgrades the existing economic structure by developing the high-tech and the tertiary sectors, with those environment-friendly industries of high-tech content in particular. Furthermore, the government has started to exercise strict control over low-level duplicated construction, eliminate industries with high consumption and high pollutant emission, and backward productivity, as well as to modify the flawed investment structure and the distorted pricing mechanisms, which have often induced many poor or even ineffective investment projects and huge wastes.[89]

Fifth, China has also mapped out stricter environmental criteria. To address the exacerbating environmental pollution problem, China has advanced two new concepts, circular economy (*Xunhuang jingji*)[90] and green GDP (*Lüse GDP*), to guide its economic activities, advocating that economic development should be based on high energy efficiency and

[88] Information Office of the State Council, "China's Energy Policy 2012," 24 October 2012.

[89] Based on the speech made by Wang Mengkui (President of the DRCSC), "Growth model needs modification," *China Daily,* 11 May 2005. http://www.chinadaily.com.cn/english/doc/2005-05/11/content_440884.htm, accessed 24 April 2023.

[90] "Circular economy" was first raised in the Central Economic Working Conference in 2004 and became the centerpiece of the NPC and the CPPCC in 2005. Basically, it means man's economic activities should be carried out through the following recycling way: resources—production—consumption—recycle the resources, that is, by fulfilling "low exploitation, high utilization, low emission" so as to make best use of the inputted

environmental protection, rather than at the sacrifice of the latter. To that end, the central government admonished officials to pursue *green GDP*, which would be used as a yardstick for their performances, rather than merely based on the conventional GDP figures, and ten cities were selected for trial implementation in 2005.[91] For the first time in the CCP's history, environmental protection has been incorporated into its evaluation system.[92] However, the way of calculating green GDP has been shelved since 2006 thanks to the technical difficulties in gauging economic losses resulting from environmental pollution and the political opposition from the local government. The current Xi Administration has advocated the concept of green development, suggesting that economic growth should not be at the cost of the environment and that environmental protection should be economic. President Xi Jinping pointed out: "Protect the ecological environment like protecting eyes, and treat the ecological environment like life"; "GDP cannot be used as the only benchmark to measure economic development."[93]

Sixth, another pronounced measure conducive to environmental protection is the financial and taxing means. The government encourages those projects contributing to energy efficiency and environmental protection. In contrast, those mega projects that may bring about large energy wastes or excessive emissions will not be endorsed by the government.

Lastly, the government is set to raise the waste gas emission standards of vehicles. Originally, the designed standards of Chinese-made vehicles for carbon monoxide and hydrocarbon emissions were 10 times

resources and energies. By so doing, we can achieve the goal of the coordinated development of economic growth and resource and environmental protection, and ultimately tally with the objective of sustainable development.

[91] Xuean Wu, "Lüse GDP jichu zhengji shuifen" ("Green GDP squeeze out false performance"), *Zhongguo gongshang shibao (China Business Times)*. 18 March 2004. http://www.cbt.com.cn/cbtnews/frontend/news.asp?ID=59104, accessed 16 September 2006.

[92] Liangping Guo elucidated the major difficulties in putting Green GDP into practice. These include the lack of an incentive structure, the regulators also being regulated, hard to measure and price the environment effects, and other unknown costs. Guo Liangping, "What 'Green Storm?"—The Politics of 'Green GDP' in China," East Asia Institute Seminar, National University of Singapore, 24 June 2005.

[93] "Zhonggong Shiba Jie Wu zhong Quanhui Gongbao" (Communiqué of the Fifth Plenary Session of the Eighteenth Central Committee of the Communist Party of China), 29 October 2015.

higher than those made in America; the permissible emission standards for running cars in China was 40 times higher than that in the US, permissible hydrocarbon emission 6 times higher and permissible nitrogen oxides 8 times higher.[94] But even such standards had not been strictly applied. For the sake of both environmental protection and oil conservation, the Chinese government has released the first national-wide compulsory criterion on limiting vehicular oil consumption. From 1 July 2005, all newly designed vehicles falling short of the compulsory criterion will not be allowed to be manufactured and distributed. For those already in use, they must be up to par by 2008.[95]

4.3 Problems and Evaluations

The internal-oriented policies that China has taken to deal with energy security indicate that China is adopting a state-managed marketization approach. On the one hand, the state has played a central and even decisive role in the policy process. Most internal-oriented policies, from macro policies like renewable energy development to micro policies like setting up a mandatory standards system of quotas for energy consumption per-unit product in key industries, are initiated, decided, implemented, and overseen by the government; on the other hand, the government's policies tend to be more market-oriented in that it recurs more often to economic instruments rather than direct administrative means to implement its policies. Thanks to such an approach, the internal-oriented measures that China has taken present the following features and problems.

First of all, the Chinese state for long has preferred supply-side policies of expanding oil and gas supplies to consumption-led policies of curbing people's energy consumptions although this is changing in recent years with the government taking a more balanced policy preference. As Downs argues, "many of the initiatives China is explicitly pursuing in the name

[94] Jieping Li, "Urban Communication: Problems and Countermeasures—On the Function of TDM," *Urban Transportation*, Vol. 3, 2002.

[95] Xiaomei Mao and Xiaofang Feng, "China Released the First National Compulsory Criterion to Control Vehicles' Oil Consumption," *Xinhua News Agency*, 28 October 2004. http://www.people.com.cn/GB/shehui/1060/2950752.html, accessed 16 September 2006.

of energy security are aimed at increasing the country's oil supply."[96] The reasons why China preferred supply-side measures mainly include: Above all, the legitimacy of the Chinese government stems primarily from improving people's living standards, ensuring sufficient energy supply to meet people's demands is in accord with the goal of promoting people's life. Otherwise, restricting energy demands may stifle economic growth and accordingly people's income. This is especially the case for a transitional economy building on the energy-intensive industry rather than the tertiary sector. Also, emphasis on the supply side results from the NOCs' strong influence, as discussed before. Additionally, it is much easier for the operation to maneuver the supply end than the consumption end technically as the latter faces a variety of atomized consumers. Given that major energy suppliers are state-owned whereas the Chinese population is so huge, the operation costs of supply-side measures are far less.

Second, related to the above, consumption-led laws and regulations are much more difficult to be fully implemented. In some cases, the laws are in place, but the effects they have produced are far from what the law-makers had expected. Although the *Environmental Protection Law* and the *Energy Conservation Law* have come into force since 6 December 1989 and 1 January 1998, respectively, they fail to accomplish their goals of protecting the environment and saving more energy in China. For example, property developers often disregard energy-intensive materials and designs despite the state-set standards for energy conservation in new buildings.[97] One reason is that the central government attached no importance to these laws and regulations in the past as aforementioned. More importantly, in a country where the promotion of government officials is primarily decided by local economic growth, GDP growth is set to become the top priority of every level of government policy, and government officials have strong motives to ruthlessly pursue local GDP expansion at the sacrifice of other values such as environment protection, energy conservation, and social harmony. So eager and prone are they to exaggerate their accounts.[98] According to Premier Wen Jiabao, all the targets set in China's 10th Five-Year Plan have been attained,

[96] Eric Downs, 2004, ibid., p. 164.

[97] *China Daily*, 24 December 2004.

[98] Eve Cary, "The Curious Case of China's GDP Figures," *The Diplomat*, 5 March 2013, http://thediplomat.com/2013/03/the-curious-case-of-chinas-gd-figures/, accessed 25 December 2013.

except energy conservation and environmental objectives.[99] During the 11th Five-Year Plan, official reports show that China's energy intensity declined 19.1%, which fell short of the government's goal of 20%. Part of this failure was because more than half of the Chinese government's four trillion RMB stimulating package went to infrastructure development, which drove up energy consumption.[100]

Also, the laws pertaining to environmental protection and energy conservation have not worked to their targets because they only provide a broad framework but "lack details and relevant regulations to cope with real, specific situations."[101] The relevant administrations of environmental protection and energy conservation are too weak to work effectively. According to Dai Yande, deputy director of the ERI, "there are only three people in the energy conservation department in the NDRC, and only a dozen officials in the Energy Bureau of the NDRC to manage energy conservation for the whole country."[102] In the 1998 governmental reform, the national bureau on energy conservation and more than 100 energy conservation centers at local levels had been dismantled. Consequently, "current energy conservation administration is even weaker than that in the 1980s," thereby causing the absence of effective supervision and assessment mechanisms to promote, implement and oversee energy conservation, as well as to punish those violating behaviors.[103] Moreover, according to both laws, local governments of different levels take the responsibility to carry through them, but the laws do not provide any effective economic incentives for the users and the producers to conserve energy and protect the environment. Policies such as tax cuts and favorable loans encouraging energy saving do not exist.[104] Considering that both goals call for large investment and coordinative efforts,

[99] *Xinwen Chenbao* (*Shanghai Morning Post*), "Chinese Premier Wen Jiabao Wins Civilian Hearts, Applauded for Eight Times in his Half-Hour Speech," 5 April 2006.

[100] According to World Watch Institute, it only declined 15.37%. See Sheldon Yoder, "Energy Intensity of Global Economy Rises, Reversing Longtime Trend," World Watch Institute, http://www.worldwatch.org/energy-intensity-energy-efficiency-gross-world-product-emerging-economies-infrastructure-development, accessed 6 December 2013.

[101] Interview with Yu Cong, director of Energy Efficiency Centre of NDRC's ERI, Beijing, 19 December 2005.

[102] Xie Ye, 2004, ibid.

[103] Interview with Yu Cong, Beijing, 8 December 2004.

[104] Xie, Ye, 2004, ibid.

it is doubtful whether local officials have such incentives to pay heed to energy saving and environmental protection, especially in case of their collision with local economic growth. As Chen Qingtai, deputy director of the DRCSC contended, the governmental administration over energy conservation used to "focus on industry but ignore transport and building sectors; lay particular stress on administrative regulation while ignoring encouraging measures; underscore policy formulation but ignore policy enforcement; emphasize technical reconstruction but ignore technical innovation; the central government cares more while some local government shows indifference." As a result, after 20 years development, China still persists "the previous economic growth mode featured with high growth, high consumption and high pollution."[105]

The predicament of green GDP further verified the delicate situation that China was facing. Green GDP is defined as an aggregate accounting index equal to the conventional GDP index deduces the economic costs of environmental pollution, natural resource depletion, poor education, overcrowding, and ineffective administration.[106] Former President Hu Jintao first endorsed green GDP in March 2004. Being used as one of the key indicators in evaluating local officials, it measured not only economic growth in a locality but also how it had protected and enhanced environmental and social welfare. In 2005 State Environmental Protection Administration of China (SEPA, the precursor the MEP) and the National Bureau of Statistics of China (NBS) launched a pilot program for a green GDP accounting system in ten provinces and municipalities.[107] On 7 September 2006, the above two agencies published a report "China Green National Accounting Study Report 2004." The report said that the environmental pollution cost reached RMB 511.8 billion in 2004, equivalent to 3.05% of China's GDP in 2004, but this cost did not cover the costs of natural resources depletion and ecological damage. To clear this

105 Qingtai Chen, "zhongguo guojia nengyuan zhanglue he zhengce" (China National Energy Strategy and Policy), Xin Nengyuan Wang (New Energy), 12 July 2006, http://newenergy.giec.cas.cn/zcfg/200607/t20060712_184070.html, accessed 26 February 2023.

106 Xinhua News Agency, "Focusing on 'Green GDP': Optimising Economic Development through Environmental Protection," 7 September 2006, http://news.xinhuanet.com/environment/2006-09/07/content_5066043.htm, accessed 25 December 2013.

107 Including Beijing, Tianjin, Chongqing, Zhejiang, Guangdong, Anhui, Sichuan, Hebei, Liaoning and Hainan.

pollution, at least RMB 287.4 billion would be required.[108] However, the actual spending for pollution treatment was merely RMB 190 billion in 2004.[109] Doubtless is the significance of green GDP for shedding light on both the quantity and quality of China's economic growth notwithstanding some flaws inherent to this new accounting system. Indeed, as an important part of the implementation of the "scientific concept of development," green GDP was expected to help facilitate changing the old development model.[110]

However, in so far as GDP remains the central benchmark in evaluating officials, it is inconceivable that green GDP can be enforced smoothly. For local governments, their GDP figures are set to dwindle after deducting costs of the environment and resource inputs, which directly affects their performance and prospect for further promotion. Understandably many local officials cold-shouldered or even had an antipathy to green GDP. It was reported that several provinces were extremely reluctant to render support to the above research work and even employed some "tricks" to invalidate the green GDP index.[111] Moreover, in May 2005, two months after launching the project, Li Deshui, then the Director of NBS openly questioned the necessity of calculating the green GDP for China. Underlying Li's suspicion was the NBS's complaint about the dominance of the SEPA, which was very high-profile in promoting this concept.[112] This was just the tip of the iceberg of the divergent interests within the central ministries, posing another threat to green GDP. As a result, the initial plan of putting a framework for a green GDP accounting system into

[108] Xinhua News Agency, "Focusing on 'Green GDP'," ibid.

[109] Xinhua News Agency, "An Interpretation of China's First Green GDP Report: What Do 3.05% and 1.8% Mean?" http://news.xinhuanet.com/fortune/2006-09/07/content_5063137.htm, accessed 28 December 2013.

[110] Yongnian ZHENG and Minjia CHEN, "China Promotes Green GDP for More Balanced Development," Briefing Series—Issue 16, China Policy Institute, Nottingham University, December 2006.

[111] Zhongguo Xinwen wang (China News Net), "Behind the Curtain of Publishing China's Green GDP: Some Localities Requested not to Publish the Results," 11 September 2006. http://www.chinanews.com/other/news/2006/09-11/787916.shtml, accessed 28 December 2013.

[112] Jiaoming Pan, "Li Deshui Strongly Questioned, Green GDP Had Been Utopiaed in the Dispute Between Ministries," *Shangwu Zhoukang (*Business Weekly*)*, 20 May 2005. http://finance.sina.com.cn/g/20050620/14151702992.shtml, accessed 29 December 2013.

nationwide operation within 3–6 years had to be shelved in 2007 and was further canceled in March 2009.[113] Other than technical reasons arising from the difficulty of quantifying environmental and ecological costs, Rauch and Chi held that the failure of the use of green GDP in China was attributed to its governance structure for environmental management, the degree of additional data collection required, and the lack of consistent rules for environmental valuation. In particular, the governance structure on the central level remains insufficient and fragmented, and in terms of central-local relations, power devolution from Beijing to provinces is detrimental to environmental causes.[114]

Although there were repeated calls for hardening the benchmark of environmental protection in evaluating government officials—the latter would be deprived of the chances for being promoted or even demoted once they were not qualified in this index, no breakthrough has been made in reality. Looking at all the places enforcing performance evaluation in light of the environmental protection index, it is liable to find that all their party and government leaders were either "passed" or "excellent"; none had been warned due to unqualified performance in environmental protection, neither were they fouled out.[115]

The Xi-Li administration has launched a new wave of reforms, aiming to lay a more solid basis for China's long-term sustainable development through a series of new policies. The Chinese government put forward such a vision of building a "beautiful China" (*meili Zhongguo*) in the 18th Party Congress. Under growing pressure to address air pollution thanks to the frequent heavy smog that smothered large swathes of the country in 2013, China unveiled a much more ambitious and specific air pollution battle plan in September 2013, through which it is expected that air quality could be completely ameliorated within five years. According to the plan, the Chinese government vows to spend about RMB 1.75 trillion (around 286.06 billion dollars) to slash the density of inhalable particulate matter by 25% in the northern Beijing-Tianjin-Hebei region

[113] *China Economic Review*, "Green GDP Project Cancelled," 4 March 2009, http://www.chinaeconomicreview.com/dailybriefing/2009_03_04/green_gdp_project_cancelled.html, accessed 19 December 2013.

[114] Jason N. Rauch and Ying F. Chi, "The Plight of Green GDP in China," *Consilience: The Journal of Sustainable Development*, Vol. 3, No. 1, 2010, pp. 102–116.

[115] Zhongguo Xinwen Wang, "Behind the Curtain of Publishing China's Green GDP," ibid.

and more than 10% nationally by 2017. To that end, Beijing strives to use both hands at the same time. On the one hand, it plans to reduce the proportion of coal in China's total primary energy use to less than 65% by 2017, have a roughly 20% cut in energy consumption per unit of industrial value-added by 2017 based on 2012 levels, gradually replace decentralized coal-fired boilers in chemical engineering, papermaking, dyeing, and tanning industry clusters, clear heavy-polluting "yellow-label" vehicles from roads across the country by 2017, and further tighten control over high-polluting and energy-intensive industries and eliminate outdated production capacity in the sectors of iron and steel, cement, electrolytic aluminum, and sheet glass. On the other hand, China will boost the supply of natural gas, coal-based substitute natural gas, coal bed methane, and nuclear power, speed up construction of desulfurization, denitrification, and dedusting facilities in coal-fired plants, steel mills, and cement plants, improve the quality of fuel oil, and promote the transformation and upgrading of industries. Meanwhile, Beijing will impose heavier penalties for violations of environmental, energy conservation, and safety requirements, and implement environmental protection standards more strictly to phase out excess production capacity.[116]

The Xi-Li administration is making more unprecedented efforts than any of its predecessors to curb environmental pollution and conserve energy use. Similar to their predecessors, their prescriptions remain an SMMA, or a top-down approach, heavily relying on the state's power to tackle the environmental and energy challenges. Although public supervision can play an effective role in disclosing and protesting environmental degradation, thus far it seems the government is not ready to bring the role of the public into full play, which apparently will undermine the efforts for that purpose. However, compared with the previous practices, the Xi-Li administration has not only taken more vigorous measures but also has a vision to zero in on the heart of the problems by the following two means.

First, to industrial producers which are also the primary polluters, for the first time, the Chinese government has started to allow for the bigger role of economic means, especially letting the market play a decisive role, along with administrative means in adjusting their behaviors so

[116] Based on *Xinhua News Agency*, "China Reveals Multi-Pronged Air Pollution Battle Plan," 12 September 2013, http://news.xinhuanet.com/english/china/2013-09/12/c_132715799.htm, accessed 30 December 2013.

as to tackle environmental pollutions and encourage energy saving. In the Third Plenary Session of the Eleventh Central Committee that attracted worldwide attention, Beijing for the first time claims that it will accelerate the development of ecological civilization system and protect the ecological environment by virtue of institutional mechanisms. The core of the mechanisms includes strengthening the system of property rights and the system of use control of natural resources and assets, allowing the market to play a decisive role in resource allocation, enforcing the system of compensation for the use of natural resources and ecological compensation system, and drawing the ecological red line. On the issue of environmental protection, anyone who goes one step beyond the prescribed limit will be punished.

Second, to party and government officials, Beijing has also worked out a new plan for reforming the official evaluation system. President Xi Jinping affirmed that "Never should we take GDP growth as the biggest achievement. Instead, indicators on ecological civilization such as resource consumption, environmental damage and ecological benefits should be included in the social development assessment system and be given more weight."[117] In light of the top leader's guidance, the Organization Department of the CPC Central Committee issued a circular on improving the evaluation of local authorities on 9 December 2013. The new rules give greater emphasis to indices related to the waste of resources, environmental protection, excess capacity, and production safety while GDP will no longer be the main determinant of local officials' success or failure.[118]

It remains to be seen whether the Xi-Li administration can effectively tackle the energy use inefficiency and environmental degradation problems. To be fair to say, as both officials and industrial producers are the keys to both energy and environmental issues and the government can grasp the crux of the problems, the prospect of resolving the two problems has greatly been enhanced under the Xi-Li administration. This is so particularly in the case of a continuously robust economy. However, China thus has a long way to go before it can attain the "security" ambit. Particularly, apart from the resource-based and environmental constraints,

[117] Zhou Shengxian, "Towards the New Era of Ecological Civilization," ibid.

[118] Xinhua News Agency, "Organization Department of the CCP Central Committee Issued Circular on Improving Evaluation of Local Authorities," 9 December 2013, http://news.xinhuanet.com/2013-12/09/c_118484309.htm, accessed 29 December 2013.

China must get over the following hurdles before it can stand up well against the big challenges if it expects to achieve its goal in 2020.

First, for a transitional economy relying on manufacturing, strictly implementing energy conservation and environmental protection regulations in China is almost bound to affect economic growth. To what extent can Beijing tolerate sacrificing economic growth purely for the sake of the environment in view they are so concerned about social stability, which may be jeopardized by the growing number of unemployed due to slow economic growth? Second, local governments still have strong incentive to foster faster GDP growth so as to generate more income, meet local spending, and reduce poverty. For that purpose, they would be unwilling to shut down those low-end energy-intensive factories causing industrial pollution or even inclined to introduce such investments into their localities and promote their growth.

A third enormous challenge is to change the conventional mindset that is infatuated with self-sufficiency. Such a passion is liable to bring about fear towards oil trade, but with higher dependence on foreign imports, China has to take more initiatives to make better use of the international energy market. As a renowned Chinese expert Hu Angang maintains, the energy development and market strategy in China should divert from the conventional one of "highly self-reliant and self-sufficient" to the new one of "basically self-sufficient with active imports and promotion of trade."[119]

4.4 Conclusion

This chapter has analyzed the countermeasures that China has taken to cope with energy security. These policies are consistent with the features of the state-managed marketization approach. On the one hand, most of these policies are formulated and implemented in a top-down manner, showing that the central government has maintained a strong hand in governing the petroleum sector. For instance, it is up to the state to decide which company can get access to oil and gas exploration and development, which one has the right to import crude oil from abroad, and

[119] Angang Hu, "Chinese Energy Strategy for the 21st Century: Production, Consumption, Trade and Security," in Kurt W. Radtke & Raymond Feddema (eds), *Comprehensive Security in Asia: Views from Asia and the West on a Changing Security Environment*, Netherlands: Brill, 2000, p. 345.

when to adjust oil prices in China. On the other hand, marketization and state decontrol is underway. For instance, more private firms are allowed to flood into the petroleum sector; the oil prices in China have largely been integrated with the international ones; the energy companies can decide where to invest and are responsible for project profitability.

The Chinese government's way of managing crude oil imports typifies the SMMA. On the one hand, initially when China has been turned into a net oil importer in 1993, the government has granted only two joint ventures (formed by PetroChina and Sinochem Import and Export Corporation, as well as by Sinopec and Sinochem Import and Export Corporation) the right to engage in state-owned imports of crude oil that have no quota limit, and later Zhuhai Zhenrong (1995) and CNOOC (2004) have gained such a right. In the meantime, to fulfill its commitments as a WTO member state, the Chinese government has to allow more than 20 non-state trading enterprises, including both private and state-owned enterprises, to import some quantities of crude oil. Meanwhile, it has set an annual quota for the import of non-state crude oil, and the quotas cannot be exceeded, but the quotas can increase year by year. Moreover, the government requires that crude oil imported from non-state trade can only be processed by refineries of PetroChina and Sinopec.

Likewise, while the Chinese government has maintained an examination and approval system over foreign direct investments by Chinese companies, the threshold has eventually been lowered.

The SMMA reflected in internal-oriented energy policies in the past indicates China's inclination towards the supply-side measures. The supply-side inclination implies that the state has to primarily rest on the NOCs to cope with its energy security concerns. The NOCs are also willing to expand their oil and gas supplies. As a result, the consumption-led policies have long been laid aside although they have been underscored in recent years.

The use of such an approach has left China's internal-oriented policies indented and uncoordinated. They are indented in the sense that these policies are in a wide spectrum between marketization and state control. Meanwhile, China's energy policies are uncoordinated in the sense of the inconsistent or conflicting elements in the policy matrix and the disjoint of policy-making and enforcement.

With a supply-side view dominant in its mindset, Beijing mainly rests on the NOCs to deal with its energy security. The NOCs have spared no effort to expand oil and gas supplies. Their roles seem to be compatible as long as domestic oil and gas demands can be satisfied. Yet, as China has eventually realized the consumption-side implications for energy security and shifted its policy focus on consumption-led measures, policy effectiveness is set to be compromised as long as it does not change its high dependence on the NOCs to deal with energy security. Role incompatibility between them would be a more common modality.

The Chinese government is not only heading forward to introduce more market elements into the energy sector but also making efforts to reform the formal institutions to better stand up against the intense global competition. The following chapter will draw on two cases to better understand how China deals with energy security.

CHAPTER 5

Use of SMMA in the Chinese Market: Two Cases

The previous chapter has highlighted the "fragmented authoritarian" nature of China's oil and gas policy-making, and the great influence the NOCs can exert. By introducing two domestic-oriented cases—Chinese oil pricing reform and the west-east gas pipeline (WEGP) project, this chapter looks into the interplay between the central state and the NOCs, and possibly the MOCs, specifically, their preferences and strategies.

The two cases illustrate that the Chinese government has both political and economic concerns with respect to certain energy policies or projects, but because under different settings the priority of concerns may be different, the role the government has played also differs. The NOCs' role propensity has changed with policy changes of the central government. Since the 1998 industrial overhaul, their role propensity for either market actors or SPSOU has strong correlations with oil and gas prices. The interactions between the state and the NOCs largely determine the approach to that matter.

5.1 Case One: The West-East Gas Pipeline Project

The WEGP case was selected not only because these pipelines have made significant contributions to China's energy security, but also because it is a vivid example from which we can watch closely the interplays of different actors. On the supply side, the WEGP is the second largest project that

S. Chen, *China's Approach to Energy Security*,
https://doi.org/10.1007/978-981-99-3573-4_5

can help alleviate China's energy hunger, expand its use of natural gas and thus reduce reliance on foreign energy imports. On the demand-side, the expansion of natural gas uses contributes to improving China's energy structure and environmental protection. Moreover, launching and operating the pipelines is set to involve a variety of actors, such as different ministries of the Chinese government, the NOCs, MOCs, and end users, as well as a host of issues, such as finding sufficient gas supplies, identifying right partners, fixing a price acceptable for both producers and consumers, and so on. By examining their concerns, this case helps dig out the strategic considerations of the government and the bargaining power of the NOCs.

The next part first gives an overview of the different WEGP projects, followed by my rendition of the motives of the NOCs and the Chinese government in the second and third parts. The fourth session will discuss the tussles pertaining to the involvement of foreign investments.

5.1.1 A Survey of the WEGP Projects

The WEGP is a set of natural gas pipelines traversing thousands of kilometers from the western part of China to the east. These pipelines used to be owned and operated by CNPC, but on 9 December 2019, all the oil and gas pipeline assets within China, including the WEGP, have been diverted from CNPC, Sinopec, and CNOOC and lumped together to form a pipeline company, called National Oil and Gas Pipeline Network Company (PipeChina). The 1st and 2nd WEGPs are already in full operation while the 3rd WEGP is under construction, and China officially started to build the 4th WEGP on 28 September 2022. Altogether the total transmission capacities of the four WEGPs would reach 77 Bcm every year.[1]

Designed to transport natural gas from the Tarim basin in Xinjiang and the Ordos basin in Shaanxi to the eastern regions covering Shanghai and the Yangtse River Delta region, the first WEGP was touted as a

[1] Yongping Ran, et al., "Quanchang yue 3340 Gongli! Xiqidongshu Sixian Gongcheng Quanxian Kaigong" ("The Total Length Is About 3340 Kilometers! Construction of the Fourth Line of West-to-East Gas Transmission Project Started"), Renmin Ribao (*People's Daily*), 28 September 2022. https://wap.peopleapp.com/article/6878977/6743150, accessed 29 October 2022.

major energy artery for the country's booming economy.[2] PetroChina is the operator and 95% owner of the first WEGP project.[3] Construction of the 1st WEGP was commenced in 2002, while full operation started on 1 January 2005. The total length of this pipeline is about 4,200 km (2,584 miles), spanning through 66 counties of ten provinces and cities,[4] and crossing through one desert, several high mountains, and three large rivers (see Map 5.1). Natural gas supplies for this pipeline mainly come from the Tarim Basin gas fields in Xinjiang while the Changqing gas area in Shaanxi province serves as a secondary gas source. Moreover, the WEGP-1 has also been fed with coal bed methane from the Qinshui Basin in Shanxi since 15 September 2009.[5] According to the amended plan, the designed capability is 12 Bcm/year for 30 years, but it has been upgraded to 17 Bcm/year since 2010.[6] The WEGP is connected to the Shaan-Jing pipeline by three branch pipelines. Starting from 15 September 2009, the pipeline is also supplied with coal bed methane from the Qinshui Basin in Shanxi.[7]

Lest that there would be insufficient gas to feed the WEGP, the designers devised the pipeline passing through Jingbian so as to tap into gas resources in the Ordos basin.[8] Accordingly, the construction of the WEGP was undertaken in two phases. The first stage witnessed the completion of the 1,516 km eastern section from Jingbian in Shannxi Province to Shanghai which commenced to supply natural gas from 1

[2] *China Daily* (HK Edition), "West-East Gas Pipeline JV Collapses," 4 August 2004, http://www.chinadaily.com.cn/english/doc/2004-08/04/content_357425.htm, accessed 25 April 2023.

[3] Winnie Lee, "China Launches Complete West-East Gas Pipeline," *Platts Oilgram News*, Vol. 82 No. 191, 5 October 2004, p. 3.

[4] The WEGP runs across Xinjiang, Gansu, Ninxia, Shannxi, Shanxi, He'nan, Anhui, Jiangsu, Shanghai and Zhejiang in the order.

[5] Jim Bai, Tom Miles, "PetroChina Pumps Coal Seam Gas in West-East Pipeline," Reuters, 16 September 2009. http://uk.reuters.com/article/2009/09/16/petrochina-gas-methane-idUKPEK27598720090916, accessed 2014 April 16.

[6] Wenjun Lu, "WEGP Will Add a 10Bcm Increase of Gas Transmission Within This Year," *Xinhua Net*, 15 July 2011. http://news.xinhuanet.com/fortune/2011-07/15/c_121673550.htm, accessed 2014 April 16.

[7] Jim Bai, Tom Miles, 2009, ibid.

[8] Jinglian Zhang and Xiangbo Li, "'Xiqi dongshu' yu woguo shiyou anquan" ("WEGP and China's Oil Security"), *Tianranqi diqiu kexue* (*Natural Gas Geoscience*), Vol. 14, No. 1, February 2003, p. 75.

January 2004, and at the second phase, the 2,484 km western section has taken shape in 2005. The pipeline has reached its designed pumping capacity of 12 Bcm of gas per year from 2007.

The Second West-East Gas Pipeline, consisting of one trunk line and eight branches, has a total length of 8,704 km and a designed capacity of 30 Bcm per year. Starting at Horgos in Xinjiang, it has been connected to the Central Asia–China Gas Pipeline and ends at the Hong Kong Special Administrative Region after traversing 14 provinces, autonomous regions, and municipalities (see Map 5.1). Besides natural gas produced in the Tarim, Junggar, Tuha, and Ordos basins, the pipeline also delivers natural gas imported from Central Asia to the Pearl River Delta (PRD) and Yangtze River Delta (YRD) areas and the central west part of China. China National Oil and Gas Exploration and Development Corp. (CNODC), a joint venture of CNPC and PetroChina, started to build the WEGP-2 in February 2008, and by 30 June 2011, the whole trunk was completed and put into operation.

In order to accommodate greater gas flows from Central Asia, CNPC commenced in October 2012 to build a third WEGP, which partially runs parallel to the second WEGP. The WEGP-3 comprises one trunkline, eight branches, three gas storage sites, and one LNG liquefaction plant. It starts from Horgos, Xinjiang, and ends in Fuzhou, Fujian province, stretching for 7378 km and passing through ten provinces and regions including Xinjiang, Gansu, Ningxia, Shaanxi, Henan, Hubei, Hunan, Jiangxi, Fujian, and Guangdong. It is expected to deliver 30 Bcm annually and to be completed in 2015. Connected with Line C of the Central Asia–China Gas Pipeline, which is under construction, the WEPP-3 will mainly be used to transport gas from the Central Asia pipeline, supplemented by incremental production of gas from the Tarim basin and coal bed methane in Xinjiang (Table 5.1).[9]

5.1.2 Motives of CNPC in Constructing the West-East Gas Pipelines

The WEGP-1 was first initiated by CNPC. In light of the SPC's *Notice of Tapping into National Natural Gas Program* in March 1998, CNPC put forward a plan to complete a trunkline from Xinjiang to Shanghai before

[9] Christopher E. Smith, "China Starts Construction on Third West-East Gas Pipeline," *Oil & Gas Journal*, 23 October 2012.

Map 5.1 The First Three West-East Gas Pipelines (*Source* Adapted from Juan Du, "Third Line to Boost Gas Supply," *China Daily*, 17 October 2012. http://www.chinadaily.com.cn/bizchina/2012-10/17/content_15823188.htmn, accessed 15 April 2014)

2005.[10] On 3 October 1998, the SPC approved the CNPC's request to conduct the feasibility study.

Doubts and oppositions cropped up soon after the initiation of this project. Opponents' major concerns include: Were the proven resources in the Tarim basin reliable? Did China have a large enough gas-consuming market? Would the prices of the long- trudged gas be accepted by end users?

[10] Liang Liao and Haihong Chu, "DangZhongyang yingming juece, shiji gongcheng angran shangma—xiqi dongshu gongcheng huozhun lixiang jishi" ("Wise Decision of the CCP Central Commission, Centenary Project Being Started—Report of the Approval Process of WEGP"), *Shiyou shang bao* (*Oil China*), 1 October 2004. www.oilchina.com/xxzx/sysb_xl.jsp?bsm=041662650.00002AD9.59E2, accessed 16 April 2014.

Table 5.1 Brief information of the West-East Gas Pipelines

	Length (km)	*Composition*	*Total investment (billion yuan)*	*Starting point*	*Final destination*	*Capacity (Bcm/year)*	*Years of service*	*Start to build*	*Start in operation*
1st WEGP	4200 (2584 miles)		43.5 ($5.7 billion)	Lunnan of Xinjiang	Shanghai	12, upgraded to 17	30	2002–7	2005–1
2nd WEGP	8653	a main line and eight sublines	142 ($21.88 billion)	Central Asia & Xinjiang	HK	30	30	2008–2	2012–6
3rd WEGP	7378 (4584 miles)	1 trunkline and 8 branches	125	Central Asia & Horgo of Xinjiang	Fuzhou, Fujian	30		2012–10	2015
4th WEGP	2445		36	Russia & Yining of Xinjiang	Zhongwei, Ningxia	45		2022	

Source Made by the author

CNPC tried to dispel the suspicions, giving the assurance that a sufficient amount of gas resources was in place and a long-term gas supply could be guaranteed. According to Sanzhong Yan, vice president of CNPC, the second nation-wide resource assessment showed that 8.39 Tcm of natural gas rests in the Tarim basin, accounting for 22% in China's total natural gas resources of 38 Tcm. At the time of interview, 562 Bcm proved gas reserves and 412 Bcm recoverable gas reserves had been discovered in the Tarim Basin. On a basis of 12 Bcm output per year, the reserves could be lasted for more than 14 years. It was projected that another 600 Bcm proved gas reserve could be on the horizon in the next five years, which could guarantee 30 years of stable gas supply with an annual output of 20 Bcm.[11] Hence, it was reliable to choose the Tarim basin as the primary gas base for the WEGP-1.

To ensure there were sufficient resources, CNPC decided to use the Changqing area in the Ordos basin as a supplemental source of gas supply for the WEGP-1. Changqing had the country's largest gas reserves at that time, which reported a 316.9 Bcm increase from 2000 to 2001.[12] Moreover, CNPC was studying the possibility of introducing natural gas from Central Asia and Russia in the future to feed the pipeline as a relay source.

The WEGP-1's target market locates in the Yangtze River Delta (YRD) region, the economic powerhouse in China, where they face grave energy and environmental constraints. The PRD regions have to rely on non-indigenous energy resources to feed their over 85% energy demands, most of which is coal. As a result, it has exerted considerable pressure on railway and waterway transportation. Moreover, the wide use of coal has resulted in deteriorating environmental pollutions, pushing up demands for clean energy. Projection by CNPC showed that gas consumption in the PRD regions would exceed 10 Bcm in 2005 and 20 Bcm by 2010.[13] It was said that 12 Bcm of natural gas approximately amounts to 9 million TCE, and combustion of natural gas can reduce 270 thousand tons of dust and

[11] The above data are quoted from: Junping Cui, "Eight Cliffhangers Associated with the 'West-East Gas Pipeline'," *Fazhan* (Development), No. 11, 2001, p. 52.

[12] Liao, Liang and Chu, Haihong, 2004, ibid.

[13] Junping Cui, 2001, p. 52.

soot.[14] Therefore, economic development and environmental protection in the eastern regions also call for the WEGP.

Finally, the WEGP helps enlarge domestic consumption and boost employment. It will promote the development of those industries related to natural gas industry as well as construction work such as machinery, electric power, and chemicals. Data provided by Zhang Guobao, vice Chairman of the SPC and Director of the National Leading Group of the WEGP Project, indicates that the WEGP-1 called for more than two million tons of steel, which would be able to promote technical progress and industrial upgrading of other related industries such as metallurgy, machinery, electricity, building materials, and equipment manufacturing.[15] It is also conducive to the development of the West and solidarity among different nationalities, helping them transform resource advantages into economic benefits.

Apparently CNPC would not disclose its intentions entirely but mainly showcase those likely benefits to the society. The WEGP conforms to CNPC's interest at least in the following aspects. Above all, the project could polish its balance sheet if the WEGP favors the energy market; but in case the project failed, the state would render necessary almsgiving. Considering that CNPC commands more knowledge about the resource endowments in Tarim, the gas supply should be sufficient for it to cover the costs. Nonetheless, the downstream market was still uncertain. In that regard, the key to marketing is the way the government set gas prices and transmission prices, which CNPC also holds sway. Moreover, CNPC could involve other partners in this project. By doing so, the investment risks could be dispersed. Otherwise, should the WEGP not be launched, the explored natural gas would be stranded, either still lying under the earth or being burned purposelessly. The vast expenditure it had already taken to conduct gas exploration and market survey would be ditched. Either case would cost CNPC more than materializing the WEGP.

According to its prediction in early 2005, CNPC was confident that it could break even before the end of 2006, and that gas through the WEGP would become a better-than-expected marketable good in the

[14] Liao, Liang and Chu, Haihong, 2004, ibid.

[15] Huijun Xiao and Fenghua Qing, "Xiqidongshu teda gongcheng xiangmu duiwai kaifang de lichengbei" ("WEGP: A Milestone for Mega Projects Opening to the Outside World—Interview with Zhang Guobao"), *Zhongguo Touzi* (China Investment), No. 1, 2003, p. 34.

downstream market. Take Shanghai as an example, the original plan was to utilize 700–1000 Mcm gas from the WEGP in 2006, but in practice, gas use was expected to reach 1.5 Bcm.[16] This seemed to verify that simply in terms of commercial profits, CNPC's effort to construct the WEGP was worthwhile.

Second, construction of the WEGP could help CNPC find a niche in China's huge gas market and reinforce its preemptive advantage in developing gas in China. The country is trying to replace coal with other types of energy so as to clean up the environment. Nature gas in China's energy consumption mix was just in a manner of one percent at that time, considerably lower than the world average of more than 20%.[17] Thereby, there is great potential for the expansion of gas consumption in China. As discussed before, after the 1998 restructuring, the domestic market in Eastern China has been monopolized by Sinopec. By constructing the WEGP, CNPC not only can wedge into Sinopec's "influence of sphere" but can be better footed in the gas market than other latecomers.

Third, the WEGP is conducive to improving the performance of the CNPC management. Construction of such a mammoth project per se would profoundly influence China's economic development. This would provide more chances for CNPC, the major undertaker of the WEGP, to engage in state economic affairs.

CNPC has wrapped up the first and second WEGPs. Construction of the third and fourth WEGP is under way, but the host company has been relayed by PipeChina. Building these pipelines is not only conducive to making full use of fast-growing gas discoveries in the Western region but also help to quench the energy hunger in the east, and diversify China's import sources of gas. For example, the WEGP-3 was proposed to transport the newly-discovered natural gas in Tukmanistan and Uzbekistan, totaling 20–30 Bcm which calls for another pipeline for delivery.[18] They also help consolidate CNPC's position in the Chinese gas market.

16 Xi qi dong shu wang (west gas transported to the east webpage), "Xiqi dongshu: wei Zhongguo nengyuan shichang dailai xin keti" ("WEGP: Bring New Topic for China's Energy Market"), 10 January 2005. www.westgas.com, accessed 16 April 2014.

17 Ye Xie and Jing Fu, "Gas Pipeline May Be Profitable Next Year," *China Daily*, 30 December 2004.

18 *Dizhi Zhuangbei* (Equipment for Geotechnical Engineering), "Xiqidongshu sanxian gongcheng qudong neibu lunzheng" ("Internal Demonstration for WEGP-3 Project Was Started"), No. 4, 2009, p. 5.

Keeping a firm hand on the gas sector and the major arteries, this company not only can hold great sway on technical standards and relevant regulations but also has successfully found a new economic engine for its own growth—developing gas market in China.

5.1.3 Motives of the Chinese Government in Launching the WEGPs

The launch of the WEGP first and foremost caters to the need of tackling the bottlenecks that China is facing. One is an unreasonable energy use structure, typified by the predominance of coal. Another bottleneck is an uneven distribution of energy resources: the eastern region is China's economic center as well as major energy-consuming zone, whereas most energy resources are concentrated in the western region. As a result, transporting those resources from the west to the east has posed considerable pressure on the transportation system. In theory, the WEGP-1 would greatly improve China's situation by increasing energy supply, mitigating pressures on the railway system, and boosting gas consumption from less than 3% to 8% in China's energy mix.[19]

In 1995, the Chinese government worked out a guideline for the development of oil and gas in the outline of the Ninth Five-Year Plan, namely "Stabilizing the east, developing the west, promoting oil and gas simultaneously, opening wider to the world" (*Wenzhu Dongbu, Fazhan Xibu, Youqi bingju, kuoda kaifang*). In light of this guideline, the SPC commissioned the CNPC and CNOOC to draw up plans for introducing pipeline natural gas and LNG respectively in December 1995. In the following April, a forum convened by the SPC on natural gas planning called for expediting pipeline construction. In the meantime, the ministry had conducted several research projects on plans and strategies for natural gas development and utilization. Experts undertaking the research projects suggested that China consider developing domestic natural gas first and importing some from neighboring countries at an appropriate time in the future. In early July 1998 when CNPC was still in the process of conducting preliminary studies on building a long-distance gas pipeline linking the east with the west, the then President Jiang Zemin paid a visit to Tarim Oilfield. Having heard that all associated natural gas

[19] Huijun Xiao and Fenghua Qing, ibid., p. 35.

had to be directly lighted thanks to the absence of necessary infrastructure, he said, "Since oil and natural gas are resources that human beings are yearning for, it makes one's heart ache to see that 700 Mcm of gas has to be burned unpurposedly every year." He also instructed that CNPC should either build a transmission pipeline or use natural gas to generate electricity or develop a local petrochemical industry so as to make use of natural gas.[20]

To justify building such a costly pipeline, sufficient natural gas is a necessity. In view of the above-mentioned controversies, the government organized some experts and high-ranking officials to conduct on-the-spot surveys in the Tarim basin. Based on the surveys, Premier Zhu nailed down the project at the premier meeting on 14 February 2000. Meanwhile, he also highlighted three problems that should be resolved at the stage of feasibility study, namely, attracting enough end users, drawing upon foreign investment, as well as ensuring enough backup resources.

Despite the above ambiguities, the Chinese government granted a green light to the WEGP out of both economic and political considerations. Economically, the WEGP is conducive to alleviating energy hunger in the coastal regions, and substituting a large proportion of coal so as to reduce pollution and optimize energy-consuming structure. The government has set the goal to enhance the share of gas in China's energy mix to 10% by 2010, from 2.1% in 2001.[21] As a bridge connecting resources and markets, the WEGP can produce remarkable social and economic benefits. If calculated with the transmitted gas of 12 Bcm in the WEGP, 16 Mt of coal equivalent can be replaced each year, thereby curtailing the emissions of 270 thousand tons of dust, and leading to a 50% increase in gas consumption in China's primary energy structure. Furthermore, because the thermal efficiency of natural gas is substantially higher than that of coal, on the basis of 12 Bcm natural gas, 4.37 Mt of energy (coal equivalent) could be saved each year. If computed in light of 300 yuan per

[20] Based on Zeng Peiyan (former vice premier), "Xiqidongshu: zhujiu nengyuan da dongmai" ("WEGP: Being Casted as an Energy Aorta"), *Zhongguo Shichang* (China Market), No. 37, 2010.

[21] Liang Yu, "Gas Pipeline Project Delayed," *Beijing: China Daily*, 9 October 2001, http://www.chinadaily.com.cn/en/doc/2001-10/09/content_87458.htm, accessed 25 April 2023.

ton of coal equivalent, over 1.3 billion yuan for fuel could be saved annually.[22] Although this calculation was done after the start of the WEGP, it does show the great benefits of improving China's energy structure and environment.

In making the decision of launching that project, political concerns seemed to override economic considerations in propelling Beijing to approve the WEGP. To begin with, the economic feasibility of this project was a big question mark before it was kicked off. On one hand, there is much uncertainty about the gas reserve in Tarim which might be inadequate to feed the pipeline. Also, China justifies an investment decision in terms of the evaluation of gas reserves or geological reserves while paying inadequate attention to the commercial exploitability of reserves.[23]

On the other hand, before the project kicked off, under the circumstance that not a single binding contract had been signed with end users,[24] the gas pipeline continued to be launched just on the basis of the market size by non-binding letters of intent and regardless of the great risks, which was an unusual practice that few private energy companies would undertake.[25] As the IEA experts attested to it, "Unlike oil production for which investment can be made stepwise and usually precedes the conclusion of sales contracts, investment in gas production cannot go ahead without long-term commitment between prospective producer and consumer."[26] Insufficient long-term commitments even persisted at the moment when the whole pipeline would be put in place. This was also one of the major reasons that foreign investors finally opted out of the project. Such an absence was not only because of the inadvertence of PetroChina to develop the downstream market in advance but also owing

[22] The above data are quoted from: Zhipeng Chang and Shuyun Liu, "Xiqi dongshu jiang dailai shenme?" ("What Will the WEGP Bring?"), *Xinhuanet*, 29 December 2004, http://news.xinhuanet.com/newscenter/2004-12/29/content_2392131.htm, accessed 25 August 2006.

[23] International Energy Agency (IEA), "Developing China's Natural Gas Market—The Energy Policy Challenges," Paris: International Energy Agency, 2002, p. 24.

[24] *Xinhua ribao* (Xinhua Daily), "Zhong shiyou zhuanjia xi shi 'xiqi' redian wenti" ("CNPC Experts Explain the Hot Issues on West Gas In Length"), 18 December 2003.

[25] IEA, 2002, p. 24. Ibid.; "China Rushes into Gas Projects before Creating Markets," *World Gas Intelligence*, 2 April 2003, p. 8, *Dow Jones Factiva*. IEA, 2002, p. 24. ibid.

[26] International Energy Agency, 2002, ibid., p. 92.

to the unwillingness of the major end users to accept the high price and afford the risk of long-term commitment.

Third, before the launch of this project, the gas supplied by the WEGP would have few comparative advantages compared with other types of fuels and the landed gas from offshore. According to the NDRC, the city-gate price of the gas through the WEGP comprises wellhead price and transmission price. The wellhead gas price is regulated by the government, albeit it is up to NDRC to specify a benchmark price, on the basis of which both producer and consumer decide the specific wellhead price, which could fluctuate within a range of 10% of the benchmark price. The transmission price is set by NDRC too. Marketing the gas through WEGP is conducted in a form of "marketing depending on which province and what volume," namely, the farther away from the gas source a province is, the higher the transmission cost it needs to pay, whereas within the boundaries of the same province, the city-gate price is the same. Also, the final city-gate price takes the gas volume a user consumes into consideration.

In February 2002, the NDPC formulated the city-gate prices for different provinces/cities: RMB1.35/cm for Shanghai,[27] RMB1.37/cm for Zhejiang, RMB1.31/cm for Jiangsu, RMB1.24/cm for Anhui, and RMB1.16/cm for Henan. Thus, the average city-gate price of natural gas from the WEGP would be RMB1.29/cm, with RMB0.45/cm for upstream and RMB0.84/cm for transmission and storage.[28] Later, because of the joint boycott by local gas distributors, PetroChina could hardly clinch any binding long-term contract with downstream end users. The NDRC had to re-adjust the prices by lowering two cents of the average gas price by, albeit the average gas price supplied by the WEGP was RMB1.27/cm. The wellhead price remains RMB0.48/cm, but the transmission price was reduced to RMB0.79/cm.[29]

[27] According to IEA, China's way to price natural gas in term of cubic meter is still not compatible to the international practice which uses heat value. The deficiency of China's practice is that it does not take account of the gas quality which virtually varies significantly in terms of pressure and temperature even for the same volume. See IEA, *Developing China's Natural Gas Market*, 2002, ibid., p. 24.

[28] IEA, *Developing China's Natural Gas Market*, 2002, ibid., p. 218.

[29] Wang, Yichao, "The sequela of the WEGP," *Caijing* (*Finance*), Vol. 21, 1 November 2004.

We may take Shanghai, the largest prosperous city as an example to spell out why the WEGP is commercially uncompetitive. According to PetroChina's Executive Director Fucheng Wang, natural gas through the WEGP was primarily to be consumed by power plants, fertilizer makers, and residents, and 60% of the gas would gradually be utilized by power plants.[30] The city-gate price in Shanghai set by the NDRC was RMB1.32/cm (about USD16.5 cents), but different types of users paid the gas with different prices. For instance, the price for power plants in Shanghai was RMB1.15/cm, RMB1.28/cm for industrial users, and RMB1.46/cm for urban residents.[31] In contrast, the city-gate price of the natural gas from the East China Sea supplied by CNOOC was only RMB0.88/cm, and the imported LNG from Australia was also cheaper than the gas from Xinjiang.[32] The gas price through the WEGP was much higher obviously because of the huge investment and its long-distance transmission. It was reported that the wellhead price in Kela-2 gas field in Tarim is RMB0.48/cm and that in Changqing gas field is RMB0.66/cm. Nevertheless, the average transmission cost reached RMB0.88/cm, much higher than the wellhead prices.[33]

The largest target consumer for WEGP is power plants, but because the gas price was much higher than that of coal, gas-fueled power generation would only lead to financial losses for power plants. "Analysts estimate that electricity fueled by natural gas from the pipeline will be about 70% more expensive than electricity fueled by coal," and IEA holds that natural gas "must be available at RMB0.7–0.9/cm to be competitive for the chemical industry and RMB1.10/cm to be competitive for the electric power sector."[34] The natural gas price for power generators suggested by Goldman Sachs was RMB0.9–1.0/cm. If that price could not be lowered, consumers might continue using coal or oil.[35] Thus, from the above

[30] "Shell, Exxon in US$5.6b Gas Plan," *Xinhua*, 19 December 2001, http://www.chinadaily.com.cn/en/doc/2001-12/19/content_98670.htm, accessed 25 April 2023.

[31] Data Source: Fuyong Li, "Xiqi dongshu jiage yuanyi" ("Cliffhangs of the WEGP Price"), *Zhongguo gongshang shibao* (*China Business Times*), 22 September 2004.

[32] Fuyong Li, 22 September 2004, ibid.

[33] Fuyong Li, 22 September 2004, ibid.

[34] *China Economic Review*, "China—Energy—Pipeline Price Barrier," 1 April 2003, *Dow Jones Factiva*.

[35] *China Economic Review*, "China—Pipeline Operator to Charge Different Rates," 1 May 2003, *Dow Jones Factiva*.

comparison, the gas supplied by the WEGP has no comparative advantage compared with other sources of natural gas and other fuels, which implies that the WEGP was commercially uncompetitive at that time.

Furthermore, the above natural gas prices were set by the government rather than by the market. If decided by the market, the price of natural gas through the WEGP would be higher.[36] If the government did not take measures to make the end-use price affordable, either through providing subsidies to the distribution companies, forcing the transmission companies to reduce their tariffs, or raising the cost of coal combustion, end users would have no incentive to shift from coal to gas. Nonetheless, thus far the government has no such encouraging policies. In an interview, Wang Fucheng also admitted that as the gas was more expensive than coal being used for power generation, the government needed to take some corresponding measures to promote the use of gas.[37]

The questionable economic feasibility of the WEGP implies that the Chinese government was primarily motivated by its political concerns to construct this project. Above all, the ascending geopolitical significance of Xinjiang after the cold war has made Beijing alert to attach more importance to this region. During the cold war, Sino-Soviet confrontation made Xinjiang relatively sealed from its neighbors, and it used to act as a strategic buffer to counter against the menace from the Soviet Union. While the border trade between Xinjiang and Central Asia after the end of the cold war contributes to local development, it has also exposed Xinjiang to foreign influence. Among them, the US presence and increasing influence in Central Asia has greatly stung China. It is much concerned about the strategic encircling by the US and its allies, which would squeeze China's maneuvering capability and endanger its national security. With the emergence of "human rights superior to sovereignty" and its practice in Kosovo, China was afraid that the US might intervene in its internal affairs when it had to calm down the riots within China. The war launched by the US in Afghanistan and later its military station

[36] Zhipeng Chang and Shuyun Liu, 10 January 2005, ibid.

[37] "Shell, Exxon in US$5.6b Gas Plan," *Xinhua*, 19 December 2001, http://www.chinadaily.com.cn/en/doc/2001-12/19/content_98670.htm, accessed 25 April 2023.

in Central Asia has only increased Chinese nervousness of the US presence in Central Asia.[38] Hence, Xinjiang has represented its geopolitical importance for China's national security.

Second, the WEGP delivering gas from the energy-rich western regions to the energy-starved east coastal areas also complies with the state's strategy of West region development. The increasingly widened gap between the affluent east and the impoverished West pressurizes the government to take countermeasures.[39] If letting such a gap continue, the ruling of the CPC treasuring social stability would be adversely jeopardized. Thus China has embarked on the vast campaign of western region development.[40] The overarching purpose is to consolidate domestic social and political stability, and the legitimacy of the government, in a manner that contributes to curtailing the economic disparity.[41] To that end, the WEGP not only poses a golden opportunity for firms in the West to fully tap their production potentials but also helps the West to turn the Western resources into wealth and to ease the Eastern energy hunger. The project "is regarded as the centerpiece of China's attempt" to develop the west and improve the environment in the east.[42] As Premier Zhu said, "The WEGP is an emblematical project hallmarking the launch of the west region development. It is also a fairly important step on the course of implementing the strategy of west region development."[43]

Indeed, the WEGP projects have brought a plethora of economic benefits to the western region, particularly Xinjiang. First, the western

[38] David Shambaugh, "China's Ambivalent Diplomacy," *Far Eastern Economic Review*, 15 November 2001.

[39] By 1978, the per capita income gap between the east and the west was only about 200 yuan (US$24), but twenty years later (1998) this gap captured 3,600 yuan (US$433.70), tripling that in the west. "West Faces Challenges, Opportunities," *Xinhua News Agency*, 6 March 2000, http://www.chinadaily.com.cn/chinagate/doc/2000-03/06/content_248035.htm, accessed 25 April 2023.

[40] The west development campaign targets twelve provinces and autonomous regions including Chongqing, Gansu, Guangxi, Guizhou, Inner Mongolia, Ningxia, Shannxi, Shichuan, Tibet, Qinghai, Xinjiang, and Yunnan. These areas cover around 60% of China's land and involve 25% of its total population.

[41] *South China Morning Post*, "Jiang Says Helping Poor Key to Stability," 5 February 2002.

[42] Ye Xie, "World Top 3 Look at US$18b Gas Plan," *China Daily*, 6 June 2001. www.chinadaily.com.cn/en/doc/2001-06/06/content_61963.htm, accessed 25 April 2023.

[43] Liao, Liang and Chu, Haihong, 2004, ibid.

region would receive vast investments from these projects. According to Zeng Peiyan, former vice premier, the total investment reached RMB140 billion, among which RMB28.4 billion, 46.3 billion and more than 70 billion were invested to develop gas fields for the WEGPs, construct the pipelines, and build matching facilities like gas pipeline networks, respectively. Among the total, 67% of all the E&P investments and pipeline investments were spent in the central and western regions, and Xinjiang alone received more than RMB46 billion to build the supporting facilities. Second, the western regions have enjoyed tax preferences in the WEGP projects. During 2004–2009, among RMB7 billion in taxes and fees created in the process of exploring and developing gas fields in the Tarim Basin, 5 billion was left to Xinjiang; 0.5 billion was returned to Xinjiang in the form of tax rebates from the pipeline transmission businesses. Other regions along the pipeline also enjoy such tax rebates. The adjustment of local taxes such as resource tax would further enhance local fiscal coffers in the western region. Third, many places in the western region are able to get access to clean energy. To conquer the long-lasting problem of fuel scarcity, China added another RMB1 billion to build a branch pipeline to Kashi, Kezhou, and Hetian in Xinjiang. The supply of natural gas has greatly improved the lives of local people and attracted an array of big firms. Since 2000, CNPC has spent RMB3.2 billion to build trunk pipelines for 1611 km specifically for Xinjiang. Fourth, some industries such as refining, chemicals, and electricity generation in Xinjiang and other regions have been able to realize a leap-frog development. Large-scale production bases of crude oil refining, ethylene, aromatic hydrocarbon, and fertilizers have sprung up in Urumqi and Southern Xinjiang. Tens of millions of crude oil refining capacity and millions of tons of ethylene production have been installed in Dushanzi, making it the largest integration project in refining and chemicals. Moreover, the western regions have also gained considerable benefits from expanding job opportunities.[44] Now petroleum and petrochemicals have become a top pillar industry in Xinjiang. In 2008, the added value of this industry reached RMB10.86 billion, accounting for 60.7% of the total industrial added value in this autonomous region. Spurred by the development of

[44] This paragraph is based on Zeng Peiyan (former vice premier), "Xiqidongshu: zhujiu nengyuan da dongmai" ("WEGP: Being Casted as an Energy Aorta"), *Zhongguo Shichang* (*China Market*), No. 37, 2010.

oil and natural gas, local GDP of Xinjiang climbed up to RMB420.3 billion in 2008, from RMB136.5 billion in 2000.[45]

Third, the Chinese government also expected that the WEGP could contribute to political stability in Xinjiang. This autonomous region houses 13 minorities with the ethnic majority of 8.82 million Uighur people.[46] For long the Uighur separatism has become a thorn in the Chinese side. Infiltration of the Turks which aims to establish a united Turkestan state becomes the latest threat. Because some radicals attempt to achieve their goal in a devastating way, such as terrorist bombing and riots, in the eyes of Beijing, separatism has greatly undermined China's stability and the CPC's legitimacy in Xinjiang. In view that Xinjiang's secession from China would not only extensively and profoundly affect the Chinese economy, and make China lose an extensive defensive shield against foreign invasion, but also may incur a "domino effect" in other regions such as Tibet,[47] Beijing has constantly placed social stability and minority solidarity in the first place.

As the CPC is well aware that its survival is associated with its obligation to protect territorial integrity, it has adopted some placatory policies to alleviate the rebellion activities. One important means is to boost investment in Xinjiang in the logic that improving the local economy would dilute the strength, magnitude, and frequency of the opposition. Thus, it is suggested that China must maintain a higher level of economic development in Western China than that of neighboring countries to prevent any potential social unrest.[48] As mentioned above, the WEGP was

[45] Yuanyuan Qu, "'Xiqidongshu' wu tiao xian zhicheng yizhang yongqi wang, rang rizi biande gengmei" ("Five Lines of the WEGP Were Woven into a Gas Network, Making Our Life More Beautiful"), *Xinjiang Nengyuan wang* (Xinjiang Energy Net), 8 February 2012, http://xjny.ts.cn/content/2012-02/08/content_6824569.htm, accessed 15 May 2014.

[46] Chinese official web: http://www.china.com.cn/chinese/2005/ethnic/837134.htm, accessed 15 May 2014.

[47] Chung, Chien-peng, "China's 'War on Terror'," *Foreign Affairs*, Vol. 81, No. 4, July/August 2002, p. 10.

[48] For official views, see, the comments by President Jiang Zemin in a report by Li Lianghui, "Jiaqiang bianfang budui zhiliang jianshe yu jianshe qiangda de bianfang" ("Beef Up Quality Building of the Frontier Troops and Construct a Powerful Frontier Defense"), *Zhongguo junshi kexue* (*China Military Science*), No. 4, 1997, p. 51; Zeng Pengyan (Deputy secretary general of the Central Economic and Financial Leading Group and minister of the State Development Planning Commission at that time), "Zhongguo jiang jiakuai shishi xibu da kaifa zhanlüe" ("China Will Speed Up the Implementation of the

regarded as beneficial to the Xinjiang people. Amidst the huge investment in the WEGP, the Western provinces and autonomous regions ushered in RMB34 billion, among which over RMB20 billion was accredited to Xinjiang; Once the WEGP reaches its designed capacity, the natural gas in Tarim will engender more than RMB1 billion in financial revenues per annum.[49] Hence, facing the external threat both from the US and the Muslim radicals, the CCP government deems it necessary to ensure the stability in Xinjiang.

Finally, the WEGP can be used as a transit to Central Asia. The geographic advantage of being adjacent to the Caspian region, the alleged second Middle East, provides China with the unique opportunity to diversify sources of energy importation. If China could import natural gas from Central Asia, the WEGP could be reinvigorated even when the gas resources in Tarim depleted. Indeed, a lot of Chinese energy experts recommended importing oil and gas from Russia and Central Asia by establishing land-based pipelines and linking them with the WEGP.[50] The plan of importing natural gas from Kazakhstan, Turkmenistan, and Uzbekistan through the WEGP has already been materialized since 2011 with the full operation of WEGP-2. The deal of importing natural gas from Russia which involves building a gas pipeline linking China and

Western Development Strategy"), *Zhongguo jingji baodao* (*China Economic Herald*), 1 March 2000. For academic views, see, Futian Song, "Jiakuai xinjiang weiwu'er zizhiqu fazhan jige wenti" ("Several Issues on Stepping Up the Development of the Xinjiang Uighur Autonomous Region"), *Jingji yanjiu cankao* (*Economic Research Reference*), 10 April 2000.

[49] CCTV, "Xiqi dongshu dui dongxibu shehui jingji fazhan de shenyuan yingxiang" ("The Profound Influence of the WEGP on the Social and Economic Development in East and West Regions"), 10 January 2005.

[50] See Zhijian Pan, et al., "Guo neiwai youqi ziyuan xingshi fenxi" ("Analysis of Domestic and Foreign Oil and Gas Resources Situation"), *Guoji shiyou jingji* (*International Petroleum Economy*), Vol. 10, No. 11, 2002, pp. 28–31; Xiaoguang Tong, "Zhongguo zai eluosi dong Xiboliya diqu de youqi hezuo ruhe qibu?" ("How Should China Start the Oil and Gas Cooperation in the Eastern Siberia?"), *Shijie shiyou gongye* (*World Petroleum Industry*), Vol. 9, No. 5, 2002, pp. 27–29; Shiqing Wu and Siyang Chen, "2001 nian Zhongguo tianranqi gongye zongshu" ("Summarization of China's Natural Gas Industry in 2001"), *Guoji shiyou jingji* (*International Petroleum Economy*), Vol. 10, No. 6, 2002, pp. 17–19.

Russia, after a 16-year marathon talk, will reportedly be clinched soon in May 2014 during President Putin's visit to Beijing.[51]

However, it deserves noting that the government's abovementioned considerations may still stand true, but environmental and energy security concerns may play a more decisive role in making decisions of building subsequent West-East Gas Pipelines. Expanding the use of natural gas not only can help mitigate China's growing reliance on oil imports, particularly from the unstable Middle East but also has become more urgent to cope with the deteriorating environmental pollution, culminated by the frequent attack of heavy smog in many cities in China.

5.1.4 Involvement of Private Investments

The Chinese government preferred to allow the involvement of foreign investors in the hope of reducing risks. First, thanks to the potentially tremendous risks inherent to such a gigantic project, the government expected that the involvement of MNCs would not only help conquer a series of technical challenges, but also bring their advanced experience in project management, and sustainable development and conservation, thus enhancing the coefficient of success of the WEGP. Second, the participation of MOCs could also substantially alleviate the Chinese starvation of capital, so could it disperse the investment risks. Third, the Chinese leadership expected that the WEGP could not only promote the growth of the fledging gas market in China but also would promote institutional reform in this sector. Fourth, opening to foreign investors tallied with the goal of forging an image of being more open after China's entry into the WTO.[52] Moreover, countries like Russia and the US have developed nationwide pipeline networks. China can learn a lot from their experiences of ensuring the safety of pipelines and maintaining them.[53] It was said that

[51] This was regarded as a move by Russia to try to find new market to mitigate the pressure of being sanctioned by the West. Katya Golubkova and Vladimir Soldatkin, "Russia Says Long-Sought China Gas Supply Deal Is Close," *Reuters*, 9 April 2014, http://www.reuters.com/article/2014/04/09/russia-china-gas-idUSL6N0N11XM20140409, accessed 25 April 2023.

[52] Huijun Xiao and Fenghua Qin, "WEGP: A Milestone for the Open Strategy—An Interview with Guobao Zhang, Vice President of National Planning Commission and Director of National WEGP Project Leading Group," *Zhongguo Touzi* (*China Investment*), No. 1, 2003, p. 35.

[53] Xiao, Huijun and Fenghua Qin, ibid., p. 35.

Premier Zhu personally stood out to conciliate the Chinese companies, maintaining that the pipeline locates within China, resources are within China, so is the market; hence there is no need to worry about the security problem stemming from a joint venture (JV) with MOCs.[54]

To attract foreign investors in investing the WEGP-1 project, the Chinese government made the following promises: The project would be fully open to foreign investors, involving not only the construction and operation of the WEGP but also midstream and downstream city pipeline networks; rather than being exclusively state-owned, foreign investors could become a majority shareholder and no limitation would be imposed to their shareholding rights; The WEGP project enjoyed those preferential policies for both infrastructure building and China's Western Development. In terms of taxes, those energy and communication projects involving foreign investors could enjoy tax breaks, and the WEGP also enjoyed deductions and exemptions of royalty fees for the rights of exploration and exploitation, tax exemption of imported equipment, and preferential policies on expanding the business scope and requisition of land.[55] Many of these preferential policies were unprecedented, showing Beijing's eagerness to attract foreign investments for this grand project.

The MOCs had their own calculations. They knew that the Chinese side was in urgent need of their involvement in such a risky project. As a Beijing-based foreign oil analyst said, "If the fields can be operated by the Chinese companies, why should they invite foreign partners?"[56] By taking advantage of their technical and managerial edges, they expected to squeeze into the Chinese gas market. In the eyes of the MOCs, a safer way of reducing investment risks was to put the JV under their control, but they knew it was unlikely thus far in China. So they proposed setting up a "half *vs.* half" JV. Under such a model, the foreign party and the Chinese party have an equal say regarding decision-making in the entity.

54 Wang, Yichao, 2004, ibid.

55 Refer to: *Huagong Wenzhai (China Chemicals)*, "Xiqidongshu gongcheng jiang quanmian duiwai kaifang" ("The WEGP Project Would Be Fully Opened to Foreign Investors"), No. 8, 2000, p. 44.

56 *China Daily*, "World Giants Get Foot in Door to Oil, Gas Reserves," 5 July 2002, http://www.chinadaily.com.cn/en/doc/2002-07/05/content_126692.htm, accessed 25 April 2023.

It was said that CNPC had repelled the involvement of foreign investors in the WEGP because, in its eyes, such a strategic trunkline should be firmly under its control on the grounds that the security of the pipeline could be ensured. Under the pressure of the government, CNPC proposed that foreign investors' total share in this project be less than 30%.[57] But after deciding to launch the WEGP, PetroChina commenced to construct the pipeline alone in 2002.

Once having made up its mind to engage foreign investors, Beijing had to arbitrate between the two options: CNPC preferred scheme of a JV where foreign investors could hold 30% equity shares at most, and MOCs preferred proposal of a 50:50% JV. The negotiation commenced in July 2000. Until 29 December 2001 did CNPC sign a non-binding interim agreement with Shell-led consortium. Later Sinopec, Exxon Mobil, and its partner decided to participate in this project. On 4 July 2002, the day when the construction of the WEGP was slated to be started, CNPC and its partners signed a *Framework Agreement on the Joint Venture*. According to the agreement, CNPC acquired 50% rather than what it preferred 70% of the shares, while the three foreign partners received 45% rather than 50% of the shares in total,[58] and the left 5% went to Sinopec. Each party's stakes in the project included gas field development, pipeline construction, and gas marketing. Therefore, PetroChina still held a controlling portion in the WEGP, but its concession also made the participation of foreign MOCs possible. "It is unprecedented for China to open its most lucrative oil and gas reserves to foreign companies in exchange for involving foreign partners in the risky project," given that previously most inland blocks that China had offered to foreign investors were "no more than infertile."[59]

The deal could have become a win-win solution for both sides should it have been carried out.[60] Nonetheless, both sides still disagreed on

[57] Yichao Wang, "Xiqi dongshu houyizheng" ("The Sequela of the WEGP"), Beijing: *Caijing* (*Finance*), Vol. 21, 1 November 2004.

[58] That is, Shell and Hong Kong & China Gas, Gazprom and Stroytransgaz, Exxon Mobile Hong Kong China Light and Power each got 15%.

[59] *China Daily*, "World Giants Get Foot in Door to Oil, Gas Reserves," 5 July 2002, http://www.chinadaily.com.cn/en/doc/2002-07/05/content_126692.htm, accessed 25 April 2023.

[60] *China Daily*, "World Giants Get Foot in Door to Oil, Gas Reserves," 5 July 2002, ibid.

profit-sharing of upstream natural gas, split of investment, and gas marketing and financing. Also, PetroChina persisted in "learn as the project proceeds" without the need of fully resolving the problems of getting adequate gas supplies and end users, which the foreign consortium deemed very unusual and a great risk.[61] Hence, even two years later, cooperation in the WEGP between PetroChina and Shell-led consortium had not been started, nor had the MOCs injected any cash into this project. Without the investment from the foreign partners and without any legal take-or-pay contract, PetroChina persisted embarking on this project on its own in 2002, placing the project at risk.[62] Foreign investors drop out of the WEGP when PetroChina sent "letters of termination" to the Shell-led foreign consortium in March 2004.

According to Zhang Guobao, Vice Minister of NDRC, the Chinese host and the overseas investors primarily differed in the tenure of the JV, and the distribution of shares in the upstream resources.[63]

For PetroChina, it "has sufficient cash and many financial resources such as banking loans and corporate bonds to fund the project."[64] At the time before the project was kicked off, PetroChina finally agreed to accept the involvement of foreign investors thanks to pressures from the government, citing their participation could reduce risks. As one senior PetroChina official said, "We had worried that there are not enough consumers in the gas market, and wanted foreign companies to share the risks."[65] Yet when the situation turned around, PetroChina became more uncompromising in the negotiation with the MOCs.

The continued oil price hikes as well as high-priced coal since 2004 not only contributed to CNPC's revenues but also made the gas through

[61] Arthur YAN, "China's Local Governments, State Energy Companies, and the Development of the West-East Gas Pipeline," presentation in the Northeast Asia Energy Cooperation Workshop Program, "Investment in China's Local Energy Infrastructure," workshop sponsored by James A. Baker III Institute for Public Policy, 11 April 2005, Houston, TX, http://www.rice.edu/energy/research/asiaenergy/docs/ArthuYan_041105.pdf, accessed 16 May 2014.

[62] *China Daily*, "Rosy Future for West-East Pipeline," 6 January 2005.

[63] Ye Xie, "PetroChina Goes Solo on Gas Line," *China Daily*, 5 August 2004, http://www.chinadaily.com.cn/english/doc/2004-08/05/content_359058.htm, accessed 25 April 2023.

[64] *China Daily*, "PetroChina Goes Solo on Gas Line Project," 5 August 2004, http://english.people.com.cn/200408/05/eng20040805_151916.html, accessed 16 May 2014.

[65] *China Daily*, 5 August 2004, ibid.

WEGP much more competitive in the downstream market.[66] The average price of natural gas through the WEGP for power generation is around RMB1.10/cm. According to the estimation by IEA, this is approximately equivalent to the cost when using coal at the current price of RMB400/ton. Under the circumstance of oil price hikes, compared with fuel oil, the comparative advantage of natural gas as the fuel for power generation was more striking.[67] So at this moment "it is not the problem of insufficient consumers, but a problem of insufficient gas."[68] Without the participation of foreign investors, PetroChina had already completed the construction of the pipeline before breaking up with the MOCs, so the foreign partners had lost their bargaining power. They had wanted to invest in the pipeline in exchange for reaping profits in the lucrative gas sector, but PetroChina was unwilling to slice up more cakes to outsiders, considering that "China's gas market is taking off and is growing by 15 percent annually."[69] Thus, it is no doubt that one senior PetroChina official said that "Foreign companies can contribute very little to this project now."[70]

Lobbied by CNPC, the Chinese government also seemed to support PetroChina's way of dealing with the CNPC this time. On one hand, the Chinese authority appears to be detached from the specific project operations and let the NOC negotiate with other partners. Hence, the government was poised to act as a middleman. On the other hand, since the WEGP has been completed, and the downstream market shows a sanguine prospect, the risks that Beijing had worried about accordingly disappeared. This also complies with the features of the natural gas market; namely, the great risks primarily lie in the preliminary stage of building the costly infrastructure and developing the downstream market.

[66] According to the *2004 Annual Report of PetroChina Company Limited*, the yearly average crude oil prices of U.S. WTI, North Sea Brent and Minas respectively rose 10.47$/b, 9.41$/b and 7.47$/b; affected by the international crude prices, accordingly the fulfilled average domestic crude oil prices in 2004 were higher than those in 2003, so were the finished oil prices within China. PetroChina, *2004 Annual Report of PetroChina Company Limited*, 2004, http://www.petrochina.com.cn/chinese/tzzgx/ftp/2004ndyj_eng.pdf, accessed 16 May 2014.

[67] Wang, Yichao, "The Sequela of the WEGP," 1 November 2004, ibid.

[68] *China Daily*, 5 August 2004, ibid.

[69] *China Daily*, 5 August 2004, ibid.

[70] *China Daily*, 5 August 2004, ibid.

Once the infrastructure is in place and consumers have accepted the natural gas, the risks have greatly been minimized. PetroChina's success in constructing such a mammoth project on its own has greatly improved its lobbying power. Moreover, barring the MOCs from dividing the final dividends also contributes to promoting the interest of CNPC. Under such circumstances, the government had no reason to let foreigners partition the alluring "cake".[71]

However, the Chinese government turned a green light to private capitals for their participation in building the third WEGP project, which was the biggest project and the first gas pipeline that was open to private capital in China.[72]

5.2 Case Two: Oil Pricing Reform

Oil prices not only have a profound impact on the national economy but involve interest redistribution among upstream producers, downstream refiners, and consumers. Price liberalization, often the first step in establishing a market economy, means that "prices had to be decontrolled and subsidies eliminated, in order to establish a demand-and-supply driven system of price determination."[73] As Friedan and Rogowski argue that global price signals can work as shadow prices in countries embracing protectionism, and influence the preferences of domestic interest groups towards liberalization.[74]

[71] Foreign investors' dropout might be because the MOCs were afraid that the fixed investment return rate could not reach 15%, the rate the MOCs required PetroChina to guarantee, but it rejected to ensure. See *China Daily*, "PetroChina Drops Foreign Partners on Pipeline," 4 August 2004, http://www.chinadaily.com.cn/english/doc/2004-08/04/content_357832.htm, accessed 25 April 2023. That foreign investors worried about their investment returns was because they were afraid that end users would be unavailable, and China lacks a natural gas professionally supervisory institution as well as a clear-cut natural gas industrial policy.

[72] Dan Bao, "Xiqidongshu sanxian gongcheng kaigong, minzi shouci jinru youqi guandao lingyu" ("WEGP-3 Was Kicked Off, Private Capitals Were First Allowed to Enter the Oil and Gas Pipeline Area"), *Renmin Ribao* (People's Daily), 17 October 2012.

[73] Jeffrey D. Sachs and David Lipton, "Poland's Economic Reform," *Foreign Affairs*, Vol. 69, 1990, p. 55.

[74] Jeffrey Friedan and Ronald Rogowski, "The Impact of the International Economy on National Policies: An Analytical Overview," in Robert Keohane and Helen Milner, (eds.), *Internationalization and Domestic Politics*, New York: Cambridge University Press, 1996.

China's oil pricing reform in the general move towards price liberation notwithstanding some turns and twists in that process. In fact, in conjunction with its economic transition from the command economy to the market economy, China has advanced the goal to put domestic oil prices in line with international ones (*gen guoji jiegui*). However, due to the incomplete conditions for market competition, price liberation in China falls into a catch-22 process for the state-owned sectors.[75] As a result, the government has to turn to price control, making the oil pricing reform "one-step forward, two steps back." According to Kennedy, conflicting views regarding price deregulation exist within the government organs and firms, domestic and foreign, state- and private-owned; the business is not merely passive price-takers, but it would proactively influence government policy.[76] Hence, it is meaningful to examine China's oil pricing system because that can help discern the government's considerations and its interactions with the NOCs in the process of reforming the pricing system and implementing its policies. This case study aims to analyze why the oil pricing mechanisms intertwine regulation with deregulation by focusing on the government's considerations as well as the NOCs' motivations. Emphasis is laid on the oil pricing systems since 1993 when China turned into a net oil importer.

I argue that political concerns and economic concerns coexist in Chinese oil pricing reform. The politically driven policies lead to market distortions, which calls for market solution. But market underdevelopment in China means that market solutions only wreak chaos. As a result, the government has to resort to administrative means. To get out of such a vicious circle, the government should put on more effort to develop the oil market.

5.2.1 Before 1998: Pre-integration Phases

Before 1998, there were three different types of oil pricing systems. In the first stage from 1949 to 1981, oil was sold at a single, state-controlled price, regardless of quality. The government played a role akin

[75] Kun-Chin Lin, "The State as Market Surrogate: Pricing Goods and Services for Oil and Petrochemical Industries in China," Conference Paper at the Annual Meeting of the Association for Asian Studies, New York, 28 March 2003.

[76] Scott Kennedy, "The Price of Competition: Pricing Policies and the Struggle to define China's Economic System," *China Quarterly*, No. 49 (January 2003), pp. 1–30.

to a rentier state, often defining oil prices according to political objectives. The second stage followed the "three-tiered price system" wherein market elements were first fetched in from 1981 to 1994. In this period, 1993 saw a large portion of state deregulations, but the state re-regulated the oil pricing policy in the third stage signaled by the two-track system which began from 1994.

1. The Three-Tiered Price System

The "three-tiered price system" denotes that oil companies could sell their surplus crude oil at market prices only after they fulfilled the centrally mandated plan of 100MT quotas. It was created in 1981 primarily to address the capital constraints that the NOCs faced for oil development and exploration. In terms of crude oil, the three different prices were "in-quota" low prices, "in-quota" high prices, and market prices.[77] The surplus crude oil could be exported through Sinochem or sold domestically at market prices.

In terms of petroleum products, since 1982, the pricing system had two levels: "in-quota" low prices and market prices for those refined oil products beyond the quota set by the state. The former prices mainly served the military, agriculture, and some large SOEs. The central government also released control over oil trade in some provinces with surplus hard currencies and in the special economic zones.[78]

From the role point of view, while the government expected that the petroleum industry could continue serving China's low-cost production and foreign exchange accumulation, it had to placate the oil companies by allowing more market room for them and ease up their capital hunger. Therefore, it had to balance the EEP role and the SPSOU role. For the NOCs, in general, they were subordinate to the government and had no much autonomy during this period. Because oil prices were under strict state control while most feedstock the oil industry relied on must be acquired through the market, many oil companies were at a loss. By 1993, the loss-making situation in the whole industry did not turn

[77] Quoted from Haijiang Henry Wang, *China's Oil Industry & Market*, New York: Elsevier, 1999, p. 56.

[78] David Pietz and Chris Ellsworth, *Fueling China: Oil and Gas Demand to 2010*, Wakefield, MA: Energy Security Analysis, Inc., January 2000, pp. 12–13.

around notwithstanding some releasing measures taken by the government. Consequently, cash starvation not only stranded oil production in the existing oilfields but also resulted in the sluggish discovery of new oilfields. Yet the government still had to be saddled to continue subsidizing this sector with RMB4–5 billion.[79]

2. Price Deregulation

To help the petroleum industry go out of the conundrum, the government decided to play the role of EEP in 1993. It removed the low-price quotas, and two-thirds of crude oil was sold at deregulated rates close to or above international levels.[80] Also, except in a few sectors such as agriculture and the military, subsidized prices of oil products were phased out and the proportion of market-priced refined oil products rose to about 65% in 1993 from less than 10% in 1983.[81] Hence, the "three-tiered" pricing system de facto changed into a "two-track" oil pricing system, in which the market played a decisive role in determining the prices of most crude oil and refined oil products.

Why did the government change its role in 1993? The role transformation virtually complied with its goal of establishing socialist market economy in China, and this oil pricing reform was regarded as a building block to that goal. As a result, 90% of agricultural products and 88% of manufactured goods were permitted to float in the market at the end of 1993, and only 12% of retail prices concerning only 5% of consumer goods were still controlled by the state.[82] "The prices of utilities (electricity, telephone, transport, etc.) remain under genuine state control, but the same can be said of many capitalist countries."[83]

More specifically, concerns over the long-term faltering operation of the petroleum industry had prompted the central government to

[79] Bi Jingquan, "Gaige shiyou jiage guanli tizhi cujin shiyou gongye fazhan" ("Reform the Oil Price Management System to Promote Development of the Petroleum Industry"), *Jiage lilun yu shijian* (*Price Theory and Practice*), 1994, Vol. 7.

[80] Philip-Andrews Speed, *Energy Policy and Regulation in the People's Republic of China*, The Hague/London/New York: Kluwer Law International, 2004, p. 69.

[81] Henry Wang, *China's Oil Industry & Market*, New York: Elsevier, 1999, p. 57.

[82] Jean-Jacques Laffont with Claudia Senik-Leygonie, 1997, p. 15, ibid.

[83] Jean-Jacques Laffont with Claudia Senik-Leygonie, 1997, p. 15, ibid.

make policy adjustments. And the marketization tide followed by Deng's Southern Tour in 1992 provided an excellent opportunity to deregulate the oil sector.[84] Moreover, it was the first large-scale experiment on oil price decontrol in the petroleum industry after China had long stuck to the highly state-controlled system. As Goldstein argued, the 1993 deregulation was a "shock treatment on oil pricing" whose policy goals were: "first, reducing the waste of energy resources; second, giving greater weight to market forces than administrative powers; and third, pumping funds into China's cash-starved oil producers."[85]

Nevertheless, such a "shock treatment" seemed unworkable in China in the sense that it was the oil price levels rather than the pricing mechanisms that had been integrated with the world. Furthermore, only part of oil prices rather than the entire oil products merged with the world prices. Consequently, the two-track system still left many loopholes for oil smuggling.

3. 1994–1998: Price Re-regulation

While the decentralization move fueled a rapid economic growth, it also caused serious economic problems. Inflation climbed up to a very perilous 26% in February 1994 from 23% in January,[86] much higher than the alert baseline of 5%.[87] The serious inflation not only affected civilians' life but

[84] After Deng's Southern Tour, a series of decentralization measures brought about a dramatic upswing for the Chinese economy. "The number of production goods regulated by the State Price Administration was reduced from 737 to 89 and price ceilings were removed for many goods" (see Richard F. Garbaccio, "Price Reform and Structural Change in the Chinese Economy: Policy Simulations Using a CGE Model," *China Economic Review*, Vol. 6, No. 1, 1994, pp. 1–34). Among them, the oil prices were also deregulated in a great measure.

[85] Carl Goldstein, "China's Oil Shock," 12 November 1992, ibid.

[86] Carl Goldstein, "No So Slick," *Far Eastern Economic Review*, 7 April 1994, Vol. 157, Iss. 14, pp. 66–7.

[87] The consumer price index (CPI) is an index to measure the average price movements of various goods and services purchased by households throughout the country. The index shows changes in the total amount of expenditure required to purchase the equivalent goods and services purchased by households in the base year, setting the consumption structure (Source: Statistics Bureau, Ministry of Internal Affairs and Communication, Japan, http://www.stat.go.jp/english/data/cpi/1585.htm#Q01, accessed 25 April 2023). According to the Chinese economist, Xu Hongyuan, CPI within 5% is normal, 5–9% indicates moderate inflation, and above 9% is serious inflation (Source: Wen Xiu, "Experts

also increased production costs. In 1993, market prices rose by month and the national retail price index went up 13.2%, while the cost of living index in 35 large and medium cities accrued 19.6%; and in 1994, prices kept surging.[88] Consequently, protests emanated from those sectors that had to undertake the steep rise in input costs.[89]

Sinopec was most severely affected. It used to enjoy the "in-quota" low-price crude oil for its refineries. When the state abolished the "in-quota" low prices in January 1993, the costs that 35–40% of crude oil Sinopec required to feed its refineries increased 134%.[90] However, Sinopec could not make up for the rising costs through marketing its refined oil products because most downstream profits went to the pockets of provincial oil companies, which bought most refined oil products from Sinopec at controlled prices but could sell them at much higher market prices. Hence, Sinopec vehemently protested the high costs it was suddenly forced to pay for its inputs.[91]

Nevertheless, the government was confronting a policy dilemma: on the one hand, China needed to curb the price spikes so as not to compromise economic growth and social stability; on the other hand, if China maintained refined oil prices lower than international ones, then the petroleum industry still could hardly recover from money-losing.[92]

Facing such a policy dilemma, Beijing prioritized its internal stabilizer role by taking a command approach to resume its reign over the price setting in 1994. Not only was the two-track pricing system abolished but it was under state control to decide the prices of both crude

Talk about China's Inflation Alert Line, Prices First Rise then Decline in the Next Half Year," *China Economy*, http://www.ce.cn/new_hgjj/hgplun/more/200409/04/t20040904_1670718.shtml, accessed 16 May 2014).

[88] Bi Jingquan, "Reform the Oil Price Management System to Promote Development of the Petroleum Industry," *Price Theory and Practice*, 1994, Vol. 7.

[89] Richard F. Garbaccio, "Price Reform and Structural Change in the Chinese Economy: Policy Simulations Using a CGE Model," *China Economic Review*, 1994, Vol. 6, No. 1, p. 1.

[90] Carl Goldstein, "Energy: Lost Privileges," *Far Eastern Economic Review*, 29 July 1993, Vol. 156, Iss. 30, pp. 50–52.

[91] Carl Goldstein, 29 July 1993, ibid.

[92] Goldstein has set out these contradictions: (1) raising subsidized energy prices vs fighting inflation; (2) injecting competition and breaking up the state energy behemoths; boosting domestic oil production to minimize import dependence vs ceding control of its oilfields to foreigners. See Carl Goldstein, "Not So Slick," 7 April 1994, ibid.

oil and refined oil products in each city and province, as well as the differences between wholesale and retail prices. Therefore, the market was abolished. After the reform, prices of the previous "in-quota" low and high crude oil were increased from RMB205/t and RMB535/t respectively to a unified price of RMB700/t, which was the first-grade crude oil. In the second grade, the previous ex-plan crude oil and the crude oil from four small oilfields with operation difficulties were sold at a uniform price of RMB1250/t.[93] Moreover, the average crude oil price captured RMB1020/t after state adjustments from May 1994 to December 1996, thus ending the history of long-term low-priced crude oil.[94] However, as shown in Table 5.2, the domestic crude price was still below the international price.

The refined oil pricing system was also changed after the reform. The ex-plant prices and retail prices of the "in-quota" and "outside-quota" refined oil in the 35 central cities were merged respectively and defined by the state. The central government only stipulated the pricing principle on the wholesale prices in the 35 cities and the wholesale and retail prices in other regions, whereas it was up to each provincial pricing authority to decide the specific retail prices. In general, the average price of domestic refined oil products was higher than the international one (see Table 5.2).

The state put stringent control over oil flows as well. The SPC carried out uniform allocation over domestic oil production as well as imports of

Table 5.2 Price comparison between Domestic and International Crude and Refined Products in 1994

Type of oil	*International*			*Domestic*
	US$/b	*US$/t*	*RMB/t*	*RMB/t*
Crude oil	18.00	129.24	1124.39	818.00
Gasoline	23.40	197.20	1715.64	2350.00
Diesel	20.20	151.50	1318.05	1900.00

Source Yan Xuzhao and Huang Wangping, "Jiakuai jianli WoGuo heli de shiyou jiage xingcheng jizhi" ("Step up to Establish Reasonable Petroleum Price Framing Mechanisms in China"), *Guoji Shiyou Jingji* (*International Petroleum Economy*), January 1995, Vol. 3, No. 1

[93] Bi Jingquan, *Price Theory and Practice*, 1994, Vol. 7, ibid.

[94] Fan Qiufang, "Plan of Further Perfecting the Shaping Mechanisms of Oil Prices," 1999, ibid.

crude and refined oil. Except for self-use, reasonable wear and tear, and state-planned exports, the crude oil produced by CNPC must be delivered to the refineries or petrochemicals of Sinopec for processing. Each oilfield was not permitted to exchange oil for electricity or other utilities nor did they need to supply crude oil to their localities. For the oil refineries, they were forbidden to process crude oil supplied by clients in various forms and directly sell refined oil to the market.[95] In addition, oil import and export businesses were assigned to certain companies, while other entities without state licenses were forbidden to conduct oil trade.

In particular, the government resorted to an internal stabilizer role by directly imposing a temporary import ban on both crude and refined oil in the early 1994. The ban was resulted from the glut of imported oil in the domestic market. Compared with 1992, the imported refined oil products in 1993 were more than doubled from 7.68 Mt to 17.41 Mt, while crude oil imports rose from 11.35 Mt to 15.64 Mt.[96] As a result, Sinopec suffered a lot as coastal regions preferred consuming the cheaper imported oil of better quality than purchasing oil from northern China. What is more, the import surge forced China to be a net oil importer and pay a bill of US$2.3 billion in 1993.[97] That was why Sinopec strongly pressurized the government to intervene in this issue.

In sum, the government assertively imposed an import ban to protect domestic petroleum industry, and increased the prices of both crude and refined oil, thus alleviating the capital-starvation problem in the petroleum industry to some extent. The state's re-regulation also straightened out the oil market and effectively beat oil speculations.

However, due to a mismatch between domestic and foreign energy markets, a price gap emerged every time when international oil prices fluctuated, which still left loopholes for illegal oil smuggling. Furthermore, price setting by the state brought about new problems. First, it reduced market actors' autonomy and strangled fledging competition among energy companies, thereby making them liable to rely on the government when they were in the red. Second, according to the new pricing mechanisms, crude and refined oil prices were different

[95] Chu Juehai and Li Hui, *Shiyou qihuo jiaoyi* (*Oil Futures Trading*), Beijing: Zhongguo jinrong chubangshe (China Financial Press), 2004, pp. 71–72.

[96] Li Shuqing, "Shiyou gongji yu shiyou jiage" ("Oil Supply and Oil Price"), *Shiyou huagong jishu jingji* (*Petrochemical Technological Economy*), Vol. 12, No. 3, 1996.

[97] Carl Goldstein, "Not So Slick," 7 April 1994, ibid.

among different provinces but the same within each province, which could not fully incorporate transport costs since each province is so large. Third, oil prices could hardly reflect supply–demand fluctuations due to changes in climates or seasons, considering that some refined oil products such as low-freezing-point diesel oil had retained the same price for a whole year.[98] Therefore, oil prices could hardly function appropriately for resource allocation.

Why did the government take such a command approach in 1994? The major reason was because the Chinese leadership was afraid that high inflation and rising prices would jeopardize social stability. In the reform and opening-up process, Beijing has always emphasized the importance of properly dealing with the relations among reform, development, and stability, and any reform should not undermine social and political stability. For the newly established Jiang Administration, stability was more than a daunting challenge deserving as a top priority. It could be said that the government had tried the marketization way in deregulating the petroleum industry in 1993, but it failed to attain the national goals, so the Chinese leadership turned back to the administrative approach, a way Beijing is familiar with.

However, after the reform, the serious inflation problem was not resolved but persisted. Inflation became so serious in the 1990s that the central government had to secure a "soft landing" solution.[99] The government expected to protect domestic market, but it adopted a radical way to remove all market oil prices, which made it suspicious about the government's sincerity to move towards market economy. Moreover, in those areas entailing government regulation, such as petroleum industrial policies, overseas development strategy, and oil market construction, state regulation was not in place. Hence, "the oil price controls appears to have only one obvious beneficiary: the state oil monopoly."[100]

[98] Research Group on *New Oil Price Mechanisms* headed by Lu Nan, "Shenhua shiyou jiage gaige silu de xuanze" ("Options for the Plan of Deepening Oil Price Reform"), *Zhongguo Wujia* (*China Price*), February 1995.

[99] Soft landing can be defined as inflation reduction without economic growth and employment collapse. Industrial Economics Institute of China Social Sciences Academy, 2000, p. 22, ibid.

[100] Haijiang Henry Wang, *China's Oil Industry & Market*, 1999, p. 60, ibid.

5.2.2 1998–Present: Price Integration

The fourth stage comes the epoch of oil pricing in line with international oil prices from 1998 to date. To that end, the Chinese government is inclined to act as an EEP, but in that process, it feels too risky to merely leave oil pricing power to the market. Hence, it has to struggle between the two roles of EEP and internal stabilizer.

The 1998 pricing reform started in June 1998 after the State Council promulgated the *Plan of Crude Oil and Refined Product Price Reform*, which stipulated that the prices of domestic crude and refined oil should progressively be in line with international oil prices.[101] Since integrating with international oil prices might expose China to oil price volatilities and foreign risks, why is China willing to expose itself to foreign risks?

This is mainly because oil pricing reform was part and parcel of the overall petroleum industry overhaul in 1998. According to Huifang Han, vice director of the Department of Price, SDPC, oil price integration is determined by oil resource endowment and the status quo of the petroleum industry in China. As China has to count on foreign oil imports, price integration could instruct domestic firms to make full use of the international market. This in turn could not only ensure oil supplies to China but also contribute to protecting domestic energy resources. Also, with its entry into the WTO, the Chinese energy market is set to be connected with the world one. Hence, only integrating with the international market could boost the development of domestic firms so that they could compete with oil multinationals.[102]

Another factor that incurred this reform arose from the domestic and foreign price gaps, which provided chances for illegal oil trafficking. Oil trafficking seriously hurt the interests of the NOCs, which exerted great pressure to dismantle the artificial price distortion and integrate domestic prices with international ones. Due to the sharp price gap (average domestic price was \$34.2/b and only \$17/b in the international market in March 1997), in the first half year of 1997, the Chinese Customs seized

[101] Details of the pricing mechanism can refer to: *Oil & Gas Journal*, "China's Oil Price Reforms a Major Step in Deregulating Its Petroleum Sector," 10 August 1998, Vol. 96, No. 32.

[102] The following paragraph is based on: *Jiage Lilun yu Shijian* (*Price: Theory & Practice*), "Jianli yu guoji shichang jiage bianhua xiang shiying de shiyou jiage jizhi" ("Establish the Oil Pricing Mechanisms Adaptive to the Price Changes in the International Market"), Vol. 7, 2000, pp. 10–12.

illegal smuggling of 62,000 metric tons of refined oil valued RMB133 million (US$16 million).[103]

The 1998 oil pricing reform had pushed the NOCs closer to the market, in tandem with some protective measures.[104] While this demonstrates the determination of the Chinese authority to proceed with its reform and open-up policy, such a move did engender some shock effect on the long-protected NOCs. They had to pay close heed to production cost reduction and volatile market changes. Nonetheless, unlike what some analysts contended,[105] such a sweeping effect was not a fatal blow against the NOCs, because they have strengthened their monopoly power in the Chinese market. As both Kennedy and Lin suggest, the NOCs are not merely price-takers; rather, they try to influence state policy-making either through intermediaries such as business associations or through direct lobbying.[106] As a result, China's retail and wholesale market was inaccessible to the multinationals until around mid-2000s, and the NOCs have de facto gained stronger power to influence oil price formulation.

The 1998 oil pricing reform displayed Beijing's endeavor to harmonize one pair of internal contradictions. While China's deeper involvement in the global market has increased international competition, it has been exposed to foreign percussions more frequently, which the government still holds misgivings for fear that foreign influence might imperil social stability. Hence, the Chinese government virtually fell into a predicament: while it had to integrate the domestic oil market with the outside, it expected that the foreign impact could be under its control. Therefore, the government "was reluctant to completely deregulate product prices out of a desire to maintain prices that are not 'too low' to protect the domestic oil industry and not 'too high' to prevent social instability and to curb inflationary pressures."[107] By the same token, the SDPC also underscored that domestic crude oil should be sold at a slightly lower price

[103] *China Business Information Network*, "China Cracks Down on Oil Smuggling," 28 July 1997.

[104] Measures include: exclude the onshore upstream from fully opening to foreign investors; allow the NOCs to aggressively preempt domestic retail stations before the market openness deadlines; and adopt the "go out" strategy.

[105] *China Business Information Network*, "China Pegs Crude Oil Prices to International Market Rates," 8 June 1998.

[106] Scott Kennedy, "The Price of Competition," 2003, ibid.

[107] Erica S. Downs, 2004, ibid., pp. 180–181.

than overseas crude oil for the purpose of encouraging Chinese refineries to purchase domestic crude oil.[108] This was perhaps a conciliatory carrot to Sinopec in order to reduce obstacles against the pricing reform considering that Sinopec had to pay a higher bill for feedstock and that most of its refineries were uneconomic in scale and uncompetitive vis-à-vis foreign counterparts.

The 1998 import ban was another typical case indicating the NOCs' lobbying power and the government's backup for the NOCs. China imposed another ban on gasoline and diesel imports in September 1998 to protect the NOCs lest they be edged out by the flood of cheaper oil from foreign countries. Before the 1997–1998 financial crises, the continuous price decline enlarged the gap between Chinese domestic and international oil prices. In the second half of 1998, domestic gasoline and diesel prices were two to three times higher than the comparable products in Singapore.[109] The lower international oil prices and oil glut in neighboring countries had stipulated large oil imports into China, both legally and illegally. As a result, large quantities of domestic refined oil products sat unsold. Accordingly, domestic crude oil producers had to cut their production. Moreover, the worldwide oil price decline also adversely affected Chinese oil exports and foreign exchange earnings. Consequently, the foreign cheaper oil threatened the viability of the NOCs. Rather than making full use of foreign cheaper oil resources to fuel the economy, Beijing opted to fence off domestic petroleum industry from international competition by imposing an import ban and making great efforts to crack down oil smuggling. Were the domestic market to be fraught with foreign oil products, it not only meant the loss of billions of dollars in revenues from the petroleum industry but also would lead to a multitude of unemployment.

The oil pricing mechanism since 1998 exposed a grave deficiency, in that Chinese oil prices were based on the average price at the Singapore market in the last month, thereby any oil product suppliers or even consumers could conjecture the price tendency in the next month; as a result, the over-transparent pricing mechanism had brought about over-speculations in the domestic petroleum market.

[108] *Oil & Gas Journal*, "China's Oil Price Reforms a Major Step in Deregulating Its Petroleum Sector," 10 August 1998, Vol. 96, No. 32.

[109] Lu Huaibin, "China's Oil Market in 1998: A Market in Transition, But to Where?" *CERA Decision Brief*, April 1999.

In order to address the over-transparency problem, the central government made two changes on the basis of the pricing mechanisms on 17 October 2001. First, domestic refined oil prices would not directly be pegged with international market rates. Rather, when the international refined oil prices fluctuated within the range of 8%, domestic oil prices would be kept intact. Only when they moved beyond the above scope would domestic prices be adjusted. Second, domestic refined oil prices would be integrated with the market prices in Singapore, Rotterdam, and New York, rather than barely Singapore prices. Accordingly, refined oil prices would be adjusted at an uncertain time rather than in each month.[110] And it was up to the NDRC to decide when and in what range to formulate domestic prices of gasoline and diesel. The crude oil pricing system remained the same, albeit it was composed of benchmark price and premium.[111] This mechanism was not so transparent as the previous one and it had assigned more power to the government to control oil prices. The new mechanism was widely regarded as favoritism towards the NOCs and thus a kind of anti-market arrangement.[112]

Meanwhile, Beijing took more measures to defend the interests of the NOCs with its accession to the WTO. In October 2001, the Chinese government stipulated that all gas stations being built in China must be controlled or fully invested by either CNPC or Sinopec, implying that private investors could invest in gas stations only in the form of joint ventures with either of the two giants. But at the same time, the government has formally released control over fuel oil prices and let it float in the market. In 2004, the state further abolished the quotas of fuel oil import and export.

In October 2006, the government stopped pegging refined oil prices with prices in the Singapore, Rotterdam, and New York markets and decided to use the average price of crude oil in Brent, Dubai, and Minas as the benchmark, plus domestic average processing costs and reasonable profits.

[110] Based on Chu Juehai and Li Hui, 2004, p. 78.

[111] The benchmark price is in line with the FOB cost plus tariff of comparable crude oil in the international market in the last month.

[112] Kun-Chin Lin, 2003, p. 14, ibid.

In May 2009, the government decided not to adjust domestic prices of gasoline and diesel unless the average prices of crude oil in the international markets fluctuated beyond a 4% range within 22 consecutive working days. When crude oil prices in the international market stayed lower than $80/b, the NDRC would decide prices of gasoline and diesel by taking account of a normal processing profit rate; when crude oil prices climbed up to more than $80/b, the NDRC would start to deduct the processing profit rate till it equaled zero; when crude oil prices went over $130/b, the NDRC would try to make as few changes as possible in raising prices of gasoline and diesel so as to ensure smooth operation of the national economy. The NDRC decided the highest retail prices for gasoline and diesel in each province (autonomous region and municipality) and central city, on the basis of crude oil prices in the international market, domestic average processing costs, taxes, reasonable distribution expenses, and appropriate profit. Crude oil prices in China would be decided in light of the average prices of crude oil in Brent, Dubai, and Cinta, each having the same weight.

Apparently, WTI, one of the most often referenced benchmarks in oil pricing, was not in the new pricing mechanism. Neither has the new reform resolved the over-transparency, time-lag, and rigidness problems of the oil pricing system. Consequently, domestic oil prices just passively follow international prices, and distributors and consumers could take advantage of the long adjustment cycle by hoarding oil products when international oil prices went up and selling them after government price adjustments.

To promote greater market transparency, the Xi-Li cabinet revised the pricing regime in March 2013. The reform shortened the retail fuel price adjustment cycle from 22 to 10 working days, cancelled a four percent floating band for oil price changes, and adjusted the varieties of crude oil used to calculate price changes for domestic oil products. The new pricing rule is a positive step towards marketization of domestic oil products considering that domestic oil prices can reflect changes in international crude oil prices in a more timely manner than before.

Since the second half of 2014, profound changes have taken place in the world oil market, with oil prices falling rapidly from $110/b to less than $40/b. Since the average production cost of domestic oil fields is about $45–55/b, low oil prices would result in heavy losses for domestic oil-producing companies, which will not only dampen their enthusiasm for exploitation but also increase the import of crude oil, thus further aggravating China's external dependence and threatening its energy security.

In order to reduce the impact of excessive fluctuations of oil prices in the international market on the domestic market and ensure China's long-term energy security, the Chinese government has taken measures to improve domestic oil pricing mechanisms and further promoted market-oriented reform. In 2016, the NDRC formulated the "*Shiyou Jiange Guanli Bangfa*" (Measures for the Administration of Oil Prices), which has been put into force since then. According to the new regulations, prices of crude oil in China will simply follow international ones. For gasoline and diesel, its maximum retail price is based on the price of crude oil on the international market, taking into account domestic average processing costs, taxes, reasonable circulation costs, and appropriate profits.[113] Gasoline and diesel prices are adjusted every 10 working days according to changes in crude oil prices in the international market. At the same time, the Chinese government decided to establish a risk reserve for oil price regulation. The unadjusted amount of refined oil prices is all included in the risk reserve, and a special account is set up for storage, which is mainly used for energy saving and emission reduction, improving the quality of oil products and ensuring the safety of the oil supply.

The new pricing mechanisms, particularly the injection of a floor price of US$40 and a cap price of US$130 in a creative way, typify the use of SMMA. On the one hand, market forces are allowed to play a decisive role in the price formation of refined oil in China. On the other hand, the market's role in price formation has its limits, that is, it should be

[113] Specifically, when the price of crude oil in the international market is US$40/b or less, the price of gasoline and diesel is calculated according to the price of US$40/b and the normal processing profit margin; When the price of crude oil is higher than US$40/b and less than US$80 (inclusive), the price of gasoline and diesel shall be calculated according to the normal processing profit margin; When it is higher than $80/b, the processing profit margin will be deducted until the price of gasoline and diesel is calculated on the basis of zero processing profit; When it is higher than US$130/b (inclusive), the price of gasoline and diesel will not or seldom be raised in principle in accordance with the principle of taking into account the interests of producers and consumers and maintaining the smooth operation of the national economy. Under such circumstances, the government will adopt appropriate fiscal and taxation policies to ensure the production and supply of refined oil. See NDRC, *Shiyou Jiange Guanli Bangfa* (Measures for the Administration of Oil Prices), 13 January 2016, https://www.ndrc.gov.cn/xxgk/zcfb/tz/201601/W020190905506573420251.pdf, accessed 2 November 2022.

within the price band. Beyond that, the Chinese government will intervene and not let the market take its own course. By so doing, Beijing expects that the new pricing system can work to kill three birds with one stone. First, it can play a positive role in stabilizing commodity price expectations, alleviating the excessive downward or upward pressure on domestic PPI, helping to ensure the security of the domestic oil supply, and promoting the stabilization of economic growth. Second, it can alleviate or even avoid the adverse consequences on the domestic petroleum industry and the overall national economy, brought about by the sudden collapse or big surge of oil prices in the international market. Third, by helping improve the competitiveness of alternative energy, it will be conducive to the development of renewable energy industry and promotes the adjustment of energy consumption structure and energy conservation and emission reduction.

5.2.3 *Changes of Market Milieu and NOC's Mixed Roles*

In practice, the NOCs can avail themselves to take advantage of domestic oil pricing mechanisms. In order to gain more initiative in affecting oil price formulation, both oil giants often work out tight oil provision plans, which is one of the principal reasons why refined oil starvation often occurs in China,[114] as any unexpected event would easily breach their tight plans. For instance, the refined oil shortage spread throughout China in November 2003, and both CNPC and Sinopec seemed proactive to allocate oil resources, but the situation was even more serious. One energy expert from CNPC frankly admitted that the oil shortage was at least partially because the two oil giants deliberately curbed oil

[114] Since September 2003, refined oil supplies in China have become very tight. Oil out-of-stock problem began from East China and soon spread to most other regions where gasoline and diesel oil wholesale business were stopped, and many petroleum stations had no oil or just provided limited supplies. For the oil starvation symptoms happened in China, refer to: *Renmin Wang* (*People's Daily Online*), "Youhuang bian 'you huang': ziyuan quekou chu xian, tizhi pingjing you zai" ("Oil Shortage Turns into 'Oil Flurry': Resource Gap Appears, but System Bottleneck Still Exists"), 22 July 2004, http://www.china.org.cn/chinese/EC-c/616541.htm, accessed 21 June 2006; *Xinxi Shibao* (*Information Times*), "Guangzhou Youzhan gaoji" ("Guangzhou Petroleum Stations in an Emergency"), 4 August 2005.

supplies.[115] Only when the NDRC raised oil prices did the nationwide oil shortage disappear. The price increase enabled the NOCs to make RMB30 billion, but the whole society had to shoulder a burden of more than RMB210 billion.[116] Similar cases occurred in March 2005, March 2006, and October 2007, when the international crude oil price kept surging, both CNPC and Sinopec lobbied NDRC to raise refined oil prices through deliberately curbing oil supplies.

Ironically, even during the oil starvation period, the NOCs still have large quantities of refined oil to export. According to the statistics of Chinese Customs, the monthly average gasoline exports in the first half of 2005 were above 0.4Mt, whereas it was only 0.2–0.3Mt in the same period of last year.[117] This is primarily driven by higher profits stemming from oil exports. One profit source is from the foreign and domestic price gap. At that time, the NDRC would not adjust refined oil prices unless the international prices fluctuate beyond 8%, whereas international prices were often higher than domestic refined oil prices. In the year 2004, domestic refined oil prices were invariably over RMB1000/ton lower than the international prices,[118] while in 2005, the price gap tended to be larger (see Table 5.3). The other profit source is from export tax rebates. The state levied only about 4% of value-added taxes on refined oil exports, but for oil sold in the domestic market, the taxes reached 17%.[119] Another underlying fact is: if all the oil resources were to be sold in the domestic market, competition would be more intense, which was likely to push down oil prices.

Hence, the NOCs do try to take advantage of the pricing system. It merits noting the fact that the NOCs' behaviors largely hinge upon two

[115] Chen Ting and Chen Jibao, "Shui lai jianguan san da shiyou guatou" ("Who Can Regulate the Three Petroleum Monopolies?"), *21 Shiji Jingji Baodao* (*21 Century Economic Report*), 30 December 2003, http://www.nanfangdaily.com.cn/southnews/zt/jjtk/xlzg/200312300114.asp, accessed 6 March 2008.

[116] Chen Ting and Chen Jibao, "Who Can Regulate the Three Petroleum Monopolies?" 30 December 2003, ibid.

[117] "NDRC Changed Thinking, Domestic Refined Oil Pricing Is Accelerating to Integrate with International Market," *Xinhua Agent*, 27 June 2005, Ibid.

[118] Data Source: *Xinhua News Agency*, "Fagaiwei silu gaibian, guonei chengpinyou dingjia jiasu yu guoji jiegui" ("NDRC Changed Thinking, Domestic Refined Oil Pricing Is Accelerating to Integrate with International Market"), 27 June 2005.

[119] Chen Ting and Chen Jibao, "Who Can Regulate the Three Petroleum Monopolies?" 30 December 2003, ibid.

Table 5.3 Retailing price comparison in June 2005 (Yuan/ton)

	Gasoline	*Diesel Oil*
Singapore FOB	5844	5822
China Domestic	4600–4700	4200–4300

Source Xinhua, "Fagaiwei silu gaibian, guonei chengpinyou dingjia jiasu yu guoji jiegui" ("NDRC changed thinking, domestic refined oil pricing is accelerating to integrate with international market"), 27 June 2005

preconditions, one of which is the existence of profit room for the NOCs to make, and the other is that no serious social unrest would be incurred. In the event that either condition has changed, the NOCs may behave very differently. Recent changes in the oil market arising from oil prices and government policies are bound to affect the NOCs' behaviors and role propensity.

The first change arises from the surging world crude oil prices. Since 2003 world oil prices keeping mounting up and hitting records (see Chart 5.1). By February 2008, Oil hit a new all-time trading high of $100.10 a barrel. As domestic refined oil prices were strictly controlled, their adjustments could hardly catch up with changes of world oil prices. Domestic oil product prices were constantly lower than the international ones. The price gap was often so enlarged due to slow response from the government to adjust domestic prices that domestic refineries have to process crude oil at a loss. As a result, the hiking oil prices and the growing price gap have exerted considerable pressure on China's refineries, particularly Sinopec.

Second, as China progresses towards meeting its WTO obligations, several changes have taken place in its oil market, which is becoming increasingly open and competitive. First, tariffs on oil have been significantly reduced or removed. Tariffs on crude oil were removed in 2000, while tariffs on oil products have been progressively lowered and will be removed by 2008. Second, quotas and licenses will be gradually eliminated. In 2002, for the first time, non-state actors obtained licenses to import 8.28 million tons (Mt) of crude oil and 4.6 Mt refined oil, and this quota is expected to increase by 15% each year. In 2004, quotas and licenses on oil imports were abolished. Finally, free entry is granted for the distribution sector. China has already opened the refined oil retail market to private investment since December 2004, and the wholesale market

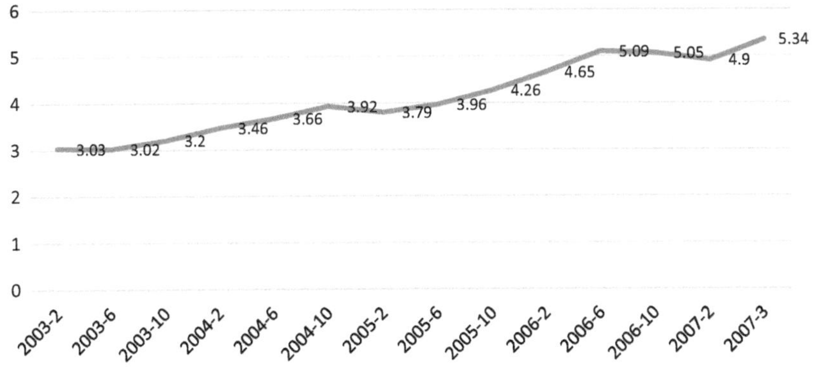

Chart 5.1 No. 93 Gasoline Prices after Government Adjustment in Beijing (RMB/litre) (*Source* Tenxun Xinwen (Tenxun News), http://news.qq.com/zt/2007/DieselSh/, accessed on 6 March 2008)

since December 2006. As a result, all the geographic, quantitative, or ownership restrictions on wholesale distribution have been removed. In order to ensure China's oil supply and prevent domestic crude oil outflow, from November 2006 the government decreased the refined oil import tax from 6 to 2% and started to levy a tariff of 5% on crude oil export.

Third, changes have also been affected by government policy changes. In December 2006, the Ministry of Commerce issued two new regulations—*Crude Oil Administration Methods* and *Refined Oil Administration Methods*. Promulgation of the two documents has turned a green light on all kinds of economic entities to gain access to the petroleum market of China. In particular, it will gradually break the two NOCs' (CNPC and Sinopec) monopolies of a concentrated wholesale business of refined oil. Due to such a monopoly, the percentage of oil product sales volume by Chinese social petro stations was less than 30% of the aggregate market volumes by the end of November 2006, notwithstanding the fact that the number of social petro stations accounted for 56.3% in China's total petro stations.[120]

[120] Hai Song, "2007 nian guoneiwai shiyou jingji redian zhanwang zhi: guonei chengpinyou shichang de kaifang, zhunru ji jianguan" (Prospects of Hot Issues Concerning Petroleum Economy at Home and Abroad in 2007: Openness, Entry and Monitoring of Domestic Refined Oil Market), *Guoji Shiyou jingji* (International Petroleum Economy), Vol. 2, 2007.

These changes have produced a mixed effect, leading the NOCs to perform different roles in different issue areas. On the one hand, they have to act as market actors as growing competition is set to fall upon. Moreover, as discussed in Chapter 3, the growing competition in the domestic market does not amount to a nightmare for the NOCs since they have taken some preparatory measures to consolidate their market status.

On the other hand, it should be admitted that the NOCs have played the SPSOU role as well. As aforementioned, the world oil prices were keeping surging, and domestic oil product prices were far below international ones despite several times price adjustments, leading to great losses for China's refineries. For instance, in September 2005, the internal gasoline price approximated RMB5505/ton, while that price within China was only RMB3946.6/ton, the gap reached RMB1558. According to an insider from Sinopec, the company would lose more than RMB800 in order to process one ton of crude.[121] According to Sinopec reports, its refinery business in the first half year of 2005 reached RMB1.3 billion, and soon rose to RMB5.1 billion in the third quarter.[122] By 2006, this loss rocketed up to RMB40–50 billion.[123] While the huge losses in the refinery prompted the NOCs to lobby the government for subsidies, they still have to continue such a business. As Wang Tianpu, vice president of Sinopec puts it, "A few years ago when international oil prices were low, some small refineries could also earn money; in recent years, however, in light of the current refined oil prices in China, there is no way to make money, so they shut down their businesses. If we also acted that way, bus driver would have no oil to pump, and all machines which consume oil would not be able to operate. Consequently, the whole country would fall into 'oil shortage crisis'."[124] In that sense, the NOCs indeed have played a role as SPSOU to ensure China's oil supplies. The NOCs have to assume that role not only because they are state-owned but also because they

[121] http://www.carcn.net/2005/9-6/200596164612.html, 6 September 2005.

[122] "Caizheng wei Zhongshihua lianyou jukui maidan" (Central Coffers Had to Foot the Bill for Sinopec's Huge Losses), 17 September 2005, www.bjt.net.cn/news/asp?newsid=132473, accessed 29 December 2005.

[123] *Beijing Daily*, "Gaoe lirun cong he er lai? Shiyou san jutou shoudu huiying gongzong zhiyi" ("Where Did the Huge Profits Come From? The Three Oil Giants Responded to the Public Skepticism"), 6 January 2007.

[124] *Beijing Daily*, 6 January 2007.

are aware the government can just increase oil prices suddenly, due to its concerns about social affordability and economic costs on many firms, particularly against a backdrop of surging inflation and the incoming Olympics, the greatest event which the government calls for the NOCs' support.

5.3 Conclusion

The above two cases suggest that the state has both political concerns and economic concerns regarding oil pricing and the gigantic WEGP, and under different settings, the government inclines to different roles. For the NOCs, they act as market actors or SPSOU largely hinging upon the impact of oil and gas prices on their commercial interests. And their interaction fundamentally determines the approach the state would take to cope with that issue.

In the case of Chinese oil pricing reform, on the one hand, the state has taken measures to move towards integrating domestic oil prices with international ones. On the other hand, the state has tried hard to keep oil prices under control, for fear that the unbridled oil prices would jeopardize economic growth and social stability.

Before 1993 when China enjoyed a self-sufficient status, the growth of the oil sector was always put in a secondary place. The government set oil prices for the sake of stability, although it also allowed bargaining to solicit compliance and political support. Consequently, China's oil prices were often arbitrarily let down to the international levels, which invariably led to tremendous capital constraints that stymied the sustained growth of the oil industry. When its growth ran into great difficulty due to market distortion arising from central policies, the state had to take releasing measures to ease up the pressure, but those measures never solved the market distortion problem. Although market prices were allowed under the "three-tiered price system," state control of oil prices was the dominant form. The NOCs fundamentally acted as SPOUS, just following the mandates of the state. Hence, the approach to oil pricing is an SCA.

In 1993, the state acted as EEP in order to salvage the cash-starved oil industry, and the NOCs were eager to act as market actors so as to pump funds for their development. Hence, the state released control over the oil sector in a great measure, and the market played a decisive role in determining oil prices with some portion of state-priced oil. As a result, the approach to oil pricing is an MDA.

In the year 1994–1998, Beijing anxiously worked as an internal stabilizer because of the serious inflation. The upstream producers (CNPC and CNOOC) were excited about high crude prices, which conversely exerted great pressure over the refineries (Sinopec). Seemingly they had divergent interests in this regard, but because Sinopec was the major client consuming most of their crude, the loss of Sinopec also affected their interest. Moreover, the glut of imported oil into the Chinese market impacted all the NOCs, so they inclined to the SPSOU role, expecting the state could help them weather through the crisis and coordinating government's effort to clamp down on oil smuggling. Thus, the state resumed holding its reigns over oil pricing, put stringent over oil flows, and even imposed import ban in 1994. The approach is a SCA.

Since 1998, the Chinese government tries to synergize a couple of goals: oil prices integrating with the world and oil price risks under its control. To that end, it has to pay attention to both economic efficiency promotion and internal stabilizing. The Jiang-Zhu administration was devoted to promoting economic efficiency. In conjunction with its overall economic reform (SOE, price, tax reforms), its growing dependence on foreign oil imports and the government's strategy to integrate the Chinese economy with the world entail Chinese oil prices being in line with international ones; at the same time, the government needed to prevent the risks emanating from oil price release to its economic growth. In the Hu-Wen administration, as discussed in Chapter 2, while acting as EEP, the state concerns much about the aggravating developing gap among regions and social groups. The NOCs' monopoly is regarded as one contributory factor resulting in a growing gap. It is apparently a grave challenge for the government to well handle the relationship between the monopolies of the NOCs and the state's goal to forge some Chinese multinational corporations.

After being restructured in 1998, the NOCs became more profit-centered with marketization underway. Though their interests are more divergent because of distinct major businesses, the NOCs' role propensity seems to correlate with oil and gas prices. When oil and gas prices are high, they are more inclined to acting as market actors, expecting the state could let them enjoy more autonomy. When oil prices are low, the NOCs tend to act as SPSOU, hoping the government compensate for their financial losses. For instance, in the last few years when world oil prices have long stayed in high levels, all the NOCs advocate the state to fully integrate domestic oil prices with the global ones. Because domestic refined oil prices are arbitrarily set below international ones, Sinopec's oil refining business suffered RMB7.88 billion losses in the first quarter in 2006. So it strongly appealed to the state to decontrol refined oil prices. Under its pressure, the Chinese government provided RMB10 billion subsidies to Sinopec to compensate for its losses in 2005, and another 5 billion in 2006. Their profit-centered tendency inevitably induces collision with their role as SPSOU. When such a conflict did come about, the NOCs strove hard to shun away from their social obligations, as evidenced in the oil shortage crisis in the previous years.

Hence, the interactions between the state and the NOCs create the specific policies: on the one hand, crude oil prices have been pegged with international ones, but it is still up to the NDRC to decide when and how to adjust refined oil prices, and refined oil prices are kept lower than international ones so as not to affect its economic competitiveness and social stability. On the other hand, the state vigorously backs the NOCs to preempt domestic distribution market before its openness to the world, and even imposed another import ban to protect domestic NOCs in 1998. Thus, China is taking a mixed approach to deal with oil pricing-related problems.

In terms of the WEGP, the state prioritized political concerns over economic concerns in deciding to build the pipeline, but in the process of implementing its decision, its economic concerns overtook political concerns. Acting as a market actor pursuing monopoly, CNPC in the whole process was very active to materialize the project, but it had little enthusiasm to let foreign investors participate. In the negotiation process, CNPC persisted in constructing the pipeline on its own before getting adequate gas supplies and signing enough "take-or-pay" contracts with end users. Hence, a state–market condominium was used in both the decision-making stage and the implementation phase. Finally, after seeing the project would take shape soon, the government followed CNPC's will to terminate negotiations with foreign investors. A MDA approach was adopted.

It is true that Beijing most of the time prioritizes political concerns over economic concerns, but it is not always so as what Downs argued. Take the WEGP as an example, the state prioritized economic concerns in building the pipeline because it was afraid of the incapability of the NOCs to undertake such a giant project and the corresponding risks. Therefore, despite the opposition of CNPC, the state insisted upon infusing foreign investments to enhance the success coefficient of the pipeline.

Meanwhile, it may have different implications in different cases when it comes to the view that political concerns override economic concerns. In the case of the oil pricing reform, this implies that out of consideration of the overall economic growth and social stability, the state deems it necessary to have certain control over oil prices to some extent, rather than directly subject domestic oil prices to the international market prices. Whereas in the case of the WEGP, the implication is that the state persisted to construct the project irrespective of the questionable economic viability. All in all, maintaining social stability and economic growth seem to become the priority of the Chinese government. It may be because both are directly linked with the legitimacy problem of the ruling party.

Both cases also show that the NOCs' considerations do not necessarily coincide with the states. In case the NOCs are required to choose between their own economic interests and social obligation, they might prioritize their own interests after becoming independent production entities. As Kennedy puts it, "[Large SOEs] have utilized their relative access to government to influence various policies of concern to them, the most important involving pricing and international competition."

CHAPTER 6

SMMA and China's Foreign Quest for Oil and Gas

In order to meet its surging appetite for oil and gas, China has to rely on foreign energy imports thanks to inadequate indigenous resources. Its growing dependence on foreign energy resources is a prime factor that has prompted Chinese NOCs to make forays into foreign countries. Currently, their presence can be found in every continent. In 2013 alone, the central energy SOEs spent US$11.66 billion on overseas Mergers and Acquisitions, which accounted for more than 1/5 of all the M&A by Chinese enterprises.[1] What are China's motivations behind its foreign energy quest? Why does China avoid fully relying on trade, and what role the NOCs has played?

Most studies take a static view to examine China's oil diplomacy, regarding the NOCs merely acting as an extension of state policy. Following that logic, it is liable to conclude that behind every behavior

[1] Yunfei Ma, "Zhongguo nengyuan qiye haiwai touzi 'tu' shenme" (What Do the Energy Companies Want to Gain' from Foreign Investments?) *Zhongguo Jingji Daobao* (China Economic Herald), 22 July 2014.

This chapter is largely based on Shaofeng Chen, "Motivations behind China's Foreign Oil Quest: A Perspective from the Chinese Government and the Oil Companies," Journal of Chinese Political Science, Vol. 13, No. 1, Spring 2008, pp. 79–103, with amendments and updates.

S. Chen, *China's Approach to Energy Security*,
https://doi.org/10.1007/978-981-99-3573-4_6

of the Chinese energy firms, particularly the NOCs, stands the Chinese government. However, it is a misperception to equalize China's foreign oil quest to oil diplomacy. Although oil diplomacy is an important part of China's foreign oil quest, the latter also includes commercial deals made by Chinese companies.

This chapter intends to elaborate on how China has resorted to an SMMA to conduct its foreign energy pursuit by analyzing the role that the Chinese government and the NOCs have played and their motivations in that process.

6.1 Overall Picture of China's Foreign Quest for Oil and Gas

The use of an SMMA has first and foremost been reflected in China's oil diplomacy, which can be defined as foreign activities led by the central government aiming to secure foreign oil and gas resources or promote interstate oil and gas business cooperation. Oil diplomacy often takes the form of intergovernmental deals with the assurance of the government's credibility. Different from it, commercial deals on oil and gas, strictly in economic terms, are profit-centered, firm-to-firm deals based on cost-benefit comparison. State-direct involvement is rare. As such, apart from commercial interests, oil diplomacy often goes hand in hand with other non-economic purposes such as ensuring energy supply security, protecting against US containment, boosting interstate relations, and so on.[2] Therefore, promoting commercial deals on oil and gas can be one of the objectives of oil diplomacy.

Chinese oil diplomacy initially came about after China has become a net oil importer since 1993, but inadequate attention had been paid to the oil security issue at that time.[3] It was not until 1996 that the central government unveiled a plan to attain around one-third of its energy demands through overseas exploitations and acquisitions.[4] Chinese oil diplomacy first aroused foreign attention when CNPC outbid Amoco,

[2] Philip C. Saunders, *China's Global Activism: Strategy, Drivers, and Tools*, Institute for National Strategic Studies, National Defense University, 4 October 2006.

[3] This is because on the one hand, the percentage of oil imports was trivial, and on the other hand, the oil prices had stayed in low levels for quite a long time.

[4] *Petroleum Intelligence Weekly*, "China's CNPC Leaps on to Global Oil Production Stage," 9 June 1997, p. 3.

Texaco, and Unocal in Kazakhstan in 1997. Some commentaries regarded China's involvement in the new great game in Central Asia as a "Chinese threat" at that time.[5] Since the turn of the new century, the leadership has taken more initiatives to help state firms expand businesses abroad when they envisage an irrevocable supply–demand gap in China.

The central goal of China's oil diplomacy is to secure sufficient oil and gas and diversify its supply sources although there are other motivations, which will be discussed in the following section. On the one hand, acquiring hydrocarbon resources to prop up the economy is a high priority in China's foreign policy. The major form China prefers is to gain direct control over foreign hydrocarbon resources or lock up long-term supplies through contracts or pipelines. In an interview, former Chinese Foreign Minister Li Zhaoxin said, "Our diplomatic work should provide vigorous support to those efforts seeking international energy cooperation."[6] On the other hand, China also endeavors to diversify oil import sources. It has made every effort to acquire hydrocarbon resources in a spate of countries. With around 50% in Chinese crude oil imports, the Middle East has become the primary source. In view of the long-term instability in that region, China feels it is a great risk to its oil security and thus endeavors to reduce its over-reliance on the Persian Gulf. Hence, its oil diplomacy targets countries all over the world, including those shunned by Western multinational oil corporations (MOCs). Under the diversification strategy, Africa, Central Asia, and Russia have eventually gained more weight in China's oil diplomacy equation. Particularly, Russia-Central Asia, Middle East-North Africa, and South America have been selected as three strategic zones for oil exploration and production (E&P). A special focus has been placed on Russia, Kazakhstan, Turkmenistan, Iran, Iraq, Sudan, Venezuela and Indonesia.[7]

[5] For example, *Dow Jones News*, "Resourceful Competitors," *The Wall Street Journal*, 28 July 1997.

[6] *21 shiji jingji baodao (21 Century Economic Report)*, "Dapo E, Mei, Ri, Yin de baoweiquan, Zhongguo nengyuan de wuhuan waijiao" (Breaking Through the Besiege of Russia, US, Japan and India, the Five-circle Diplomacy of China Energy), 2 April 2004.

[7] Development Research Center of the State Council of P. R. China, "Zhongguo shihua hangye jidu fenxi baogao" (Quarterly Analysis report on Chinese Petrochemical Industry), 3 March 2003, http://www.drcnet.com.cn.

How does China conduct oil diplomacy? First of all, strong government involvement is integral to oil diplomacy. The Chinese leaders sometimes vigorously support some projects in person, especially the mega or competitive ones calling for state-to-state transactions, or those conducive to boosting interstate relations. In 2002, former president Jiang Zemin's visit to Libya paved the way for signing a cooperative agreement between CNPC and Libya National Oil Company. Gaining oil and gas resources for China had become one of the priorities of former President Hu Jintao's foreign tours. In January 2004, China signed oil cooperation agreements with Egypt, Gabon, and Algeria respectively during Hu's visits to the above countries. His subsequent visit to South America also saw China's substantial investments in the energy sector, with Argentina alone attracting 20 billion dollars from China.[8] Seeking energy deals with foreign countries has also been a top priority of President Xi Jinping in his state visits to Mongolia, Venezuela, Brazil, South Africa, Kyrgyzstan, Turkmenistan, and so on. The Sino-Russia 30-year gas deal worth US$400 billion that attracted worldwide attention was clinched during Putin's state visit to China in May 2014 since President Xi Jinping took office.

Second, in order to secure oil and gas resources, China's oil diplomacy has de facto been incorporated into its overall strategy with energy-rich regions and countries. In the 2006 China-Africa Cooperation Forum, China called off more than USD10 billion debts of African countries. Before that, it canceled its RMB10.9 billion debts since 2000 and undertook over 900 projects in Africa.[9] The strategic relationship and free trade agreement (FTA) also work to that end. Thus far, China has signed 16 FTAs with more than 20 countries and regions, such as ASEAN, Australia, and New Zealand. Negotiation with the Gulf Cooperation Council to build a FTA was launched in 2005, but thus far it has not

[8] *Beijing Morning Post,* 15 December 2004 (in Chinese).

[9] Kunzhe Liu, "Zhongguo waijiaobuzhang zhuli tan jiu da ZhongFei guanxi wenti" (China's Foreign Minister Assistant Talked About Nine Issues Regarding China-Africa Relations), *China Youth Daily*, 30 October 2006. http://world.people.com.cn/GB/14549/4971637.html, accessed 20 December 2010.

been concluded.[10] These actions have facilitated Chinese energy cooperation with them by creating a favorable atmosphere for its NOCs' entry or energy deals directly.

China has employed a variety of means for its oil diplomacy, such as cultivating special relations with energy-rich countries, foreign aid, project assistance, FTA, and so forth. For instance, China has established strategic partnerships with Saudi Arabia, Argentina, Indonesia, Kazakhstan, and Venezuela. It helped construct railways in Nigeria, metro system in Iran, port facilities in Gabon, etc. Its permanent membership of UN Security Council is another card that it can capitalize on for its oil interest. One case often cited was the Chinese rejection of a UN proposal to sanction Sudan when a humanitarian crisis happened in the Darfur region.

Third, in practice, the central government endorses the NOCs' venturing abroad. CNPC, Sinopec, and CNOOC are taking the lead to venture abroad. Their presence can be found almost everywhere across the globe. In recent years, the NOCs have consecutively gained oil exploration or exploitation rights in countries like Venezuela, Nigeria, Iran, Angola, Sudan, Iraq, Kazakhstan, Indonesia, Australia, Libya, and so on. CNPC is a heavyweight in "going abroad." With oil and gas projects in more than thirty countries and regions, the equity oil that CNPC received from overseas increased from 47.21 Mt to 76.33 Mt during 2013–2021, while equity gas was doubled from 15.05 Bcm to 31.5 Bcm in 2021.[11]

In terms of Sinopec, its overseas equity oil production grew from 18.4 Mt in 2010 to 28.29 Mt in 2021, while its equity gas production hit 9.96 Bcm in 2021.[12] Besides upstream business, this company was also very active in conducting petroleum services and refining and chemical engineering projects. In 2010 Sinopec had 11 refining and chemical engineering projects in Saudi Arabia, Kazakhstan, etc. with contract value totaled USD5.5 billion, and executed 448 service contracts in 35 countries valued USD9.48 billion.[13]

[10] Official website of the Ministry of Commerce of China, http://fta.mofcom.gov.cn/gcc/gcc_special.shtml, accessed 31 October 2022.

[11] The above data are quoted from: *CNPC Group Co. 2013 Annual Report* and *CNPC Group Co. 2021 Annual Report* respectively.

[12] The above data are quoted from: *Sinopec Group Co. 2010 Annual Report* and *Sinopec Group Co. 2021 Annual Report,* http://www.sinopecgroup.com/group/Resource/Pdf/GroupAnnualReport2021.pdf, accessed 20 December 2010.

[13] Based on the website of Sinopec, www.sinopec.com.cn, accessed 23 January 2015.

In the case of CNOOC, the setback in a bid for Unocal vis-à-vis Chevron in 2005 has not stalled the company's efforts to go international. Instead it has worked hard to raise its international profile, extending its global presence in Asia, Africa, Oceania, North America, South America, and Europe, and covering conventional oil and gas and unconventional shale oil and gas, oil sands, and coal bed methane. In February 2013, it completed its US$15.1 billion acquisition of Canada's Nexen, which enables CNOOC to get access to offshore production in the North Sea, the Gulf of Mexico, and off Western Africa, as well as producing properties in the Middle East and Canada.[14] In December 2013 the consortium composed of Shell, Petrobras, Total, CNPC, and CNOOC won a 35-year production-sharing contract to develop the Libra oilfield in offshore Brazil. CNOOC reports that overseas resources accounted for 44.8%, 36.2%, and 30.5% of its total reserves, production, and oil and gas sales, respectively.[15]

Fourth, energy itself is also a tool with which China employs to achieve its other objectives. "China's energy market has been used as a carrot to influence countries to adopt policies which are favorable to China's perceived national interests."[16] One case is the transaction with Saudi Arabia. China made a deal with the Saudis by allowing it to co-fund a refinery in China to barter for Chinese entry into Saudi upstream market. Such a calculation to use energy as a tool to promote inter-state relations is striking in China's relationship with Iran, Libya, and so on. This kind of market-exchange-for-resource has been a new strategy favored by the Chinese government as it takes no transport risks.

Fifth, it should be pointed out that China's foreign oil quest basically follows market rules, but on some occasions, political consideration outweighs commercial viability. When making a deal of oil purchase or oil asset procurement, private firms usually prioritize commercial interests over other considerations. In the case of the Chinese NOCs, they also attempt to synergize all potential benefits and reduce possible risks.

[14] Euan Rocha, "CNOOC Closes $15.1 Billion Acquisition of Canada's Nexen," *Reuters*, 25 Feruary 2013.

[15] Website of CNOOC, http://www.cnooc.com.cn/col/col8041/index.html, accessed 23 January 2015.

[16] Philip Andrews-Speed, Xuanli Liao and Roland Dannreuther, *The Strategic Implications of China's Energy Policy*, New York: Oxford University Press, 2002, p. 80.

Nonetheless, when they envisage a project that may generate high political benefits but has no commercial feasibility, the NOCs bolstered by the central government may continue the deal irrespective of the economic costs.[17]

6.2 Motivations of China's Foreign Quest for Oil and Gas

In practice, three options are available for a country to obtain foreign oil and gas, albeit, by trade, by force, and by directly producing oil and gas overseas and shipping it back home. Why does China deem it necessary to conduct oil diplomacy? Why not directly rely on trade or resort to forces? And why does China prefer a way of direct control mainly in the form of "equity oil" or locking up long-term supplies?[18]

Using forces, which used to be the way employed by colonialists to secure foreign resources, is out of question for today's China. China has to seek other options: trade and/or oil diplomacy. This has elicited the following question. *Why does China deem it necessary to conduct oil diplomacy, rather than rely on international trade*? China's oil diplomacy has mainly been motivated by both the government and the NOCs. They have identical interests in foreign quests for oil and gas, but their motivations and interest priorities are different.

6.2.1 Government Motivations

The Chinese government's support for oil diplomacy is in line with its domestic and foreign strategic concerns with respect to energy security,

[17] According to the Chinese law, any Chinese state firms' foreign investment must get the approval from various organs depending on the investing amount and the categories. From 1 July 2006, the State Administration of Foreign Exchange of China has phased out the restriction that domestic firms could apply for a maximal 5 billion USD per year for overseas investment, and only those investments exceeding 10 million dollars require the examination and approval of this institution. See James T. Areddy, "China Turns on Green Light for Domestic Firms' Large-Scale Overseas Investment," *Washington Street Journal*, 9 June 2006; *Zaobao*, "China Will Remove the Restriction of Foreign Exchange for Chinese Firms' Foreign Investment", 18 February 2006, available at: http://www.zaobao.com/stock/pages14/china060218a.html, accessed 21 August 2006.

[18] Locking up long-term supplies can be fulfilled by signing long-term supply contract, or by building pipelines.

economic development, social stability, and foreign strategy. To some extent, it is also a result of learning effect.

China's oil diplomacy has largely been led by the government's perceptions of energy security and its reliance on the global energy market.[19] As discussed before, in the eyes of Beijing, the international oil market could be manipulated by the West or OPEC, speculated by hedge funds, and agitated by price volatility. Either risk from the lack of oil and gas, oil price fluctuation, and oil supply disruption would deal a heavy blow to the Chinese economy. Hence, China deems it necessary to secure more foreign energy resources and diversify its import sources.

Some Chinese officials pointed out that in the present international oil market, it is not true that as long as one has money, (s)he can purchase oil of any volume at any time. On the contrary, even if one is willing to pay high, (s)he may not get oil from the market, and this saying "is popular in the countries that already control the supplies."[20] Its essential concern lies in American dominance in both hydrocarbon-rich regions and major sea lanes in the world. China is reluctant to envisage such a scenario where its energy development has to depend on the established MOCs because in the leadership's deep mind, they tend to regard reliance on the MOCs would undercut their "deep-rooted instinct for self-reliance, nurtured during decades of isolation."[21] Hence, Beijing worries that it could not obtain sufficient oil and its sea lane supply chains might be interrupted in times of emergency.

The second strand to understand Beijing's support for oil diplomacy relates to its development strategy. It is apparent that China aspires to become a strong power in the world. For that end, the central government deems it imperative to foster the competitiveness of some large SOEs with strategic importance. Large and competitive firms are one important benchmark that gauges a nation's level of technology, industry

[19] Wang rightly points out, "the oil industry and market are primarily sensitive to government oil policy, which emanates largely from a greater macroeconomic policy, which, in turn, depends on the character and intentions of those holding power." Haijiang Henry Wang, *China's Oil Industry & Market*, Amsterdam, New York, Oxford, Singapore etc.: Elsevier, 1999, p. 22.

[20] He Jun, an energy consultant in Beijing, see Joseph Kahn, "China's Costly Quest for Energy Control," *New York Times*, 27 June 2005.

[21] David B. Ottaway and Dan Morgan, "China Pursues Ambitious Role in Oil Market," *Washington Post*, 26 December 1997.

strength, and international competitiveness, and determine a nation's capacity for sustained development.[22] And petroleum is regarded as a pillar industry that should be in the hands of the state. Their importance is particularly reflected by their tax payments.[23] Therefore, under the aegis of the government, the NOCs have enjoyed a monopolizing status in the Chinese energy market, and this status has further been consolidated in the 1998 restructuring.

Yet, the uncompetitiveness of the Chinese NOCs versus the MOCs has intensified the government's concerns. As shown in Table 7.1, Western oil giants dominate the global petroleum industry and are much stronger than the Chinese NOCs. Because of the MOC's dominance in the international market, the oil or gas fields that the Chinese NOCs can acquire abroad are generally of small acreage which has been mined for years or call for high costs of exploitation. Even so, China is confronting other countries' fierce competition. Hence, Beijing deems it necessary to provide the NOCs with state support to acquire oil and gas abroad.

The weakness of the NOCs has further aggravated the government's concerns about the social consequences. The growing unemployment has vexed Beijing for a long. With millions of workers being laid off due to the industrial restructuring of the SOEs, this problem has become more pronounced.[24] If measured by reference to the MOCs, the NOCs still have redundant staffs although quite a large number of staffs were slashed in previous reforms. For instance, in the year 2003, BP created US$10.44 billion in net profits with 107,000 staffs, whereas Sinopec, staffed with 855,000, only generated US$1.05 billion net profits.[25] With

[22] Wengang Liu, *Jingji Quanqiuhua yu Zhongguo Qiye "Zouchuqu" Zhanlue* (Economic Globalization and the "Go out" Strategy of Chinese Firms), Beijing: Press of Economic Science, 2003, p. 42.

[23] The NOCs often contribute around 25% of the tax revenues, which outshines many other SOEs. Ding, J.M. "Decipher the Ranking of Top 100 Tax Payer in 2004 (China)", Xinhua News Agency, 11th September 2005. www.xinhuanet.cim/fortune/200509/11/content_342845.htm, accessed 20 December 2010.

[24] Barry Naughton, "China's transition in economic perspective", in Merle Goldman and Roderick MacFarquhar, *The Paradox of China's Post-Mao Reforms*, Cambridge, MA: Harvard University Press, 1999, pp. 30–44.

[25] BP's net profit can be found in BP, *BP Annual Report and Accounts 2003*, while its staff number is found in the Web site of British and Colombian Chamber of Commerce: http://www.britishandcolombianchamber.com/membersdirec.htm#ene; Sinopec figures are available at http://www.sinopecgroup.com.cn/. Exchange rate: 1 USD = 8.27 RMB.

China's fulfillment of the WTO commitments, competition is set to be more intense. However, given the already massive underemployment, the government can hardly push its reform simply by cutting the number of staffs again. Developing business in foreign markets is evidently conducive to resolving the overstaff problem (Table 6.1).

A fourth line of thinking of oil diplomacy pertains to China's overall foreign strategy and its perception of other countries' ways of dealing with energy security. With its growing reliance on foreign oil and gas, Beijing soon picked up the internationally common practice of diversifying import sources. Securing energy resources from its neighbors like Russia, Central Asia, and Southeast Asia not only serves to quench its oil and gas hunger and deepen its economic interdependence with those countries but also provides a leeway for China to protect against a potential US containment. China's oil diplomacy in the Middle East, Latin America, and Africa, though primarily driven by energy needs, intends to serve other strategic goals, such as promoting its "one China" policy. Beijing has sped up efforts to squeeze Taiwan's international space. For the Chinese leadership, business is not merely business, which can hardly divorce from politics. Thus, it spares no effort to strive for more states to support its one-China policy, as well as the desired oil and gas from them.

Table 6.1 China's oil companies in comparison vs. western oil companies

Fortune 500 global rank	*Company name*	*Country*	*Revenue (US$ billion)*	*Profit (US$ billion)*
2	British Petroleum	UK	285.06	15.37
3	ExxonMobil	US	270.77	25.33
4	Royal Dutch/ Shell Group	Netherlands/ UK	265.19	18.54
10	Total	France	152.64	11.95
11	Chevron Texaco	US	147	13.3
12	ConocoPhillips	US	118.72	8.13
30	ENI	Italy	79.31	9.89
31	Sinopec	China	75	1.26
46	CNPC	China	67.7	8.76
117	SK	South Korea	37.7	1.47
125	Petrobras	Brazil	37	6.11
133	Petronas	Malaysia	36.1	9.36

Source CNN, "Fortune Global 500," 2005, http://money.cnn.com/magazines/fortune/global500/2005/index.html, accessed 26 April 2023.

The Chinese way of conducting oil diplomacy is also a result of learning effect. The US is often referred to as a model in this regard. As Venn points out, "(h)ow governments perceived each other's actions, objectives and priorities, and what they envisaged to be in their national interest, played a significant part in the evolution of their petroleum policies."[26] In Beijing's view, each successive US administration, for the sake of energy security, has constantly taken a firm grip over the principal energy producing regions so as to maintain its unipolar status in the world.[27] China believes that the US has gained the commanding heights in the international oil and gas market through the two wars against Iraq and Libya. While seeing it as a typical example that government should play an indispensable role in guaranteeing stable oil and gas supplies, Beijing also worries that the US "would use its influence in oil-rich countries to limit China's ability to gain access to oil from these areas."[28] Out of such a concern, it was said that the Iraq War has induced Beijing to change its oil strategy from over-reliance on the Middle East to diversifying oil sources in the world.[29] Moreover, the failure to acquire the Kashagan oil field and Unocal "convince Chinese that the US is blocking China's access to oil."[30] Citing that many countries are conducting oil diplomacy, like Japan, India, and even the US, China tends to believe that it is not business that only China is doing. "The U.S. can resort to forces to capture oil, why China has to deprive its own rights to do fair oil business with other countries."[31]

Then why *does the Chinese government prefer a way of direct control of foreign oil resources mainly in the form of "equity oil" to international*

[26] Fiona Venn, *Oil Diplomacy in the Twentieth Century*, Basingstoke: Macmillan, 1986. p. 12.

[27] Zhongming Gong and Jiayu Cheng, "Cong shijie nengyuan fazhan qushi tansuo weilai Zhongguo nengyuan zhanlue" ("To Probe Into China's Future Energy Strategy in Light of World Energy Developing Trends"), *Keji bu Diao yan baogao* (*Research Report by Ministry of Science and Technology*), Vol. 38, 8 June 2004.

[28] Erica S. Downs, "The Chinese Energy Security Debate," *The China Quarterly*, Vol. 177, March 2004, pp. 21–41.

[29] *Washington Post*, 14 July 2005.

[30] Kashagan Field is an oil field located in Kazakhstan. Bo Kong, "An Anatomy of China's Energy Insecurity and Strategies," 2005, ibid.

[31] Interview with an energy expert at ERI, NDRC, who required anonymity as a precondition to accept interview. Beijing, 2 March 2005.

trade? For the Chinese government, "oil diplomacy" in the form of producing more oil abroad has both the merits of cost efficiency and risk reduction. In fact, purchasing oil through trade has brought hefty economic burdens. As shown in Charts 6.1 and 6.2, the expenses that China has to pay for the net oil imports have ascended for about 174 times from 1995 to 2021 (without considering inflation). The proportion of this expenditure to China's total trade surplus exceeded 35 percent in 2021, and in 2011 this ratio even hit 133.4 percent. In particular, the expenditure of crude oil imports has constantly stayed at very high levels. Therefore, with oil price spikes, China has to pay an exorbitant bill for oil notwithstanding some returns from oil product exports. The more crude oil from overseas production, the more financial burdens can be hacked down.

On the other hand, the Chinese government contends that producing oil overseas could help reduce risks. Apart from being averting from volatile prices, direct control of overseas oil is safer than that obtained from the international market. According to Zhou Dadi, former director of ERI affiliated with NDRC, the more oil in the hands of the Chinese NOCs in the international energy market, the greater capacity they can

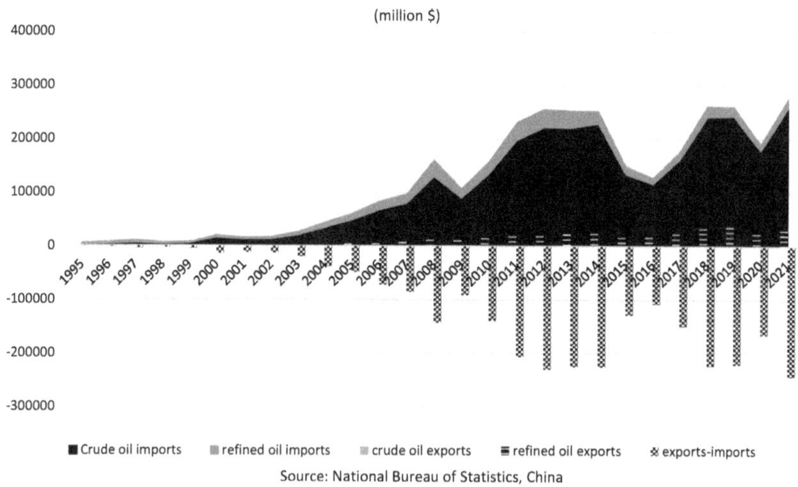

Chart 6.1 China's oil trade by value

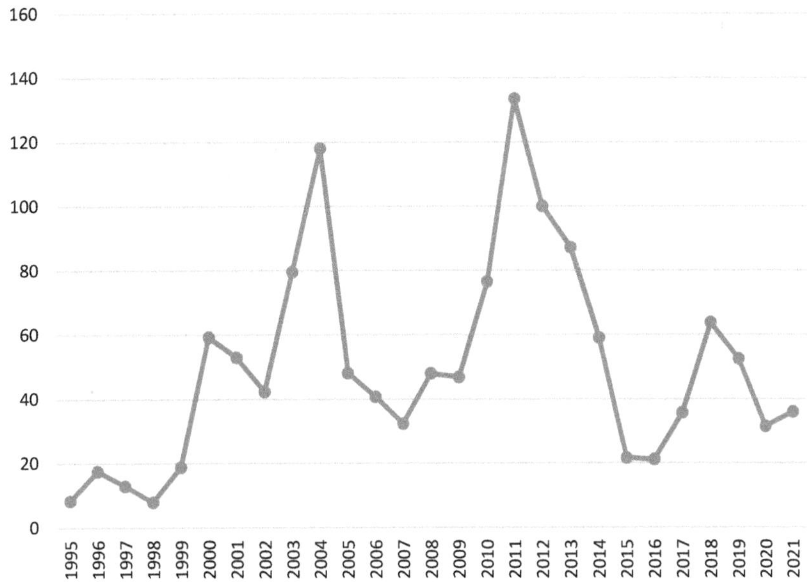

Note: Net cost of oil imports = imports of crude oil and refined oil - exports of crude oil and refined oil; Total trade surplus = total exports of commodities - total imports of commodities

Source: Drawn and calculated by the author based on data from Na

Chart 6.2 China's ratio between net cost of oil import and its total trade surplus

sustain oil price hikes.[32] Chen Zhengdong, a member of the Economic Committee of the Chinese People's Political Consultative Conference (CPPCC) spelled out it more directly, "We should advocate the collaborative form of 'equity oil' ... In fact, as many experts pointed out, as long as we have sufficient overseas oil throughput, our economy can be buffeted and even offset from the percussions resulted from high oil prices. Therefore, it would be better to go abroad to exploit oil than to purchase

[32] Dadi Zhou and Xingshan Zhu, "Zhongguo shiyou gongying yu anquan zhanlue" (China's Petroleum Resources Supply and Security Strategy), *International Petroleum Economics*, No. 12, 12 December 2002.

oil."[33] Another possible reason is that reliance on others is liable to be held at bay. Once China has to depend on others for oil and gas, it has been exposed to external risks brought about by the rivalries' interruption, regional turmoil, terrorist attack, and so forth. For instance, the Sino-Soviet split in 1960 not only led to oil shortages in China but also dealt a heavy blow for the development of its petroleum industry.

Pertaining to the above, the strong influence of the Western governments on the international energy markets and the dominance of the Western MOCs, along with the limited tradable oil resources in the global oil market, not only confronts China the risks of being denied access to oil imports but also expose it to the risk of price manipulations. In 1997, Y. Zhou, the then President of CNPC, stated that "oversea exploration and development is a better way for China to achieve a stable oil supply because of price fluctuations make oil imports a high risk."[34] Therefore, in the eyes of Beijing, direct control of oil resources is a safer and more economic way to ensure China's oil security.

6.2.2 *Corporate Motivations*

Unlike the government whose overarching concern is to ensure China's oil and gas supplies, the NOCs primarily concern about their long-term development and global competitiveness. As mentioned before, domestic oil and gas reserves cannot sustain China's surging appetites. Considerations about long-term development have compelled the NOCs to expand businesses abroad. One interviewee kept reminding the author of the dire consequences for an oil company should it have no oil.[35] The likelihood of world oil depletion enhanced their sense of urgency to gain a foothold in the global energy market.

Venturing abroad also derives from the NOCs management's perception of the impending challenges they would confront. Accession into the WTO has obliged China to progressively open its energy market to the

[33] *CNPC*, "Zhengxie weiyuan qiwang Zhongguo shiyou gongsi jiakuai zouchuqu bufa" (CPPCC Member Expects China Oil Companies Can Speed up the 'Going Abroad' Step), 16 March 2005, available at: http://www.cnpc.com.cn/xwygg/1200503180025.htm, accessed 22 November 2006.

[34] "China Exploring Oversea Petroleum Business," www.chinaeco.com, 8 September 1997.

[35] Interview with Shi Pengfei, one Sinopec financial official, Beijing, 19 January 2005.

MOCs. The upcoming openness was bound to intensify competition in the domestic market, which might further undermine their monopolizing status and hefty returns. In turn, they might be harder to get loans from the state banks given that the banks are also undergoing reform. In view of these challenges, the management of the NOCs feels more imperative to expand business abroad. By so doing, they can reap great benefits as to be discussed in the following.

The management of the NOCs itself also has strong incentives to go abroad so as to improve their performance. Their further promotion largely depends on the performance of the NOCs under their charge. They are aware that the central leadership expects them to secure more foreign oil and gas to meet domestic soaring consumption. Hence, the NOCs' going abroad coincides with the management's drive of further promotion and the state's desire of securing more energy supplies for the sake of energy security.[36]

As discussed in previous chapters, corporatization has created certain conditions motivating the NOCs to maximize their commercial interests. The advance of market economy leaves much room for firms and individuals to pursue their own interests. In particular, the management and employees' welfare is more closely associated with the NOC's performance. As listed companies, they need to be accountable to shareholders. In that sense, the NOCs have a propensity to be market actors with strong incentives to maximize profits.[37] By building their muscles, the NOCs aspire to become strong athletes that can emulate with their counterparts across the globe.

Then *why do the NOCs prefer direct control of oil mainly in the form of "equity oil" to international trade?* This is primarily motivated by the NOCs' cost and benefit comparison.

The NOCs are more likely to reap windfall benefits when producing oil overseas due to the Chinese oil pricing system, particularly when world oil prices go up. According to Chinese experts, securing the rights of

[36] *Economist Intelligence Unit—Executive Briefing*, "China Energy: Mix Motives behind CNOOC's Bid," 27 June 2005.

[37] It merits noting that the NOCs are state owned, but their profits have never been shared by the public, and the resource taxes they pay to the government are much lower than the MOCs to their parent states. While reaping windfall profits, the NOCs still keep pressurizing the government to raise oil and gas prices, which the Chinese public feel indignant about. Hence, compared with other industries, employees in the monopolizing sectors get much higher incomes.

producing oil abroad, notwithstanding some risks, can bring a variety of benefits. The most striking one consists in receiving oil with much lower costs.[38] Normally the cost for each barrel of oil through self-producing abroad is merely 7–8 dollars, and less than 10 dollars of the C.I.F.,[39] which is tremendously lower than the oil at a price of over 30 dollars in the international market.[40] It is manifest that the costs of producing oil abroad are much lower than crude oil imports. Virtually, other than that, lower costs are also in terms of the gap between foreign and domestic crude oil production. On average, the onshore oil production cost in China was $12/b, much higher than the international average of US$8/b. In some regions like Xinjiang the costs reached US$10–13/b; although those in the northeast were US$5–7/b, they were rising due to declines in output.[41] That is to say, producing oil abroad is even more economical than tapping oil in Western China. That means the NOCs can gain more with less costs in foreign markets regardless of other risks.

The lower costs the of crude oil, the more profits the NOCs can obtain. Because refined oil prices are still formulated by the government by reference to the international oil prices, the NOCs can raise their profits through curtailing crude oil costs. When world oil prices rise up, the more directly produced crude oil, the more profits they can reap. Even if oil prices dived down, the NOCs still could press for the government to set prices that could cover their costs. Virtually, the continuing high oil prices have encouraged the NOCs' all-out overseas oil and gas hunt.

There are other benefits for the NOCs when producing oil abroad. They have realized that "going out" is the expedient way for them to gain

[38] Haiyan Guo, "Zhongguo zhuanjia jianyi guojia qixinxieli zhichi shiyou qiye" ("Chinese Experts Recommend that the State Make a Concerted Effort to Support the Participation of Oil Enterprises in Overseas Competitions"), *Zhongguo Gongshang Shibao* (*China Industry and Commerce Times*), 20 November 2000; Yuqing Zhang, "Shishi 'zouchuqu' fazhan zhanlue" ("Implement the 'Go Abroad' Development Strategy"), *Hongguan Jingji Guanli* (*Macroeconomic Management*), No. 10, 2000, p. 5.

[39] Cost, Insurance and Freight (C.I.F.) is an international commerce term, meaning that the selling price includes the cost of the goods, the freight or transport costs and also the cost of marine insurance.

[40] Jianhua Jiang, *Zhonguo Shiyou Gongye—Quanqiu Kaifang Shichang Tiaojian xia de Zhanlue Yanjiu* (Chinese Petrochemical Industry—Studies on the Strategies in Open Global Market), Doctoral dissertation of Graduate School, The Chinese Academy of Social Sciences, 2001, p. 68.

[41] Data quoted from Eric Downs, *China's Energy Security*, 2004, p. 92, ibid.

a competitive edge and vie with oil multinationals. This is because doing business abroad can help them forge the capability of operating globally so as to become real multinational oil companies, enhance their expertise, acquaint with international rules, find a niche in foreign markets, gain managerial and marketing experiences, export Chinese labor and technologies, and so on. Thereby, the NOCs are eager to "go out." Their active overseas oil quest is not necessarily driven by "state exhortation and diplomatic and financial support."[42]

Although both the government and the NOCs have common interests in acquiring more oil and gas abroad, their interest priorities are different. As mentioned above, the NOCs primarily concern about their long-term development and global competitiveness. For that end, they expect that the government can render both diplomatic and financial support if necessary. For the state, its overarching concern is to ensure China's energy supply security. So it expects that the NOCs could forsake their windfall interests if necessary.

However, it is possible that the NOCs may run counter against the state's policies whenever they are required to relinquish their commercial interests. For instance, they may be reluctant to ship the oil and gas back home whenever they expect higher returns in foreign markets. The likelihood of the NOCs' defection behavior tends to be larger with the ongoing marketization. This problem has also been intensified by the problem of asymmetric information between the government and the NOCs regarding the costs and profits of their foreign operations. Even if the NOCs are willing to ship the oil and gas back to China, it is questionable as to whether they have the capability to transport it home safely in time of war.

That the NOCs are more profit-seeking can be illustrated by the competition between them, which exists both within domestic and foreign markets. Cases do exist like contests to snap up gas stations in China between CNPC and Sinopec as illustrated by Lin,[43] competition between PetroChina and Sinopec in Sudan and Libya as well as between

[42] Kenneth Lieberthal and Mikkal Herberg, April 2006, pp. 17–19, ibid.

[43] Kun-Chin Lin, 2003, ibid.

CNOOC and Sinopec in Brazil, regardless of the government's directives not to compete against each other in overseas oil bids.[44] Out of expectation of the government, their fierce competition only resulted in massive losses of state assets. The following will further elaborate on how the Chinese government and the NOCs go out to contest for oil and gas through two case studies on the Russian oil pipeline and the failed acquisition of Unocal by CNOOC.

6.3 USE OF SMMA AND ENERGY COOPERATION UNDER THE BRI

As an integral part of China's Belt and Road Initiative (BRI), energy cooperation has been considered as the "highlight and pioneer" of the BRI.[45] Although energy does not appear in BRI's five cooperation priorities,[46] it pertains to a variety of cooperation areas under BRI. Given the BRI covers two important fossil fuel producing regions abundant in fossil fuels (the Middle East and Russia-Central Asia) and two important fossil fuel consuming regions (Asia and Europe), energy cooperation under the BRI will be highly complementary. As such, the implementation of the BRI is slated to involve massive energy trade, numerous energy investments, and energy infrastructure constructions. In particular, building a more efficient and better-integrated energy network across the world has become one of the top priorities of the BRI. According to the Global Energy Interconnection Development and Cooperation Organization, by 2050 energy investments in Belt and Road Initiative economies are expected to hit $27 trillion, covering investments in facilitating power supplies and constructing grid infrastructure.[47]

[44] Kang Wu and S. L. Han, "Chinese Companies Pursue Overseas Oil and Gas Assets," *Oil and Gas Journal*, Vol. 103, Iss. 15, 18 April 2005.

[45] Jinping Zhao, *Reshaping the Economic Cooperation Pattern of the Belt and Road Initiative*, Singapore: Palgrave Macmillan, 2021, p. 151.

[46] The cooperation priorities include: promoting policy coordination, connectivity of infrastructure and facilities, unimpeded trade, financial integration, and closer people-to-people ties.

[47] Shuiyu Jing, "BRI Energy Investment to Hit $27 Trillion by 2050," *China Daily*, 27 April 2019, http://www.chinadaily.com.cn/a/201904/27/WS5cc3ef61a3104842260b8bba.html, accessed 5 November 2022.

To strengthen energy cooperation in jointly building the BRI, the NDRC and the National Energy Administration (NEA) have published a white paper in May 2017, called Vision and Actions on Energy Cooperation in Jointly Building Silk Road Economic Belt and 21st-Century Maritime Silk Road. This white paper has highlighted seven cooperation priorities: policy coordination, unimpeded trade, energy investment cooperation, energy production capacity cooperation, energy infrastructure connectivity, sustainable energy for all, and a better global energy governance structure.[48]

In May 2019, the energy authorities from 30 participating countries and five observer countries officially established the Belt and Road Energy Partnership (BREP), which aims to "promote policy exchanges and cooperation intention communication among participating countries, build bilateral and multilateral project cooperation and technology exchange platforms, to promote pragmatic cooperation in the energy field."[49] They agree to hold the Belt and Road energy ministerial conferences every other year and launch some training projects for energy ministers and energy cooperation talents as needed.

After years of construction, the BRI has made tremendous progress. In 2020, the volume of trade in goods with countries along the belt and the road reached US$1.35 trillion, an increase of 0.7% over the previous year, accounting for 29.1% of China's total foreign trade; non-financial foreign direct investment in countries along the belt and the road totaled US$17.79 billion, an increase of 18.3%, accounting for 16.2% of China's foreign direct investments. The turnover of contracted projects in these countries reached US$91.12 billion, accounting for 58.4% of China's foreign contracted projects.[50] Moreover, a large number of mega overseas projects and industrial park construction have made steady progress,

[48] NEA, Vision and Actions on Energy Cooperation in Jointly Building Silk Road Economic Belt and 21st-Century Maritime Silk Road, 12 May 2017, http://www.nea.gov.cn/2017-05/12/c_136277478.htm, accessed 5 October 2022.

[49] Belt and Road Energy Cooperation, "The Belt and Road Energy Partnership (BREP) was Officially Established in Beijing," 25 April 2019, http://obor.nea.gov.cn/pictureDetails.html?id=2336, accessed 4 November 2022.

[50] The above data quoted from: Qiyu Feng, "Woguo yi Qianshu Gongjian 'Yidaiyilu' Hezuo Wenjian 205 fen" (China Has Signed 205 Cooperation Documents for the Joint Construction of the "Belt and Road Initiative"), *Jingji Ribao* (Economic Daily), 1 February 2021. http://ydyl.china.com.cn/2021-02/01/content_77175407.htm, accessed 6 November 2022.

such as the China-Laos Railway and the Yawan Railway in Indonesia. As a major land-based trade channel linking the east and the west, the China Railway Express to Europe is playing an important role in helping expand China–Europe trade. Foreign enterprises from countries along the belt and the road have set up 4294 new enterprises in China, with a direct investment of US$8.27 billion.[51]

The implementation of the BRI complies with the SMMA. On the one hand, not only has the BRI been mapped out and directed by the Chinese government but also it calls for intergovernmental policy coordination. Indeed, as of January 2022, the Chinese government has signed more than 200 cooperation documents on jointly building the "Belt and Road Initiative" with 147 countries and 32 international organizations.[52] On the other hand, the Chinese government has eventually realized whether the BRI can make a success largely hinges upon the market, or whether the investment projects have commercial feasibility. Hence, Beijing has toned down the role of the government and encouraged companies to play a larger part in the process of constructing the BRI.

This shift has been triggered not only by the COVID-19 pandemic severely hitting the world economy and thus causing more troubles for the BRI but also by the intensifying Sino-US strategic competition. Thanks to the relentless suppression and hi-tech ban imposed by the US, the Chinese government has put forth the "dual circulation" (*shuang xunhuang*) strategy to try to minimize the likely severe percussions on China brought about by the US decoupling move. This "dual circulation" strategy, aiming to re-zoom into domestic "new Infrastructure" (*xin jijian*) investment development, has been considered a herald of China's policy change. The Chinese official document emphasizes that the BRI "will abide by market rules and international norms, give play to the decisive role of the market in resource allocation and the primary role of enterprises,"[53] but in practice, the government and government-led

[51] Qiyu Feng, 2021, ibid.

[52] Xiyao Xie & Yilin Yan, "Woguo yi yu 147 ge Guojia, 32 ge Guojizuzhi Qianshu 200 duo fen Gongjian 'Yidaiyilu' Hezuo Wenjian" (China Has Signed More than 200 Cooperation Documents on Jointly Building "Belt and Road Initiative" with 147 Countries and 32 International Organizations), *Xinhua News Agency*, 19 January 2022, http://www.gov.cn/xinwen/2022-01/19/content_5669215.htm, accessed 6 November 2022.

[53] NDRC, MFA, MOCOM, Vision and proposed actions outlined on jointly building Silk Road Economic Belt and 21st-Century Maritime Silk Road, March 2015.

platforms, instead of companies, often played a decisive role in the past. This is understandable given that the BRI was in its infant stage and needs to get nurtured. However, the wind vane has started to change in recent years. Besides "companies as the main actors," "following international rules" and "market-oriented as the key principle," China's 14th Five-Year Plan and 2035 Long-term Vision, for the first time, has underscored that the BRI should stick to "financial (lending/debt/loan) sustainability" and "promoting a variety of financing structure."[54] This is in stark contrast with the previous practices wherein "Chinese governments have coordinated all sorts of domestic resources to provide a better BRI mechanism."[55] Accordingly, the actual overseas lending has witnessed a retrenchment. While underscoring the central role of enterprises in implementing the BRI, China's foreign energy quest has indeed showcased a more marketization trend, which will be illustrated below.

6.4 The "Marketization" Side of China's Foreign Energy Quest

While placing a strong hand in managing and regulating the Chinese enterprises' outward direct investments, the Chinese government has taken some measures tilting towards the "marketization" side. First, it has removed the limitation on foreign exchange use for Chinese firms' foreign investments.[56] The government has also broken up the SOEs' monopoly in oil import rights. On 27 August 2014, Xinjiang Guanghui Petroleum Co Ltd, a wholly owned subsidiary of Guanghui Energy, was granted an import quota of 200,000 metric tons of crude oil for 2014. It has thus become the first private firm that has obtained such a license,

[54] Xinhua, "Zhonggong Zhongyang guanyu Zhiding Guomin Jingji he Shehui Fazhan Di Sishi ge Wunian Guihua he 2035 nian Yuanjing Mubiao de Jianyi" (Advisory of the CPC Central Committee on the formulation of the 14th Five-year Plan for National Economic and Social Development and the Long-term Vision for the year 2035), 3 November 2020, http://www.gov.cn/zhengce/2020-11/03/content_5556991.htm, accessed 9 November 2022.

[55] Yuki, "China's Energy Belt & Road Initiative: Priorities are Shifting," *Energy Iceberg Analysis*, 16 December 2020. https://energyiceberg.com/chinese-energy-belt-and-road-initiative/, accessed 10 November 2022.

[56] *Zaobao*, "Zhongguo jiang quxiao qiye haiwai touzi yonghui xianzhi" ("China Will Remove Foreign Exchange Use Limitations for Chinese Enterprises Foreign Investments"), 18 February 2006.

which used to be dominated by Sinopec Group and PetroChina since 1998.[57] The government's move apparently is conducive to enhancing competition within the Chinese market.

Second, over the past decades, the official ODI regulatory regime has been more open and streamlined. As illustrated in Chapter 3, the initial regime was extremely rigid, but at present, firms with an ODI project, as long as it is neither in sensitive industries nor in sensitive countries and regions, are not subject to the government's examination and approval. Third, the NOCs have competed against each other in their foreign energy quest. For instance, PetroChina and Sinopec bided for the same project in Sudan and Libya, and so did CNOOC and Sinopec in Brazil.[58] Consequently, fraternal rivalry often resulted in bidding wars and pushed up the price that the Chinese winner had to pay, which is the last scenario that the Chinese government is willing to see.

Fourth, the NOCs are major actors in engaging in China's oil diplomacy, but it is inaccurate to consider that every overseas investment by the NOCs falls into the category of China's oil diplomacy, or has been driven by the whim of the state. As a matter of fact, the NOCs are far from puppets operating under the control of the Chinese government. They enjoy a high degree of independence from the Chinese government. As an IEA report finds, "their actions appear mainly to be driven by commercial incentives to take advantage of available opportunities in the global marketplace. This independent, commercially driven behavior is particularly pronounced in upstream investments and operations, while policy drivers seem to play a larger role in some, though not all, transport (pipeline) projects."[59]

Fifth, it is true that the Chinese NOCs prefer a cooperation mode of "equity oil" that they can have direct control, but it may be too rash and biased to conclude that they pose a threat to other countries, neither is what the NOCs are doing abroad a boon for China's energy security. One notable concern is: Because the NOCs have operations and great stakes in

57 Juan Du, "Private Firm Guanghui Gets Oil Import License," *China Daily*, 29 August 2014.

58 Shaofeng Chen, "Marketization and China's Energy Security," *Policy and Society*, Vol. 27, 2009, p. 258.

59 Julie Jiang and Jonathan Sinton, "Overseas Investments by Chinese National Oil Companies: Assessing the Drivers and Impacts," *International Energy Agency Information Paper*, February 2011.

some so-called "rogue states," the Chinese government is less willing to dance with Washington's foreign policy, thereby undermining America's policy effectiveness. Leaving aside the normative question about whether China should follow every step of the US, we also need to take note of the positive side of Chinese NOCs' investments in those countries, which have expanded global oil and gas supplies to the global energy market that many countries are relying on. Likewise, it is hard to assert that China is the only beneficiary from its NOCs' venturing abroad in view that most equity oil virtually has flown into the international market, rather than being shipped back to China.[60] For instance, almost all the equity oil produced by the Chinese NOCs in the Americas was sold locally, and their decisions are mainly driven by market considerations. "No evidence suggests that the Chinese government currently imposes a quota on the NOCs regarding the amount of their equity oil that they must ship to China."[61]

Sixth, besides the NOCs, a growing number of private energy-related firms from China have embarked on ODIs in energy projects abroad. Guanghui Energy stands out in this regard. In August 2009 Xinjiang Guanghui Industry Co Ltd, a privately owned company based in Xinjiang, purchased a 49% stake in Kazakhstan-based Tarbagatay Munay LLP or TBM for US$40.52 million, enabling it to possess a 49% stake in TBM's Zaysan oilfield with 31-year exploration rights.[62] Its stake in TBM was further expanded to 52% in September 2013.[63] In order to develop the oilfield, Guanghui Energy built a Jimunai gas pipeline linking China and Kazakhstan, and this pipeline has been put in use on 20 June 2013.[64] China's Landbridge Group, a private company from Shandong province,

[60] Chen Shaofeng, "Has China's Foreign Energy Quest Enhanced Its Energy Security?" *The China Quarterly*, Vol. 207, September 2011, pp. 600–625.

[61] Julie Jiang and Jonathan Sinton, February 2011, ibid.

[62] *China Knowledge*, "Xinjiang Guanghui to Acquire Kazakhstan TBM Oil Assets," 24 August 2009. http://news.alibaba.com/article/detail/energy/100161228-1-xinjiang-guanghui-acquire-kazakhstan-tbm.html, accessed 26 January 2015.

[63] *The Reuters*, "Guanghui Energy Co Ltd Announces Acquisition of Stake in Tarbagatay Munay LLP by Sub-subsidiary; Announces Acquisition of Stake in Xinjiang-based Company by Subsidiary," 13 September 2013.

[64] Webpage of Guanghui Energy, "Jimunai Gas Pipeline," http://www.xjguanghui.com/Typ.aspx?id=040303&Type=NYKF_SYTRQKTKF_ZHSLBLKJMNTRQGD&nid=187, accessed 26 January 2015.

invested in Australia's petroleum sector through its takeover of Brisbane-based WestSide Corporation with about US$200 million in November 2014.[65] This is the first acquisition of a foreign-listed energy company by a Chinese privately owned company. Compared with the state-owned NOCs, private firms have their own advantages to invest in the energy sector in foreign countries in that they are more flexible and exposed to less discrimination and political obstacles from Western countries. The NOCs often come across such suspicion due to their government background. However, private companies from China also encounter some difficulties in "going abroad." Prominent among them are difficulties in financing, which is crucial to an ODI over energy projects that often call for substantial capital. In order to help resolve such a problem, China Minsheng Bank provided tailor-made financial services to China's small and medium enterprises.

6.5 Conclusion

An SMMA is used in Chinese firms' oil quests. On the one hand, the government has played an important role in that process particularly as manifested in its oil diplomacy or incorporating securing energy resources into its foreign policies. While encouraging the NOCs to venture abroad by providing necessary support, the government has also controlled the "gate" through which firms have to pass through by stipulating various requirements. To some extent, the government's intervention has a strong impact on the Chinese firms' success or not in their foreign energy quest.

Meanwhile, along with a more streamlined official ODI regulatory regime, the government has gradually reduced its intervention in the Chinese firms' forays into other countries and regions. While the NOCs remain the principal forces in "going abroad," the private companies become more proactive, constituting new forces competing with the NOCs. Also, the Chinese companies enjoy greater autonomy in their energy quest. Most of the time, it is the Chinese companies rather than the government that is taking the "driver" seat in venturing abroad.

[65] Australian Trade Commission, "China's Landbridge Makes a Strategic A$200m Investment in Australian Gas," 4 November 2014.

CHAPTER 7

SMMA in China's Foreign Energy Quest: Three Cases

The preceding chapter has illustrated the motivations of China's foreign quest for oil and gas from the perspectives of the Chinese government and the NOCs. In summary, China's foreign energy quest has been the mixture of the government's strategic concerns as well as the NOCs' commercial motivations. With time passing by, the role of the latter has been looming larger. This chapter further elaborates on how the Chinese government and the NOCs go out to contest for oil and gas through three case studies on the Russian oil pipeline, Sino-Kazakhstan oil pipeline and the failed acquisition of Unocal by CNOOC.

The case on the Russian oil pipeline is associated with China's energy security not only because the oil through this pipeline would expand China's source of oil supplies, but also because it could contribute to the diversification of oil import sources and alleviating China's concern of "Malacca Strait dilemma." Furthermore, this is a typical case exemplifying the more intensified interstate competition over energy resources against a backdrop of surging oil prices. As such, we can see what strategic concerns the countries concerned had exhibited and how they strove to achieve their goals.

Similar to the case on Russian oil pipeline, the case on Sino-Kazakhstan oil pipeline pertains to China's oil security. It has great significance on China's oil security not only because the oil through this pipeline has helped expand oil supplies to satisfy the country's surging demand,

S. Chen, *China's Approach to Energy Security*,
https://doi.org/10.1007/978-981-99-3573-4_7

but also because it has contributed to diversifying oil import sources, easing overreliance on the Middle East, and alleviating China's concern of "Malacca Strait dilemma." More importantly, the case of China's action in Kazakhstan exemplifies Chinese contradiction in making a decision. In deciding whether to build this pipeline, Beijing changed its tune once and again. As such, we can see what strategic concerns Beijing had exhibited.

The CNOOC acquisition case pertains to China's energy security in the following senses.[1] First of all, this was the first big internationalization move by a Chinese NOC, an effort which had strong impact on the business world, not only because it was the largest overseas acquisition of China, but also because it directly targeted the American market and confronted American oil giant. Such an internationalization effort conforms to the Chinese government's industrial policy of forging some large SOEs into real multinationals. Second, the 18 billion dollars deal, should it have succeeded, would have enhanced the competitiveness of CNOOC and China's oil security, in view that there would be more oil and gas assets under the control of the Chinese firms. Third, to some extent, this acquisition could be regarded as a touchstone on the perception of energy security held by the US as well as the way it treats other countries when it comes to strategic assets.

The three cases involved Russia, America, and Kazakhstan. All of them are important energy players and the first two are large energy markets in the world. Russia and Kazakhstan are developing countries heavily relying on oil and gas exports, while the US is a developed country with the largest oil consumption. Through the three cases, readers can have more in-depth understanding concerning how the Chinese government and NOCs deal with big powers and developing countries in their foreign energy quest.

7.1 Case One: Sino-Japanese Contest for Russian Oil Pipeline

Competition revolving around the construction of Russia's oil pipeline to Asian Pacific has undergone turns and twists. This process can be classified into three stages: The first stage was from 1994 to 2001, when the pipeline was proposed and the marathon negotiations proceeded between

[1] Hereafter CNOOC refers to CNOOC Limited.

China and Russia. The second stage was signaled by Japan's involvement from halfway in 2002. Since then, China, Russia, and Japan started the trilateral competitions, in which Japan, by virtue of its massive silver offensive, succeeded to persuade Moscow to build an oil pipeline to the Sea of Japan. And in the last stage, the competition centered on the priority to build the trunk pipeline to Japan or the offshoot line to Daqing of China. Thus far, Russia has decided to build a trunkline to the Pacific and a branch line to China (see Map 1 in the Appendix). It kicked off the construction of the pipeline to Skovorodino in April 2006. As the focus of this study is on China, this case study will only briefly introduce Japan and Russia's intentions. Emphasis is placed on setting out how China actively engaged in vying for the Russian oil pipeline,[2] and what its calculations are.

7.1.1 Initial Stage: China's Impassiveness to Russia's Pipeline Proposal

Sino-Russian energy cooperation started from 1994 when Russia first proposed an oil pipeline linking Siberia to northeast China.[3] Russia's offer was primarily because of its plan to develop its energy-rich Siberia and Far East and the constraint by its economic predicament at that time. Among the world aggregate reserves, Russia enjoys 13% of oil and 45% of natural gas, most of which locates in Siberia and Far East: of the 2250 Bcm proven natural gas reserves, 92% are in Siberia,[4] and the percentage of oil in Siberia and Far East reaches 76.2% (See Table 7.1). In reality, about one

[2] Compared with other transportation means such as rail, ship, or vehicle, the advantages of pipeline lie in its less for-ever land occupancy, larger transport capability, smaller wear and tear, lower costs and so on. It is said that railway transportation, the major means to transport refined oil in China, would not only engender higher costs, but also affect the quality of refined oil. Source: *Shiyou Xinxi wang* (*Petroleum Information Net*), "Youqi chuyun: xunsu jueqi de 'guandao jingji'" ("Oil and Gas Storage and Transport: Rapidly Rising Pipeline Economy"), 1 July 2005, available at: http://www.infopetro.com.cn/Dissertation/ShowDissertation.aspx?cid=6&id=5579, accessed 18 November 2006.

[3] Before that motion, the Russian government advanced a package plan to develop the Siberia and Far East region in 1993. See *Zhongguo Guojia dili* (*China National Geography*), Beijing, December 2004, p. 69.

[4] Yishan Xia, "China-Russia Energy Cooperation: Impetus, Prospects and Impacts," The James A. Baker III Institute for Public Policy of Rice University, May 2000, p. 6.

Table 7.1 Regional distribution of petroleum reserves in Russia

	Million tons	%
West Siberia	7340	73.5
Ural	890	
North Russia in Europe	700	
Volga coastal regions	620	
East Siberia	160	1.6
Far East	100	
North Caucasus	90	
Continental shelf	80	1
Total	9980	100

Source Russian Economy, Vol. 9, 2003 (in Russian). Cited from Diao Xiuhua, 2005, ibid.

half of Russian government revenues derived from energy exports.[5] The geographical proximity, rapprochement of bilateral relations, and mutual energy complement facilitated China as an objective market.

Initially the Chinese government acted as an EEP when considering the plan of building a pipeline linking Russia and China. It was mainly out of economic concerns that delayed the negotiation process. Russia made that proposal in 1994, but only until July 2001 did the two governments clinch an agreement to build the oil pipeline. Why did the negotiation last for 8 years?

Technically, prudent feasibility study takes time but it is a must for such a huge project. However, there were more complicated reasons for such a delay. It was China's impassiveness that led to the deadlock of negotiation. In order to tackle the funding issue for building the pipeline, Russia proposed establishing a joint stock company; it even agreed to headquarters that company in Hong Kong so as to marshal sufficient capitals to finance the pipeline. However, its proposal was rejected by China.[6] The then Jiang Zemin—Li Peng Administration thought it was too costly to construct such a pipeline to China, and preferred oil imports from the

[5] Yishan Xia, *China-Russia Energy Cooperation*, May 2000, p. 8, ibid.

[6] Interview with Xia Yishan, senior energy expert at China International Studies Institute, affiliated with Ministry of Foreign Affairs, Beijing, 10 January 2005.

Middle East; thereby China lost a precious opportunity to enter Russian oil market.[7]

One of the major reasons why the Chinese government acted as an EEP was because of the low oil prices in the last decade. As shown in Chart 7.1, from 1994 to 2001, the average crude oil price (based on Dubai in light of which most Chinese oil imports were calculated at that time) was merely US$19.53/b. During the 1990s, the oil prices stayed below US$20. Therefore, at time of low oil prices, it was hard for Beijing to consider building a commercially unfeasible oil pipeline (uneconomic on the basis of the oil prices at that time). Secondly, the Asian financial crisis further curtailed Chinese domestic oil demand, though temporarily, which was also a retarding factor. Thirdly, because of China's meager coffers at that time, building such an exorbitant mega project could hardly move into the center in the government's timetable. Moreover, China was still in the dream of going back to self-sufficiency initially since it became a net oil importer in 1993. With such an impassive attitude, it was conceivable that both sides could hardly reach any deal.

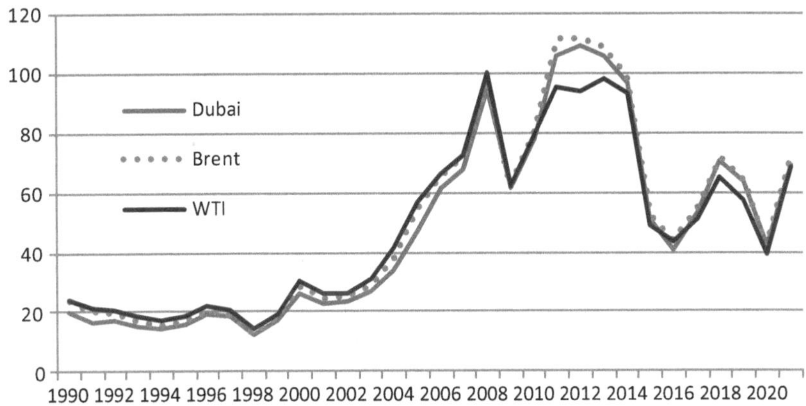

Chart 7.1 Spot crude oil prices (*Source* BP, Statistical reivew of world energy, 2022)

[7] Jibao Chen, "Zhongguo nengyuan 'wuji' waijiao" ("China's 'Five-pole' Energy Diplomacy"), *21 Shiji Jingji Baodao* (*Nanfangdaily*) 17 March 2004, http://www.nanfangdaily.com.cn/jj/20040318/chj/200403170017.asp, accessed 18 November 2006.

7.1.2 *Tussle Between Chinese Companies and China's Changing Attitude*

Negotiation warmed up when Sinopec proposed a pipeline from Russia to the refineries in Northern China (at that time they belonged to Sinopec) via Mongolia in a report to the central government in 1997, which was coincidentally in accord with the pipeline Russia had initiated. Moscow advocated a pipeline through Mongolia on the ground of 200 km shorter in length and thus of less cost. Later CNPC propounded a competitive alternative line leading from Angarsk directly to Daqing. Both companies had wanted to use crude oil from Russia to feed their refineries in Xinjiang and Daqing respectively. Therefore, the route issue is entangled with the interest strife between Sinopec and CNPC in China. Facing their tussles, the Chinese government had to make a decision between the two.

Beijing's security concern finally made it lean towards a pipeline avoiding Mongolia. The SPC and Ministry of Foreign Affairs decided not to adopt the line proposed by Sinopec, despite the fact that the line, if adopted, would be far shorter, and accordingly more construction-cost-efficient. China held that the oil pipeline should not pass any third country. Beijing worried that the line would be controlled by a third nation as it took the risk of cutting down the pipeline. The government was convinced by the likelihood that oil transit countries may blackmail the pipeline-linked nations. For instance, Russia was pressurized to raise the transit fees by Ukraine and Belarus when they could not afford the oil they consumed.[8] Sometimes, they even walked off with oil by merely drilling a hole in the pipeline. Therefore, the Chinese think tanks argued for an oil pipeline directly leading to Northeast China.

At that time, CNPC mainly acted as a market actor to win an oil pipeline terminating at Daqing. It vigorously braced for that pipeline because it owns all refineries there. By transporting oil from Russia to Daqing, CNPC expects to invigorate Daqing. As the largest oilfield in China and the chief profit generator for CNPC, Daqing Oilfield has entered its aging stage. After maintaining 27-year high yields of 50 Mt oil production annually during 1976–2002, annual crude oil production fell down to 40 Mt for another 12 years (2003–2014) and further declined to

[8] The oil export from Russia to West Europe must pass across by Ukraine and Belarus.

30 Mt afterward.[9] The Daqing syndrome provided CNPC with a playing card. This syndrome arose from the waning producing capability, which not only aroused concerns about China's oil supply security, but engendered serious social problems. At the end of the 1990s, an array of SOEs were on the brink of bankruptcy. The situation in Northeast China was more grievous as it used to be the industrial base of China. With the shut down of many factories, Northeast China was confronted with a large number of the unemployed, partly due to the waning oil production in Daqing. Therefore, to gain government support for a pipeline to Daqing, CNPC deliberately played up the impact of the Daqing syndrom on social stability and China's oil security.

CNPC's market actor role could be verified by its strong stance in negotiating on how to finance the pipeline. The costs were estimated at 2.9–3.0 billion.[10] At last, both sides agreed that each was responsible to foot the bill of the segments within their own territories respectively. Therefore, Russia was required funding 1,452 (1,600) km of the pipeline whereas CNPC only need fund 795 (800) km.[11] As a compromise, CNPC promised to provide loans to Russia. Such an arrangement was apparently in China's favor.

The Chinese government, prioritizing its sociopolitical and strategic concerns, was prone to a role of internal stabilizer since the turn of this century. After the pipeline drawn up from Angarsk to Daqing was formally placed on the intergovernmental negotiation table in 2001, Beijing turned to have more interest in that project. There were many factors that prompted such a change. For instance, the dream of coming back to self-sufficiency evaporated after years of struggle; and international oil prices began to bounce up as Asian countries eventually recovered from the setback of the financial crisis. Other than the economic concerns, however, Beijing's zest was overridingly out of its sociopolitical and

[9] Hui Qi, "Daqing Youtian: Tingqi Gongheguo Youmian Jiliang" (Daqing Oilfield: Standing up the Backbone of the Oil Vein of the Republic), *Jingji Ribao* (Economic Daily), 20 September 2019.

[10] Erica S. Downs, *China's Energy Security*, 2004, p. 121, ibid.

[11] There are two different versions on the length of the pipeline. Figures outside the two parentheses can refer to: Erica S. Downs, *China's Energy Security*, 2004, p. 121, ibid; The other can refer to: Wei Cai, "Zhong Ri E Guanxian zhi zheng de beihou" ("Behind the Pipeline Strife Among China, Japan and Russia"), *Sanlian Shenghuo Zhoukan* (*Life Week*) 22 September 2003, http://old.lifeweek.com.cn//2003/1015/6735.shtml, accessed 26 April 2023.

strategic concerns. First of all, this pipeline can be utilized to lubricate Sino-Russian strategic partnership. Though great efforts had been made to promote bilateral trade so as to be commensurate with their warming political relations, Sino-Russia trade only gained a modest growth in the 1990s. In 2001, trade volume only reached US$10.7 billion, far below the goal of US$20 billion set by the two governments.[12] It was paled by the US$80.5 billion trade volume between China and the US in the same year.[13] Once the oil pipeline was in place, it would remarkably boost bilateral trade. Moreover, maintaining the pipeline is preconditioned by the bilateral trust. In that sense, this project was conducive to Sino-Russian strategic partnership.

Second, the Daqing syndrome indeed stirred the central government's nerve since a bulk of oil fields in the East and South China have entered their aging stages and the oilfields in the far west failed to meet the government's expectation to act as China's new oil producing bases. In the 1990s, in the exploitation of Daqing Oilfield, the proportion of water injection production was increasing. The Chinese government was aware that Daqing Oilfield has gradually become aging. Because Daqing Oilfield has become a source of crude oil for major refineries in China, particularly for refineries in areas through crude oil pipelines laid to Jilin, Liaoning, and other places. With the production reduction of Daqing Oilfield, there will be problems in the supply of raw materials for these refineries. So the Chinese petroleum administrative department started to contact Russia since the 1990s to explore pipelines from Russian oil fields in Siberia to Daqing to make up for the decline in Daqing crude oil production. By virtue of an oil pipeline to Daqing, China intended to salvage the erstwhile heavy industrial center in view that building and maintaining such an ambitious pipeline would create many job opportunities. Further, those SOEs related to oil processing could be invigorated.

Third, China's interest in Russia's oil resources is also because it conforms to its efforts to diversify oil import sources. The overriding cause that prompts China's efforts o diversification lies in its growing reliance on the oil imports from the Middle East as well as on the passage through the teMalacca Strait, as discussed in Chapter 2.

[12] Gennady Chufrin, "Russia's Economic and Strategic Interests in North-East Asia," *Asia Europe Journal*, Vol. 1, May 2003, p. 254.

[13] General Administration of Customs of China, *China Customs Statistics*, 2002.

Russia had its strategic considerations to build an oil pipeline from Siberia to the Pacific. First, building this pipeline and developing related industries, such as refinery, would not only help to fill the energy gap in Russian Far East, but also contribute to economic development there. Second, it would also help diversify the Russian oil and gas export market, reinforce Russia's presence in the booming Asian energy market, and reduce its dependence on the European oil and gas market.

When the Chinese side became more enthusiastic, the Angarsk-Daqing route went smoothly. In September 2001 when Chinese Premier Zhu Rongji visited Russia, both governments agreed to jointly conduct feasibility studies of the pipeline.[14] It was expected that the pipeline could be in place as early as 2005. They also confirmed a plan to pipe 20 Mts of oil per year to China after 2005 and 30 Mts after 2010.[15] Following the Sino-Russian Treaty of Good-neighborliness, Friendship, and Cooperation signed by President Jiang and President Putin in 2001, both countries made the *Sino-Russian Joint Statement* in December 2002. The Statement reemphasizes, "The two heads of state believe that ensuring the scheduled implementation of the agreed Sino-Russian crude oil and natural gas pipeline cooperation projects and coordinating the implementation of promising energy projects is essential to ensuring the long-term stable supply of oil and gas."[16] Just when the dust on the Angarsk-Daqing pipeline seemed to be settled, Japan started to meddle in. With Japan's involvement in the competition, the weather vane began to turn around.

7.1.3 China's Counteractions Against Japanese Contest

Thanks to China's surging demand for oil driven by its rapid economic growth, Japan was very worried that China was "grabbing" too much oil. As a result, Russia would have insufficient oil to supply Japan. During the end of 2002 and early 2003, the then-Japanese Prime Minister Junichiro Koizumi met with Putin twice to discuss energy cooperation. Both countries signed the "Russia-Japan Energy Cooperation Plan," in which Japan

[14] *BBC Monitoring Asia Pacific*, "Russia to Keep Promises to China, Others on Energy Programs," London, 14 April 2004, p. 1.

[15] *Nezavisimaya Gazeta*, 6 September 2001.

[16] *Xinhua*, "President Jiang Zemin and President Putin Sign the Full Text of the Sino-Russian Joint Statement," 3 December 2002, http://m.law-lib.com/law/law_view.asp?id=74890&page=1, accessed 17 November 2022.

proposed to Russia to build the Angarsk-Nahodka oil pipeline through which crude oil would flow to Japan. Japan also pledged to import 1 million barrels of oil a day from Russia and promised a loan of US$7.5 billion to help Russia develop oil fields and build oil pipelines on the condition that Russia would lay the Angarsk-Nahodka pipeline. The intention of the Japanese was not only to find new sources of oil imports, but also to increase its influence in the Far East through energy cooperation with Russia, thereby affecting the Sino-Russian comprehensive strategic partnership of cooperation and ruining the Angarsk-Daqing pipeline. As a result of Japan's intervention, Russia decided to re-consider the direction of the crude oil pipeline.

By offering remarkable financial and technical assistance, Japan succeeded to lure Russia to change tack. At the end of 2004 the Russian government made a formal decision to construct a new Tayshet-Skovorodino-Perevoznaya Bay pipeline with an annual output capacity of 80 Mt. This pipeline, whose construction costs were estimated at 11.5bn dollars,[17] basically followed the Japanese preferred route, but Moscow's decision did not stipulate whether it would lay a branch pipeline to Daqing or not.[18] At this juncture, Japan won this pipeline after fusillading lobbying activities with its deeper pocket.

By taking advantage of Sino-Japanese competition, Russia strived to maximize its national interest. "Russian government has been jumping back and forth between the two alternatives, even talking of merging both projects together so to satisfy both Japan and China."[19] However, Russia had to opt for one major oil pipeline because of the uncertainty of sufficient oil resources to be discovered and the unaffordability of the tremendous costs to build two lines. Although the strident territorial dispute between Russia and Japan in 2005 had some awful impact on Russia's decision, Russia held that a pipeline to the Sea of Japan is more in accord with its interest.

[17] London: *BBC Monitoring Former Soviet Union*, "Russia Takes Decision on Building First Stage of Siberia-Pacific Oil Pipeline," 27 April 2005.

[18] London: *BBC Monitoring Former Soviet Union*, "Russia's New Far Eastern Oil Pipeline to Skirt Chinese Border," 31 December 2004.

[19] *Mosnews Information Service*, "Russia Not to Build an Oil Pipeline to China," Moscow, 1 March 2004, http://www.mosnews.com/money/2004/03/01/chinapipe.shtml, accessed 26 April 2023.

On 31 December 2004, President Putin personally decided to build the East Siberia-Pacific oil pipeline, that is, the "Taishet-Nahodka Line," which pushed the original "Angarsk-Daqing Line" more than 400 kilometers northward, far away from Lake Baikal, so as to resolve the likely environmental pollution problem on Lake Baikal that many Russians were concerned about.

The uncertainty of the Daqing pipeline prompted the Chinese government and CNPC to explore other options. Japan's involvement from the midway had provided CNPC with ammunition to lobby for government support. It started to act as a SPSOU in the sense that CNPC tried to win the pipeline regardless of the economic costs it would incur for China. For the Chinese government, Tokyo's overt support had furnished it with every reason to render government diplomatic and financial support. Hence, it played a role of internal stabilizer. The government-SOE collaboration thus contributed to the debut of the following measures.

First of all, as a countermine against Russia's caprice and competition from Japan, China decided to revive the originally shelved plan of building an oil pipeline linking Kazakhstan with China.[20] Because the Sino-Kazakhstan pipeline intersects a pipeline from Mosk, Russia, to Chardzhou, Turkmenistan, at Atasu, connecting with Russia's West Siberia pipeline network, Russia thus could export oil to China through this pipeline.[21] Moreover, the Sino-Kazakhstan pipeline could even be extended to the Middle East.[22] China's return to build this pipeline amounted to sending a message to Russia and Japan that it was not so reliant on Angarsk-Daqing pipeline. The reviving of the China-Kazakhstan project was "partly as high oil prices made it attractive to the

[20] It was shelved in 1999 due to concerns about insufficient oil reserves to justify costs of construction. *Oil and Gas Journal*, "CNPC Shelves China-Kazakhstan Oil Pipeline," Vol. 97, Iss. 35, 30 August 1999, p. 44.

[21] Once the pipeline is in place, Kazakhstan's Caspian Sea crude oil can be delivered to the Xinjiang refining base. Thus far, only the Atyrau-Kenkiyak part has been completed, the Atasu-Dushanzi section is due to be completed by the end of 2005. *BBC Monitoring Asia Pacific*, "China, Kazakhstan Move to Build Oil Pipeline," London, 29 July 2004, p. 1.

[22] Mengdi Gu, "China Wants More Pipelines for Improved Oil Import Security," *Oil & Gas Journal*, 3 January 2005, Vol. 3, Iss. 1, p. 59.

Kazakhs, but largely because of Moscow's lukewarm attitude on which route to use to transport Siberian oil to Asia."[23]

The second strategy that China adopted was to take measures to foster mutual trust. During Putin's visit to Beijing in October 2004, China agreed with Russia's entry into the WTO. Furthermore, both countries have completed the final demarcation of the 4,300-kilometer-long borders in October 2004. Final settlement of territorial dispute contributes to enhancing mutual trust and deeper collaborations.[24]

The third strategy is to accept Rosneft's request of "exchange loans for oil." In order to raise funds to complete the acquisition of all shares of Baikal Financial Group so as to acquire 76.79% absolute control of Yugansk Oil and Gas Company, a subsidiary of Yukos, in December 2004 Rosneft put forward a cooperation proposal of "loan for oil" to the Chinese side, hoping to borrow US$6 billion from China, and the Russian side would repay it by selling oil. Despite the risks associated with such a large one-off loan and misgivings in the Chinese financial circle, Ma Ka and Zhang Guobao, the then chairman and vice chairman of NDRC, along with You Quan, then Deputy Secretary-General of the State Council, had worked hard to coordinate and persuaded different ministries concerned to accept the "loan-for-oil" program.[25]

Finally, in order to win the pipeline, China agreed to carry out large-scale investments in the Far Eastern region despite high risks. Learning from Japan and its previous experience of ignoring Russian local communities, China embarked on large-scale investments to help Russia develop its energy industry and construct infrastructure. Premier Wen Jiabao agreed to expand Russian oil exports to China through railway transport and to cooperate with Russian companies in oil E&P, and nuclear

[23] "Hong Kong Paper Reviews Importance of China-Kazakhstan Oil Pipeline Project," London: *BBC Monitoring Asia Pacific,* 4 July 2005.

[24] Sergei Sevast'ianov, "The Russian Far East' Security Perspective: Interplay of Internal and External Challenges and Opportunities," in *Siberia and the Russian Far East in the 21st Century: Partners in the "Community of Asia"*, Vol. 1, Crossroads in Northeast Asia, edited by Iwashita Akihiro, the Slavic Research Center, 2005, p. 27.

[25] Zhang Guobao, "Zhong E Yuanyou Guandao Shiwunian Tanpan Jishi: Riben Jiaoju hou, Putin Zuizhong Paibang" (A Record of 15 Years of Negotiations on the Sino-Russian Crude Oil Pipeline: After Japan Disrupted it, Putin Finally Made the Decision), *Zhongguo Jingji Zhoukan* (China Economic Weekly), No. 2, 2018.

plant construction.[26] In September 2004, he further promised that China would invest $12 billion in Russia by 2020, focusing on energy development, infrastructure construction, manufacturing, and high-tech fields.[27] China hoped these measures could help change Russian's mentality that China just treated it as an energy base.

On 26 April 2005, the Russian Ministry of Industry and Energy issued Decree No. 91, approving the construction of the "Taishet-Nahodka Line," or the Eastern Siberia-Pacific pipeline. The whole pipeline would be built in two stages. The first leg, around 2390 km, stretching from Taishet in Siberia to Skovorodino near the Chinese border, would be completed by mid-2008. From Skovorodino, 20 Mt of oil would be exported to China and the left 10 Mt to the Pacific coast by rail, while the pipeline would be extended to both directions at later stages. The remaining 1800 km or so, from Skovorodino to Perevoznaya Bay, would be constructed hinging upon the oil resources available.[28] However, even at this time, Russia did not clarify whether it would build the pipeline to Daqing, China. In view that Skovorodino is close to the Chinese border, Japan worried that Russia would build an offshoot line to China first; and if the oil discovered in Russian Far East annually could not reach 50 Mt, the second stage to Perevoznaya might be shelved *sine die*.

The cooperation of "loan for oil" has prompted Russia to take a positive attitude towards building a pipeline to China. On 8 July 2005, President Putin said for the first time that Russia would give priority to laying a branch line to China when building the Far East crude oil pipeline. Although President Putin repeatedly proposed to build a pipeline to China since then, the Russian government had not specified the construction of a pipeline to China in any document officially signed by the two governments. It remained uncertain whether the Sino-Russian crude oil pipeline would be built.

Russia was well aware that China was eager to have the Sino-Russian crude oil pipeline. Moscow tries hard to maximize its interests in the

26 "China Willing to Promote Energy Cooperation with Russia," Lanham: *WorldSources Online*, 21 September 2004.

27 "Wen Sees Rise in Russian Energy Links Ahead of a Moscow Visit, the Premier Pushes for an Increase in Oil Imports," Hong Kong: *South China Morning Post*, 22 September 2004.

28 Eric Watkins, "A Pipeline Stage issue," *Oil & Gas Journal*, 13 June 2005, Vol.103, Iss. 22, p. 33.

negotiations, often linking the Sino-Russian crude oil pipeline to other projects of concern to Russia. For example, Russia required that Units 3 and 4 of China's Tianwan Nuclear Power Station would still use Russia's technical equipment; they wanted to invest in refineries and gas stations in Tianjin, rather than merely export crude oil to China; it was required that China would import 15 million tons of coal from Russia every year, and hoped that the Chinese side would expand its import of Russian electricity, and so on.[29]

The deadlock in the bilateral negotiations was not broken until the global financial crisis erupted in 2008. It was in the context that the Russian economy was severely hit by the global financial crisis that China and Russia finally came to an agreement in Feburary 2009. Both countries signed a package of deals, including the US$25 billion financing loan contract, Sino-Russian crude oil pipeline construction and operation contract and long-term crude oil trade contract (Russia will supply 15 million tons of crude oil to China through the pipeline for the next 20 years from 1 January 2011). The pipeline went into trial operation on 1 November, 2010, and has been officially put into operation since 1 January 2011.

On 21 May 2014, the Chinese and Russian governments signed the Memorandum on Sino-Russian Natural Gas Cooperation Project, and CNPC and Gazprom signed the Sino-Russian Eastern Line Gas supply purchase and sale contract. The contract stipulated that China and Russia would jointly build the Sino-Russian East Line natural gas pipeline, and the gas transmission volume would increase year by year after it was completed and put into operation, eventually reaching 38 billion cubic meters per year, for a total of 30 years. On 2 December 2019, the China-Russia East Line natural gas pipeline was officially put into operation.

On August 13, 2016, the second line of the Sino-Russian crude oil pipeline, parallel to the Sino-Russian crude oil pipeline, began construction and was officially put into operation on 1 January 2018. The oil transportation capacity of the two parallel pipelines is 15 Mt/y, totaling

[29] Zhang Guobao, "Zhong E Yuanyou Guandao Shiwunian Tanpan Jishi: Riben Jiaoju hou, Putin Zuizhong Paibang" (A Record of 15 Years of Negotiations on the Sino-Russian Crude Oil Pipeline: After Japan Disrupted it, Putin Finally Made the Decision), *Zhongguo Jingji Zhoukan* (China Economic Weekly), No. 2, 2018.

30Mt/y. As of 1 January 2021, the first and second lines of the Sino-Russian crude oil pipeline have transported a total of 200 Mt of Russian crude oil to China.[30]

7.1.4 SMMA and the Case

The case of the Sino-Russian crude oil pipeline complies with SMMA. On the one hand, the Chinese government indeed played a pivotal role in facilitating this deal, not only through its own coordination and negotiations with the Russian counterparts as well as the provision of large loans, but also through deepening its strategic partnership with Russia. On some crucial moment, it was the government, or more specifically the officials of the State Council and the NDRC, that had made the final decisions. Hereupon there was one episode conducive to comprehending the government's role. In order to avert the vicious competition among Chinese domestic enterprises, which was likely to be exploited by the Russian side, the Chinese government let PetroChina solely represent China to negotiate with Russia and restrict other Chinese companies from getting involved.

On the other hand, the Sino-Russian crude oil pipeline first and foremost is a commercial deal, which can be verified by the following facts.[31] First, the Russians have tried their best to maximize their own national interest and have not given special care to China notwithstanding their special strategic relationship. In the process of negotiations, Russia often raised extra requirements, resulting in a very prolonged process of negotiations before they were able to clinch a deal.

Second, in view of Russia's vast energy resources and its proximity with China, the Chinese government has long been keen on entering Russian energy market and building closer energy ties with its neighbors. At the time when Rosneft was eager to hunt for strategic partners, PetroChina

[30] Runmin Zhu, "Jin'e guo Qianyi, Zhong E Hezuo zai Jiama" (The Amount of Money Exceeds 100 Billion Yuan, and the Cooperation Between China and Russia Will be Increased), *Zhongguo Shiyou Shihua* (China Petrochem), 22 Feburary 2022, http://www.chinacpc.com.cn/info/2022-02-22/news_6150.html, accessed 19 November 2022.

[31] The following facts are based on: Zhang Guobao, "Zhong E Yuanyou Guandao Shiwunian Tanpan Jishi: Riben Jiaoju hou, Putin Zuizhong Paibang" (A Record of 15 Years of Negotiations on the Sino-Russian Crude Oil Pipeline: After Japan Disrupted It, Putin Finally Made the Decision), *Zhongguo Jingji Zhoukan* (China Economic Weekly), No. 2, 2018.

merely bought US$500 million of its strategic investor shares, only half of India's investment. It did not go on a buying spree because it thought that Rosneft's share price was overvalued more in terms of commercial interests at that time. The top figures of NDRC were frustrated after knowing that; they thought PetroChina should have grasped this rare opportunity to own more upstream assets of Rosneft.

Third, the commerciality of the China-Russia energy cooperation can be verified by the terms of their contract entitled "long-term Trade contract for importing 48.4 million tons of Russian crude Oil" signed by PetroChina and Rosneft on 8 January 2005. According to the contract, Russia could obtain a loan of US$6 billion from China, and the loan was based on the international Libor interest rate plus 300 points commercial loan interest rate, which was not low and in full accordance with commercial principles, with a loan period of six years. Accordingly, Russia would repay the loan with the proceeds from crude oil trade; it would supply 48.4 million tons of crude oil to China through railways between 2005 and 2010. The price of oil purchased by PetroChina from Russia was also calculated in full accordance with international oil prices.

Finally, despite restrictions imposed by the Chinese government, Sinopec, another state-owned oil giant, was reluctant to be marginalized in China's oil cooperation with Russia and had privately bought US$200 million Rosneft shares. Sinopec was also in private contact with Rosneft to navigate the possibility of building another pipeline from Russia to Yanshan in Beijing via Mongolia. Apparently, this was not in line with Beijing's original intention of importing crude oil from Russia to make up for the decline in production in Daqing, fearing that this plan would derail the pipeline to Daqing under plan. Therefore, Zeng Peiyan, the then vice premier of the State Council required Sinopec to terminate negotiating with Russia, and Sinopec had to quit. This is one of the episodes showcasing the commercial drive of the Chinese energy enterprises.

7.2 Case Two: Sino-Kazakhstan Oil Pipeline

7.2.1 Stage One: Sino-Kazakhstan Pipeline Scheme—1997

China and Kazakhstan embarked on their collaboration in energy transportation in 1997 when the two governments reached an agreement on oil and gas cooperation. In the same year, CNPC outbid Texaco,

Amoco, and Russian firms for a 60% stake in the state-owned Aktyubinsk Oil Company, and won an exclusive right to develop Uzen oilfield, the second largest oilfield in Kazakhstan. To win the two deals, CNPC agreed a purchase price believed to be in excess of $5 billion and $71 million of debts. In addition, it had to pay $320 million in cash upfront and guarantee the pensions and housing of some 5,000 employees.[32] It was reported that CNPC overpaid as much as 30% for Aktubinsk and Uzen.[33] In addition, CNPC backed by the Chinese government,[34] offered a term of promising to build not only a pipeline from Kazakhstan to China despite its questionable commercial feasibility, but also a pipeline to Iran. Apparently it was hard for private companies to offer such generous provisions.[35]

With two principal considerations regarding a pipeline from Kazakhstan, Beijing primarily played a role as an internal stabilizer. Economically, this would be China's first pipeline from overseas which could help diversify its import sources. It was believed that the pipeline would provide another route of foreign oil imports that would avoid the passage from the sea, thus enhancing the country's oil security. Moreover, such a proposal was put forward in a context where China's hope to find a substantial oil patch in its vast Western deserts fell apart. Politically, the pipeline was expected to help bring about stability in Xinjiang, and create a friendly neighboring environment. China was eager to have peace and stability in its northern borders as it had to shift much of its attention to the crisis across the Taiwan Strait followed Lee Teng-hui's visit to the US. It had to take a rainy day to avoid fighting in two fronts. Hence, a safe backyard was entailed.

The overbid that CNPC offered indicated that the company mainly acted as a SPSOU. CNPC embarked upon its new strategy to "go out,"

32 David B. Ottaway and Dan Morgan, "China Pursues Ambitious Role in Oil Market," *Washington Post*, 26 December 1997, p. A01.

33 "China Finance—Buyers Beware of Upcoming Oil Listings," *Economist Intelligence Unit—Viewswire*, 29 September 1999, *Dow Jones Factiva*.

34 According to *Washington Post*, CNPC won the bid largely due to "the Chinese leader's personal involvement (former Chinese Premier Li Peng, who was said to have made repeated calls to Kazakhstan's president), the use of government funds to sweeten the bidding and the offer to build two multibillion-dollar pipeline as part of the deal." See David B. Ottaway and Dan Morgan, 1997.

35 David B. Ottaway and Dan Morgan, "China Pursues Ambitious Role in Oil Market," 1997.

which was part of its efforts to forge itself as a competitive multinational. As this was its initial efforts of venturing abroad and it confronted several more powerful rivalries from the west, CNPC figured out that the only possibility to win the deal was to offer more.

7.2.2 Stage Two: Pipeline Plan Shelved—1999

From 1997 to 1999, both parties completed the feasibility study report on the pipeline construction. According to the agreement signed between CNPC and the Kazakhstan state oil company KazMunaiGaz, the 3,000 km-long pipeline (625 mile) from Atasu, in northwestern Kazakhstan, to China's northwestern Xinjiang region, would be completed in three phases. The first section, on the western end of the trunkline, has a length of 450 km and links Atyrau to Kenkiyak in northwest Kazakhstan. This section has been put into operation since December 2002. The second section connects central Kazakhstan's Atasu with the Chinese border checkpoint at the Alataw Pass in the northwest part of the Xinjiang Autonomous Region. A third section of the pipeline was to be built for linking up Kenkiyak to Atasu.

However, both the Chinese government and the Chinese oil company changed their roles to Economic Efficiency Promoter and market actor respectively. CNPC announced to shelve the pipeline in 1999, saying that insufficient oil reserves being found in Aktubinsk and Uzen made the pipeline unjustifiable.[36] One possible reason set out by Downs was the change of Chinese premier from Li Peng to Zhu Rongji, who was prone to procuring oil through international trade.[37] This is true, but one more important reason is that international oil prices between 1997 and 1999 fell down to historic low levels. As indicated in Chart 7.1, due to the increase of OPEC's production quota and the impact of the Asian financial crisis which dealt a blow on oil demands in Asia, oil prices plummeted and stayed below 20 dollars per barrel in the late 1990s. At that time, the cost for building the pipeline was estimated to

[36] *Oil & Gas Journal*, "CNPC shelves China-Kazakhstan Oil Pipeline," Vol. 97, Iss. 35, 30 August 1999.

[37] Erica S. Downs, *China's Energy Security*, PhD dissertation, Princeton University, Publication Number: AAT 3,110,228, 2004, p. 117.

reach 3 billion dollars.[38] China might think it too economically costly to construct a pipeline compared with off-land oil imports. Another reason was because both the Chinese government and CNPC had prioritized building an oil pipeline from Russia first, which both governments and their oil companies concerned were actively pushing forward to realize.[39]

7.2.3 *Stage Three: Pipeline Restarted—2003*

Interestingly, China revived the pipeline in 2003. During the Chinese President Hu Jintao's visit to Kazakhstan in June 2003, China and Kazakhstan struck a deal on the phased construction of an oil trunk-line between the two countries. Hence, the construction of the Sino-Kazakhstan pipeline has regained momentum thanks to the push from both countries' leadership. In September 2004, the second section, from Atasu to Allah Mountain Pass, was officially launched and put into operation from December 2005. And the third phase, connecting Kenkiyak and Kumkol, was under construction from December 2007, and was completed and put into operation in July 2009, connecting the whole line from western Kazakhstan to Xinjiang.

The Chinese government adjusted its role to internal stabilizer due to the following factors. First and foremost is because the geopolitical situation in Xinjiang and Central Asia has been changed after September 11th. Domestically, Xinjiang is an strategic region both in its location and its resource potential. Geographically, Xinjiang, bordering eight nations, not only constitutes a security problem for China, but is a significant security hinterland for its national security. Particularly, China perceives that Uyghur Islamism and separatism has posed a threat to Chinese security, as any separation would embolden separatists in Tibet and Taiwan. The demise of the former USSR and the establishment of Central Asian states have triggered off an awakening among the Muslims of Xinjiang about their Islamic identity. In particular, "Uyghur militants are acquiring much

[38] Renmin Wang (People Daily Online), "Promoting Plural Energy Supply," *People Daily Online*, 29 September 2004.

[39] Junfeng Chen, "Jiemi Zhong Ha shiyou guandao, chenggong tupo junshi jingqu" (Decipher Sino-Kazakhstan Oil Pipeline, Successfully Broke the Military Forbidden Areas), *Guoji Xianqu Daobao* (*International Herald Leader*), 23 December 2005, available at: http://news.xinhuanet.com/world/2005-12/23/content_3960592.htm, accessed 17 March 2008.

wider connections to the worldwide Jihad movement than ever before, forcing Beijing to cast an equally wide net to contain them."[40]

Economically, Xinjiang is rich in mineral resources. It is rich in gold, copper, and ore, and approximately two-fifths of China's oil, more than 40% of China's total coal reserve, and 40% of its wool come from this province.[41] It is believed that there are rich oil and gas reserves in Xinjiang, if fully tapped, it would greatly enhance China's oil security. It is reported that Xinjiang has estimated oil resources of 20.9 billion tons, or 30% of the nation's total onshore oil resources.[42]

Given this strategic and economic significance of Xinjiang, China needs to ensure the stability there. While taking stricter control over Xinjiang, it has adopted some placatory policies to alleviate the rebellion activities. One important means is to boost investment in that region in the logic that improving the local economy would dilute the strength, scale, and frequency of the oppositions. Thus, Chinese officials and scholars suggest that China must maintain a higher level of economic development in western China than that of neighboring countries to prevent any potential social unrest.[43] The Sino-Kazakhstan pipeline contributes to Xinjiang at least in the following aspects: (i) creating more job opportunities; (ii) The Alataw Pass will become a hub of railway, road, and pipeline

[40] Ahmed Rashid, "China Forced to Expand Role in Central Asia," *Central Asia-Caucasus Analyst*, 19 July 2000.

[41] "Rich Mineral Resources," 11 January 2008, available at: http://www.aboutxinjiang.com/topic/content/2008-01/11/content_2389669.htm, accessed 17 March 2008.

[42] *Xinhua News Agency*, "Oil, Gas Supply Line Built Along Silk Road," 17 September 2005, http://china.org.cn/english/BAT/142534.htm, accessed 17 March 2008.

[43] For official views, see, the comments by President Jiang Zemin in a report by Li Lianghui, "Jiaqiang bianfang budui zhiliang jianshe yu jianshe qiangda de bianfang" ("Beef up quality building of the frontier troops and construct a powerful frontier defense"), *Zhongguo junshi kexue* (*China Military Science*). No. 4, 1997, p. 51; Zeng Pengyan (Deputy secretary general of the Central Economic and Financial Leading Group and minister of the State Development Planning Commission at that time), "Zhongguo jiang jiakuai shishi xibu da kaifa zhanlüe" ("China Will Speed Up the Implementation of the Western Development Strategy"), *Zhongguo jingji baodao* (*China Economic Herald*), 1 March 2000. For academic views, see, Futian Song, "Jiakuai xinjiang weiwu'er zizhiqu fazhan jige wenti" ("Several Issues on Stepping up the Development of the Xinjiang Uighur Autonomous Region). *Jingji yanjiu cankao* (*Economic Research Reference*). 10 April 2000.

transportation in the near future, which also means a great many commercial opportunities[44]; (iii) The refinery at Dushanzi in Karamay is forging itself as the largest one in China. Crude oil from Kazakhstan is conducive and imperative to that goal since all the crude oil from Kazakhstan will be delivered there. Currently the designed capacity of this pipeline is 20 million ton/year, which was 15% of China's 2005 total crude imports, but this capacity can be easily enlarged by adding more pumping stations.[45]

Second, externally, while the border trade between Xinjiang and Central Asia after the end of the cold war contributes to local development, it has also exposed Xinjiang to foreign influence. Among them, the America's presence and increasing influence in Central Asia has greatly stung Beijing. According to Chien-peng Chung, the Chinese government worried about the US's influence in three senses. Diplomatically, it feared that Central Asian states would be less willing to accommodate China's political demands, and tilt towards the US. Economically, Beijing worried that its oil companies would lose the game in the competition for concessions from Central Asian governments with American petroleum companies supported by the US government. Security-wise, with bases close to Xinjiang, it was much concerned about the strategic encircling by the US and its allies, which would squeeze China's maneuvering capability and endanger its national security.[46] With the emergence of "human rights superior to sovereignty" and its practice in Kosovo, China was afraid that the US might intervene in its internal affairs when it had to calm down the riots within China. The Sino-Kazakhstan pipeline not only helps lubricate the relationship with Kazakhstan, but also with other Caspian states in view that their extracted crude oil can be delivered to China via this pipeline too. In fact, once the Sino-Kazakhstan pipeline is ready for use, China will be in a more advantageous position to be linked into three separate Kazakh petroleum basins, and it was reported that relevant plans are under way regarding constructing additional oil

[44] *Xinhuashe (Xinhua News Agency)*, "Oil Pipeline Links China, Kazakhstan," 15 November 2005.

[45] James Fishelson, "From the Silk Road to Chevron: The Geopolitics of Oil Pipelines in Central Asia," *Vestnik*, Iss. 7, Winter 2007.

[46] Chien-peng Chung, "The Shanghai Co-operation Organization: China's Changing Influence in Central Asia," *The China Quarterly*, Vol. 180, 2004, pp. 989–1009.

and natural gas pipelines that would transport the energy resources from Kazakhstan, Uzbekistan, and Turkmenistan.[47]

Third, China's oil imports surge dramatically since 2000, and it is unlikely that such a growing trend will abate in the near future (see Chart 7.2). To improve its oil security, the country is striving to reduce its dependence on the Middle East. As China's first major artery of overland energy delivery, the Sino-Kazakhstan oil pipeline doubtlessly contributes to meeting China's surging demand, reducing its reliance on imports from the Middle East as well as imports via sea lanes, and giving it its first large-scale access to non-waterborne imported oil.

Fourth, pertaining to the above, Japan's tussles and Russia's caprice centering on the plan of constructing an oil pipeline from western Siberia to China has led both the Chinese government and CNPC to figure out other available options. In addition, in order to tackle the problem of insufficient crude oil from nearby Kazakh fields to justify and sustain the pipeline, the two parties, in conjunction with Russia, decided to

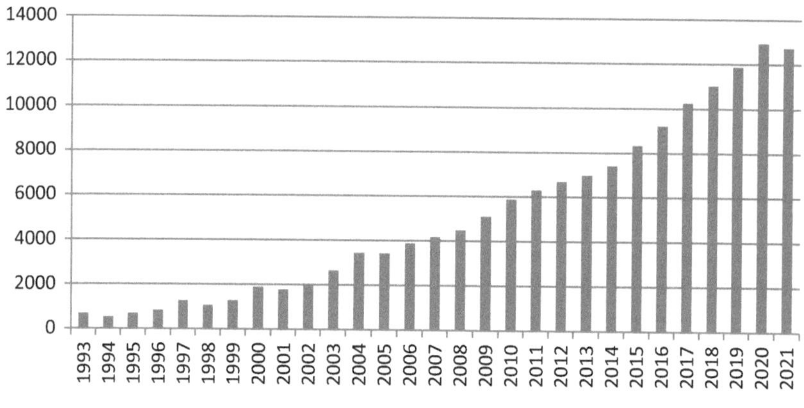

Chart 7.2 China's oil imports (*Source* BP, Statistical reivew of world energy, 2022)

[47] *Strategic Forecasting*, "China, Kazakhstan: Pipelines and the Balance of Power," 11 December 2007, available at http://www.stratfor.com/analysis/china_kazakhstan_pipelines_and_balance_power, accessed 8 March 2018.

pump half the oil through the pipeline from Russia.[48] Thus, the previous concern about inadequate oil resources seemed to have been resolved.

By the early 2000s, CNPC has preferred a role of a market actor concerning building the Sino-Kazakhstan pipeline out of considerations of its corporate strategy and the change of oil prices. As indicated in Chart 5.1, the world crude oil prices started to pick up and kept breaking new record highs since 2000. The oil price spikes have stimulated CNPC's interests to conduct more E&P in the Caspian region, and also made the pipeline linking China and Kazakhstan more justifiable. Another factor prompting CNPC's role adjustment pertains to its own corporate strategy. Since 1997, CNPC has invested more than $2.6 billion in Kazakhstan. Its efforts have got rewarded in the sense that more heart-stirring oil reserves have been found in Kazakhstan. Thus, Kazakhstan has become one of CNPC's three key energy bases abroad after years of operations.[49] In October 2005, CNPC purchased the Canadian-based PetroKazakhstan Inc., owner of the Kumkol field, which has laid a more solid resource foundation for sustaining this pipeline. As Kazakhstan is politically stable and this pipeline does not go through a third country, the safety of this pipeline can be ensured and CNPC could save a large sum of transit fee. Moreover, the pipeline complies with CNPC's corporate strategy to use Xinjiang as China's key energy base and to create the largest refinery of China in Karamy.

7.3 Case Three: CNOOC vs. CHEVRON—Acquisition Battle Over Unocal

On 23 June 2005, CNOOC announced the acquisition of Unocal Oil Company, the ninth largest oil company in the US, for US$18.5 billion. This was the largest overseas M&A involving a Chinese company by that time. CNOOC's bidding, however, was subject to regulatory approval from US and the support of Unocal shareholders over the rivalry Chevron

[48] F William Engdahl, "China Lays Down Gauntlet in Energy War: The Geopolitics of Oil, Central Asia and the United States," *Asian Times*, 22 December 2005.

[49] The other two are Sudan and Venezuela. See, *San Lian Shenghuo Zhoukan* (*Life Week*), "Zhongguo de haiwai luxian tu, jike caiyao zouchuqu" (China Oil's Overseas Route Map, Going Out Because of Energy Hunger), 16 December 2005, available at: http://www.oilnews.cn/gb/zhuanti/2005-12/16/content_646011.htm, accessed 8 March 2018.

Corporation. Moreover, a series of US government scrutiny that CNOOC faced would not be encountered by Chevron. This case primarily focuses on whether it was a commercial bid or a political deal, or what role CNOOC and the Chinese government had played in the bid.

The issue of why CNOOC was willing to spend US$18 billion, 1.5 billion higher than its rival, Chevron, to acquire Unocal, had engendered controversies with regard to its intention. Some including Chevron claimed that this was first and foremost because CNOOC, backed by the Chinese government, was carrying out the government's energy strategy aiming to control more foreign oil resources. Echoed by the Chinese government, CNOOC claimed that its proposal was made barely on commercial ground.[50] Others asserted that it was a mix of both political and commercial intentions. Yet, the debate should not be halted at whether the Chinese government endorsed the deal, but should further consider what kind of support and in what manners. In this case, CNOOC primarily acted as a market actor driven by its own corporate interest, while the Chinese government basically acted as an EEP and took an off-hand approach in the whole bidding process.

7.3.1 CNOOC's Bid for Unocal: Politics Driven?

My account of CNOOC's market actor role starts from analyzing the reasons that politics-driven proponents argued for. One reason they claimed was that CNOOC overbid its competitor a lot though Chevron was much more powerful. The second reason was the state-owned identity of CNOOC, which was 70% owned by the Chinese government. Further, a large sum of capitals that CNOOC used for the deal came from its parent corporation and the Industrial Commercial Bank of China (ICBC), both of which were backed by the Chinese government.[51] The following will analyze these contingencies one by one:

[50] Proponents of such a view like: Matt Pottinger, "Behind the Cnooc Deal: Cnooc's Fu Shows Complex Trends in Chinese Firms," *Wall Street Journal* (Eastern edition), New York, N.Y., 24 June 2005, p.C.4.

[51] Some like Senator Charles Schumer also argued that the Chinese would not allow an American company to take over a Chinese company. But as the Editorial of *New York Times* suggests, that such a question "ignores the way American companies have been buying up stakes in Chinese companies." Even Chevron has a wide stake in China. Other cases include Bank of America. See *Editorial* of *New York Times*, "Chinese Strength, U.S. Weakness," 26 June 2005.

First, it was meaningless to separately talk about the CNOOC's "overpayment" problem as it was associated with other factors: evaluation of the values of Unocal's visible and invisible assets, judgment on future oil and gas prices trend, the spillover price that CNOOC had to afford to counterbalance the huge political pressures from the Congress.

(1) When it comes to the evaluation of Unocal's assets, it was liable to make two mistakes. First, it was easy to overlook that Unocal's assets had different importance for different buyers. Just like a cup of water that has different marginal utilities for a person who lives beside a river and for one who is stranded in a desert, so were Unocal's assets to Chevron and CNOOC. This difference was in both quantitative and qualitative terms. The second mistake was to ignore Unocal's invisible assets. Specifically, for Chevron, Unocal's hydrocarbon resources might serve to add flowers to the brocade, helping Chevron to strengthen its reserve bases, but for CNOOC, Unocal's hydrocarbon resources amounted to offering fuel in snowy weather; they could not only bolster CNOOC's take-off strategy, but also could act as a springboard to internationalize its business. Moreover, CNOOC would gain considerable benefits from Unocal's invisible assets like managerial expertise, wide distribution networks, deep water operating techniques, part of which might be of value for Chevron too, but not so much as those to CNOOC. According to CNOOC's President Fu Chengyu, the invisible and visible assets of Unocal included at least the following:

- Unocal's oil and gas values far exceeded 20 Bd, according to CNOOC's conservative way.
- Unocal's actual recoverable hydrocarbon reserves, which reached 4.428 billion barrels of oil equivalent (BBOE), were much higher than 1.754 BBOE, the reserves registered at the New York Security Exchange.
- Accordingly, CNOOC would have profiteered should it have succeeded in the takeover. At that moment, the average price to purchase one barrel of reserve was 12–14 dollars in the international market, and 16 dollars in North America. If CNOOC acquired Unocal at a bid price of 19 Bd, the average price to purchase a barrel of reserve was only 10.8 dollars, if computed in light of the registered 1.754 billion barrels; but if calculated according to the actual reserves of 4.428 billion barrels, the average price was only 4.3 dollars.

- The actual price that CNOOC needed to pay would be even cheaper in view of 4.428 Bd cash flows in Unocal. Hence, CNOOC virtually just needs to spend around 15 Bd for the deal. Calculated in light of 1.754 BBOE, the average price was only 8.55 dollars per barrel, whereas it was as low as only 3.4 dollars per barrel in light of 4.428 BBOE.
- Unocal owned an integrated technical and managerial team which CNOOC was yearning for.
- Unocal's deep-sea E&P know-how would help CNOOC to be more sophisticated.
- Unocal owned 138 thousand square kilometers explorable acreages in the world.[52]

Therefore, CNOOC's 18.5 Bd bid for Unocal was cost-efficient. Suppose Chevron's offer—17 Bd was a benchmark, we might consider the excess 1.5 Bd as the price to afford Unocal's invisible assets and to surmount the political oppositions from the US Congress.

(2) It is hard to know exactly what CNOOC's judgment was about future oil prices, but as aforementioned, the average price to purchase a barrel of reserve was only 10.8 dollars, if computed in light of Unocal's registered 1.754 billion barrels and CNOOC's bid price of 19 Bd. Apparently, that price, even plus the E&P costs (7–8 dollars), was far below the then world oil price of over 50 dollars/b.[53] Although debates existed on the issue whether global oil supply could satisfy demand, but most energy experts at that time tended to believe that world oil supply would come to a peak in one of the years from 2005 to 2010, with the most likelihood being in 2003 or 2004.[54] In the long run, it was widely believed that world oil prices would stay at high levels unless any other type of energy

[52] The above points are based on: Liang Du and Zhiqiang Wang, "Liu wen Fu Chengyu – Younike shougou an fangsi" ("Six Questions to Fu Chengyu—Reflections on the Case of Unocal Acquisition"), Beijing: *Zhongguo Qiyejia* (*China Entrepreneur*), Vol. 17, 12 September 2005, http://www.cnemag.com.cn/magazine_view.asp?a_id=1456, accessed 6 September 2019.

[53] The average E&P costs can refer to footnote 39.

[54] *Zaobao*, "Global Oil Production Peaks, Oil Will Dry Up Soon?" Singapore, 1 July 2004, http://www.zaobao.com/special/newspapers/2004/07/nanyang010704.html, accessed 10 August 2005.

comparable to oil could be found.[55] Even if oil could be substituted, transition to non-oil era calls for 50 years, or at least 25 years.[56] Moreover, even if global oil supply and demand could reach an idealistic balance, world oil demand still risked being disrupted by unexpected natural disasters or political crisis in oil producing regions. Whichever happened, it would drive up global oil prices.

Gas prices and its future supply and consumption in China were vital components for CNOOC to take into account when deciding to join the competition. It was Unocal's rich gas assets that attracted CNOOC to join the bid, considering that the bid, should it have succeeded, would greatly facilitate the implementation of CNOOC's corporate strategy of expanding gas market in China. As to be discussed below, CNOOC envisaged that gas has a very sanguine prospect in China's future energy equation, but the supply–demand gap of natural gas is so huge that 100 billion square meters were predicted to be in shortage in supply by 2020.[57] Affected by world surging oil prices, natural gas becomes a new cosset and its prices also tend to ascend. Therefore, in the long run, both oil and gas prices would stay at high levels.

Second, regarding CNOOC's state ownership identity, it is too easy to equalize a NOC as the host government's subordinate who must absolutely follow the state's directives. After all, the historical memory from the command economy has left a shadow that the NOCs had no initiatives to forge ahead but just follow the line the government had set beforehand. Nevertheless, we need to raise a question mark for such an "innate" conception: Must a SOE be the arms of the state's policy? And should the state ownership constitute the very reason to reject CNOOC's takeover? In retrospect of the M&A cases happened in the US, it was noticeable that some state-owned energy companies from Europe and the Middle East had the records to successfully acquire oil/gas assets from American energy companies. One typical case was the takeover of more than ten thousand petroleum stations and some refinery plants of America by CIGO, a Venezuelan SOE.[58] Therefore, "if state-owned companies were

[55] It is worth noting that the shale revolution was not perceptible at that time.

[56] "Global oil production peaks, oil will dry up soon?" ibid.

[57] *Zhongguo Gongye Bao* (*China Industry News*), "Zhonghaiyou: haiwai shougou bao Guojia nengyuan anquan" ("CNOOC: Overseas Takeover Ensures National Energy Security"), 19 February 2004.

[58] Du Liang and Wang Zhiqiang, 2005, ibid.

banned from buying US assets, more than a few European, Latin and Asian companies would have to divest what they already own."[59]

As discussed in the first chapter, the SOEs in the market economy milieu are not necessarily the extension of state policies. To say the least, no company can divorce it from their host governments' support when going abroad. It is widely believed that one of the US' motivations to launch the Iraq war was for energy. And the fact that most American energy companies have got the oil and gas developing contracts in Iraq reconstruction seems to verify this. Herein the key to this M&A case lied in whether the Chinese government had rendered any specific support to reinforce CNOOC's bargaining power.

Third, regarding the financing problem, did the Chinese government provide CNOOC with preferential financial support to facilitate the deal? To answer the question, besides the will, it is necessary to consider CNOOC's capability to afford the deal.

Apparently CNOOC had no such a defraying capability. It bid for Unocal with an offer of US$18.5 billion in cash (US$67 per share), but it only had US$3 billion in cash available.[60] Suppose it used all the 3 billion cash for the deal, 15.5 billion would have had to rely on other channels, such as borrowing, issuing corporate bonds, selling corporate shares, government subsidies. Except government direct subsidies, whichever other means would have placed CNOOC in arrears, and the debt would have been "2.8 times of its earnings before interest, taxes, depreciation and amortization, a more highly leveraged position than other companies in the industry."[61] In view of this, S&P and Moody's, two world famous credit assessment institutions, placed CNOOC into the observation list, indicating that the possible acquisition might engender some negative impacts on its balance sheet.[62] These institutions seemed to hold some reservations about CNOOC's acquisition.

[59] *Wall Street Journal* (Eastern edition), "China's Oil Thirst," 24 June 2005, p.A.12.

[60] *Economist Intelligence Unit—Executive Briefing*, "China Energy: Mixed Motives Behind CNOOC's Bid," 27 June 2005.

[61] "China Energy: Mixed Motives Behind CNOOC's Bid," ibid.

[62] It received a credit level of "BBB +" and "A2" from the two institutions respectively in the end of 2004. See *Zhongguo Qiyejia* (*China Entrepreneur*), "Shougou Younike, Zhonghaiyou zai Fu Chengyu shidai de maoxian zhi lu" ("Acquiring Unocal, CNOOC's risky tour under the leadership of Fu Chengyu"), 22 July 2005.

As far as the specific capital sources for CNOOC's bidding were concerned, as shown in Chart 7.3, apart from its own US$3 billion and 3 billion bridge loans from Goldman Sachs and JP Morgan Chase & Co., the other 13 billion come from ICBC and CNOOC Corporation, its largest shareholder.[63] Some implications might be inferred from its financing sources. (1) In legal procedures it was unclear whether CNOOC got support from the government. According to the administrative regulations concerned in China, any project abroad exceeding 30 million dollars must get the NDRC's approval.[64] China was posing strict control over capital account. The acquisition calling for huge foreign currencies (13 billion) obviously entailed the approval of the Chinese foreign exchange administration bureau. Because the acquisition was not materialized at last, it was unclear whether the Chinese government would endorse CNOOC's action. (2) The involvement of Goldman Sachs and JP Morgan, two worldwide distinguished investing companies, showed that they held a positive outlook towards the deal, or they tended to believe the acquisition of Unocal could foster CNOOC's future growth.

(3) Majority of funds had to count on the state-backed SOEs. Regarding the funds from ICBC, it is necessary to take several factors into account. On the one hand, suppose the acquiring party was a Chinese private firm, the state-owned bank might not be so "generous" to provide such a huge loan. Such a large loan could hardly be proceeded without the government's approval. On the other hand, the bank itself has to find a foothold in the market, especially after foreign banks flow into China. Hence, the Chinese banks also vie for those clients of "good quality" to ensure their loans are safe and can make higher profits. CNOOC is undoubtedly such a first-grade client because of its substantial cash flows. Moreover, in terms of the specific terms of the loan, the amount reached US$6 billion with the market loan rate. Therefore, it is hard to conclude

[63] Bridge loans are "short-term funds that 'bridge' the gap between today's need for immediate cash to pay bills and the final closing of a pending investment deal or long-term financing package. Firm owners can go to banks for such a loan if they have a solid cash-flow position and the bank feels comfortable with the level of monthly sales as sufficient to support the loan for 60, 90 or 120 days. The bridge can also be provided by a factor, a firm that agrees to provide front-end cash on specific accounts receivable that meet certain credit requirements on the part of the payer." See David Newton, "Securing a Bridge Loan," *Entrepreneur*, 28 April 2003, http://www.entrepreneur.com/article/0,4621,308255,00.html, accessed 23 March 2019.

[64] Website of NDRC: www.sdrc.org.cn.

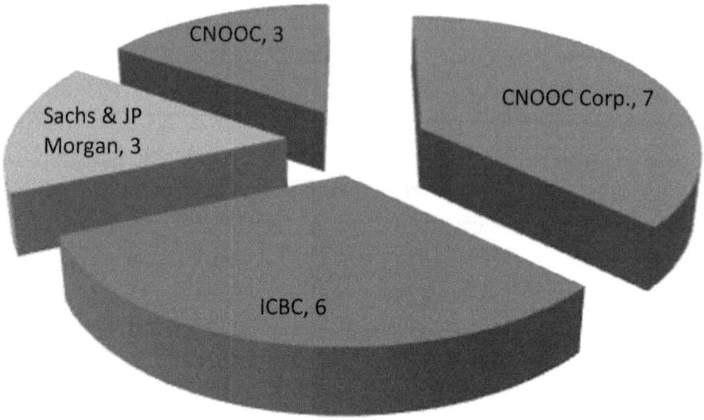

Chart 7.3 Composition of CNOOC's financing (*Source* Marshall W. Meyer, "Is CNOOCC's Bid for Unocal a threat to America?" knowledge at Wharton, 21 November 2005, https://knowledge.wharton.upenn.edu/article/is-cnoocs-bid-for-unocal-a-threat-to-america/)

that the Chinese bank loan to CNOOC was overwhelmingly politically motivated, but it was more of mixed motives, including ICBC's intention to improve its loan quality.

Another doubt is related with the CNOOC Corporation, which provided CNOOC with US$4.5 billion loan for 30 years with an interest rate of 3.5%, and 2.5 billion bridge loan with no interest rate liability. It was natural to relate to their relations: Is it a legally common practice that the parent corporate can finance its holding company with less or no interest than the concurrent loan interest rate from the bank? According to Nan Li, "it is legal and common, especially if the parent corporate has a higher credit rating than its holding company."[65] Hence, it was unjustifiable to rebuke CNOOC Corporate for the loan provisions.

To sum up, the "overbid" problem should not be exaggerated, and the state ownership identity was more of an excuse. After analyzing each part of the CNOOC's financing package, it seemed that the government tended to connive at CNOOC's action, which was attested to from the warning of the spokesman for the Chinese Foreign Ministry that the US

[65] E-mail correspondence with Nan Li, a doctor in financial economics from University of Chicago, 27 February 2006.

should stop politically intervening in the commercial deal. But all in all, the Chinese government appeared to take a "hands-off" policy towards the Unocal case, starkly contrast to its boldly diplomatic activities in other occasions like the above Russian oil pipeline case.

7.3.2 *Why a Hands-off Policy?*

Why did the Chinese government take a relatively "hands-off" approach in this deal? This was primarily because of its inclination to the EEP role. First, the Chinese government has picked up CNOOC as a litmus test since its setup in 1982, endorsing it to operate in line with western corporate governance. Thus, CNOOC has the least obligation among the NOCs to serve China's energy security. After years of cooperation with foreign firms, the company has become one of the enterprises deemed as the most Westernized.[66] The Chinese leadership is full aware that sooner or later, the Chinese companies need to venture abroad by themselves and acquiring Unocal was a precious opportunity for CNOOC to gain M&A experience. As Andrews-Speed said, "China's energy strategy is to make its oil companies into major players globally. But to accomplish that, they may have to show that the companies are not in fact following a government strategy."[67] Second, the Chinese leadership might have believed that the US was a free market where business was business and the one who bid higher would win the deal.

Third, as the US strongly opposes China's oil diplomacy with those countries hostile to America, the Chinese government might treat CNOOC as a touchstone to observe the response of the US on the sensitive energy security issue. "If U.S. or free-world energy assets are off-limits, China will be only too happy to cut deals with the world's pariah states."[68] But if the bid was rejected at the excuse of national security, "China could be motivated to build more ties to rogue states and step up its courtship of major oil producers in Africa and Latin America."[69] Moreover, the Chinese government tended to accept CNOOC's view that

[66] *Wall Street Journal*, "China's Oil Thirst," 24 June 2005, ibid.

[67] Joseph Kahn, "A Deft Balance in Orchestrating China's Oil Offer," *New York Times*, 7 July 2005.

[68] *Wall Street Journal*, "China's Oil Thirst," 24 June 2005, ibid.

[69] Joseph Kahn, "China's Costly Quest for Energy Control," *New York Times*, 27 June 2005.

M&A is a fast and convenient way to build muscles for the NOCs. In order to forge some Chinese MOCs that can act as China's flagships to jostle in the globe, the government encourages the Chinese firms to "go out" in order to "acquire technology, expand their markets and emulate Western multinationals."[70]

The substantial foreign reserves have laid a solid basis for the Chinese government's inclination to an EEP role. As of the end of 2005, Chinese foreign exchange reserves climbed up to 818.9 Bd.[71] Such a huge reserve risk being evaporated should the US dollar depreciate, so China had to find other channels to spend the money.

7.3.3 CNOOC's Bid: Commercially Driven?

CNOOC's economic considerations outweighed its political concerns in its efforts to acquire Unocal. Politically, the success of the acquisition would be a trophy for the CNOOC management, which was a building stock for further promotion. Moreover, this acquisition coincided with the state's strategies of fostering some SOEs that can compete globally, and securing more energy supplies for the sake of energy security.[72] However, economic concerns seemed to overtake political ones in this case. Apart from the managerial and technological benefits, my argument is based on the following:

First, the acquisition over Unocal can help CNOOC to shake off resource constraint, thus helping fulfill its strategic objective to "build an integrated energy company with international competitiveness and modern management system by 2008."[73] To that end, it has taken the developing natural gas market in China as a key strategy for its sustained development. Thus far, CNOOC has been undertaking the LNG projects in Guangdong, Fujian, Zhejiang, and Shanghai. It also signed cooperative agreements on LNG projects with Hainan, Qinhuandao of Hebei

[70] Joseph Kahn, 7 July 2005, ibid.

[71] People's Bank of China, accessed 26 February 2006. http://www.pbc.gov.cn/diaochatongji/tongjishuju/gofile.asp?file=2005S6.htm, accessed 5 August 2012.

[72] *Economist Intelligence Unit—Executive Briefing*, "China Energy: Mix Motives behind CNOOC's Bid," 27 June 2005.

[73] See its webpage: http://www.cnooc.com.cn/defaulten.asp, accessed on 5 August 2012.

province, and Wenzhou of Zhejiang province. CNOOC's zest in developing China's gas market is largely based on its perception that boosting gas consumption not only complies with the government's policies of improving the environment and reducing coal and oil dependence, but also can avoid price fluctuations as compared with oil. At that time, natural gas oddly only accounted for 2.5% in China's energy consumption, much lower than 20% in developed countries.[74]

That Unocal's assets could be a useful complement to CNOOC was the principal reason why it courted Unocal. Specifically, it favored Unocal's rich hydrocarbon resources in Asia. Among the 1.75 billion barrels of proven oil and gas reserves possessed by Unocal, 70% was located outside America, particularly 56% (among which 73% composed by gas and 27% by oil) was in Asia, such as Indonesia, Thailand, Myanmar, Bangladesh, Vietnam, Azerbaijan, and Caspian countries.[75] If CNOOC had succeeded to acquire Unocal, its output would have been doubled.

Second, the geographic distribution of Unocal's assets catered to CNOOC's natural gas strategy in China very well since Unocal's rich gas in Southeast Asia could be an ideal source for the Chinese market. However, that did not mean that it would only serve Chinese market. Currently CNOOC sells crude oil in the domestic market at the international prices. Hence, in an integrated global market where countries face the same prices, there is no strong impetus for CNOOC to ship the oil produced abroad back home in the peaceful time, unless selling the oil is profitable. In the war time, it risks being intercepted by foreign forces. Virtually most oil produced by CNOOC in foreign countries has been sold through the Singapore oil hub. To say the least, it is a natural propensity for any company to hunt for a market where their goods could be sold at a higher price. Since it takes time and money to develop a new market and CNOOC has gained a foothold in China's coastal gas market, it is blameless for it to take such a strategy that gas resources in Southeast Asia could be linked with its distribution networks in China. This is particularly the case considering that many MOCs are scrambling to go

[74] This paragraph is based on: *Jingji Ribao* (*Economic Daily Online*), "Shiyou san jutou shuo you dao qi" ("The Three Oil Giants Talking About Oil and Gas"), 19 May 2005, http://www.cnooc.com.cn/, accessed 5 August 2012.

[75] Figures are based on: "China Energy: Mix Motives Behind CNOOC's Bid," ibid; and David Barboza and Andrew Ross Sorkin, "Chinese Oil Giant in Takeover Bid for U.S. Corporation," *New York Times*, 23 June 2005.

after the Chinese energy market, and for natural gas, it calls for large-scale facilities before it can be widely used.

Third, CNOOC also made efforts to dismiss the misgivings of the US congressmen that the US national and energy security would be jeopardized. It promised that Unocal's North American assets would be sold back to the US market.[76] As to the second assertion, both Unocal spokesman and some American geophysicists denied such a possibility that Unocal's seismic technologies would be taken away by CNOOC,[77] and the latter also agreed to divest such sensitive technologies that might be utilized for military purpose if the US thought it necessary.

Therefore, in the process of pursuing for a takeover of Unocal, CNOOC was first and foremost driven by its own commercial interests and acted as a market actor. The Chinese government primarily worked as an EEP notwithstanding its connivance at or some implicit support for the NOC's bold acquisition, but its acquiesce was more related with its regulation.

7.4 Conclusion

The oil and gas hunger has compelled China to rely more on the world energy market, but Beijing regards it as an unfair arena for latecomers. Driven by such a perception and its strategic concerns regarding energy security, development strategy, social stability, and foreign policy, the Chinese government encourages Chinese companies to go out actively, and decides to wield state power to shore up the NOCs' quest for oil and gas abroad, when necessary. Taking advantage of the state's growing concern over energy security, the NOCs have striven to expand businesses abroad in order to catch up and sustain their long-term development. Hence, their common interest has brought about China's vigorous foreign energy quest. Again, the NOC's commercial interests in acquiring oil producing rights and the state's cost-effective and risk-minimizing thinking have contributed to shaping China's preference of gaining direct control over oil and gas assets.

[76] Amounted to 33% of its global output and 26% of its proved reserves. "China Energy: Mix Motives behind CNOOC's Bid," ibid.

[77] Robert Collier, "Backlash to Chinese Bid for Unocal," *The San Francisco Chronicle*, 24 June 2005.

China takes a SMMA in its foreign energy quest. On the one hand, some Chinese firms' all-out efforts to venture abroad have been endorsed by the Chinese government. Sometimes Beijing forcefully bolsters up them to go out with policy and even financial support in the hope that they could be forged as Chinese flagship firms able to emulate MOCs while helping to ensure China's energy security. Other than CNPC, Sinopec and CNOOC, Sinochem, the Chinese Aviation Oil Corp. Ltd, and China International Trust & Investment Corp. are also new active players embarking upon oil and gas deals in foreign markets. In addition, according to Xu Dingming, director of Energy Bureau of NDRC, the government encourages domestic private firms to expand overseas oil market with various kinds of policy support.[78] To shore up the Chinese firms' go out, Beijing even partially opened domestic market to the MOCs in exchange for their support.

On the other hand, the state requires the NOCs to submit to the center's foreign policies. In the early stage when China embarked on oil diplomacy, it even made special regional arrangement for the three NOCs to expand businesses overseas. CNPC mainly focused on Russia, Central Asia, Africa, and North and South America. Sinopec zeroed in on the Middle East and CNOOC concentrated on Southeast Asia and Australia. In order to reduce competition among the NOCs and enhance Chinese firms' success in overseas oil bidding, the government tries to promote their co-biding efforts.

In principle, the central government endorses the NOCs' actions to secure oil concessions, or at least gives implicit support, but the way in which and the extent to which the state involves in different situations are distinct. Letting the NOCs go unfettered, on and off the CCP leadership directly participates in facilitating energy deals with foreign parties. In the first case, in order to win the Russian pipeline, the Chinese government has taken a variety of measures such as summit meeting, diplomatic promoting, economic package, and financial aid; Whereas in the CNOOC bidding for Unocal case, the government seemed to take a hands-off policy, just giving the bridle to CNOOC to contend for the deal, though it was suspected to have helped bankroll the attempted acquisition.

[78] *Diyi Caijing ribao* (*First Finance Daily*), "Guojia guli minqi haiwai youyuan kaicai, zijin he zhengce cheng zhang'ai" ("The State Encourage Private Firms to Exploit Oversees Oil, Capital and Policy Be the Obstacles", 14 December 2004. http://www.china.org.cn/chinese/jingji/728087.htm, accessed 5 August 2015.

Why did the state present two contrasting attitudes and played different roles in the three different cases? This was mainly because the government had different concerns when facing different situations. Though the Chinese government tries to balance its strategic concerns and economic considerations, as most other governments do, once the two can hardly be synergized, it has to compromise one over the other. In the Sino-Russia oil pipeline case, initially, acting as economic efficiency promoter, the Chinese government was indifferent to the Russian proposal due to the then low oil prices, its low reliance on foreign oil imports and the economic infeasibility, and thus negotiations mainly remained in the corporate level. With growing reliance on foreign oil, rising oil prices, and Tokyo's involvement, political concern eventually gained weight in the Chinese government agenda. Beijing came to realize the importance of the Russian oil pipeline with respect to diversifying oil sources, strengthening bilateral relations, and reinvigorating the aging Daqing oilfield. Thus, the government spared no efforts to act as an internal stabilizer to help CNPC contest for the pipeline.

In the Sino-Kazakhstan pipeline case, the roles of the Chinese government and NOCs and their considerations changed in different stages. In the first stage, CNPC acted as a SPSOU, trying to outcompete other competitors through overbid. The Chinese government-backed CNPC's move as building the Sino-Kazakhstan pipeline was considered conducive not only to enhancing China's energy security, but also to promoting peace and development in Xinjiang. In the second stage, the proposed pipeline was shelved as the Chinese government and CNPC changed their roles to Economic Efficiency Promoter and market actor respectively. This change was largely due to the reshuffling of the state council and the sagging oil prices, which had made the project economically unviable. In the third stage after 2003, thanks to the geopolitical situation in Xinjiang, China's irreversible dependence on foreign oil imports, and the logjam of the Sino-Russia pipeline, Beijing's preference tilted towards the role of internal stabilizer while CNPC readjusted its preference as a market actor. In the whole process, changes of the international oil prices had a significant impact.

In the CNOOC bidding for Unocal case, economic concern outweighed political concern. The Chinese government expected that the takeover of Unocal would transform CNOOC thoroughly, namely, from an inward-looking enterprise whose business overwhelmingly concentrated on the Chinese market to an outward-looking multinational that could emulate with the MOCs in the international market. To that end, Beijing acted as an EEP and restrained itself from direct involvement. The hands-off policy might be out of its perception that any public intervention resorting to state power might be counterproductive. Of course, other reasons include the institutional settings (the competition took place in America which has the acquisition law against foreign government involvement); competition structure (Besides haggling with Russia, China faced strong competition from Japan); timing (oil price hiking vs. price flat time, and low vs. high foreign oil dependence), and even national leadership's ideology (liberals vs. realists), and so forth.

The Chinese NOCs have primarily driven by their commercial interests though they are endorsed by the government to secure more oil and gas equities. Hence, the NOCs sometimes have conflicting interests in their "going out" process. This can be illustrated in the first case where both Sinopec and CNPC scrambled for a Russian oil pipeline to their own refineries. At last, the central government adopted CNPC's proposal, though economically it was more expensive, based on the considerations that Sinopec's scheme via a third country faced the risk against oil supply security, and that CNPC's plan could avoid that problem and help dispel the possible instability stemming from large unemployment.

In the process of their foreign oil quest, the NOCs, however, do not merely acted as market actors. When they envisage fierce competition from others, they may shift their role to SPSOU, striving hard even irrespective of economic costs. CNPC's contest for a pipeline from Russia with Japanese firms typifies such examples.

The Chinese companies seem to have left outsiders an image of getting all ammunition ready and just waiting to be shot, but ironically, the government lacks a systematic strategy in this regard. Its policies and regulations concerned often are not well coordinated. For instance, thus far the government has maintained strict control over foreign exchange uses; and any Chinese firms' large investments and M&A in overseas markets must go through the Chinese bureaucracies' stretched examination and approval, thereby leading to the likely loss of the best investing opportunities.[79]

[79] *Zhongguo Binggou Jiaoyi wang* (*Mergers-China*), "Dangdai Kuaguo binggou langchao yu Zhongguo qiye 'zouchuqu'" ("Contemporary Transnational M&A wave and Chinese firms' 'go out'"), 27 December 2005, http://www.mergers-china.com/guwen/zjzxdetail.asp?id=1811, accessed 5 August 2015.

CHAPTER 8

Is China's Approach Distinctive?—Comparative Analysis with the US and India

China has been thrust into the world spotlight thanks to its surging appetite and growing reliance on foreign energy resources. In 2021, China's imports of crude oil and natural gas hit 513 Mt and 168 Bcm, accounting for 72.05 percent and 45 percent of China's oil and natural gas consumption respectively.[1] Moreover, after turning into a net importer of coal since 2009, China purchased 323 Mt, or around 5 percent of coal demands from abroad in 2013.[2] It is a wide consensus that emerging economies, particularly China and India have become a pivotal force contributing to a lion's share of world energy demand growth.[3] More worrisome, China's surging demand seems unbridled thanks to the undergoing industrialization and urbanization. Will China follow the "standard international rules" to deal with its energy challenge? Is there any distinctiveness of China's approach to energy security?

[1] China's National Bureau of Statistics & General Administration of Customs

[2] Data based on *Zhonghua Gongshang Shibao* (China Business Times), "Mei you qi duiwai yicundu gaoqi, qunian meitan jinkouliang chuang xin gao" (Dependence on foreign coal, oil and gas heightened, import of coal broke new record last year), 24 Jan. 2014, http://energy.people.com.cn/n/2014/0124/c71890-24212885.html, accessed 26 April 2023.

[3] See, for example, *BP*, "BP Energy Outlook 2030," January 2013; OECD & IEA, "OECD Green Growth Studies: Energy," 2011. http://www.oecd.org/greengrowth/greening-energy/49157219.pdf, accessed 26 April 2023.

S. Chen, *China's Approach to Energy Security*,
https://doi.org/10.1007/978-981-99-3573-4_8

There are a lot of discussions focusing on the issue whether China's approach would destabilize the international energy market or pose a threat to energy security of other countries and regions with the US in particular. Yet relatively few research has been conducted to analyze the distinctiveness of China's approach to energy security. Apparently one's standpoint to the first issue largely depends on their answer to the second one.

To answer the question with regard to the distinctiveness of China's SMMA, two points merit attention. First, in view that there are no such "standard international rules" applicable to every country in the world,[4] a frame of reference matters in order to pinpoint the peculiarities of China's approach. As Vaclav Smil argues, "There is no global energy solution, only local ones," and "what we produce and use depends on where we are."[5] Nevertheless, we may still be able to make some comparison in light of the nature of their approaches to energy security adopted by different countries. Under such circumstances, selection of a measuring stick may hold sway on the conclusion. Other than different cultures, traditions, international status, and political, economic, and social systems, countries are at different development stages and with varying energy endowments and demands. What we can do is to choose some sub-optimal references. The US has been chosen considering that the US has often been drawn upon as a "model" or a "benchmark" of free market economy that other countries should "duplicate," including the way of running the energy sector. India is selected largely because both China and India are the two largest developing countries with large energy consumption, similar energy supply and demand situations and close population size, and both countries are regarded as two emerging economies that have an influential impact on the international energy markets and on the global economy as a whole.[6]

[4] World Energy Council, "Global Energy Issues," Speech by Chairmen of the e8, Evian, France, May 30 and 31, 2006.

[5] *Wall Street Journal*, "There Is No Global Energy Solution, Only Local Ones: Noted Scholar Vaclav Smil Says What We Produce and Use Depends on Where We Are," 8 April 2014.

[6] Daniel Yergin, "Innovation, diversification, cooperation vital to energy security," *The Asahi Shimbun AJW (Asia and Japan Watch)*, 12 August 2012, http://ajw.asahi.com/article/globe/economy/AJ201208120013, accessed 22 August 2014.

Second, rather than staying static, China's SMMA per se is evolving. Unlike most developed economies whose approach to energy security remains relatively stable, China is witnessing more drastic change of annual energy supply and demand and Beijing is in the midst of learning and pushing forward domestic reforms.

Is China's SMMA distinct from others? If so, in what sense is it special? Debates arise primarily centering on the following issues: Do China's perception of energy security under the SMMA differ from that of the US and India? Are China's measures of ensuring energy security distinct from the US and India? Who are the major players serving energy security in the three countries? Do their behaviors differ from each other? And is the role that the Chinese government has played in ensuring energy security distinct from that of the American and Indian counterpart? The following will conduct comparative analyses centering on the above questions.

8.1 Perceptions of Energy Security in China, US, and India

Different countries have different understanding about energy security.[7] As analyzed in Chapter 3, ensuring a sufficient supply of oil has constantly prevailed in China's perception of energy security although in recent years more weight has been given to improving energy use efficiency and environmental protection. However, in the eyes of Beijing, energy insecurity would still primarily originate from oil supply disruption and oil price hikes. Based on such perceptions, understandably China seems to make every effort to place more oil concessions under its control. Is China's emphasis on the supply side of energy security different from the US or India?

In the case of the US, its oil production peaked in 1970 and continued to fall since then while domestic oil consumption continued to rise. As a result, its import ratio continued to increase till a peak in 2005. With a growing reliance on foreign oil imports, the current situation in China is quite similar to the US between 1970 and 2005. How did Washington define energy security at that time? There are several features of its perception. First, the US has pinpointed oil supply security as the

[7] Sascha Müller-Kraenner, *Energy Security*, London: Routledge, 2008, chapter 2.

key. Second, energy security is a crucial component of preserving American national security and its superpower status. Third, the US pursuit of energy security has been blanketed with an ideological tint, namely promoting democracy or at least not to harm such a value. According to Joseph Romm, the core of the energy security problem in the US is primarily a problem of oil, and energy security is an important component of national security.[8] Conceivably the oil crisis in the 1970s has a profound impact on perceptions of energy security in the US. Thus a prevalent view of energy security is the ability to accommodate disruptions of supply in energy markets.[9] Such disruptions may stem from geopolitical, military, or civil developments and may not be able to be offset in the near term. According to *Transatlantic Trends 2007*, an annual opinion survey comparing American and European attitudes on transatlantic relations, 88 percent of Americans and 78 percent of Europeans in 2007 considered energy dependence to be a threat that was likely to affect their personal life. To avoid disruption of energy supply, the shortcut is to reduce US reliance on foreign energy imports, a philosophy embodied in the strategy of energy independence which was formulated by then President Richard Nixon in response to OPEC's oil embargo. The plan aimed to reduce the US imports of oil and other forms of energy from other countries. Since then, each successive administration of the US espoused energy independence as a national objective although some officials may have their reservations. Revolving around that goal, policymakers in Washington tend to define energy security as having the flexibility to choose not to import oil from unstable and or unfriendly countries and regions.[10] Former Secretary of Energy Spencer Abraham

[8] Joseph Romm, Defining National Security: The Nonmilitary Aspects. Washington: Council on Foreign Relations, 1993.

[9] See, for example, Lutz Kilian, "The Economic Effects of Energy Price Shocks," *Journal of Economic Literature,* Vol. 46, No. 4, December 2008, pp. 871–909; Michael Toman, "The Economics of Energy Security: Theory, Evidence, Policy," in A.V. Kneese and J.L. Sweeney, eds., *Handbook of Natural Resource and Energy Economics*, Vol. 3, Amsterdam: Elsevier B.V./North Holland, 1993; and World Economic Forum, "The New Energy Security Paradigm," *Energy Vision Update*, Spring 2006.

[10] Congress of the United States, Congressional Budget Office, "Energy Security in the United States," a Congressional Budget Office (CBO) report, May 2012.

underscored the importance of increasing domestic energy production and energy use efficiency within America.[11]

In many aspects pertinent to energy, India is very akin to China. Having very poor energy resources, India is the fourth largest primary energy consumer, after China, USA, and Russia, and it is projected that India's energy demand would grow by three to four times within next two decades, thus turning India into the third largest energy consumer by the year 2020.[12] With 44 percent in 2020, coal remains the predominant form of primary energy use in India, followed by oil (25%), traditional biomass (13%), and natural gas (6%).[13] Moreover, having no access to electricity, a large chunk of population needs to rely on firewood for their living in India. With a growing dependence on imports of oil, India has also turned into an importer of coal. Like China, its imports of oil mainly come from the Middle East. How has India perceived energy security? Former Prime Minister Manmohan Singh described India's energy security as a serious problem, second only to food security.[14] The petroleum and natural gas minister, Dharmendra Pradhan reiterated the goal of making India self-sufficient in energy resources.[15] According to the Integrated Energy Policy of India, "We are energy secure when we can supply lifeline energy to all our citizens irrespective of their ability to pay for it as well as meet their effective demand for safe and convenient energy to satisfy their various needs at competitive prices, at all times and with a prescribed confidence level considering shocks and disruptions that can be reasonably expected."[16] India's Prime Minister Narendra Modi upholds a banner of justice, saying that "India's Energy Plan aims to ensure energy

[11] David Myszewski, "News: Stanford Scholars Host Energy Conference," *The Stanford Review*, Vol. XXVII, Iss. 2, 24 Oct. 2001.

[12] ANI, "India pursuing all options to achieve energy security: Manmohan Singh," 3 December 2013. http://www.dnaindia.com/india/report-india-pursuing-all-options-to-achieve-energy-security-manmohan-singh-1928968, accessed 22 June 2014.

[13] IEA, *India Energy Outlook 2021: World Energy Outlook Special Report*, IEA, Paris, 2021, https://www.iea.org/reports/india-energy-outlook-2021, accessed 31 December 2022.

[14] Jiali Ma, "China, India stoke energy bond," *China Daily*, 2 Feb. 2010.

[15] EIA, "Country Analysis—India," updated 26 June 2014.

[16] Deloitte, "Energy Access for the Poor," Background paper of India Energy Congress 2013, "Securing tomorrow's energy today: Policy & Regulations", New Delhi, 7-8 February 2013, http://www.indiaenergycongress.in/iec/Energy%20access%20for%20the%20poor%20-%20020213.pdf, accessed 22 June 2014.

justice. We plan to achieve 'One Nation One Gas Grid' & shift towards gas-based economy. A self-reliant India will be a force multiplier for the global economy and energy security is at the core of these efforts."[17] Therefore, currently India is pursuing four major policy objectives: energy access, energy security, energy justice and mitigation of climate change, and energy security takes a central position in Indian government policy making.

From the above analysis, China, India, and the US at least have the following commonalities in perceiving energy security. (a) In general, their perceptions of energy security have been evolving over time. (b) In their eyes, oil security has remained the core of energy security. (c) The supply-side view that emphasizes sufficient energy supply seems predominant in their perceptions. The three big powers have attached great importance to disruptions of energy supply thanks to the adverse impact on national security and economic development. Hence, ensuring sufficient energy supply is a top priority for them. (d) They are very much concerned about energy price changes and affordability of households and enterprises.

In the meantime, there are some explicit or implicit distinctions among their perceptions. First, compared with China and America, reducing energy poverty is a key component of India's energy security concern. Thus far more than 300 million Indian people get no access to electricity and over 800 million only have limited electrical access, and thanks to energy poverty, 300,000–400,000 deaths occur each year resulting from burning traditional wood and animal waste indoors for cooking and heating.[18] Thus the Indian government has to redouble its efforts to tackle this issue.

Second, the US tends to highlight the percussions of oil supply disruption on its national security and military operations largely due to its status as the world hegemon and its widespread military bases across the globe. The heightened sense of vulnerability as a consequence of the

[17] "India's energy plan aims to ensure energy justice: PM Modi," Modi's speech at the Fourth edition of India Energy Forum CERA Week, 26 October 2020, https://www.narendramodi.in/prime-minister-narendra-modis-address-at-the-inauguration-of-india-energy-forum-552078, 8 December 2022.

[18] Kristopher Settle, "India Combats Energy Poverty through Natural Resources," *Energy Biz*, 08 Aug. 2013. http://www.energybiz.com/article/13/08/india-combats-energy-poverty-through-natural-resources, accessed 22 June 2014.

9.11 terrorist attack in 2001 has made many Americans quite apprehensive about their growing reliance on oil imports from the Middle East. According to Rasmussen Reports, a majority of Americans believe that "money spent on Middle Eastern oil eventually finds its way to funding terrorist activities".[19] This shift in mindset has led the US to place more emphasis on "security" and "independence" rather than "conservation" or "reliability".[20]

Third, in China's perception, more weight has been placed on the demand side, paying more attention to the externalities of energy development and utilization. Hence, Beijing underscores the importance of balancing economic growth, environmental protection, and energy conservation. Of course, apparently there remains a gap between central decrees and local implementation in practice. In contrast, as to be elaborated in the following, New Delhi and Washington seem to lay less emphasis on the demand-side ramifications. The reasons behind that may encompass: Above all, this pertains to the role of the state. Widely known is a Chinese strong state playing a very active role in intervening in the economy and energy conservation, less so in India and a small state in the US Related with the above, the second reason is that in the US, it is primarily the business and households that have played a crucial role in energy conservation although the American government may contribute to that. In response to the Arab oil boycott in 1973, energy use efficiency had been considerably improved as a result of American consumers changing their habits and government requirements for more fuel-efficient vehicles, but such efforts came to an end with oil price plunge during the last two decades of last century.[21] A third and perhaps more important reason is that China's energy use inefficiency is rather low compared with India, let alone developed countries. Also, environmental pollution is so severe to the extent that it may undermine social stability in China. India has been plagued by severe environmental pollutions too,

[19] *Rasmussen Reports*, "71% Say Finding New Energy Sources More Important than Conservation," 2006.

[20] Michael E. Webber, "Chapter 8- The USA: The Key Global Driver," in Andreas Wenger, Robert W. Orttung & Jeronim Perovic (eds.), *Energy and the Transformation of International Relations: Toward a New Producer-Consumer Framework*, New York: Oxford University Press, 2009, p. 224.

[21] Michael E. Webber, 2009, ibid, p. 224.

but India's top priority is to cope with the more grave challenges of meeting surging energy demand and promoting economic growth.

8.2 Measures of Ensuring Energy Security

To different extent, the three big powers have eventually leaned to take the most common measures of enhancing energy security, including stockpiling, technological innovation, improving energy conservation and energy efficiency, diversification of energy consumption mix, acquiring more equity oil, cultivating a close relationship with energy exporting countries, and so on. In the meantime, the measures they have taken have different priorities and features.

8.2.1 Similarities

To a large extent, the measures that China has implemented to enhance its energy security resemble those of India and the US although the effectiveness of implementing these measures varies in different countries. In fact, their similarities intertwine with distinctions, and in most cases the similarities are the resultant symptoms caused by different factors in the three countries.

On the supply side, corresponding to their perceptions, the three big powers have attached more importance to ensure sufficient energy provisions. First of all, prominent in their measures is their embrace of Winston Churchill's maxim that "Safety and certainty in oil lie in variety, and variety alone." Diversification has thus become an overarching guiding principle in their pursuit of energy security. Externally, all the three big powers stress the importance of diversifying sources of imports and strive hard to reduce their dependence on oil imports from the Middle East. While the "shale revolution" has helped the US to curtail its oil dependence on the Persian Gulf, Washington has also capitalized on its global powerhouse to serve its energy interests. Without such leverage, both China and India are proactive in securing more overseas hydrocarbon assets so as to hedge against high oil crisis and ensure energy supply security. India's former petroleum minister Murli Deora said, "Acquisition of exploration and oil producing properties overseas is a key strategy to reduce our dependence on world's oil reserves".[22] Hence, Indian oil companies have made their presence in places as far apart as the Middle East, Africa, Australia, Russia, Central Asia, and Latin America.[23] Internally, they are making efforts to diversify different types of energy resources. Interestingly, despite the strident percussions brought about by Fukushima Daiichi nuclear disaster in 2011, both China and India continued to map up ambitious plans of expanding the use of nuclear power. Meanwhile, distinctions centering on this principle are also straightforward. Due to their different energy consumption structures and production capacities, what China and India have tried to diversify is mainly to reduce their over-reliance on "dirty" coal and oil whereas the US has primarily targeted oil. As a result of their efforts, China and India have diversified the sources of oil imports, but the trend of their growing dependence on oil imports from the Middle East tends to be irreversible; In contrast, the US has successfully reduced its reliance on the Persian Gulf. Furthermore, its dependence on imported oil has also witnessed a decline since peaking in 2005 thanks to its declined consumption and shifts in supply patterns.[24]

Second, the three countries have resorted to strategic petroleum reserves to prevent oil supply disruption and curb oil price volatilities. The US begun to stockpile oil for its strategic petroleum reserve after the first oil embargo in the early 1970s while both China and India have not started their SPR until 2004 and 2005 respectively. Conceivably the US has been much more seasoned in operating SPR while the two largest developing countries are still in the midst of building their oil stockpiles.

[22] Rakteen Kaktiya, "ONGC, Oil India ordered to buy 'big' assets overseas," *Bloomberg*, 18 Mar. 2010.

[23] But it was said that China is more successful than India in oil investment abroad for a number of reasons, such as more consolidated central energy authority, more support from the central government and state-own banks, and more effective diplomatic efforts. See Hong Zhao, "China and India: The Energy Policies," *EAI* (East Asian Institute, Singapore) *Background Brief*, No. 462, 2 July 2009.

[24] The dependency rate (net imports to total consumption) was around 40% in 2012. Oil consumption declined mainly due to the economic downturn, energy efficiency improvement, changes in consumer behavior, and patterns of economic growth. Shifts in supply patterns of oil was a result of the growing use of biofuels and shale revolution. See, Energy Information Administration, "How dependent are we on foreign oil?" 10 May 2013, http://www.eia.gov/energy_in_brief/article/foreign_oil_dependence.cfm, accessed 18 July 2014.

Third, in order to reduce their reliance on fossil fuels, the three big powers are making great efforts to promote other types of energy resources. They are taking the lead in developing renewable energy. For instance, China, the US, and India are the top, second, and fourth largest wind markets with a cumulative wind power capacity of 288,320 GW, 121,985GW, and 38,625GW as of 2020, respectively.[25] India has singled out nuclear power, hydro and solar power for its pick-up energy that goes along with government support; the US has accentuated the development of bio fuels, nuclear, solar, and wind power, while China prioritized nuclear, hydro, solar, and wind power. In the case of India, it plans to install another ten new reactors, expecting to expand its nuclear power generation capacity to 22,480 MW by 2031.[26] Starting from the 1990s, India has significantly increased wind power. India's installed wind capacity rose from 13.2 GW in 2010 to 49.7 GW in 2020, expecting to further hit 119 GW by 2030.[27] To fulfill their goals, all the three countries have provided a set of financial incentives and policy support for renewable sources of energy.[28]

On the demand side, one front is concerned about energy use efficiency, in which they all have witnessed various degrees of improvement in the past decades. While they all have benefited from technical progress, the driving forces behind their progress have some variances. In India, this is mainly because the Indian economy is largely based on the service industry; in the US this is contributed by technical innovation in private businesses, while China's progress in that regard was mainly brought about by industrial restructuring, particularly large-scale privatization of SOEs in the early 2000s. Nonetheless, energy efficiency in both China and India remains low in the world, and it is also relatively low in the

[25] US Department of Energy, *Wind Market Reports: 2021 Edition*, https://www.energy.gov/eere/wind/wind-market-reports-2021-edition, accessed 12 January 2023.

[26] Umesh Ellichipuram, "India to build nuclear plants to increase generation capacity," Power Technology, 30 July 2021, https://www.power-technology.com/news/india-nuclear-power/, accessed 13 January 2023.

[27] IEA,"Installed capacity in India, 2000-2020, and projections up to 2040 in the Stated Policies Scenario," 26 October 2022, https://www.iea.org/data-and-statistics/charts/installed-capacity-in-india-2000-2020-and-projections-up-to-2040-in-the-stated-policies-scenario, accessed 13 January 2023.

[28] For some of the specific supportive schemes, see, for example, WindPowerIndia: www.windpowerindia.com; US Environmental Protection Agency: http://www.epa.gov/statelocalclimate/state/topics/renewable.html, accessed 13 January 2023.

US compared with other developed countries. It was said that up to 75 percent of the electricity used in the US would be saved if the US could take proper measures.[29]

Energy inefficiency also results from the subsidy practices in the three countries. They have not only utilized subsidies to tap into their own unconventional oil and gas resources and renewable energy, but also consistently provided more subsidies to fossil fuels, although they did it in different ways and are considering reforming such measures. It is widely recognized that energy subsidies distort the market, encourage inefficiencies and contribute to the production of green gas emissions. Nonetheless, many countries including China, India, and the US remain dogged in providing energy subsidies. According to IMF, worldwide fossil fuel subsidies were US$5.9 trillion or 6.8 percent in 2020; this figure is expected to rise to 7.4 percent of GDP in 2025.[30] Among the net importers of energy resources in the world, India provided the largest amount ($21 billion) of subsidies to fossil fuels in 2009, while China ranked the fifth with around $19 billion.[31] In the case of the US, it has provided $4 billion in annual subsidies and tax breaks for the oil companies.[32] Other energy producers and purchasers also enjoy financial support in the form of tax incentives, direct spending, research and development funds, and other support mechanisms.[33] During 2002–2008, subsidies to fossil fuels hit $72 billion in the US, while those to renewable energy were only $29 billion; moreover, most forms of subsidies to fossil fuels have been written into the taxation law as permanent provisions,

[29] National Audubon Society, "Curbing Global Warming: Fact Sheets," http://policy.audubon.org/sites/default/files/documents/curbingglobalwarming.pdf, accessed 30 August 2014.

[30] International Monetary Fund, "Fossil Fuel Subsidies," https://www.imf.org/en/Topics/climate-change/energy-subsidies, accessed 13 January 2023.

[31] Qi An, "Guoji huashi ranliao butie xianzhuang pingshu" (Review of the status quo of international subsidies to fossil fuels), *Zhongguo Nengyuan* (China Energy), No. 4, June 2012.

[32] Jason Raznick, "Should The Government Really End Oil Subsidies?" *Forbes*, 1 Feb. 2011. http://www.forbes.com/sites/benzingainsights/2011/02/01/should-the-government-really-end-oil-subsidies/, accessed 25 August 2014.

[33] For detailed analysis, see Texas Comptroller of Public Accounts, *The Energy Report*, 6 May 2008, chapter 28.

which is in stark contrast with subsidies to renewable energy that would be phased out after some time.[34]

With on average 1.4 percent of GDP since the financial year (FY) 2008, fuel subsidies have become a massive financial burden for India. In the financial year 2012–2013, 1.75 percent of GDP, or INR 1000 billion (USD 16 billion) were used to compensate oil marketing companies for retail under-recoveries accrued during this period.[35] India has primarily adopted a method of cross-subsidization, selling gasoline, aviation oil, etc., over wealthy people at prices higher than their costs whereas fuel oil was sold to low-income people at prices below costs. While becoming an unbearable financial burden, the regulated prices of electric power, petroleum and other liquids, and natural gas have discouraged private investments, making the situation worse. However, India's energy subsidies have become a publicity stunt capitalized on by most candidates to win more votes. As over 300 million citizens in India are still grappling with no access to electricity and over 800 million remain with limited electrical access, energy subsidies have to some extent mitigated the energy poverty challenges.[36] Taking both factors into account, it is conceivable that removing energy subsidies in India would be very difficult. Luckily, New Delhi has embarked on the first reform step by deregulating gasoline prices in June 2010 (to take effect in 2012). In January 2013, it started a phased deregulation of retail diesel prices each month,[37] and finally has deregulated diesel prices since 18 October 2014.[38]

According to IEA, China's average fossil fuel consumption subsidization rate (as a proportion of the full cost of supply) in 2012 was 3.4%; as a comparison, this rate in India reached 17.6%. In 2010 China's oil subsidies hit $8.1 billion, climbed up to $18.8 billion in 2011, and then

[34] Qi An, "Guoji huashi ranliao butie xianzhuang pingshu" (Review of the status quo of international subsidies to fossil fuels), *Zhongguo Nengyuan* (China Energy), No. 4, June 2012.

[35] Kieran Clarke, Shruti Sharma and Damon Vis-Dunbar, *India Energy Subsidy Review*, Vol. 1, Iss. 1, Feb. 2004, https://www.iisd.org/gsi/sites/default/files/ffs_india_review_february2014.pdf, accessed 26 April 2023.

[36] Kristopher Settle, "India Combats Energy Poverty through Natural Resources," *Energy Biz*, 8 Aug. 2013.

[37] US Energy Information Administration, "Country Analysis- India," updated 26 June 2014, http://www.eia.gov/countries/cab.cfm?fips=IN, accessed 22 November 2014.

[38] Fitch Ratings, "India's Diesel Deregulation Positive For Oil Companies,"21 Oct. 2014.

fell to $12.9 billion in 2012.[39] As energy subsidies spur energy waste and even aggravate social disparity, both Beijing and New Delhi have realized the importance of eventually having an overhaul of the present modus operandi, allowing more foreign and private investments into energy sectors and pushing forward energy pricing reform.[40] However, as noted by Dansie et al., the two countries (along with Russia) present a similar pattern of two steps forward and one back.[41]

The other front on the demand side pertains to environmental pollution. China, the US, and India are the top three largest emitters of carbon dioxide emissions in the world. As such, they play a crucial role in fighting climate change. However, reducing greenhouse gas (GHG) emissions has been nowhere on their agendas for a long period of time in the past.[42] While the Bush administration opted against Kyoto-type policies and thus far the US has not ratified the Kyoto Protocol, both China and India insisted that as developing countries, they have the rights of development and developed countries should take greater responsibilities in cutting emissions because of their historical contribution to climate change. As a result, not only developing China and India saw a big rise in carbon dioxide emissions, but also in the US such emissions increased by about 5% between 1990 and 2012 largely due to increased energy use.[43] During 2006–2012, US carbon dioxide emissions declined every year, but from 2012 to 2014, such a trend of steadily falling emissions was reversed.[44] Of course, it may be unfair to deny their efforts to curb GHG emissions. For example, the Obama administration has committed itself to reduce

[39] Data based on: IEA, *World Energy Outlook* 2013, "Energy Subsidies", http://www.iea.org/subsidy/index.html.

[40] For the recent development, see IEA, "Recent Developments in Energy Subsidies," http://www.iea.org/media/weowebsite/2013/Developments_EnergySubsidies.pdf, accessed 27 August 2014; Kieran Clarke, Shruti Sharma and Damon Vis-Dunbar, *India Energy Subsidy Review*, Vol. 1, Iss. 1, Feb. 2004.

[41] Grant Dansie, Marc Lanteigne and Indra Overland, "Reducing Energy Subsidies in China, India and Russia: Dilemmas for Decision Makers," *Sustainability*, No. 2, 2010, p. 485.

[42] Carbon dioxide (CO2) is the primary greenhouse gas emitted through human activities.

[43] EPA (US Environmental Protection Agency), "Overview of Greenhouse Gases—Carbon Dioxide Emissions," http://www.epa.gov/climatechange/ghgemissions/gases/co2.html, accessed 22 November 2014.

[44] US Energy Information Administration

GHG emissions in the range of 17% below 2005 levels by 2020.[45] Nine Northeastern and Mid-Atlantic states in the US worked out a Regional Greenhouse Gas Initiative on 18 January 2007, trying to cap GHG emissions on a local basis.[46] The far-reaching deal stricken by President Xi Jinping and President Obama in November 2014 culminates their efforts to limit greenhouse gases, with China committing to cap its fast growing carbon emissions by 2030 or earlier and Obama unveiling a plan to cut US emissions 26 to 28 percent below 2005 levels by 2025.[47] Altogether GHG emissions by the two giants account for about 45% in the world.

In India, New Delhi was consistently reluctant to be subject to any compulsory targets of cutting GHG emissions for fear it would jeopardize its economic development and poverty alleviation goals. Recent overtures may show that India tends to be more proactive. In 2008, its Ministry of Environment and Forests mapped out a National Action Plan on Climate Change, listing 20 initiatives that India was undertaking to combat climate change with reforestation as a priority. In 2009 India announced that it would cut its carbon intensity by 24% by 2020 in comparison to the 2005 level.[48] Such a goal calls for India's more efforts than its existing policies, but even so, "the target may not be demanding enough to deliver the aims of the Copenhagen Accord".[49] More worrisome is that India's energy intensity significantly rose from 0.1355 kilowatt hour per rupee since the Lehman crisis to 0.1518 in early 2014.[50] India's new environment minister, Prakash Javadekar has precluded the possibility that India would be subject to any compulsory target of emission reduction, and his government's priority remains

[45] The White House, "President to Attend Copenhagen Climate Talks," November 25, 2009.

[46] RGGI Inc., "Regional Greenhouse Gas Initiative," http://www.rggi.org/, accessed 26 April 2023.

[47] David Nakamura and Steven Mufson, "China, U.S. agree to limit greenhouse gases," *The Washington Post*, 12 Nov. 2014.

[48] *The Guardian*, "India to reduce carbon intensity by 24% by 2020," 2 Dec. 2009.

[49] Grantham Institute for Climate Change Report GR4, "An Assessment of India's 2020 Carbon Intensity Target," Imperial College, London, April 2012.

[50] Raj Kumar Ray, "India's energy intensity rises 10.5% since FY06," *The Financial Express*, 1 April 2014.

poverty alleviation and economic development. With that, India's emissions are projected to double, surpassing those of the US and China in coming decades.[51]

At last, all the three countries are keen to build close ties with oil exporting countries. As two emerging economies with a surging appetite for energy resources, both China and India strive to improve relationship with energy exporting countries, such as Saudi Arabia, Russia, Iran, Sudan, and so on. Presence of their energy companies can be found in every continent in the world to acquire more oil and gas concessions. While cooperating with each other, both Asian giants also compete in their foreign energy quest.[52] The US has gained a foothold in energy acquisition in its backyard. Particularly Washington has woven a dense oil and gas network with North and South American countries. Salameh argues that the US' hemispheric energy policy involving Canada, Mexico, and the rest of Latin America has become a cornerstone in enhancing its energy security and reducing its dependence on the Persian Gulf region.[53] On the basis of shale revolution, energy imports from the Western hemisphere have contributed to fulfilling energy independence in the US, a goal being pursued for several decades. Moreover, by capitalizing on its hegemonic status, the US has built an alliance network in the Middle East, reinforcing its strong influence on the oil producing center, and re-consolidating the central role of the US dollar in the international monetary system after the collapse of the Bretton Woods System in 1971.

8.2.2 Distinctions

Regarding the distinctions of their measures, apparently the US is more seasoned to deal with its energy security challenges. Not only it has developed strategic partnership with major oil suppliers such as Saudi Arabia and Canada, but also it has taken the lead to establish the IEA whose

[51] Coral Davenportsept, "Emissions From India Will Increase, Official Says," *The New York Times*, 24 Sep. 2014.

[52] For details, see Hong ZHAO, *China and India: The Quest for Energy Resources in the Twenty-first Century*, London & New York: Routledge, 2012.

[53] Mamdouh G. Salameh, 'The new frontiers for the United States energy security in the 21st century', *Applied Energy*, Vol. 76, No. 1, September-November 2003, pp.135–144.

central mission is to ensure energy security,[54] joining hands with its allies to cope with oil disruption. It thus could be said that the powerful alliance system woven by the US also contributes to enhancing its energy security. Apparently neither China nor India possesses such leverage.

Particularly striking in the US countermeasures is its emphasis of resorting to its foreign strategy or even military means to help ensure its energy supply security. Although energy pursuit has been more factored into Beijing's and New Delhi's foreign strategies, it seems that neither of them has gained such leverage. Although it is controversial, an important driver motivating the Bush administration to launch military strike and topple the Saddam Hussein regime was largely for the sake of the abundant Iraqi oil reserves.[55] As an Indian commentary says, "When the US felt vulnerable about energy supplies, it was busy pushing the interests of its oil majors, using the Central Intelligence Agency (CIA) to topple governments, or sending gunboats to tame recalcitrant countries."[56]

The shale revolution taking place in the US has not only greatly enhanced its energy security and international industrial competitiveness, but also significantly reshaped the global energy landscape. Although the shale revolution can hardly attribute to the American government policies, it can still harvest its fruits. Thanks to shale revolution, the US has successfully not only fulfilled its long-pursuing goal of energy independence, but also transformed itself into a net oil and gas exporter. Consequently, the US has less concern about oil and gas supply security; neither does it need to rely on oil imports from the Middle East. In contrast, both China and India have deep concerns about oil supply disruptions, and particularly they have a growing dependence on the Middle East oil.

Another distinction regarding the energy policies taken by the three countries is the extent of marketization. While the US has often been touted as the emblem of free market economy, both China and India, as two developing countries, are still in transition from the previous planned

[54] IEA, "Energy security: Reliable, affordable access to all fuels and energy sources," http://www.iea.org/topics/energysecurity/, accessed 25 April 2023.

[55] Neela Banerjee, "Arabs have a litmus test for US handling of Iraqi oil," *New York Times*, 6 April 2003.

[56] *Rediff Business*, "How India can ensure fuel security," 1 Apr. 2013. http://www.rediff.com/money/slide-show/slide-show-1-column-how-india-can-ensure-fuel-security/20130401.htm#4, accessed 29 August 2014.

economy to market economy. In terms of oil pricing reform, crude oil prices in the three countries have already been in line with international prices, but China has introduced a mechanism for regular, automatic adjustment of prices of petroleum products in line with international prices of crude oil whereas in India this is not the case.[57] Moreover, with more leverage in hand,[58] the US apparently has held more sway on international oil prices than either China or India. In the case of access to petroleum market, foreign investors have to collaborate with Chinese counterparts in order to get access to China's upstream E&D market, but the downstream distribution sector has fully opened to foreign investments. In the US and India, they have no such restrictions, but their governments often conduct reviews on foreign investments in the name of safeguarding national security, as evidenced by the CNOOC bidding Unocal case. With the intensifying Sino-US strategic competition and India's growing suspicion towards China, the Chinese investment is facing more obstacles in the US and Indian markets.

Due to the characteristics intrinsic to their political systems, energy policies in the US and India are not that consistent relative to China's. Party rotation may not necessarily bring about policy changes in some cases, but more often than not, different ruling parties will formulate different policies in the first two countries. Take the US as an example, the current Biden administration has largely continued the Trump administration's "America first" policy, but changed the latter's pro-fossil energy policy. Under the Biden administration, it has strengthened supervision of the energy companies' oil drilling activities on the environment.

57 Anand Kalyanarama, "All you wanted to know about Fuel Pricing," *The Hindu Business Line,* 14 December 2020, https://www.thehindubusinessline.com/opinion/columns/slate/all-you-wanted-to-know-about/article33330388.ece, accessed 29 December 2022.

58 The leverage that the US has gained at least include: its status as the largest economy, crude oil producer, and largest oil consumer, having the largest SPRs, most developed commodities market, US dollar centric international monetary system, strongest military forces with military bases across the globe, alliance with a host of oil producing countries, leadership in IEA, highly competitive oil multinationals, and so on.

8.3 Major Players Serving Energy Security in China, US, and India

As illustrated in Chapter 4, the three state-owned NOCs (CNPC, Sinopec and CNOOC) are the major players predominant in China's oil and natural gas sectors, both upstream and downstream markets, while PipeChina is responsible for owning and operating oil and gas trunk pipelines and other state-owned companies such as Sinochem, CITIC Group, and local government-owned Yanchang Petroleum, have also expanded their presence in China's petroleum sector.

By contrast, the major players in the American oil and natural gas industrial chains are private energy firms, particularly the IOCs such as ExxonMobil, BP, Royal Dutch/Shell, Chevron, and Conoco Phillips. With a strong presence in both upstream and downstream sectors in numerous countries, the IOCs are mainly headquartered and responsible for oil and gas provision in the US. Thanks to their hefty revenues, they have become even more influential than some states. Meanwhile, there are also some energy SOEs owned, controlled, and wholly or partially managed by governments at the levels of US states, counties, municipalities, and other subdivisions.[59] In general, the petroleum and natural gas markets in the US are much more competitive.

In India, public and private energy companies are competing in the oil and natural gas sectors. Like China, India's petroleum production and refining activities are dominated by three state-owned companies, Indian Oil Corporation Limited (IOCL), Oil and Natural Gas Corporation (ONGC), and Oil India Limited (OIL). IOCL is India's largest oil and gas company as well as the country's most profitable state-owned company, followed by ONGC. As the largest oil and gas exploration and production company in India, ONGC alone accounted for about 69 percent of India's domestic oil production in 2012 and has become its largest profit making public sector undertakings (PSU). OIL is an Indian public sector company responsible for the production of crude oil and natural gas. The three PSUs are competing with other two state-controlled companies, Bharat Petroleum and Hindustan Petroleum, and two private-owned companies, Reliance Petroleum and Essar Oil.

[59] OECD, "State Owned Enterprises and the Principle of Competitive Neutrality," DAF/COMP(2009)37, 20 Sep. 2010, http://www.oecd.org/daf/competition/46734249.pdf, accessed 26 April 2023.

Bharat Petroleum is the second largest oil and gas company in India, while Hindustan Petroleum owns the largest lubricant refinery in India, engaging in producing a wide variety of petroleum fuels in the country. With Maharatna status, Gas Authority of India is the largest state-owned natural gas processing and distribution company in India. GAIL (India) Ltd, formerly known as Gas Authority of India Limited, is the largest state-owned natural gas processing and distribution company, owning the largest pipeline network in India. Reliance Petroleum, a subsidiary of the Reliance Industries Limited, owns the Jamnagar Refinery, the largest refinery in the world.[60]

Unlike China which does not allow a controlling status for foreign investors, private and foreign investments have been permitted to bid on small oil fields with up to 100 percent foreign control in India since 1999, but production in upstream oil by most private firms is still relatively low except Cairn India, a subsidiary of British company Cairn Energy, which controls more than 20 percent of India's crude oil production. In the refining sector, India's state-owned firms own about 62 percent of its total refining capacity while the remaining 38 percent is under the control of private sector. In China, there are numerous small-scale local government-owned or private refining firms that possess 10–15 percent of China's refining capacity, and most of them are facing the risk of being shut down due to surplus production in this sector.[61] Another difference between China and India is the presence of international companies in the refining sector. In order to gain a foothold into China's downstream oil market, NOCs from Kuwait, Saudi Arabia, Russia, Qatar, and Venezuela have entered the Chinese market by setting up joint ventures with Chinese NOCs to build integrated refinery and petrochemical projects. In contrast, so far, international oil companies have few stakes in the Indian oil market.[62]

[60] This paragraph about Indian oil and gas companies is based on: *Walk Through India*, "Top 10 Largest Oil And Gas Companies in India," 9 January 2023, http://www.walkthroughindia.com/industry/top-10-largest-oil-and-gas-companies-in-india/, accessed 14 January 2023.

[61] *Reuters*, "China tried to close local small refineries," 2 May 2011, available at: http://cn.reuters.com/article/wtNews/idCNCHINA-4229120110502, accessed 31 August 2014.

[62] Related information in this paragraph is based on: EIA, "Country Analysis – India," updated 26 June 2014; and EIA, "Country Analysis—China," updated 4 Feb. 2014.

In terms of marketing and distribution of petroleum products, China's CNPC and Sinopec are the principal actors responsible for wholesale and retail businesses of such petroleum products as gasoline, kerosene, and diesel according to a geographic division. Individual refineries have no discretionary powers to dispose of their products, including outlets, prices, and so on, except that they could sell paraffin/wax and asphalt with permission from either CNPC or Sinopec.[63] That also means local oil distributors have no other channels but the two NOCs to purchase wholesale oil for their retail businesses. After China's entry into WTO, IOCs were authorized to run petrol stations in China in the form of joint ventures with Chinese NOCs. Similar to the situation in China, marketing and distribution of petroleum products in India is dominated by three state-owned energy companies, which have a market share of 92.7 percent altogether.[64] The Indian government did not authorize the entry of private investors to carry out retailing of fuel until 2002. Subsequent reform of allowing private participation was subject to some restrictions. Currently, Reliance Industries Ltd. (RIL), Shell, and Essar are also undertaking the retail marketing related to petroleum products.

In the area of oil and gas pipelines, 51,349 miles of crude oil pipelines, 86,486 miles of oil products pipelines, and 1,566,495 miles of gas pipelines traverse the US.[65] China has 14,658 miles of crude oil pipelines, 11,795 miles of oil products pipelines in its domestic network, and nearly 32,000 miles of main natural gas pipelines at the end of 2012. In India, less than 5900 miles of crude oil pipelines and over 9,200 miles of natural gas pipeline span in this country in 2013.[66] Hence,

[63] Si Zhi Guo (Kaku Shi Shi), "Trends of Petroleum Distribution Business in China," The Institute of Energy Economics, Japan (IEEJ), May 2003, http://eneken.ieej.or.jp/en/data/pdf/195.pdf, accessed 1 September 2014.

[64] Calculated by the author according to data from: *Infraline Energy*, "Marketing and Distribution of Petroleum Products in India," Updated in July 2011, http://www.infraline.com/ong/petroproducts/MandD.aspx, accessed 1 September 2014.

[65] Bureau of Transportation Statistics, Research and Innovative Technology Administration (RITA) , U.S. Department of Transportation (US DOT), "Table 1–10: U.S. Oil and Gas Pipeline Mileage," http://www.rita.dot.gov/bts/sites/rita.dot.gov.bts/files/publications/national_transportation_statistics/html/table_01_10.html, accessed 2 September 2014.

[66] Relevant data on China and India in the above are based on: EIA, "Country Analysis—India," updated 26 June 2014; and EIA, "Country Analysis—China," updated 4 Feb. 2014.

both China and India have been dwarfed by the US in pipeline infrastructure. In the US, those oil and gas pipelines are owned and managed by a plethora of private companies, whereas in China, the trunk oil and gas pipelines used to be fully controlled and managed by the NOCs, particularly CNPC,[67] but China has separated pipeline business from the three NOCs and lumped together these pipeline assets to establish the National Oil and Gas Pipeline Network Company (PipeChina) since December 2019. Local transmission networks are still operated by various local distribution companies. Like China, India's oil pipelines (both crude oil and products) are mainly controlled and operated by the NOCs. The state-owned Indian Oil Corporation Lmt. (IOCL) controls the largest pipeline networks, such as the Haldia-Barauni, Barauni-Kanpur product lines, and the Mundra-Panipat crude oil pipeline. Other than IOCL which owns 66.6% crude oil pipelines, ONGC possesses 15.3% and OIL 18.1%. Regarding petroleum products pipelines, other important players include Bharat Petroleum Corporation Limited (BPCL, 1389 km) and Hindustan Petroleum Corporation Limited (HPCL, 2134 km).[68] In terms of gas pipelines, there are several actors, both public and private ownership, but the two largest ones are GAIL and Reliance Gas Transportation Infrastructure Limited (RGTIL). As a state-owned gas transmission and marketing company, GAIL operates over 70% of India's pipeline networks, particularly the two major gas pipelines in northwestern India with a combined length of 3328 miles: the Hazira-Vijaipur-Jagadishpur (HVJ) line and the Dahej-Vijaipur (DVPL) line. RGTIL, owned by RIL, is the biggest private investor in the gas transmission business. In 2009, it completed an 881-mile East–West pipeline. Other players like Assam Gas Company and Gujarat State Petronet Limited (GSPL) are also operating pipelines which mainly serving northeastern India and Gujarat, respectively. Most LPG pipelines are dominated by GAIL, which owns 85% of India's LPG pipelines (2,000 kilometers in length) while IOCL controls the remaining pipelines.[69] City gas distribution has mainly been undertaken by a small number of major players,

[67] CNPC manages 67% of China's total crude oil pipeline, and holds over three-fourths of the gas transmission in China. See EIA, "Country Analysis—China," updated 4 Feb. 2014.

[68] http://www.cerebralbusiness.com/OilnGasKB/Content/10260/10260/1/Pipeline-Transportation

[69] EIA, "Country Analysis—India," updated 26 June 2014.

such as GAIL, Indraprastha Gas, Mahanagar Gas, Gujarat Gas, and GSPC Gas.[70] Therefore, the NOCs have predominant market shares in controlling pipeline networks in both China and India. Nonetheless, in China, pipeline segments are highly concentrated in the hands of CNPC and Sinopec and almost closed to private companies, whereas in India, the market is much more dispersive among different enterprises with a high participation of private firms.

In terms of foreign energy quest, in the US a variety of firms of different ownership, particularly the IOCs, are venturing abroad with an aim to snatch more market share in the largest petroleum market. In both China and India, the state-owned NOCs, are the major actors which are desperate to acquire foreign energy assets. In India, the major state-owned actors include ONGC, Bharat Petroleum Corporation Ltd (BPCL), IOCL, and OIL, as well as Hindustan Petroleum Corporation Limited (HPCL) and GAIL. At the same time, there are a number of private firms from both countries engaging in some foreign energy asset acquisitions. In India, private companies such as Reliance and Essar are making efforts to secure more overseas energy resources. For instance, Reliance possesses two blocks in Peru, three in Yemen, two each in Oman, Kurdistan, and Colombia, one each in East Timor and Australia. Essar's oil and gas assets abroad include two blocks in Madagascar since 2006, one block in Nigeria (2010), and one block in Vietnam (2007).[71] However, in both countries, oil and gas resources acquired abroad by private firms encounter some barriers to enter their domestic markets. In China this is because private firms have not been allowed to directly import crude oil into China, and this policy has slightly been loosened in September 2014. In India, this is largely because the artificially low prices of refined oil have simply made it very uneconomic for private firms to send crude oil back home.

[70] Western Australia Trade Office—India, "An overview of India's oil and gas market," April 2011.

[71] Isabelle Saint-Mézard (Asia Centre) and CSFRS (Conseil Supérieur de la Formation et de la Recherche Stratégiques), *The International Dimensions of India's Energy Security*, Note in the framework of the SECI project (Energy Security from China and India) in partnership with the CSFRS, February 2014.

8.4 Role of the State and Government-Business Relationship

Central to the debate concerning the fundamental distinctions between China's approach to energy security and other countries' is the role of the state and their government-business relationship. Although scholars have created different concepts to depict the role of the Chinese state, the state capitalism thesis has gained wide currency in the Western world.[72] Its central argument is to underscore the Chinese state's strategic intentions and policies that champion state-owned firms and sovereign wealth funds, provide state funding to the SOEs to help them lock in long-term contracts, and use the domestic market to bolster the Chinese government's domestic political positions. What this view has incisively discerned is the Chinese state's strategic concerns and how it braces up the SOEs, but it is problematic to presuppose the state organs as a unitary entity. In fact, the Chinese state is not so strong that it can be immune from particularistic interests. Nor is the state 'staffed by agents of change who are unified by a common purpose and technical orientation'.[73] As an alternative interpretation, the author has developed the SMMA to portray the role of the Chinese state, which is neither complete state control nor full marketization, but encompassing both components.

Although the US has been touted as the epitome of the market economy, in no event that the American government takes an off-hand approach in running its petroleum sector and ensuring its energy security. First of all, an important means is to provide subsidies, both at the federal and state levels, to the oil and gas industry. "In the United States, the federal and state governments have supported the oil and gas industry since the early twentieth century through fiscal, military, scientific, and other forms of support."[74] Supposing oil prices staying at US$50 per barrel, Erickson finds that tax preferences and other subsidies in the US

[72] For details about their debates, see, Shaofeng Chen, "State-Managed Marketization: A Revisit of the Role of the Chinese State in the Petroleum Industry," *The Copenhagen Journal of Asian Studies*, Vol. 30, No. 2, 2012, pp. 29–60.

[73] Steven Chan, et al., 'Looking beyond the developmental state', in Steven Chan, Cal Clark and Danny Lam (eds), *Beyond the Developmental State: East Asia's Political Economies Reconsidered*, London: Macmillan Press & New York: St. Martin's Press, 1998, p.2.

[74] Nancy Pfund and Ben Healey, "What would Jefferson do? The Historical Role of Federal Subsidies in Shaping America's Energy Future," San Francisco, CA: DBL

not only make nearly half of yet-to-be-developed oil investments profitable, but also potentially increase oil production by 17 billion barrels over the next few decades.[75] With $4.86 billion, the subsidies provided by the White House to oil and gas during 1918–2009 prevails that to other energy forms, including nuclear, biofuel and renewables.[76] Despite its pledge to remove 'inefficient' and 'wasteful' subsidies to fossil fuels since 2009, the US continues to subsidize the oil and gas industry.[77] It was estimated that around US$ 20.5 billion of subsidies has been poured by the US federal and state government every year.[78]

A second form of support by Washington is to render massive support for R&D in the American oil and gas industry. The principal duties of the US Energy Department are to support research and policy options to ensure its domestic supply of oil, and invest in "research, technology and processes to make oil drilling cleaner and more efficient, including enhanced oil recovery and improved offshore drilling practices."[79] While its 17 National Laboratories directly conduct R&D on cutting-edge technologies, the Energy Department and also provides funds to support American petroleum companies, universities, and research institutes for their energy-related R&D activities. More than that, the US Environmental Protection Agency also spares no effort to fund the above actors' R&D projects.

Investors, September 2011, https://www.dbl.vc/wp-content/uploads/2012/09/What-Would-Jefferson-Do-2.4.pdf, assessed 18 December 2022.

[75] Peter Erickson, Adrian Down, Michael Lazarus & Doug Koplow, "Effect of subsidies to fossil fuel companies on United States crude oil production," *Nature Energy*, Vol. 2, 2017, pp. 891–898.

[76] Nancy Pfund and Ben Healey, "What would Jefferson do? The Historical Role of Federal Subsidies in Shaping America's Energy Future," San Francisco, CA: DBL Investors, September 2011, https://www.dbl.vc/wp-content/uploads/2012/09/What-Would-Jefferson-Do-2.4.pdf, assessed 18 December 2022.

[77] Alan B. Krueger, "Statement of Alan B. Krueger Assistant Secretary for Economic Policy and Chief Economist, US Department of Treasury Subcommittee on Energy, Natural Resources, and Infrastructure," 10 September 2009, https://home.treasury.gov/news/press-releases/tg284, accessed 18 December 2022.

[78] Ploy Achakulwisut, Peter Erickson, and Doug Koplow, "Effect of subsidies and regulatory exemptions on 2020–2030 oil and gas production and profits in the United States," *Environmental Research Letters*, Vol. 16, No. 8, 2021.

[79] Webpage of the Department of Energy: https://www.energy.gov/oil, accessed 19 December 2022.

Most prominent is the iron fist of the US government to launch military actions when it deems it necessary so as to preserve its fossil-fuel-related interests. The shadow of oil can hardly be ruled out in its invasions of Iraq. Some say that the US invasion against Iraq was for the sake of acquiring oil concessions for its oil companies. Others say that the then Bush Administration's military action was out of considerations of preventing a possible spillover caused by Saddam Hussein's decision of oil settlement with Euro, rather than dollar, which was alleged as one major determinant driving their military actions.

At last, another important role that the US government has played is to regulate the petroleum market hinging upon what goals the White House pursues. With the largest strategic petroleum reserves (SPR) in the world, the US can exercise a strong influence on the oil market by adjusting its SPR. For instance, in October 2022, Joe Biden released the SPR in a hope to curb surging inflations stemming from the Russia-Ukraine war and OPEC+'s decision of oil production cuts and better handle the alarming mid-term election pitch. Hence, the SPR serves not only to reduce short-term market disruptions, but also has become a political and geopolitical tool for the US government. Other than the SPR, the US has an array of policy toolkits that can be drawn upon to influence the energy market, such as changing its monetary policy, environmental regulations, financial rules, and so on.

Akin to the US, the Indian central government and state governments have played an important role in running the oil and gas industries. As IEA asserts, "The Indian government as a whole plays an indispensable role in the energy sector through state-owned enterprises, public policy and market regulation, indirect guidance and personal networks."[80] First of all, India has consistently pursued a goal of energy self-sufficiency or energy independence notwithstanding its meager oil and gas reserves.[81] To that end, the Indian government nationalized the hydrocarbon sector in the 1970s–1980s, and has underscored the pivotal role of state-owned enterprises in the energy sector. Consequently, this inevitably leads to "a monopolistic market structure" and "the systemic infirmities that are

[80] Sun-Joo Ahn and Dagmar Graczyk, *Understanding Energy Challenges in India: Policies, Players and Issues*, International Energy Agency, Partner Country Series, 2012.

[81] Tanvi Madan, *The Brookings Foreign Policy Studies Energy Security Series: India*, Washington, DC, 2006.

inherent in cases of majority public ownership of an enterprise".[82] Like China, India also formulates five-year plans to achieve its development goals. While its first eight five-year plans primarily aimed to expand the public sector by virtue of massive investments in basic and heavy industries, the focus was shifted to providing indicative directions rather than expanding the public sector.

Secondly, the Indian government still plays an important role in oil and gas pricing. With an Administered Pricing Mechanism (APM) based on a cost of operating capital plus formula, it was up to the Indian government to formulate the prices of oil. Since April 2012 the APM has been canceled and oil marketing companies can decide the prices of most petroleum products, but gasoline (called "petrol" in India) and diesel, two major transportation fuels, along with kerosene and LPG, two important products for the poor, remain regulated by the Indian government. Thus far, India is implementing a trade parity price formula to price gasoline and diesel. This new formula is on the basis of gasoline and diesel prices in the international market, rather than of crude oil prices, plus taxes and exchange rate between dollars and rupees. However, the Indian government still holds sway in the sense that gasoline and diesel prices may not necessarily fall down even when international crude oil prices sharply decline, and that gasoline and diesel price changes take place only in consultation with India's Ministry of Petroleum and Natural Gas (MPNG). Moreover, government taxes account for about 60 percent of the fuels' price.[83] More often than not, India's two state-owned oil giants, ONGC and OIL have to sell their petroleum products at a price much lower than international prices in order to keep the end-use prices low.

Thirdly, in the natural gas sector, the Indian government has taken a quasi-command economy approach. Allocation of natural gas is regulated by the MPNG through administrative orders, so is the pricing of gas produced by its public sector undertakings. The government's priority is to take care of the fertilizer, LPG, and power sector. Natural gas from joint ventures follows the production sharing contracts. For natural

[82] India's Planning Commission, *Integrated Energy Policy: Report of the Expert Committee*, New Delhi, 2006.

[83] For details about India's oil pricing mechanism, see Anand Kalyanarama, "All you wanted to know about Fuel Pricing," *The Hindu Business Line*, 14 December 2020, https://www.thehindubusinessline.com/opinion/columns/slate/all-you-wanted-to-know-about/article33330388.ece, accessed 29 December 2022.

gas produced from fields allocated to public sector undertakings by the government, it will be sold at prices set by the Indian government under the administered pricing mechanism.[84]

Fourthly, New Delhi has also worked out extensive subsidy programs for oil and gas products. India's MPNG is responsible to work out the subsidy scheme, based on which India's Ministry of Finance will provide subsidies to oil marketing companies in the form of cash and bonds. India's subsidies to oil and gas reached INR 67,678 crore in FY 2019, which was 5.83 times more than the value of subsidies to renewables and electric vehicles.[85] Despite mounting fiscal burden, the Indian government has not phased out its subsidy programs. Slashing subsidies to oil and gas is very likely to spark public protests, causing dissipation of votes. This is a political gamble that few ruling parties are willing to see.

From the angle of government-business relations, the pendulum has swung in favor of different sides in the three countries. In China, as discussed in previous chapters, the NOCs have enjoyed greater autonomy with the marketization process being unfolded, but this marketization process has been initiated and is under the control of the government. The principal mechanisms making the SMMA feasible can be summarized as control, autonomy, and support.[86] Moreover, the government also requires the NOCs to assume the duties of serving macroeconomic policy adjustment. They are expected to launch some big projects in order to help stimulate economic growth. Hence, the pendulum is tilting towards the Chinese state.

To a large extent the Indian government-business case is similar with China's. First of all, the state is still playing a decisive role in price setting and resource allocation. Second, public sector undertakings are predominant in the oil and gas sector. Third, the Modi Government has highlighted energy security as one of the top priorities in its foreign policies, and has been all out to support Indian state-owned petroleum

[84] Sun-Joo Ahn and Dagmar Graczyk, *Understanding Energy Challenges in India: Policies, Players and Issues*, International Energy Agency, Partner Country Series, 2012.

[85] Vibhuti Garg, Balasubramanian Viswanathan, *et al*, *Mapping India's Energy Subsidies 2020—Fossil Fuels, Renewables and Electric Vehicles*, Winnipeg: International Institute for Sustainable Development, April 2020. https://www.ceew.in/publications/mapping-indias-energy-subsidies-2020, accessed 30 December 2022.

[86] Shaofeng Chen, "Marketization and China's Energy Security," *Policy and Society*, Vol. 27, No. 3, 2009.

companies to venture abroad. By mapping out "Make in India" and "Made for the World" initiatives, New Delhi aspires to turn India into a global manufacturing hub that would overtake China. Apparently, energy security matters for that goal. Indian state-owned petroleum companies, such as OVL, BPCL, and OIL are the most active players of overseas upstream investments, but private companies also embark on acquiring upstream assets abroad. The Indian government has tried its best to bolster domestic energy firms to make forays into the international energy market. "Energy security's primacy in Modi government's foreign policy is reflected in his record number of high-profile foreign visits during which he has been cutting energy deals with energy-rich countries."[87] Therefore, the three features of control, autonomy, and support can also be applied to depict the government-NOCs relations in India.

The relationship between the US government and the IOCs-dominated oil industry is much more complicated as it is evolving over time and may differ in different cases. Nominally, relative to China and India, the US is more prone to relying on market forces and the IOCs, rather than state-directed power, to deal with energy security challenges. By and large, both the government and the IOCs in the US are running in two parallel domains, work in light of different logic and pursue different goals.[88] One is in the political logic in the political arena and the other is in the commercial logic in the economic domain. Historically in most cases, the two sides have acted independently in pursuit of their interests. Washington would try to resist the temptation to intervene too much in the IOCs' operations in the US domestic and foreign markets. That is to say, the American petroleum companies enjoy greater autonomy in oil production, investment, marketing, pricing, and other business decisions relative to their Chinese and Indian counterparts. This is not only related with the American culture, but also because the American IOCs are much more competitive and enjoying a preemptive advantages in the global

[87] 10 Pointers, "Energy Security: India's Perspective," 12 March 2022, https://www.10pointer.com/current-affairs/energy-security-indias-perspective, accessed 25 December 2022.

[88] G Hamel. "The Multinational Corporation and Home Country Foreign Policy: A Research Agenda," Working Paper No. 229, Graduate School of Business Administration, The University of Michigan, August 1980.

energy markets. Thereby, they do not want the US government to interfere too much in their business activities. However, that does not mean that the US government will leave them alone under any circumstances.

Similar to the case in China and India, the US government expects the IOCs to serve the US energy security and foreign policies; if necessary, it will provide support and or exert pressure on the IOCs to help attain its national interests. To fulfill its domestic and foreign goals, as aforementioned, the US government is likely to render military, diplomatic, and financial support to the IOCs. Krasner suggests that the US government protect the American oil companies, even through military means, in order to secure stable supplies of raw materials, particularly oil.[89] Indeed, the multinational companies are utilized by the US government as a tool to promote economic growth, secure raw materials of strategic importance, promulgate ideology, serve foreign strategy, and so forth.[90] Vivoda finds that the IOCs are in a more advantageous position in preserving existing contracts and bargaining with other players when they have their home governments on the back.[91] The relationship between the US state departments and the IOCs has been portrayed as an almost hand-in-glove one from the end of World War II to 1970s, both working hard to meet American foreign strategic objectives in the Middle East.[92]

Apparently the IOCs are subordinate to directives of the US government, but they are not passive mindless pawns. The IOCs had to abide by the US government ban of export of US crude oil for more than 40 years until President Obama lifted the ban in the end of 2015. Externally, the sanctions against other countries imposed by the US government will pose a direct deterrence to the IOCs, making them more hesitant about and even hold back from investing in the targeted country, as evidenced

[89] Stephen Krasner, *Defending the National Interest: Raw Materials and US Foreign Policy*, Princeton: Princeton University Press, 1978, p. 39.

[90] Vlado Vivoda, "International Oil Companies, US Government and Energy Security Policy: An Interest-based Analysis," *International Journal of Global Energy Issues*, Vol. 33, No. 1-2, 2010, pp. 73-88.

[91] Vlado Vivoda, *The Return of the Obsolescing Bargain and the Decline of Big Oil: A Study of Bargaining in the Contemporary Oil Industry*, Saarbrücken, Germany: Vdm Verlag Dr. Müller, 2008.

[92] US Congress Subcommittee on Multinational Corporations, "Multinational Oil Corporations and US Foreign Policy," US Government Printing Office, 2 January 1975.

by their pullout from the Russian market after the outbreak of the Russia-Ukraine war. "The IOCs act in harmony with the US foreign and energy security policy only when their interests are congruent, or under severe threat, such as that of legal action."[93] However, when the IOCs' interests are not in alignment with the US government, they will either take initiative to influence government policy-making, or simply turn a blind eye to government directives. In the former case, the American political system has provided such channels through which numerous interest groups, including the IOCs, can influence government policy formation, such as lobbying, government contracts, joint ventures with government, direct involvement in policy-making process or indirect access to policy-making through intermediaries, parliamentary representatives, trade associations, and so on. Some scholars have highlighted the important role of the IOCs in influencing the US energy security and foreign policies.[94] In the latter case, the IOCs were reluctant to scale up domestic oil production despite the Biden administration's call to do that with an aim to help curb high inflation in the US in 2022. Placing their own commercial interests on the top, the IOCs have been criticized for failing to represent the interests of American energy consumers.[95]

In face of the energy companies' possible defiance, the governments in the three big powers have different options. The Chinese and Indian governments can punish the NOCs through reshuffling the top management, fiscal transfer, tax adjustment, and cancelation of specific rights, while the US government does not have such policy tools except policy changes and tax adjustments to discipline the IOCs.

[93] Vlado Vivoda, "International oil companies, US Government and energy security policy: an interest-based analysis," *International Journal of Global Energy Issues*, Vol. 33, No. 1–2, 2010, pp. 73–88.

[94] See, for example, Robert Gilpin, *US Power and the Multinational Corporation*, New York: Basic Books, 1975; Amy Myers Jaffe and Ronald Soligo, "The International Oil Companies," Policy Report Prepared in Conjunction with an Energy Study Sponsored by the James A. Baker III Institute for Public Policy and Japan Petroleum Energy Center, November 2007.

[95] Richard E. Bissell, "The Role of the International Oil Companies," *Current History*, Vol. 74, No. 437, May/June 1978, pp. 202-205.

8.5 Do the Major Players' Behaviors Fundamentally Differ from Each Other?

An energy company's behavior is not only guided by its interest concerns, but also shaped by the institutional milieus where it is operating. Understandably, within a country different energy firms may behave differently, and an energy company may not necessarily act in unison at different times within a country or in different countries. In view of such complexity, we may paraphrase the above question: as market actors, whether they always follow market principles in their operations, both at home and abroad.

In general, "competition among private entities has been and remains the current norm for the U.S. economy".[96] Theoretically speaking, profit maximization is the first and foremost concern for private petroleum companies, and even if they undertake some social obligations, it is of their own accord. In the American market, most energy companies including IOCs are private owned. Their decisions are primarily based on market principle with profit maximization as the core, taking account of both short-run and long-run costs and interests. The IOCs have full autonomy to make decisions on whether stay in or exit from a market, whether expand or reduce investments to find new reserves or build new refinery capacities, whether an increase or decrease oil and or gas supply to the market, and so on. As aforementioned, there is a positive reinforcement effect between the government and the IOCs in the US. That is to say, the IOCs are more inclined to donate money to candidates in more favor to the oil and gas business in the presidential or congressional elections; In return, those candidates, once being elected, are more prone to supporting policies friendly to the oil and gas industry or even using people from the IOCs to fill in some top positions in the government. If the US government expects them to help ensure energy security and fulfill its foreign strategy, and if the IOCs are reluctant, the US government cannot punish them directly through reshuffling the management, reducing budgetary allocation, or other administrative measures. However, the White House still can use administrative means

[96] OECD, "State Owned Enterprises and the Principle of Competitive Neutrality," DAF/COMP(2009)37, 20 Sep. 2010, http://www.oecd.org/daf/competition/46734249.pdf, accessed 26 April 2023.

to discipline them. Setting a ban of running business in some countries is such an example. In January 2022, Biden excluded Tesla from a discussion about domestic electric vehicle production, mentioning only General Motors and Ford Motors, although Tesla is the most renowned brand of electric vehicles. Hence, the IOCs are willing to serve the US market not because of government mandates, but primarily because of their commercial motives.

Unlike IOCs in the US primarily focusing on economic returns, the NOCs from China and India, are subject to government mandates while enjoying prerogatives reserved by their governments. In conformity with the marketization and liberation trends in both economies, the NOCs, shielded from fully competitive pressures, have been required to eventually face more market competition; at the same time, as state-owned firms, they are expected to take social responsibilities and even orchestrate government actions when necessary. Thus, the NOCs have been endowed with several objectives. Besides commercial interests, externally they may be vanguards serving their home governments' foreign strategies, of their own will or against their will; internally they are required to supply sufficient hydrocarbon resources to meet domestic demands regardless of the economic costs, help absorb domestic surplus labor forces, forge themselves into their national flagship IOCs, support government stimulus plans through higher spending and job retention after the global financial crisis, etc. Apparently these goals are inherently contradictory.

With multiple goals in mind, how do the Chinese and Indian NOCs behave in practice? A notable fact is that most times these NOCs act like their private counterparts with an aim of profit maximization in their operations. Their strong commercial motives have arisen from the following two factors. On the one hand, welfares for employees of these NOCs are directly associated with the performance of their companies. With marketization going on, those traditional social welfares like housing and medical care that SOE employees used to enjoy under the planned economy have gradually been relegated to the market. On the other hand, chances of promotion for the top management of the NOCs will be largely hinged upon the performance of the NOCs. The latter may not be the only factor that affects their personal advancement, but apparently it is an influential or even decisive one. The research done by Feng et al.find that CEO labor market in the Chinese state sector exhibits characteristics similar to those of managerial labor markets in developed countries, in the sense that firm performance has a positive effect on CEO compensation, and that firm performance is positively associated with CEO promotion and negatively associated with CEO turnover.[97]

Under the circumstances where the NOCs are required to take social responsibilities which run counter to their commercial interests, the NOCs' behaviors tend to be complicated. (1) There are occasions that they were willing to take that role at the sacrifice of their economic interests in the event of severe energy crisis, harsh government orders, strong public pressure, and so on.

(2) But there are such occasions that the NOCs fell short of their governments' expectations of serving national interests, or even turned a deaf ear to governments' fiats of prioritizing public interests by using delaying tactics, working in a slipshod manner, or others. Both China and India have a growing dependency on foreign oil imports, especially from the Middle East, making them very vulnerable to high risks there. India's oil import dependency is projected to exceed 90 percent by 2031[98]; in 2009 an overwhelming 78 percent of its oil imports came from OPEC countries.[99] As such, both countries have endeavored to shore up their NOCs to secure more overseas oil and gas concessions. To that end, both governments have spent billions to facilitate their deals with foreign countries in a hope these investments could help ensure their domestic energy supply security. It was reported that India has spent more than $53 billion on foreign oil and gas ventures over the last decade,[100] while Chinese NOCs have spent a handsome around $92 billion on foreign oil and gas assets since the end of 2008.[101] Nonetheless, most crude oil has been directly sold in the best available markets. Neither the Chinese NOCs nor the Indian NOCs have delivered their crude oil received from their foreign investments to their home markets in spite of that these investments have often been touted as essential for their energy security, and

[97] Xunan Feng, Anders C. Johansson, "CEO Incentives in Chinese State-Controlled Firms," Stockholm School of Economics Asia Working Paper, No.27, September 2013.

[98] Victor Mallet, "India's Reliance on Imported Energy Threatens Long-term Recovery," *Financial Times*, 12 Sep. 2013.

[99] Keith Kohl, "India's Solution to an Oil Crisis," *Energy & Capital*, 25 Sep. 2012.

[100] James Crabtree, "The Threat of Energy Dependency in India," *ABO* (About Oil), 26 August 2014, https://www.abo.net/oilportal/topic/view.do?contentId=2291217, accessed 8 November 2014.

[101] *Resources Quarterly*, "China, and Its Rush for Foreign Oil," Vol. 1, Iss. 1, Summer 2013, pp. 26–27.

that the demands for oil are so high in both countries that even those foreign acquisitions could hardly quench their oil hunger.[102] Liberals may deem it unnecessary to ship those resources home given that we are living in an integrated global oil market, but their ways of doing things at least illustrate the NOCs' relentless pursuit of their commercial interests.

(3) The NOCs might deliberately create some situation to force the government to make policy changes by taking advantage of government regulations and their information monopoly. In the previous chapter we have mentioned the case that the Chinese NOCs deliberately created a tight market situation at the excuse of refinery maintenance so as to exert pressure on the government to raise gasoline and diesel prices.

Therefore, state ownership does not mean that the Chinese and Indian NOCs would simply dance to their governments' tune in practice. The prevalent view perceiving the Chinese and Indian NOCs as arms of the state embodies an element of truth, but it is very biased.[103] Likewise, emphasizing the NOCs' more commerce-orientation does not imply that they are on a par with private energy companies in market efficiency. In the complex relationship with the government, the NOCs enjoy some privileges conducive to their rivalry with IOCs, but assuming the role of serving national interests means they have to pay some costs. Also, some of the privileges like being bailed out may turn out a con for the NOCs' growth. Moreover, as property rights are more attenuated in an SOE than in a private firm, state ownership per se can be an impediment to the NOCs' development.[104] Specifically, state ownership and control weaken managerial incentives and internal monitoring among publicly listed firms in China.[105]

[102] For the specific analysis on China, see Shaofeng Chen, "Has China's foreign energy quest enhanced its energy security?" *The China Quarterly*, Vol. 207, September 2011, pp. 600-625; in the case of India, see James Crabtree, "The Threat of Energy Dependency in India," 2014, ibid.

[103] See, for example, Shaofeng Chen,"State-Managed Marketization: A Revisit of the Role of the Chinese State in the Petroleum Industry," *The Copenhagen Journal of Asian Studies*, Vol. 30, No. 2, 2012, pp. 29-60.

[104] Pradeep Chhibber and Sumit K. Majumdar, "State as Investor and State as Owner: Consequences for Firm Performance in India," *Economic Development and Cultural Change*, Vol. 46, No. 3, April 1998, p. 563.

[105] Chen Lin & Dongwei Su, "Does state control affect managerial incentives? Evidence from China's publicly listed firms," *Journal of Business Economics and Management*, Vol. 10, Iss. 4, 2009.

IOCs seeking profit maximization does not mean they do not need to undertake social obligations or corporate social responsibilities (CSR), such as safe and compliant operations, labor standards, environmental responsibility, and so on. Akin to citizens in the society, companies, no matter public or private ownership, should act in the morally right way and abide by government laws and regulations. Although a firm's behavior is closely related to culture and corporate governance, it is also subject to the regulatory milieu where it is operating. Accordingly, IOCs in the US serve "national interests" either out of their own moral consciousness or commercial drive, or because of government laws and regulations. For instance, IOCs have a compulsory duty to conduct petroleum reserve and can be drawn down by the federal state. Overall government-business relations in the US are more clearly defined. In contrast, Chinese and Indian NOCs serving "national interests" is largely seen as an intrinsic element of state ownership, but the NOCs' rights and obligations, positive or negative list of their behaviors remain far from being clearly defined in both China and India. This kind of murky government-NOCs relationship has its historical root, which goes beyond the topic.

8.6 Conclusion

Using the US and India as a reference, this chapter aims to analyze whether and to what extent China's approach to energy security differs from other countries. In terms of perceptions of energy security, the three countries have highlighted the central position of oil, the importance of stable oil supply, and expansion of indigenous energy production. The measures and policies they have taken are similar in the sense that both supply side and demand side are encompassed. Among the supply-side measures, diversification is the most prominent strategy; Among the demand-side measures, more and more attention has been paid to environmental protection and energy transition.

The salient distinction lies in the type of major market actors and market structure in the oil and gas sector. In the two Asian giants, it is the typical SOEs-dominant market structure where the NOCs enjoy some privileges, whereas in the US the IOCs prevail and private companies compete with each other. The IOCs' behaviors are decisively driven by commercial interests whereas the NOCs, most of the time, behave for the sake of commercial interests, but sometimes they are required to undertake social and political responsibilities.

When it comes to the role of the state and government-business relationship, the US government does not intervene as deeply in the oil and gas sector as the governments of China and India, both of which often draw upon their SOEs to serve non-commercial objectives, allocate resources among different sectors, and are even directly involved in running the petroleum industry. However, it does not mean that the US government has less leverage to regulate the petroleum industry. In particular, the US government often abuses its hegemonic role to protect its oil interest in other regions or countries. Moreover, government support, maybe in different forms, is prevalent among the three big powers. Energy companies in the three countries, no matter whether they are private owned or state owned, behave in concert with their home government's directives in case the latter caters to their commercial interests. However, these energy companies have such a propensity of prioritizing their commercial interests and sometimes even acting against the will of their home governments. Hence, in the sense of commercial drive there is no fundamental difference between IOCs and NOCs, while minor distinctions may exist with regard to their motives to serve public interests. In face of the IOCs' defiance, the White House has few punishment means at hand; In contrast, both the Chinese and Indian governments have more options, both overt and covert, to discipline the NOCs. Looking forward, distinctions of the IOCs' and NOCs' behaviors tend to be diminished in the future. As argued by Steve Westwell, former BP Group Chief of Staff, "the idea that their (NOCs and IOCs) roles and priorities are vastly different, no longer holds true in the twenty-first century."[106]

[106] Steve Westwell, "Key roles and responsibilities of IOCs in an age of uncertainty," speech at the World National Oil Companies Congress, London, 22 June 2010, http://www.bp.com/en/global/corporate/press/speeches/key-roles-responsibilities-iocs.html, accessed 13 November 2014.

CHAPTER 9

SMMA and State-SOEs-Market Relations

The book argues that the SMMA is dictated largely by the interplay between the state and the NOCs. Their interactions, however, do not take play in vacuum. Rather, there are a variety of factors that can influence the SMMA. Also, this approach has special implications for the political economy of development. Previous literature like the developmental state model is based on the assumption of a state-market dichotomy. Under China's approach, however, both the state and the market not only coexist and compete with each other, but also collaborate, and or play a role compatible with each other. Largely decided by the institutions where they are located, the SOEs are not passively subordinate to government mandates. With globalization and marketization going on, the SOEs' behaviors are not static either.

This chapter first summarizes the formation of China's approach to oil security, followed by my analysis of the major factors affecting role choices by the Chinese government and the NOCs. The third section focuses on the theoretical implications of China's approach from the perspective of state-SOEs-market relations.

S. Chen, *China's Approach to Energy Security*,
https://doi.org/10.1007/978-981-99-3573-4_9

9.1 Role Compatibility and Formation of China's Approach

As the major actors who have been playing a leading role in the Chinese oil policy process, the government and the NOCs have a cluster of their own interest concerns, which are often, though not always, overlapping. Their predominant concerns may be at odds under different settings, but both will try to build role compatibility to cope with the oil security issue. The success or failure to reach role compatibility will remarkably affect China's approach to oil security (For the roles the state and the NOCs have played and the resulted approaches in each case, see Appendix Chart 2).

All the cases show that the Chinese government has both sociopolitical/ security concerns and economic concerns with respect to certain energy policy or project, and it will try to synergize both concerns. Political concern and economic concern do not necessarily contradict with each other, but sometimes China has to prioritize one over the other. It is not necessary that the Chinese government will always prioritize sociopolitical/security concern over economic concern. Which concern predominates depends on what type of country it transacts, whether the government is confident to prevent and curb the likely risks to its national and economic security. Generally speaking, China tends to follow market rules when it is doing business with market economies, as the CNOOC acquisition case suggests. That Beijing stood against a Russian oil pipeline through Mongolia to China reflects its security concern dominance, whereas in the WEGP case, Beijing persisted in allowing foreign investment as it is confident that the whole project, which is within China, could be under its control.

Related with the above, the priority of which concern the government will take may change over time. The case of Russian oil pipeline and Sino-Kazakhstan oil pipeline well illustrate the evolution of Beijing's calculations. The change of concern priority further leads to the government's role adjustment. In the Russian oil pipeline case, Beijing did not involve itself with the project initially and much was left to the corporate level due to its economic concerns, but later the government, in conjunction with the NOCs, strove hard to win the pipeline. The economic concerns in the CNOOC acquisition case also largely determined its role as economic efficiency promoter, taking a hands-off policy in the negotiation process.

There are plenty of factors affecting the role that the NOCs are willing to take. All the cases tend to show that the NOCs' role propensities are closely correlated with oil prices they face. As domestic crude oil prices are integrated with world ones whereas the government still controls refined oil prices, the NOCs' role preferences will be impacted by the actual level of oil prices, their expectations of future oil price trend, as well as the gap between domestic crude oil and refined oil prices. High oil prices provide strong motivations for the NOCs to act as market actors, and vigorously search more oil and gas resources both at home and abroad. By contrast, when both domestic crude oil prices and refined oil prices are low, the NOCs prefer the role of SPSOU since they need to depend on the government to make up for their losses, and they are also less willing to proceed an energy project, as shown in the cases of WEGP, Russian pipeline and Kazakhstan pipeline. When the NOCs expect high oil and gas prices in the long term, they would boldly proceed a project even it is economically unfeasible at that time. Cases of the WEGP, CNPC's pursuit for the Russian oil pipeline, and CNOOC's attempt to acquire Unocal all testify this. When the gap between crude and refined oil prices is very high, CNPC and CNOOC prefer the market actor role as they can reap prolific returns, whereas Sinopec, the largest oil refiner, is inclined to the SPSOU role since it suffers most. Of course, the interest division will eventually be reduced since all the NOCs are gearing up to develop an integrated up-, mid-, and down-stream businesses.

The NOCs' role propensity seems to vary when they are in foreign markets compared with that at home. When venturing abroad, they tend to prefer the role ofmarket actor, trying to garner government support. Conversely, the NOCs appear inclined to the role of market actor at domestic market. Such a difference is comprehensible. In domestic market, they are holding monopoly, so they are willing to play the game with other actors in light of a set of extant rules obviously favorable to them. In contrast, since the NOCs, as latecomers into the international markets, confront much more competitive MOCs, they are more liable to resort to the government assistance. Saying that, of course, does not mean that every NOCs' foreign activity has the government on their back. In fact, even in different foreign countries, their role preference may be different, as indicated in the two cases of CNOOC acquisition and the Russia oil pipeline.

The NOCs' role choices will also be affected by government policy changes. When the NOCs predict that their commercial interests are to be negatively affected, they will voice their opposition before decision-making. For instance, Sinopec opposes the levy of fuel oil taxes and the construction of SPR. Yet, when such a policy is formulated, the NOCs may try to evade the adverse policy, as evidenced in the oil pricing case. Beijing has cherished the hope that the NOCs could serve domestic market well notwithstanding lower prices of refined oil, but the NOCs took advantage of the price gaps via more oil exports, which led to the repeated phenomena of large-scale oil shortages in recent years as illustrated in Chapter 4.

Hence, the NOCs are not passive policy recipient. Rather, they often take some strategies to initiate a new policy or project. One strategy is in making alliance with local governments or other NOCs. The two largest giants' joint pressure to raise oil prices typifies such cases. But there exists monopolized competition too. In that case, the NOCs often refer to the second strategy by highlighting the political/security-side significance of that project, with minority region stability, energy security, or social stability in particular, such as CNPC's lobbying for the WEGP and a Russian oil pipeline vis-à-vis Sinopec. Catering to the government's requirements by creating conditions or eliminating its concerns is their third strategy. For example, CNPC's endeavor to complete the pipeline finally changed the government's mind to involve foreign investment in the WEGP. To strive for more benefits from a policy, the NOCs will place more emphasis on the difficulties they are facing and the importance of what they concern about. They may recur to the strategies of allying with local governments or even the MOCs, highlighting security reasons, sparing no efforts to satisfy the government's requirements or reduce its certain concern,, and so on.

More than that, the NOCs may jealously guard the information they hold and or take advantage of their monopoly. As evidenced in the oil price case, the NOCs deliberately created oil shortage crisis by manipulating domestic market oil and gas supplies in order to create force the government to adjust oil prices. The NOCs' production expansion drive has coincided with local governments' proclivity to prioritizing local economic growth, even at the expense of energy efficiency and environmental protection. As a result, energy inefficiency and environmental pollution keep the deteriorating trend irrespective of the relevant laws being in place for years.

Underlying the above role changes is the fact that the NOCs are more profit-oriented. Compared with the traditional SOEs, the NOCs have leaped forward in paying closer heed to profits, but unlike the profit-centered private firms, the NOCs have not been entirely imposed by hard budget constraint since they have no need to worry about the chastisement of being cleared out of the market. The integration of Chinese economy with the world market, not only has brought about marketization of most factors of production for the NOCs, but has empowered them with more autonomy; hence, they become more self-interest-centered.

As a result of the interactions between the state and the NOCs, China's approach to oil security has taken a sketchy shape. The government, as the energy policy maker, can hardly leave aside the NOCs' interests when formulating an energy policy not only because of their strong influence arising from the state's industrial policy to prop up some Chinese multinationals, their personal contacts with central leadership, monopoly status, and financial contribution, but also because of the state's reliance on their energy expertise, market information, as well as their pivotal role as the overriding policy implementers. The NOCs, out of their own interest, most of the time, try to build consensus and stand in line with the government. Hence, both the state and the NOCs strive to play a role compatible with each other so that both can benefit from their "collaboration." The benefits, among other things, particularly consist that state policy can be enforced more smoothly, and NOCs' privileges can be held on. As such, a MDA or SCA will come into being. As indicated by the cases of oil pricing reform in 1994, the initiation of the WEGP, the Russian oil pipeline, and the Sino-Kazakhstan pipeline, when the state deems it necessary to play the role of an internal stabilizer while the NOCs are willing to act as SPSOU, their interactions will form the SCA. By contrast, when the state prefers the role of EEP while the NOCs are proactive to work as market actors, as the cases of oil pricing reform in 1993 and the acquisition battle over Unocal have demonstrated, their interactions have formed the MDA.

However, the role expectations of the government and the NOCs do not always coincide with each other. Under the circumstances of role incompatibility, the state may take a policy unwelcomed by the NOCs, while the NOCs may try to prioritize their own interests, rather than merely stay in line with the state's mandates. Thereby, state-NOC intercourse will form a mixed approach.

Therefore, the effectiveness of its "management" has to some extent been undermined by the NOCs, despite the fact that the state endeavors to get marketization under its control. Consequently, the government sometimes has to roll back from the marketization process, which in turn dampens the development of the energy sector. To prompt its growth, the state then has to introduce more market forces. The past trajectory seems to indicate that the Chinese government has fallen into a quandary. How will China go out of such a quandary? or wither China's approach to oil security? It is worthwhile to explore the major factors influencing their role choices and consequently China's approach.

9.2 Factors Affecting Role Choices

There are a variety of factors influencing the role that the government and the NOCs prefer to undertake, and consequently the quality of China's approach. These factors can be classified into four categories: external environment factors, such as macro economic situation, sociopolitical situation, macro economic policy, energy market situation; state-related factors, such as leadership, central regulatory capacity, fiscal capacity, and consolidation of the state bureaucracies; NOCs-related factors, such as consolidation of the NOCs, and social network; and other factors, such as the state and the NOCs' interest/preference expectancy towards each other and information flow.

9.2.1 External Environment Factors

External environment factors influence China's approach through creating incentives or constraints on the state and the NOCs. The macro economic situation, the subsequent macro economic policies, particularly the industrial and energy policy, and even domestic energy market situation will directly affect the central government agenda and interest preferences of the state and the NOCs. Kun-Chin Lin finds the macro economic situation in 1998 had created conditions for the oil industrial restructuring.[1] Implementation of a proactive fiscal policy to counter economic deflation caters to the NOCs' impulse to expand investments; conversely, enforcing a tight financial policy to curb inflation might deal a blow to the NOCs' large-scale investments. As our cases have illustrated, the government used to prop up those export-oriented industries at the

[1] Kun-Chin Lin, PhD dissertation, 2003, ibid.

cost of the petroleum industry. Since 1998, the government has changed the industrial policy by vigorously promoting the development of some large SOEs with strategic and fiscal values including the NOCs. Similarly, unlike previous practice which blindly paid homage to GDP figure, enforcement of stricter environment protection criteria is bound to affect the petroleum and petrochemical industry, a major pollution maker.

Energy market situation is another important factor that can influence China's approach to energy security. Straightforward is the case when oil supply shortages happened in the years 2003–2005, conflicts arose when the state compelled the NOCs to expand supplies while the latter pressed for oil price increase. In contrast, when the glut of foreign oil imports dealt a blow to the NOCs in 1994 and 1998, the state did not hesitate to impose import bans to salvage the NOCs. As a matter of fact, the global market situation also has a strong influence on China's approach. Noteworthy is the price factor in influencing their efforts to construct role compatibility as discussed above. It is easier to reach role compatibility whenever the state perceives fiercer competition over energy acquisition abroad, as the case of the Russian oil pipeline indicates.

The sociopolitical situation that China faces has an in-depth impact on China's reform agenda thanks to the state's sociopolitical/security concern. Both the state and the NOCs have common interests in preserving sociopolitical stability of China so as to maintain the CCP's exclusive ruling power. Hence, whenever events like the 1989 Tiananmen Square Movement occur, it will be easier for them to reach role compatibility, thus deciding China's approach.

9.2.2 State-Related Factors

The state-related factors range from who constitutes the leadership, what guideline it embraces, the state's interest/preference, its regulatory and fiscal capacities, as well as the consolidation of the state bureaucracies, and so forth.

Leadership matters not only because of their different personalities that will affect their perceptions of the evolving social realities, attitudes towards market, and even the past ideology, but also because of their distinct guidelines under different generations of leadership. For instance, casting off the ideological constraint, the Chinese leadership has recognized that the establishment of the "socialist market economy" entails a bureaucratic system compatible with a market economy. Nonetheless, the bureaucratic reform in 1993 under Li Peng failed owing to his "predominantly conservative mindset and other factors"; in contrast, a radical restructuring could turn into a fulfilled mission under Zhu Rongji.[2] If it can be said that Zhu prioritized market efficiency through bureaucratic, financial, and SOE reforms, then Premier Wen Jiabao paid more attention to social equality.

Crucial among these various factors is the state's regulatory and fiscal capacities as they directly associate with the policy process. As discussed in Chapter 1, bargaining widely exists in Chinese policy process between the central and the local government, as well as between the state and the NOCs. Central-local relations inevitably affect the role compatibility construction between the state and the NOCs because either of them can seek alliance with the local. The regulatory capacity issue thus correlates with the trilateral interactions among the central government, local governments, and the NOCs. In brief, the NOCs yearn for the state's protective prerogatives, while the state's regulatory capacity over local governments largely hinges upon its coffers, which in turn rests on the NOCs' fiscal contribution. Therefore, both the state and the NOCs have an interdependent relationship. The NOCs gained their monopoly status at the cost of local firms, most of which belonged to local governments. Sometimes local governments' energy projects and inclination to foreign energy imports may be a menace to the NOCs' interest. Hence, their interests may be conflicting; on the other hand, local governments have to rely on the NOCs to ensure their energy supplies, while the NOCs' operations can be greatly facilitated or impaired by local governments. Moreover, the launch of any large energy projects can hardly divorce from the collaboration of the NOC and local government. Thereby, the NOCs and local governments are also interdependent too. The state's fiscal capacity is another key variable in deciding its regulatory capacity and its inclination to reach role compatibility with the NOCs.

It is apparent that this study is based on the prerequisite that state organs keep unified with the same role. In reality there are two situations. In case the NOC just needs to interact with one single state agency on certain issue, then the 'state' can be regarded as unified. But when more than one state organ is involved, chances are that they may act "in one voice" or "in more than one voice." As the case of fuel tax levy illustrates,

[2] Yongnian Zheng, 2004, ibid., p. 106.

the Chinese state organs sometimes were at odds with each other, particularly when certain policies impaired the vested interests. Their dispute left a loophole for the NOC to take advantage. The latter can seek alliance with those bureaucracies of similar interests to justify its requirement.

9.2.3 NOCs-Related Factors

Likewise, the number of NOCs involved and the consolidation of them are important factors that can influence the strategy and policy of the state. It is true that the more NOCs are involved, the more likely the collective action problem may occur,[3] but since the number of major NOCs in the petroleum sector is merely four and they have different main businesses, it is easy to avoid that problem. Hence, when all the NOCs have identical interest towards a policy, the state is more likely to be convinced of that policy. Conversely, when only one NOC is interested in a policy, the state may be more hesitant towards it, worrying about policy unfairness to the others or the society. When different NOCs have different proposals regarding a policy or project, the state has more room to maneuver and act according to its own considerations, and a compromised arrangement may be the option. In case a NOC is reluctant to carry out the state policy, the government can turn to other NOCs. That being said, it cannot be denied that even the four NOCs have different influence on and bargaining power with the state due to their different background.[4] The consolidation of the NOCs is another important factor for bargaining with the state, which directly relates with the intensity of their preferences.

One channel through which the NOCs engage in influencing central energy policies is through their social networks or *guanxi* with central leaders. *Guanxi* can deeply influence and structure nearly all aspects

[3] Collective action problem is identified by Olson, who insightfully finds that people with a common interest will not necessary get together to strive for that goal. See Mancur Olson, *The Logic of Collective Action: Public Goods and the Theory of Groups*, Cambridge, Mass.: Harvard University Press, Revised edition, 1971.

[4] It was said that among the four NOCs, usually CNPC is the most powerful and influential enterprise, then Sinopec, and then CNOOC and Sinochem. Interview with Zhou Keyuan, a researcher on China studies, 10 July 2006, Singapore.

of Chinese society, including the political realm.[5] One reason that the NOCs have reinforced their monopoly status was reportedly because many central leaders in Jiang era had some background related to the petroleum sector.[6]

9.2.4 Other Factors

The preferences of the NOCs and the state in terms of their relations directly decide the role they will take. Although "no reliable measure exists for the intensity of preferences",[7] it by no means affects the bargaining power between the state organs and the NOCs. It merits noting that neither the state's nor the NOCs' preferences will remain unchanged. Rather, their preferences towards a policy may change over time. As the example provided by Groombridge says,

> When market prospects are favorable, industrial actors in SOEs argue that state leaders should liberalize prices in their industry and extend greater managerial residual claimant rights by restructuring property rights. Conversely, when market prospects are not favorable, industrial actors are much less interested in price reform and lobby to have state leaders bail them out.[8]

Thus, we need to consider the specific context, but the formation of preferences largely hinges upon the information they have on certain issues.

Information influences the interaction between the state and the NOCs. First, Information of a technical sort is vital to industrial policy-making. Second, information affects their role expectations towards the other. The formation of rational expectation of maximizing behavior depends on "the cost of information, the intrinsic difficulty of the

[5] D. Guthrie, "The declining significance of *guanxi* in China's economic transition," *The China Quarterly*, Vol. 154, 1998, pp. 254–282.

[6] Willy Wo-Lap Lam, *The Era of Jiang Zemin*, Singapore: Prentice Hall, 1999, p. 94.

[7] Jon Elster, *Nuts and Bolts for the Social Sciences*, Cambridge: Cambridge University Press, 1989, p. 156.

[8] Mark Allen Groombridge, *The Politics of Industrial Bargaining: The Restructuring of State-Owned Enterprises in the People's Republic of China, 1978 to 1995*, Doctoral dissertation for Columbia University, 1998, p. 9.

forecasting problem, and the benefits to be obtained from accurate predictions."[9] Finally, accurate information is also needed to monitor whether the other party follows the interaction "rules" including the shirking behavior. However, acquiring information is not without transaction costs.[10] If the costs are too high, the state bureau has to depend on firms or sector associations.[11] In reality, despite the fact that the state tries hard to facilitate information collection and processing, asymmetric information still exists between the NOCs and the state as the latter heavily relies on the NOCs to provide much information on the petroleum sector. Such a problem has further been exacerbated by the suppressed press freedom in China. When the exchanging parties face asymmetrical information, their transaction is subject to hazards.[12] The principal–agent theory illustrates that the agent has the propensity to take advantage of asymmetric information to serve its own purpose.[13] Moreover, other than by the asymmetric information problem, market exchange is to be impaired by small-numbers bargaining, bounded rationality, and the agents' opportunistic impulses as well.[14] As illustrated by the oil pricing and the WEGP cases, this is indeed the case as the NOCs fabricated information or created market distortion for the sake of their own purposes.

[9] Stephen J. DeCanio, "Rational Expectations and Learning from Experience," *The Quarterly Journal of Economics*, Vol. 93, No. 1, Feb. 1979, p. 55.

[10] *Transaction costs* are the costs incurred in making an exchange and enforcing the agreement. It usually consists of information searching costs, bargaining costs, and enforcing and monitoring costs. See Oliver E. Williamson, "Transaction Cost Economics: The Governance of Contractual Relations," *Journal of Law and Economics,* Vol. 22, No. 2, Oct. 1979, pp. 233–261.

[11] Alan Cawson (ed.), *Organized Interests and the State: Studies in Meso-Corporatism*, London, Beverly Hill and New Delhi: SAGE Publications, 1985, p. 30.

[12] Oliver E. Williamson, *Markets and Hierarchies, Analysis and Antitrust Implications*, New York: Free Press, 1975, p. 31.

[13] Sappington has discussed the principal–agent incentive problems, see D. Sappington, "Incentives in principal agent relationships," *Journal of Economic Perspectives*, Vol. 3, No. 2, 1991, pp. 45–66.

[14] Oliver E. Williamson, 1975, ibid., pp. 31–33.

9.3 State-SOEs-Market Relations in the Globalization Era

9.3.1 *State-SOEs-Market Relations: A Review*

Government-business relationship has an important influence on economic performance and distribution of economic benefits.[15] Thus, it has become a long-lasting debate as to how to institute appropriate mechanisms conducive to sustained economic development and social justice. The debates in political economy focus on a wide range of topics such as state–market relations in general, state-SOEs relations, and micro corporate governance.

Analysis of state-SOEs relations starts from the states' various motivations to create SOEs. Krapels has summarized the justification for creating NOCs: "to increase public revenue; to improve government control; and to improve government insight."[16] Even if the original goal of creating a SOE is clear and simple, the SOE often finds itself divert to other goals, and it is in this multiplicity of goals that confusion lies.[17] Hence, the SOEs have to struggle among different goals which may be unreconciled and irreconcilable. Moreover, as cases in this book illustrate, the SOEs may take advantage of the different goals (roles) to serve their own purposes. That elicits another problem of how the government ensures the SOEs' executives acting on its behalf. Based on the observations on the advanced industrial nations, Cassese finds that these countries basically failed to find adequate ways to control their SOEs without destroying their entrepreneurial nature.[18] This study has partly collaborated with such a view, partly because government-SOEs relationship is not static

[15] Fred Block, "The Roles of the State in the Economy," in Neil J. Smelser and Richard Swedberg (eds.), *The Handbook of Economic Sociology*, Princeton, N.J., Princeton University Press, 1994, pp. 691–710; Charles E. Lindblom, *Politics and Markets: The World's Political Economic Systems*, New York: Basic, 1977; Douglass North, *Institutions, Institutional Change, and Economic Performance*, Cambridge: Cambridge University Press, 1990.

[16] E. N. Krapels, *Controlling Oil: British Oil Policy and the British National Oil Corporation*, Washington D.C.: US Government Printing Office, 1977, p. 20.

[17] Raymond Vernon, "Introduction," in Raymond Vernon and Yair Aharoni (eds.), *State-Owned Enterprise in the Western Economies*, London: Croom Helm, 1981, pp. 11–14.

[18] Sabino Cassese, "Public Control and Corporate Efficiency," in Vernon and Aharoni, *State-Owned Enterprise in the Western Economies*, 1981, ibid., pp. 145–156.

and fully institutionalized, and partly because the NOCs become a more centrifugal force.

From the perspective of micro corporate governance, previous studies have highlighted some problems affecting SOE performance, for example, soft budget constraint,[19] management rewards incommensurate with their performance,[20] allocation of control rights,[21] separation of ownership and control as well as state-imposed policy burdens,[22] state asset stripping, and so on. These problems, though affect the Chinese SOE performance to a differing extent, have been gaged merely in light of economic indexes. Given the SOEs have been endowed with multiple goals (roles), it would be unjustifiable to measure them merely from the economic angle.

In the context of China, students of political economy have developed five major paradigms to study the relationship between the government and the SOEs. The first type is pluralism, which holds that various types of social groups including the SOEs and bureaucracies stand in a relatively equal line to influence state policy. Pluralism rightly perceives the rise of some interest groups like the NOCs, but apparently different social groups are unequal and state policy process is far from open in China. Second is societal corporatism, in which SOEs exert their influence on the government through their representative associations. Despite a growing impact in China identified by Scott Kennedy, even he himself admitted business associations' role should not be overstated.[23]

The third paradigm is state corporatism, which holds that the state generates great pressure on the SOEs to conform to state policies while the latter have to be subject to state directives. Walder's version of

[19] Yingyi Qian and Gérard Roland, "Federalism and the Soft Budget Constraint," *American Economic Review*, Vol. 88, No. 5, December 1998, pp. 1143–62.

[20] Jon Cauley & Todd Sandler, "Agency theory and the Chinese enterprise under reform," *China Economic Review*, Vol. 3, 1992, pp. 39–56; Zhou Mi and Xiaoming Wang, "Agency cost and the crisis of China's SOE," *China Economic Review*, Vol. 11, 2000, pp. 297–317.

[21] Yingyi Qian, "Enterprise Reform in China: Agency Problems and Political Control," *The Economics of Transition*, Vol.4, No. 2, October 1996, pp. 427–447.

[22] Justin Yifu Lin, Fang Cai, and Zhou Li, "Competition, Policy Burdens, and State-Owned Enterprise Reform," The American Economic Review, Vol. 88, No. 2, May, 1998, pp. 422–427.

[23] Scott Kennedy, *The Business of Lobbying in China*, Cambridge, MA: Harvard University Press, 2005.

"local state corporatism" articulates that local government can replace entrepreneurs to drive local firms' growth in China.[24] Similar to this paradigm stressing that the power lies in the state, the patron–client model, the fourth type, is used to describe state-SOEs relationship as mutual obligations, each expecting to gain what the other can supply.[25] This model has properly depicted state-SOE reciprocal relations, but state coercion, state rent-seeking, and SOE defection behaviors may exist as well.

Rent-seeking theory, the fifth paradigm, includes two aspects. One is disclosed by the public choice theory, portraying that the self-interested state bureaucrats and politicians are not neutral arbitrator; rather, they may take advantage of their power to line their own pocket, maximize their own budget or try to increase their chances for staying in power. Likewise, SOEs managers may conduct rent-seeking as what the principal–agent theory reveals.[26]

As this study has shown, the NOCs enjoy a rising power and influence in China's energy industry; the government keeps patronizing the NOCs, and both have their interest stakes on the other; corruption resulting from rent-seeking is prevalent. Hence, the above models have grasped some aspects of state-SOE relationship in China. Nonetheless, neither of them can fully cover this pair of complex, dynamic, and evolving relations.

Similarly, there are many debates concerning state–market relations and their different roles in promoting economic development. According to the remedy prescribed by "neoliberalism" or "Washington consensus" to post-communist countries including China, economic transition is simply a linear process, namely, from state control to free marketization. Over the past quarter century, "neoliberalism," marked by privatization and free competition, had become the "global policy paradigm," and

[24] Andrew Walder, "Local governments as industrial firms: an organizational analysis of China's transitional Economy," *American Journal of Sociology*, Vol. 101, No. 2, 1995, pp. 263–301.

[25] In his study on China's internet services, Zhang conceptualizes the state-enterprise relations with unequal power position. See Jun Zhang, "Market Transition, State Connections and Internet Geography in China," *The China Review*, Vol. 6, No. 1, Spring 2006.

[26] Ding has explored the major strategies widely employed by state-firm managers and officials to illicitly strip state assets. See X. L. Ding, "The Illicit Asset Stripping of Chinese State Firms," *The China Journal*, No. 43, Jan., 2000, pp. 1–28.

non-neoliberal policies and institutions had been deemed as "deviant".[27] "Public discourse shows an overwhelming tendency toward simplistic trust in 'the market' and skeptical rejection of the state's role in the economy."[28] According to its logic, there was a universally a priori fixed benchmark, by which latecomers could be measured, and a set of standard rules and goals, to which they were going to, or at least should integrate with.[29] Therefore, China's breathtaking transformation was just a process of integrating with the presumed globalization practices. In particular, it is claimed that the market had "a natural affinity" with private ownership, and thus "rapid privatization would generate the necessary conditions for an efficiently functioning market economy".[30]

By contrast, the developmental state model has highlighted a constructive role that the state has played in nurturing certain industries and fostering human capitals.[31] As such, it is believed that the state is a rational and unitary entity which not only has a good will to serve the public but also enjoys great autonomy and capacity to fulfill that aim. However, this model has aroused many criticisms. Neostatist scholars like Peter Evans, Linda Weiss, and John Hobson argue against its assumption that market agents are passive policy recipients, neither is

[27] Neoliberalism's prevalence is largely due to the historically prolonged economic growth resulted from large-scale privatization programs by Thatcher and Reagan respectively in the 1980s. Robert Hunter Wader, "Beyond Asian Horizon: Neoliberalism and the Emergence of a Hereditary World Oligarchy," Workshop in the First Congress of Asian Political & International Studies Association—Asia *in the New Millennium*, Singapore, 27–30 November 2005.

[28] Louis Putterman & Dietrich Rueschemeyer, "State and Msrket in Development: An introduction," in Louis Putterman and Dietrich Rueschemeyer (eds.), *State and Market in Development: Synergy or Rivalry?* Boulder: Lynne Rienner Publishers, 1992, p. 1.

[29] "Preface" by Peter Nolan, for Jin Zhang, *Catch-up and Competitiveness in China: The Case of Large Firms in the Oil Industry*, London and New York, NY: RoutledgeCurzon, 2004.

[30] Jeffery Sachs, *Poland's Jump to the Market Economy*, Cambridge, MA: Harvard University Press, 1993; Janos Konai, "The Affinity between Ownership Forms and Coordination Mechanisms," *Journal of Economic Perspectives*, Vol.4, No. 3, 1990, pp.131–47.

[31] Among the many studies along the developmental state line of reasoning, those frequently cited include Alice Amsden, *Asia's Next Giant*, Oxford: Oxford University Press, 1989; Stephan Haggard, *Pathways from the Periphery*, Cornell University Press, 1990; Chalmers Johnson, *MITI and the Japanese Miracle,* Stanford University Press, 1982; and Robert Wade, *Governing the Market,* Princeton University Press, 1990.

the state rational and unitary, possessing considerable autonomy and technical capacity, and staying immune to rent-seeking. Instead, they maintain that government-business close ties are crucial to effective market governance and successful economic restructuring.[32] Likewise, the social-institutionalists and neopluralists underscore cooperative ties between government and the private sector. They do not deny the importance of a strong state for economic development, but they stress the importance of private-sector preferences over state interests and institutions, which is opposite to the development state model that reifies the state.[33]

The above models, though having different emphases, are common in presuming a state-versus-market dichotomy, which Underhill believes is problematic. According to him, both the developmental state model and its revisionists still stay in the state-market dichotomy paradigm, which conceals the fact that the state is one of the market agents and market actors also engage in the process of governance. He thus puts forward a state-market condominium model, regarding state and market agents as "part of the same integrated ensemble."[34] This model has rightly perceived state-market reciprocal relations, and the dynamics between changing forms of governance and changing market structures. However, that model is preconditioned with democratic systems where various business groups can access to state governance. In the Chinese case, state-market condominium is at most a worthwhile pursuit. However, within that "ensemble," state–market relations are equivocal. These important questions are unclear from this model: Who is the director? Do they

[32] See Peter Evans, *Embedded Autonomy*, Princeton University Press, 1995; and Linda Weiss, *The Myth of the Powerless State*, Ithaca, New York: Cornell University Press, 1998; Linda Weiss & John Hobson, *States and Economic Development*, Polity, 1995; and Linda Weiss (ed.), *States in the Global Economy*, Cambridge University Press, 2003.

[33] R. Doner, 'Limits of State Strength', *World Politics*, Vol. 44, No. 3, 1992, pp. 398–431; E. Y. Kim, 'The Developmental State and the Politics of Business Interest Associations', *Pacific Focus*, Vol. 8, No. 2, 1993, pp. 31–60; and D. Okimoto, *Between MITI and the Market*, Stanford University Press, 1989.

[34] Geoffrey R.D. Underhill, "State, market, and global political economy," *International Affairs*, Vol. 76, No. 4, Oct. 2000, pp. 805–824; Geoffrey R.D. Underhill & Xiaoke Zhang, "The changing state-market condominium in East Asia: Rethinking the political underpinnings of development," *New Political Economy*, Vol. 10, No. 1, Mar. 2005, p. 1–24; and Geoffrey R.D. Underhill, "Markets, institutions, and transaction costs: the endogeneity of governance," Working paper in the World Economy & Finance Research Programme, WEF0025, June 2007.

compete for that role? How does one's change affect the other? Therefore, SMMA would be more appropriate to portray state–market relations in China's oil and gas sectors.

As abovementioned, institutionalists underscore the "synergy" between the state and the market, which is the basis for the catch-up of late-development countries. Particularly, institutionalists shifted their attention to the organizational differences among the capitalist economies and their subsequent economic performance. According to Onis, the East Asian model of developmental state is "the product of unique historical circumstances" with three key elements that make it extremely difficult to emulate, that is, "the single minded adherence to growth and competitiveness at the expense of other objectives, the unusual degree of bureaucratic autonomy and capacity, and the equally unique and unusual degree of public–private cooperation."[35] It is true that "state leadership and policy are relevant to East Asia's developmental history," but "the nature of society, culture, market, and evolving international economy is also important."[36]

Although new institutionalism has rightly pointed it out that both the liberalist and developmental state models took no account of the institutional context and incorporated institutional factors into analyses, it renders support to the argument that economic efficiency "appears almost as a moral imperative that justifies the disregard for conflicts of interest and inequalities of power as well as for the societally specific ways of dealing with them".[37]

This study has verified state-market interdependent and intertwining relationship. The state engages in market activities via its SOEs, while the NOCs, the major market actors in the Chinese oil and gas market, also directly involved in the process of governance. Meanwhile, as will be analyzed below, state and market compete with each other.

This study has partly corroborated the above view regarding most states' embrace of economic efficiency led by the market, which may be called as the convergent effect brought about by economic globalization,

[35] Ziya Onis, "The Logic of the Developmental State," *Comparative Politics*, Vol. 24, No.1, Oct., pp. 109–126.

[36] Steve Chan, Cal Clark, and Danny Lam (eds.), *Beyond the Developmental State: East Asia's Political Economies Reconsidered*, New York: St. Martin's, 1998, p. 8.

[37] Ayse Bugra and Behlul Usdiken (Ed.), *State, Market, and Organizational Form*, Berlin: Walter de Gruyter & Co., 1997, p. 5.

but simultaneously globalization has created some divergent effects on China's energy practices.

9.3.2 *State Managing the Market*

The Chinese government tries to "manage" the market in the process of handling its energy security challenge. Other than laying out market rules and regulations, Beijing also resorts to the means such as shaping market actors, differentiating the market for the major NOCs, setting rules for their cooperation and competition, imposing limits on market entry, partially controlling prices, setting energy import/export quotas, and so forth. As a result, the scope and substance of market activities are modified by the government. Market competition has been arbitrarily formatted.

The SMMA has exhibited that the Chinese government has fallen into a paradox with regard to the market. On the one hand, the government has to infuse more market mechanisms into the economy and expose the SOEs to market competition to some extent, because it has to win legitimacy by promoting economic development. On the other hand, the state expects that market competition could be under its control and would not bring about domestic unrest.

Likewise, the state is keen on the growth of the SOEs out of concern for boosting national industry and international competitiveness. For that purpose, the state has privatized most SOEs while keeping those with strategic and fiscal potentials in hand. For the selected SOEs, the state granted them with considerable autonomy and directed them into engaging in market competition. In order to push forward its tough reform agenda, the state even recurs to what Solinger calls "virtual globalization" by threatening the direct injection of global forces into China,[38] as described by Lin in his studies of wage regime in China's SOEs.[39]

[38] Dorothy J. Solinger, "Globalization and Human Rights for Workers in China: Convergence or Collision?" in Mahmood Monshipouri, Neil Englehart, Andrew J. Nathan and Kavita Philip (eds.), *Constructing Human Rights in the Age of Globalization*, New York: M.E. Sharpe, 2003.

[39] Kun-Chin Lin, "Explaining Evolving Wage Structure in State-Owned Enterprises in China: Evidence from the Oil Industry," Paper presented at the Workshop, "Globalization and the Workplace," ST. Anthony's College, Oxford University, 27–8 October 2006.

Nevertheless, the state is reluctant to let go the SOEs entirely thanks to its sociopolitical concerns.

Apparently China's approach to energy security is not wholly following the internationally conventional way; rather, it is also transforming the international practice, adding new ingredients to countries' used ways of dealing with energy security. In particular, China's practices in the following are pronounced.

First, Beijing aspires to reshape the NOCs into the flagship of Chinese corporations so that they can lay a solid economic base for China's rise. As the "world-system" proponents have argued, a state's position in production for global markets embodies profound implications for its politics and welfare of its citizens.[40] And the optimal shortcut is to provide state support. On the one hand, the state is directly involved in reshaping Chinese oil producers; on the other hand, it also endows them with the autonomy to operate on their own rather than intervening in their routine business through administrative decrees.

Second, the government seemed to treat the global integrated market as divided, and tap domestic market to powerhouse the Chinese oil giants so that they could be better footed in global competition. While carrying out a thorough restructuring over Chinese petroleum market with the aim to reduce competition for the newly-born oil mammoths, the state does not reject market competition and exchange activities between and within the Chinese firms themselves. Thus, domestic market has become a powerhouse for the Chinese oil giants.

In addition, the state has also vigorously bolstered the SOEs to venture abroad through both political and financial means, in the hope that they could gain more experience in engaging in global competition and contribute to China's energy security through acquiring more foreign oil and gas resources. Therefore, China's approach implies that it is hard for it to accept neoliberalists' recipe of full privatization.

The state has its own calculation regarding market competition and NOCs' growth, but as will be discussed below, the market has its own logic and the NOCs have their own concerns which may not necessarily overlap with the state's.

[40] Christopher Chase-Dunn, *Global Formation: Structures of the World Economy*, Cambridge, Mass: Basil Blackwell, 1989.

9.3.3 NOCs' Reactions on State Management and Market Power

How do the NOCs respond to the state's SMMA? The NOCs get along well with their oligarchic status quo. While enjoying considerable autonomy in business operation, the NOCs have acquired massive state support. In the policy sense they are holding a monopoly status in the Chinese energy market, and the government even renders diplomatic and financial backup in their efforts to expand business abroad.

Nonetheless, the NOCs are caught in a dilemma. While striving for state support, sometimes they feel state intervention is nothing but a hindrance against their business expansion, as evidenced by CNOOC President Fu's call for the reduction of state-owned shares after the failed acquisition over Unocal. With the pressing competition from the MOCs, the NOCs try to strive for more market autonomy, extricating themselves away from the sociopolitical obligations posed by the government.

The NOCs have to confront the affected market forces ushered in the energy industry as well as the whole economy. Sometimes the NOCs even brace for market openness in order to capitalize on the pricing system or their collaboration with the MOCs, as verified by their claim for integrating domestic oil prices with global ones and the case of the CNOOC acquisition. However, most of the time they are eager to protect their prerogatives, turning against market openness to their competitors. "SOEs as an institution mediate market forces, sometimes as a force of inertia and conservative statist interests as described by March's metaphor of the firm as an adaptive political coalition."[41] Therefore, the protected NOCs are ambivalent about market competition.

This study finds that the Chinese state is not so unitary and so powerful that it can push its will downwards with ease, and bar any pressure group outside its door. The state has been fragmented not only by its own bureaucratic structures (identified by Kenneth Lieberthal), and local governments (identified by Dali L. Yang, Yongnian Zheng, etc.), but also by the NOCs, an ascending vested interest group mainly transformed from the monopolizing power. As Lin argues, the state's preformatted

[41] Kun-Chin Lin, "Explaining Evolving Wage Structure," 27–8 October 2006, ibid., p. 31.

competition in setting domestic prices for goods and services can be undermined by the NOCs.[42]

In the previous state–market relationship accounts, firms including the SOEs were presumed to be identical and their impact on both the state and the market had not been taken into account. As a result, firms are passive. Liberals and neoliberals basically treat firms as the market, operating only in light of the rules of profit maximization and cost minimization with no other goals.[43] Under the developmental state model, firms are more a tool and a passive recipient of state policy, and at most, they follow the logic of neoclassic economics. According to North, as long as property rights are in place, firms would automatically act according to the maximizing behavior rules.[44] Therefore, his view of the business organizations differs little from the neoclassical formula of the firm.[45]

As this study has demonstrated, in spite that the NOCs are marching toward the goal of market actors, they behave with miscellaneous considerations, rather than merely economic one. For purpose of turning the SOEs into market actors, Lu suggested that the SOEs undergo organizational change from within, whose goal was to seek managerial control, meaning that managers take the responsibility for the performance of the enterprise.[46] From the perspective of role compatibility, I argue that the key lies in the transformation of roles. Ideally the state would be transformed just to act as a regulator, while the SOEs merely behave as market actors; but in the transitional period, it is apparent that this is not a one-step achievable goal for China. Therefore, during the transitional period, it is of importance to institutionalize the rules and norms of bilateral intercourse and dispute settlement so that both can form reasonable expectations, thus reducing the possibility of conflicts.

[42] Kun-Chin Lin, "The State as Market Surrogate: Pricing Goods and Services for Oil and Petrochemical Industries in China," Paper delivered at the Annual Meeting of the Association for Asian Studies, New York, 28 March 2003, p. 39.

[43] Ayse Bugra and Behlul Usdiken, 1997, ibid., p. 2.

[44] Douglass C. North, *Institutions, Institutional Change and Economic Performance*, Cambridge: Cambridge University Press, 1990, pp. 78–84.

[45] Feng Lu, 1999, ibid., p. 14.

[46] Feng Lu, 1999, ibid.

9.3.4 *Convergence and Divergence: Ungovernable Market Forces on the State and SOEs*

How does the market respond to the Chinese state's SMMA? The Chinese government attempts to control the market, whereas the market has its own logic that does not succumb to the state's will. Once released, the market would become an independent force expanding its space out of boundaries, pressing the actors within it to follow its logic, and even causing the state to surrender itself. "Once a crack is opened in the monolith that is the centrally planned economy, cumulative forces take over and prise the crack open even more widely. The crack, in the case of China, was the elimination of the state monopoly over industry, which began a process of change that became irreversible."[47] The intrinsic expanding impulse largely stems from the profit-seeking nature of the capital across the globe, from the nascent social forces pressing for leveling the playing field with the NOCs, and even from the pro-market propensity of the NOCs with a deeper pocket. Therefore, the Chinese domestic market, serving as a milking cow for the NOCs, is bound to be exposed to pressures of the international market.

In particular, economic globalization has exerted great influence upon both the state and the NOCs. Most remarkable is the convergent effects on their behaviors. Convergence is in the sense of the change of their mindset and practices. The former refers to their new focus on consumption-side implication of energy security, as well as their embrace of market mechanisms to deal with China's energy security challenge, which largely results from their relinquishment of the previous ideology that centered on class struggle. Ensuing that, the state has embarked upon transforming its role and the governance over the SOEs.

In practice, the convergent effects brought about by globalization encompass two aspects: gradual state withdrawal from specific energy firms' operation and energy policy convergence. State withdrawal has been represented by a series of measures like the injection of more market competition, state ownership reduction, tax cut, less trade barriers, market openness, and price integration. As Chapter 3 has illustrated, the roles

[47] John McMillan and Barry Naughton, "How to Reform a Planned Economy: Lessons from China," in Ross Garnaut and Yiping Huang (eds), *Growth Without Miracles: Readings on the Chinese Economy in the Era of Reform*, New York: Oxford University Press, 2001, p. 460.

that private investors (domestic firms and foreign MOCs) will play in Chinese energy market are set to loom larger. Moreover, China's growing reliance on foreign energy resources has also compelled it to gradually integrate domestic oil prices with international ones. In the time when refined oil prices were decided by the state, as Friedan and Rogowski argue, global price signals do work as shadow prices which instruct the trend of China's oil and gas prices.[48] Sooner or later, the state has to leave oil and gas pricing power to the market.

The other aspect is the energy policy convergence. As a result of the change of its mindset, the current Chinese state has started its emphasis on both supply-side and consumption-led measures to resolve China's energy security problems. Moreover, international common practices have been adopted by the Chinese government as well, such as diversification of oil import sources, construction of SPR, and formulation of stricter environmental protection and energy efficiency regulations.

The convergent effect exerted by globalization upon the NOCs particularly consists in the fact that they turn to be more profit-centered and market responsive. On the institutional level, the NOCs have been restructured largely in light of the Western practice of corporate governance. In the routine business operation, they have learned to pool foreign capitals to boost their growth through listing the core assets abroad. They are also more sensitive to price signals in the global energy market, as evidenced by their manipulating the price gap between domestic and foreign oil prices, by lobbying the government for more subsidies, and by creating tight oil supply market so as to push the government to raise oil prices. More striking is the measure to boldly whittle down vast number of workers in order to curtail costs. Globalization has also made it possible for the NOCs to ambitiously venture abroad.

Nonetheless, globalization has generated some divergent effects on the state and the NOCs. Apparently the Chinese approach to energy security is far from a MDA. Globalization has convinced the Chinese government that energy competition is worldwide. By no means is energy security in the eyes of it merely an economic issue. Its sociopolitical and security concerns over this problem have complicated its ways to

48 Jeffrey Friedan and Ronald Rogowski, "The Impact of the International Economy on National Policies: An Analytical Overview," in Robert Keohane and Helen Milner, (eds.), *Internationalization and Domestic Politics*, New York: Cambridge University Press, 1996.

handle it. As a result, the state still leaves a strong hand in managing energy businesses. The Chinese government still holds sway on oil and gas prices notwithstanding partially pricing deregulation. Visible and invisible barriers against private investors' energy market entry and energy trade are still prevalent. Particularly, the state spares no effort to shore up the NOCs' oil quest abroad.

Regarding the divergent effects on the NOCs, the fierce market competition, coupled with their ambitions, has spurred them to draw on every resource available to cautiously guard against their prerogative. Taking advantage of global competition and the government's energy security concern, the NOCs have not only triumphantly prevented the state's attempt to split them, but also successfully prevented it to fully expose them to hard budget constraints. Profit-seeking considerations and accountability to shareholders have also prompted the core parts to push cost reduction and staff discharge obligation to the non-core parts.[49]

9.4 Conclusion

The interactions between the state and the NOCs have largely dictated China's approach to energy security. To comprehend and decipher China's approach to energy security, this book tries to create a role compatibility model. The central government tries to "manage" the oil and gas market in light of its own priority concerns and calculations, whereas the NOCs have their own interest concerns that may or may not necessarily be in line with the central government's. It could be found that their priority concerns would lead them to play a role compatible or incompatible with the other's expectations, but in many cases, both the central government and the NOCs strive to navigate a role compatible with each other so as to reduce political and commercial risks and achieve a win–win outcome. This chapter has further analyzed major factors influencing the role that the government and the NOCs are more inclined to assume. Particularly, the NOCs' role propensities are closely correlated with international crude oil prices.

Inherent to the SMMA approach are some of its ramifications on the trilateral state-SOEs-market relations in the globalization era. The SMMA has shown that the state-market dichotomy paradigm can hardly

[49] Kun-Chin Lin, "Explaining evolving wage structures," 2006, ibid.

be applied to examine China's approach to economic reform. Rather, both the state and the market have formed an interdependent and intertwining relationship. The state tries to manage the market and place it under its control, whereas the market has its own logic that can discipline the state intervention. The state intends to bolster the growth of the NOCs, while the latter, after being exposed to market competition, are caught in a dilemma. While they are reluctant to part with government support, the NOCs have their own interest preferences and seek to play a role not necessarily compatible with the state's expectations.

Conclusion

This book has tried to elucidate how China perceives energy security as well as why and how China uses the state-managed marketization approach to cope with it. It is argued that the interplay between the Chinese government and the national oil companies has largely dictated the specific approach through the mechanisms of "role compatibility."

Both the Chinese government and the Chinese NOCs have Janus-faced identities in running the oil and gas industries. On the one hand, in the context of economic reform and transition from a command economy to a socialist market economy, the Chinese government, as the oil and gas policy maker, has undertaken a role of economic efficiency promoter, ushering in more market forces to the oil and gas sectors and let the NOCs be exposed to market competition for sake of economic efficiency and their competitiveness. On the other hand, the government acts as an internal stabilizer without hesitation when it anticipates that the sudden liberation of the oil and gas sectors is likely to bring about economic and social disorder.

Likewise, the NOCs, as the predominant market actors in the Chinese energy market and the leading oil and gas policy implementers, have dual faces, too. On the one hand, they prefer to act as market actors, a role contributory to pursuing their commercial interests in a milieu of market economy. On the other hand, as the government pins its hope on the NOCs to help ensure China's energy security and thus empowers them with some privileges, the NOCs choose to assume the role of state

S. Chen, *China's Approach to Energy Security*,
https://doi.org/10.1007/978-981-99-3573-4

policy & social obligation undertaker, whether by choice or force, for sake of their prerogatives in market status, political prospect of the management and government supports. Moreover, they even directly involve in the process of governance.

The growing reliance on foreign oil and gas resources has elicited China's growing concern about its energy security. As the major actors who have been playing a decisive role in the Chinese oil and gas policy-making and implementation process, the Chinese government and the NOCs have their own interest concerns. For the Chinese government, it will try hard to synergize both sociopolitical/ security concerns and economic concerns with respect to certain energy policy or project, but sometimes the government has to prioritize one over the other. It is not necessary that sociopolitical/security concern will always override economic concern. Which concern predominates depends on what type of country it transacts, and whether the government is confident to prevent and curb the likely risks to its national and economic security. For the Chinese NOCs, commercial profits are their top concern; at the same time, they have to cater to the government's non-economic demands for reasons as aforementioned. The priority concerns of the Chinese state and the NOCs are often, though not always, overlapping. Their predominant concerns may be at odds under different settings, but both will try to build role compatibility to cope with the energy security issue.

The success or failure to reach role compatibility will remarkably affect China's approach to energy security. Given that the Chinese government and the NOCs have their own priority interest concerns, they will choose to play roles that may or may not necessarily be congruent with each other. When the roles of the Chinese government and the NOCs are compatible, China will draw on either a market-dominated approach or a state-controlled approach to deal with energy security. Conversely, when their roles are incompatible, a competing paradigms approach will be used, trying to balance the state power and market force. Therefore, China's approach to energy security cannot be simply reduced to either a state-controlled or a market-dominated approach. Rather, China has employed a SMMA, a portfolio of the above approaches, to cope with its energy security. With a SMMA, the Chinese state has to push forward marketization in the oil and gas sector, but in the meantime, it tries to "manage" and put the marketization process under its control, making policy adjustments according to its own concerns and calculations. For the NOCs, while being desperate in preserving their monopoly rights, most of the time they act in light of the principle of maximization of their commercial interests. When they are required to undertake social responsibilities, the NOCs have to comply with government orders even at the expense of their commercial interests in most cases, but in some cases they are likely to go against the will of the government in a sneaky manner. All the cases tend to show that the NOCs' role propensities are closely correlated with oil prices they face, government policy changes, and what markets they are in.

Despite some distinctions, China's SMMA has no fundamental difference from the US and India. The three big powers share similar perceptions of energy security and take similar measures to tackle energy security challenges. There are two salient distinctions among them. One is related with ownership of major companies in the petroleum sector, and the other is pertinent to the role of the state and government-business relationship. State ownership does allow the NOCs in both China and India to enjoy some prerogatives in their domestic markets, but they have to confront growing market competition. As latecomers to the international energy market, they are in an inferior position to emulate with the IOCs, who have already gained a foothold in many countries with rich oil and gas resources. On the contrary, the IOCs in the US do enjoy preemptive advantages not only in its domestic market but also in the international energy market. Regarding the role of the state, government support is prevalent among the three big powers although the extent of government intervention in the petroleum industry may differ.

In theory, this research has special ramifications for state–market and government-business relations. Most preceding studies, such as the developmental state model, social institutionalism, and neopluralists tend to be built on the assumption of a state-versus-market dichotomy, but the SMMA has challenged that. Under China's SMMA, state–market relationship presents multi-faceted features. First, the state is outside the market. To a large extent, it is the Chinese state that has created the market, or introduced relevant market mechanisms into the petroleum sector. Second, the state is above the market. Not only is the state responsible to formulate rules of the game for the market, but also the state tries to "manage" the market as aforementioned, and if necessary, will rescind the preceding marketization measures. Third, the state stands by the market in the sense that market operations are under the oversight of the state. Fourth, the state is also in the market in that the state engages in market activities via its SOEs. Thereby, the state and the market have developed a symbiotic and interdependent relationship in China; they compete and collaborate with each other.

Furthermore, contrary to many preceding works that consider the SOEs as puppets of the Chinese government, the SOEs are not passive policy recipients, nor are they always subordinate to the government. Rather, the SOEs have become more profit-oriented, have their own calculations, and often take initiatives to initiate new policies and projects. The government can hardly turn a blind eye to the NOCs' interests when formulating energy policies. As a result, the effectiveness of the government's "management" of the marketization process has to some extent been undermined by the SOEs.

Appendix

See Chart 1 and Map 1.

S. Chen, *China's Approach to Energy Security*,
https://doi.org/10.1007/978-981-99-3573-4

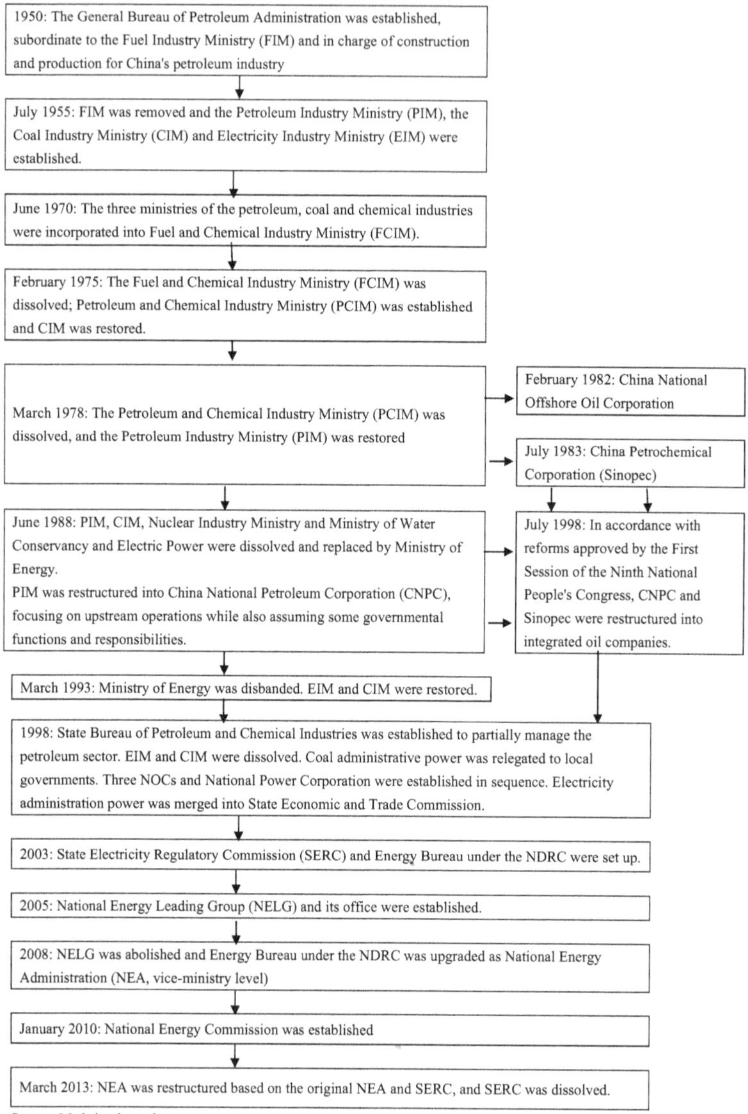

Source: Made by the author.

Chart A.1 History of China's Petroleum Industry

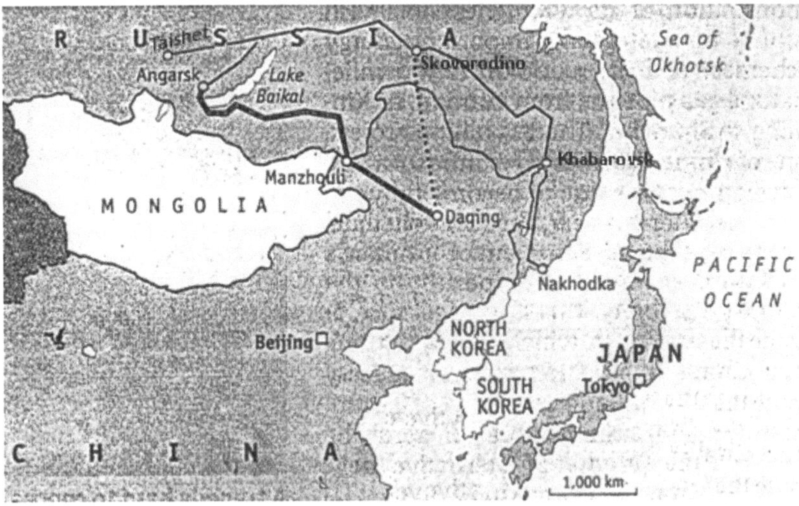

Map A.1 Russian Far Eastern Oil Pipelines (*Source* Adapted from "The oil wars: in the pipeline," *The Economist*, May 1–7, 2004)

Selected Bibliography

Primary Sources

Ai, Lin, 2006, "Bumen Liyi pengzhang, weihai gaige daju" (Sector Interests expand, Undermine Overall Reform), *Xinhua*, 11 October, http://news.xinhuanet.com/comments/2006-10/11/content_5184607.htm.

Almanac of China's Foreign Economic Relations and Trade, Beijing: China National Economy Publishing House Economic Information & Agency, various years

A research project by China Energy Comprehensive Development Strategy and Policy research group headed by the energy experts from DRCSC and NDRC, 2003, "*Guojia nengyuan zhanlue de jiben gouxiang*" (Tentative Plan of National Energy Strategy), 16 November, http://www.people.com.cn/GB/jingji/1045/2191153.html.

Asian Development Bank (ADB), 2005, *Asian Development Outlook 2005 Update*, ADB. Available at: http://www.adb.org/documents/books/ado/2005/update/default.asp.

Bai, Gang, et al., 1999, "Zhengque chuli fazhan yu wending de guanxi" (Correctly Handle the Relations Between Development and Stability), *The People's Daily Internal Reading Materials*, 6 October.

Belt and Road Energy Cooperation, 2019, "The Belt and Road Energy Partnership (BREP) Was Officially Established in Beijing," 25 April, http://obor.nea.gov.cn/pictureDetails.html?id=2336.

BP, 2004, *BP Annual Report and Accounts 2003.*

———, 2013, "BP Energy Outlook 2030," January.

———, 2023, *Statistical Review of World Energy 2022.*

S. Chen, *China's Approach to Energy Security*,
https://doi.org/10.1007/978-981-99-3573-4

Bureau of Transportation Statistics, Research and Innovative Technology Administration (RITA), U.S. Department of Transportation (US DOT), "Table 1-10: U.S. Oil and Gas Pipeline Mileage," http://www.rita.dot.gov/bts/sites/rita.dot.gov.bts/files/publications/national_transportation_statistics/html/table_01_10.html.

Cao, Yishu (vice Secretary and spokesman of NDRC), 2005, "Guanyu shiyou liutong tizhi gaige de sikao" (Reflections on Reforming Oil Circulation Mechanisms), Speech at the Forum on Reforming Oil Circulation Mechanisms in Heilongjiang), Heilongjiang, 9 July.

Chen, Deming (Vice president of NDRC), 2007, "Zhongguo nengyuan fazhan yu yazhou nengyuan hezuo" (China's Energy Development and Asian Energy Cooperation), a speech made at the 2nd Asian Energy Minister Roundtable Meeting, Riyadh, 2 May.

Chen, Xiaochun (Head of Guangdong Price Bureau) and Huang, Chengkuang, 2005, "Tuijin shiyou jiage tizhi gaige de shexiang" (A Proposal on Pushing Forward the Reform of oil Price Mechanisms), *Guangdong Economy*, Vol. 4.

China Energy Comprehensive Development Strategy and Policy research group, 2003, "*Guojia nengyuan zhanlue de jiben gouxiang*" (Tentative Plan of National Energy Strategy), 16 November. Available at Chinese official website: http://www.people.com.cn/GB/jingji/1045/2191153.html.

China Commerce Yearbook, 2005, Beijing: China Commerce and Trade Press.

CNOOC, *Zhonghaiyou Niandu Baogao* (CNOOC Annual Report), various years.

CNPC, *Zhongshiyou Niandu Baogao* (CNPC Annual Report), various years.

CNPC Group Company, *CNPC Group Co. Annual Report*, various years.

Cui Minxuan (ed.), 2006, *Zhongguo Nengyuan Fazhan Baogao* (The Energy Development Report of China), Beijing: Shehui Kexue Wenxian Chubanshe (Social Sciences Academic Press).

Deng, Xiaoping, 1982, "Qian shinian wei hou shinian zuo hao zhunbei" (Formal Ten Years Should Make Good Preparation for the Next Ten Years), *Deng Xiaoping Wenxuan* (Deng Xiaoping Analects), Vol. 3, 14 October.

Deng, Xiaoping, 1994, *Deng Xiaoping Wenxuan* (Selected Works of Deng Xiaoping), Beijing: People's Press.

Department of Energy, USA, "International Petroleum Imports and Exports (Trade) Data," http://www.eia.doe.gov/emeu/ipsr/t47.xls and http://www.eia.doe.gov/emeu/ipsr/t31.xls.

Department of Industry and Transport Statistics of National Bureau of Statistics, and Energy Bureau of NDRC, 2005, *China Energy Statistical Yearbook—2004*, Beijing: China Statistics Press.

Department of Petroleum and Natural Gas, National Energy Administration et al., *Zhongguo Tianranqi Fazhan Baogao* (2021) (China Natural Gas Development Report <2021>), Beijing: Shiyou Gongye Chubanshe (Petroleum Industry Press), 2021.

Development Research Center of the State Council of P. R. China, 2003, "Guanyu shihua hangye de jidu fenxi baogao" (Quarter Analysis Report on Chinese Petrochemical Industry), 3 March, http://www.drcnet.com.cn.
———, "Zhongguo shihua hangye jidu fenxi baogao" (Quarterly Analysis Report on Chinese Petrochemical Industry), 3 March 2003, http://www.drcnet.com.cn.
Energy Information Administration (EIA: Official Energy statistics from the U.S. Government), 2002, "International Coal Recoverable Reserves Data," Available at: http://www.eia.doe.gov/pub/international/iea2002/table82.xls.
———, 2004, Country Analysis Briefs: http://www.eia.doe.gov.
———, 2005, "China Country Analysis Brief," U.S. Department of Energy, 2 August, http://www.eia.doe.gov/emeu/cabs/china.html.
———, 2006, *International Energy Outlook 2006*, Report #:DOE/EIA-0484(2006), Release Date: June.
———, 2014, "Country Analysis—China," updated 4 February.
———, 2014, "Country Analysis—India," updated 26 June.
———, 2013, "How Dependent Are We on Foreign Oil?" 10 May, http://www.eia.gov/energy_in_brief/article/foreign_oil_dependence.cfm.
Energy Bureau of National Development and Reform Commission, 2005, "Woguo tianranqi ji shuqi guandao gongye zhanwang" (Prospect of Natural Gas and Gas Pipeline Industries in China), 28 December. http://www.sdpc.gov.cn/nyjt/dcyyj/t20051228_55011.htm.
———, 2005, "Woguo nengyuan anquan de liu de duice" (Six Countermeasures to China's Energy Security), 29 December. Available at: http://www.sdpc.gov.cn/nyjt/dcyyj/t20051229_55137.htm.
———, 2005, "Meiguo xin de nengyuan zhengce fa ji tedian" (America's New Energy Policies and Their Attributes), 5 September. Available at: http://www.sdpc.gov.cn/nyjt/dcyyj/t20051229_55137.htm.
———, 2005, "Mei Zhong nengyuan xuqiu ji nengyuan zhengce" (China and US's Energy Demands and Energy Policies), 11 July, http://www.sdpc.gov.cn/nyjt/zhdt/t20050714_46467.htm.
———, 2005, "Ran shichang lai tigao nengyuan anquan chengdu" (Let the Market Improve Energy Security), 15 September. http://www.sdpc.gov.cn/nyjt/dcyyj/t20060915_84552.htm.
———, 2006, "'Nengyuan anquan' de zhenzheng hanyi" (The True Meaning of "Energy Security"), 15 September, http://www.sdpc.gov.cn/nyjt/dcyyj/t20060915_84550.htm.
———, 2006, "Zhongguo canyu Guoji nengyuan zuzhi de hezuo xianzhuang" (The Situation of China's Cooperation with International Energy Organizations), 17 July. Available at: http://www.sdpc.gov.cn/nyjt/gjjlyhz/t20060717_76589.htm.

———, 2006, "Jiaqiang Zhong Fei nengyuan hezuo de chubu gouxiang" (Preliminary Ideas About Energy Cooperation Between China and Africa), 17 April. http://www.sdpc.gov.cn/nyjt/gjjlyhz/t20060421_67092.htm.

———, 2006, "Guojia jueding zhengshou shiyou tebie shouyijin" (China Decides to Levy Petroleum Special Revenue Taxes), 13 April. http://www.sdpc.gov.cn/nyjt/zhdt/t20060414_66291.htm.

———, 2007, "Quanqiu nengyuan anquan guan de yansheng he fazhan" (Extension and Development of Global Energy Security Conception), 2 March, http://www.sdpc.gov.cn/nyjt/dcyyj/t20070302_119668.htm.

EPA (US Environmental Protection Agency), 2014, "Overview of Greenhouse Gases—Carbon Dioxide Emissions," http://www.epa.gov/climatechange/ghgemissions/gases/co2.html.

General Administration of Customs of China, *China Customs Statistics*, various years.

General Office of the State Council, "Guowuyuan Bangongting Guanyu Jinyibu Jiakuai Meicengqi (meikuang wasi) Choucai Liyong de Yijian" (Opinions of the General Office of the State Council on Further Accelerating the Extraction and Utilization of CBM/Coal Mine Gas) (Guo Ban Fa [2013] No. 93), 14 September 2013.

Gong, Zhongming and Cheng, Jiayu, "Cong shijie nengyuan fazhan qushi tansuo weilai Zhongguo nengyuan zhanlue" (To Probe into China's Future Energy Strategy in Light of World Energy Developing Trends), *Keji bu Diao yan baogao* (Research Report by Ministry of Science and Technology), Vol. 38, 8 June 2004.

Gong, Zhongming, Jiayu Cheng and Chi Ma, 2005, "Gao Fengxian Guoji Youqi Shichang xia de Zhongguo nengyuan changyuan zhanlue sikao" (Reflections on China's Long-Term Energy Strategy in the International High-Risk Oil and Gas Market), Internal Document, Diaoyan Baogao, No. 1, Kejibu Zhongguo Keji Cujin Fazhan Yanjiu Zhongxin, 4 January.

Guangdong Planning Commission, 2005, "Wosheng Qiyou, Chaiyou Lingshou Jiage Tiaozheng Qingkuang Yilangbiao" (List of Gasoline, Diesel Oil Price Adjustments in Guangdong).

Guangdong Price Bureau, "Guangdong Wujia Ju guanyu yunyong jiage zhengce wending chuzuche hangye de tongzhi," (Notice of Guandong Provincial Price Bureau on Applying Price Mechanisms to Stabilize Taxi Sector), *Neibu Mingdian*, *Yuejia* [2005] 150 hao, 10 August 2005.

———, 2001, "Guangdong Sheng chengpinyou xiaoshou jiage biao" (A List of Refined Oil Prices in Guandong Province), Yuejia [2001] 253 hao, 16 October.

———, 2004, "Guanyu Tuijin Woguo Shiyou Jiage Xingcheng Jizhi Gaige, Baozheng Guojia Shiyou Anquan de Jianyi" (A Proposal on Pushing Forward the Reform of China's Oil Price Shaping Mechanisms in Order to Ensure Our Oil Security), 1 December.

Guangdong Sheng qi diao dui zonghechu (Guangdong provincial firm survey team), 2005, "Youjia xiaoying tuxian, qiye yingxiang jiaoda" (Oil Price Effects Emerge, Which Has Great Impact on Firms), *Guangdong Economy*, Vol. 6.

"Guoji shiyou jiage shangzhang qushi ji dui WoGuo yingxiang de chubu fenxi" ("Rising Tendency of International Oil Prices and Preliminary Analysis of Its Impact on China"), Guowuyuan Neican (*Internal Reference of the State Council of P.R. China*), 29 October 2004.

Guojia Jing Mao Wei Hangye Guihua Si (Industrial Planning Bureau of National Economic and Trade Commission), 2001, "Shiyou gongye 'shiwu' guihua" (The Tenth Five Year Plan for the Petroleum Industry), 25 June, http://www.setc.gov.cn/gjjmwznzn/gyswgh/200207310027.htm.

India's Planning Commission, 2006, *Integrated Energy Policy: Report of the Expert Committee*, New Delhi.

Information Office of the State Council, "China's Energy Policy 2012," 24 October 2012.

International Energy Agency (IEA), 1996, *The Role of IEA Governments in Energy: 1996 Update*, Paris: IEA, Organization for Economic Co-operation and Development (OECD)

———, 2000, *China's Worldwide Quest for Energy Security*, Paris: OECD.

———, 2001, *Towards a Sustainable Energy Future*, Paris: IEA, OECD.

———, 2002, *Developing China's Natural Gas Market: The Energy Policy Challenges*. Paris: IEA.

———, 2002, *World Oil Outlook to 2030*, Paris: IEA, http://www.iea.org/Textbase/work/2002/calgary/birol.pdf.

———, 2004, *Oil Crises & Climate Challenges: 30 Years of Energy Use in IEA Countries*, Paris: IEA Publications.

———, 2011, *World Energy Outlook*.

———, *World Energy Outlook* 2013, "Energy Subsidies", http://www.iea.org/subsidy/index.html.

———, 2013, "Recent Developments in Energy Subsidies," http://www.iea.org/media/weowebsite/2013/Developments_EnergySubsidies.pdf.

———, 2021, *India Energy Outlook 2021: World Energy Outlook Special Report*, IEA, Paris, https://www.iea.org/reports/india-energy-outlook-2021.

———, 2022, "CO_2 Emissions Intensity of GDP, 1990–2021," 8 March, https://www.iea.org/data-and-statistics/charts/co2-emissions-intensity-of-gdp-1990-2021.

———, 2022, "Installed Capacity in India, 2000-2020, and Projections up to 2040 in the Stated Policies Scenario," 26 October, https://www.iea.org/data-and-statistics/charts/installed-capacity-in-india-2000-2020-and-projections-up-to-2040-in-the-stated-policies-scenario.

———, "Energy Security: Reliable, Affordable Access to All Fuels and Energy Sources," http://www.iea.org/topics/energysecurity/.

International Monetary Fund, "Fossil Fuel Subsidies," https://www.imf.org/en/Topics/climate-change/energy-subsidies.

International Petroleum Economy, 2006, "2005 nian guo neiwai nengyuan zhengce zongshu" (Summarization of China Domestic and Foreign Energy Policies in 2005), February.

Krueger, Alan B., 2009, "Statement of Alan B. Krueger Assistant Secretary for Economic Policy and Chief Economist, US Department of Treasury Subcommittee on Energy, Natural Resources, and Infrastructure," 10 September, https://home.treasury.gov/news/press-releases/tg284.

Law of Renewable Energy in People's Republic of China, Taking effect from 1 January 2006.

Liaowang (Outlook), 2006, "Jingti Bumen liyi pengzhang" (Be Cautious About Sector Interest Expansion), 10 October. http://news.xinhuanet.com/legal/2006-10/10/content_5183777.htm.

Liu, Ming, 2007, "Guankui nengyuan zhengzhi" (Energy Politics in My View), *Shishi Baogao* (Current Affairs Report), 30 March. Available at: http://news.xinhuanet.com/world/2007-03/30/content_5916386.htm.

Ma, Fucai (CNPC president), 2002, "Report at CNPC Working Conference," January 19, 1999, in *CNPC Yearbook 2000*.

Ma, Kai (Chairman of NDRC and Director of the Office of the National Energy Leading Group), "WoGuo Dangqian de nengyuan xingshi yu 'Shiyiwu' nengyuan fazhan" (China's Current Energy Situation and the '11th Five-Year Plan' for Energy Development), A Report at the Conference on Current Situation Jointly sponsored by six ministries in the Central Propaganda Department of PRC, 15 August 2006, http://news.xinhuanet.com/politics/2006-08/15/content_4963795.htm.

———, 2007, "Jiaqiang nengyuan hezuo, shixian gongtong fazhan" (Strengthen Energy Cooperation to Attain Joint Development), speech at the inauguration of the "Symposium on Sino-Japanese Energy Cooperation", 12 April, http://www.sdpc.gov.cn/nyjt/nyzywx/t20070418_130115.htm.

Ministry of Commerce, China, 2004, "Zhongguo shiyou qiye haiwai tuozhan, 'zouchuqu' pojie shiyou kunju" (China Oil Firms Expand Overseas, Go Abroad to Ravel Out the Oil Predicament), 21 September. http://sg.mof com.gov.cn/aarticle/jians/200409/20040900281860.html.

———, 2004, "Zhongguo shiyou qiye haiwai tuozhan, 'zouchuqu' pojie shiyou kunju" (China Oil Firms Expand Overseas, Go Abroad to Ravel Out the Oil Predicament), 21 September. http://sg.mofcom.gov.cn/aarticle/jians/200409/20040900281860.html.

———, 2005, "Shangwubu bo 'Zhongguo shiyou weixie lun'" (Ministry of Commerce Rebukes "China Oil Threat"), 18 November. Available at.

National Commission on Energy Policy, 2004, "Ending the Energy Stalemate: A Bipartisan Strategy to Meet America's Energy Challenges," December.

National Development and Planning Commission (NDPC) of P.R. China, 1998, "Guojia fazhan jihua weiyuanhui guanyu yinfa <Yuanyou chengpinyou jiage gaige fang'an> de tongzhi" (A Notice from NDPC on Printing "Plans of Reforming Crude Oil and Refined Oil Prices"), Jidian (98) 52 hao, Neibu chuangzhen dianbao, 3 June.

———, 2001, *Energy Development Plan of the Tenth Five-Year Scheme (2001–2005) of National Social and Economic Development*, Beijing: State Development Planning Commission.

———, 2002, National Economic Department, "Zhongguo shiyou de jiben shexiang" (Basic Plans for China's Oil Reserve), *Jingji Yanjiu cankao* (Economic Research Reference), 9 January.

National Development and Reform Commission (NDRC), China, 2003, "Guojia fazhan he gaige weiyuanhui guanyu xin biaozhun qiyou jiage deng youguan wenti de tongzhi" (A Notice from NDRC on Problems Like the New-Criteria Gasoline Prices), Fagai Jiage [2003] 594 hao, 23 June.

———, 2003, "Take Measures of Strengthening Energy Saving, Make Great Efforts to Construct a Energy-Saving Society," 5 November. http://www.sdpc.gov.cn/a/news/200311051.htm.

———, 2004, "Jieneng zhong changqi zhuanxiang guihua" (Plan on Medium- and Long-Term Energy Saving), 25 November. http://www.sdpc.gov.cn/.

———, 2007, "Nengyuan fazhan 'shiyiwu' guihua" (11th Five-Year Plan for Energy Development), April. http://www.sdpc.gov.cn/nyjt/nyzywx/P020070410417020191418.pdf.

National Economic and Trade Commission, 2001, "Jieyue he tidai ranliaoyou 'shiwu' guihua" (The Tenth Five-Year Plan of Fuel Oil Conservation and Substitution), 24 December, http://trade.chinavista.com/cn/chreference.html#cn00012.

National Energy Administration, 2013, "Shale Gas Industry Policy" Guojia Nengyuanju Gonggao 2013 Nian di 5 hao (NEA Announcement No. 5, 2013), 22 October.

National Energy Policy, 2001, Report of the National Energy Policy Development Group led by V.P. Cheney, May. Available at: http://www.whitehouse.gov/energy.

National Bureau of Statistics of China, *China Statistical Yearbook*, various years.

———, *2022 Yearly Data*. www.stats.gov.cn

National Planning Commission of P.R. China, 2001, "Guanyu wanshan shiyou jiage jiegui bangfa ji tiaozheng chengpinyou jiage de tongzhi" (Notice on Perfecting Oil Price Integrating Methods and Adjusting Refined Oil Prices), Neibumingdian, Jidian [2001] 96 hao, 15 October.

NDRC, 2004, "Jieneng zhong changqi zhuanxiang guihua" (Plan on Medium- and Long-term Energy Saving), Fa Gai Huanzi [2004] No. 2505, 1 May 2004, http://www.nea.gov.cn/2011-08/18/c_131057667.htm.

———, 2016, "*Shiyou Jiange Guanli Bangfa*" (Measures for the Administration of Oil Prices), 13 January, https://www.ndrc.gov.cn/xxgk/zcfb/tz/201601/W020190905506573420251.pdf.

NDRC and NEA, 2017, *Zhongchangqi Youqi Guanwang Guihua* (The Medium and Long-term Oil and Gas Pipeline Network Planning), May.

NDRC, NEA, MOF, etc, 2021, "'Shisiwu' Kezaisheng Nengyuan Fazhan Guihua" (14th Five-Year Renewable Energy Development Plan), October, https://www.ndrc.gov.cn/xwdt/tzgg/202206/t20220601_1326720.html?code=&state=123.

NEA, 2017, *Vision and Actions on Energy Cooperation in Jointly Building Silk Road Economic Belt and 21st-Century Maritime Silk Road*, 12 May, http://www.nea.gov.cn/2017-05/12/c_136277478.htm.

Nengyuan Zhongchangqi Fazhan Guihua Gangyao (cao'an) [China Energy Mid- to Long-term Development Scheme (2004–2020) (draft)], laid out on June 2004.

OECD, 2010, "State Owned Enterprises and the Principle of Competitive Neutrality," DAF/COMP(2009) 37, 20 September, http://www.oecd.org/daf/competition/46734249.pdf.

People's Bank of China, accessed 2006 February 26. http://www.pbc.gov.cn/diaochatongji/tongjishuju/gofile.asp?file=2005S6.htm.

People's Daily, "Zhengfu jigou gaige: huantang you huanyao" (Governmental Organization Reform: Change Both Format and Substance), 18 March 2003, http://www.people.com.cn/GB/guandian/183/6103/6104/20030318/946373.html.

———, 2004, "Shijie shiyou geju zoushi yu duice" (Tendency of World Oil Structure and China's Countermeasures), *People's Daily*, 30 July.

PetroChina, *Annual Report of PetroChina Company Limited*, various years.

Project Group of Macroeconomy Research Institute, National Planning Commission, 1999, *Zhongguo Zhongchangqi Nengyuan Fazhan Zhanlue Yanjiu Zong Baobao* (Overall Report on China Mid- and Long-Term Energy Development Strategies), China Planning Press, February.

Ramsay, William C. (Deputy Director, Deputy Executive Director, IEA, Paris), 2005, *Asian Oil: Current Trends, Outlook and Issues*, Presentation at the Roundtable Conference on Regional Cooperation: Key to Energy Security, New Delhi, 6 January, http://library.iea.org/textbase/speech/2005/ramsay/asianoil.pdf.

Research Group on *New Oil Price Mechanisms* headed by Lu Nan, "Shenhua shiyou jiage gaige silu de xuanze" (Options for the Plan of Deepening Oil Price Reform), *Zhongguo Wujia* (*China Price*), February 1995.

SASAC, "Directory of Central SOEs", http://en.sasac.gov.cn/sasacdirectory.html.

SASAC, "Main Functions and Responsibilities of SASAC," http://en.sasac.gov.cn/2018/07/17/c_9258.htm.

State-Owned Assets Supervision and Administration Commission of the State Council (SASAC), "List of Central SOEs", http://www.sasac.gov.cn/zyqy/qyml/default.htm.

Shijie Shiyou (World Oil), 2006, "2006 nian shijie shiyou kangtan kaifa touzi qishi" (World Oil Exploration and Production Tendencies in 2006), February.

Sinopec Group Company, *Sinopec Group Co. Annual Report*, various years.

State Council of China, 2004, "Jinyibu gaige nengyuan changpin jiage xingcheng jizhi" (Further Reform the Price Shaping Mechanisms of Energy Products), September.

Statistics Bureau, Ministry of Internal Affairs and Communication, Japan, http://www.stat.go.jp/english/data/cpi/1585.htm#Q01.

Tang Yongbing, "shiyou qihuo – shichanghua bixian de biran xuanze" (Petroleum Futures—The Necessary Choice of Avoiding Risks for Marketization), *Jingji Ribao* (Economic Daily), 14 November 2003.

The Editorial Board of the China's Foreign Commerce Yearbook, *China Commerce Yearbook*, Beijing: China Commerce and Trade Press, various years from 1999 to 2005.

The Joint Economic Committee, Congress of the U.S., 1994, *China's Economic Dilemmas in the 1990s: The Problems of Reforms, Modernization, and Interdependence*, Armonk and New York: M.E. Sharpe.

The Sixth Plenary Session of the 16th Central Committee of the Communist Party of China, 2006, "Resolution on Major Issues Regarding the Building of a Harmonious Socialist Society," *China Daily*, 19 October. http://www.chinadaily.com.cn/china/2006-10/19/content_711520.htm.

The State Council Information Office of the People's Republic of China, *Xin Shidai de Zhongguo Nengyuan Fazhan Baipishu* (The White Paper on Energy in China's New Era), December 2020.

The White House, 2009, "President to Attend Copenhagen Climate Talks," November 25.

United Nations Development Programme, *World Energy Assessment*, New York: UNDP, 2000.

US Congress Subcommittee on Multinational Corporations, 1975, "Multinational Oil Corporations and US Foreign Policy," US Government Printing Office, 2 January.

US Department of Energy, *Wind Market Reports: 2021 Edition*, https://www.energy.gov/eere/wind/wind-market-reports-2021-edition.

Verrastro, Frank (Director of Energy Program at the Center for Strategic and International Studies), 2006, "Comments and Observations on the Topic of

U.S. Energy Independence," Testimony Before the Committee on Energy and Natural Resources, United States Senate, 7 March. Available at http://www.csis.org/media/csis/congress/ts060307_verrastro.pdf.

Wang, Mengkui (President of the DRCSC), "Growth Model Needs Modification," *China Daily*, 11 May 2005. http://www.chinadaily.com.cn/english/doc/2005-05/11/content_440884.htm.

Xinhua, 2006, "Fang 'Tesu liyi jituan'pohuai hexie" (Prevent "Special Interest Groups" from Undermining Harmony), 5 October. Available at: http://www.zaobao.com/zg/zg061005_505.html.

———, "China's 12th Five-Year Plan (2011–2015)"

———, 2020, "Zhonggong Zhongyang guanyu Zhiding Guomin Jingji he Shehui Fazhan Di Sishi ge Wunian Guihua he 2035 nian Yuanjing Mubiao de Jianyi" (Advisory of the CPC Central Committee on the Formulation of the 14th Five-Year Plan for National Economic and Social Development and the Long-term Vision for the Year 2035), 3 November, http://www.gov.cn/zhengce/2020-11/03/content_5556991.htm.

Xu, Dingming (vice director of China National Energy Leading Group Office), 2007, "Zhongguo buneng fuzhi Meiguoshi nengyuan xiaofei moshi" (China Cannot Replicate American-Style Energy Consumption Model), *Xinhua*, 4 April. http://news.xinhuanet.com/fortune//2007-04/04/content_5930223.htm.

Yearbook of China's Foreign Economic Relations and Trade, Beijing: China Foreign Economic Relations and Trade Publishing Press, various years.

Yu, Chuanguang and Shi, Xiangxing, "Guotu ziyuanbu buzhang Tian Fengshan: guanzhu shiyou ziyuan anquan" (Minister of Land and Natural Resources Tian Fengshan: Attention Must Be Paid to Oil Security), *Jiefangjun Bao* (*Liberation Army Daily*), 20 July 2002.

Yu, Fei and Meng Na, 2003, "Meiyi zhanzheng yinyun yinfa Zhongguo shiyou anquan huati" (US-Iraq War Eliciting the Topic of China's Oil Security), *Xinhua*, 7 March, http://news.xinhuanet.com/fortune/2003-03/07/content_764778.htm.

Zeng, Peiyan (vice Premier), 2000. "Zhongguo jiang jiakuai shishi xibu da kaifa zhanlüe" (China Will Speed Up the Implementation of the Western Development Strategy). *Zhongguo jingji baodao* (China Economic Herald), 1 March.

———, 2006, "Dangqian Woguo nengyuan xingshi ji nengyuan anquan wenti" (Current Energy Situation and Energy Security Problems of China), A Report at the 19th Session of the Standing Committee of the 10th National People's Congress. 2 December. http://www.sdpc.gov.cn/nyjt/nyzywx/t20060123_57789.htm.

Zhang, Guobao (vice-President of NDRC), 2005, "Xin shiji de Zhongguo nengyuan he shiyou tianranqi zhengce" (China's Energy and Oil & Gas Policies in the New Millennium), A speech made at the 6 the Sino-US Oil and Gas Forum, 9 August. http://www.sdpc.gov.cn/nyjt/nyzywx/t20050810_41382.htm.

Zhang, Xiaoqiang (vice President of NDRC), 2005, "Jiaqiang nengyuan hezuo, shixian gongtong fazhan" (Strengthen Energy Cooperation, Fulfill Common Development), speech at the International Energy Agency Minister Meeting, Paris, 2 May. http://www.sdpc.gov.cn/nyjt/nyzywx/t20050714_41370.htm.

"*Zhonggong Shiba Jie Wu zhong Quanhui Gongbao*" (Communiqué of the Fifth Plenary Session of the Eighteenth Central Committee of the Communist Party of China), 29 October 2015.

Zhongguo de Kuangchan Ziyuan Zhengce Baibishu (White Book of China's Mineral Resources Policy), 25 December 2003. http://news.xinhuanet.com/zhengfu/2003-12/23/content_1244724.htm.

Zhongguo Fazhan Guancha (China Development Observer), 2007, "Quanqiu nengyuan xingshi dui Zhongguo de yingxiang" (Impact of Global Energy Situation on China), 6 April. http://news.xinhuanet.com/theory/2007-04/06/content_5938171.htm.

Zhongguo Guowuyuan Neican (Internal Reference for State Council of China), 2004, "Guoji Shiyou Jiage shangzhang qishi ji dui woguo yingxiang de chubu fenxi" (Preliminary Analysis of the Impact of International Oil Price Surging Trend on China).

Zhongguo Heneng Hangye Xiehui (China Nuclear Energy Association), 2022, *Quanguo Hedian Yunxing Qingkuang (2021 nian 1-12 yue)* (National Nuclear Power Operation (January–December 2021)), https://nnsa.mee.gov.cn/ywdt/yjzx/202202/t20220208_968871.html.

Zhongguo Hedian Fazhan Zhongxin (China Nuclear Power Development Center) and Guowang Nengyuan Yanjiuyuan (State Grid Energy Research Institute), 2019, *Woguo Hedian Fazhan Guihua Yanjiu* (China's Nuclear Power Development Planning Research).

Zhongguo Neng Yuan Fazhan Baogao (The Energy Development Report of China), 2006, Beijing: Shehui Kexue Wenxian Chubanshe.

Zhongguo Nengyuan Tongji Nianjian (China Energy Statistical Yearbook), Beijing: Zhongguo Tongji Chubanshe (China Statistical Press), various years from 1998–2006.

Zhongguo Shiyou Huagong Jituan Gongsi Nianjian (China Petrochemical Corp. Yearbook), Beijing: Zhongguo Shihua Chubanshe (China Petrochemical Press), various years from 1999–2006.

Zhongguo Shiyou Tianranqi Jituan Nianjian (China National Petroleum Corp. Yearbook), Beijing: Shiyou Gongye Chubanshe (Petroleum Industry Press), various years 1994–2006.

Zhongguo, Yindu, Riben, Hanguo, Meiguo wuguo nengyuan buzhang lianhe shengming (Joint Statement of China, India, Japan, Korea and US Energy Ministers), 16 December 2006. http://www.sdpc.gov.cn/nyjt/nyzywx/t20061219_101585.htm.

Zhongshiyou Jingji Jishu Yanjiuyuan (Institute of Economics and Technology, of CNPC), *2021 Nian Guoneiwai Youqi Hangye Fazhan Baogao* (2021 Domestic and Foreign Oil and Gas Industry Development Report), April 2022.

Zhou Shengxian (Minister of MEP), 2013, "Towards the New Era of Ecological Civilization—Studying the Important Statement by Comrade Xi Jinping on the Building of Ecological Civilization," Webpage of the MEP, 2 September, http://english.mep.gov.cn/Ministers/Activities/201309/t20130917_260331.htm.

Zhu, Rongji, 2001. *Report on Outline of the Tenth Five-Year Plan*, presented to the Fourth Session of the Ninth National People's Congress, Beijing, China, March 5.

Secondary Sources—English Books

Ahn, Sun-Joo and Dagmar Graczyk, 2012, *Understanding Energy Challenges in India: Policies, Players and Issues*, International Energy Agency, Partner Country Series.

Alagappa, Muthiah, 1998, *Asian Security Practice: Material and Ideational Influences*. Stanford: Stanford University Press.

Allison, Graham T., 1971, *Essence of Decision: Explaining the Cuban Missile Crisis*, Glenview (Illinois) and London (England): Scott, Foresman and Company.

Amsden, Alice, 1989, *Asia's Next Giant*, Oxford: Oxford University Press.

Amuzegar, Jahangir, 2001, *Managing the Oil Wealth: OPEC's Windfalls and Pitfalls*, London: I.B. Tauris.

Andrews-Speed, Philip (eds.), 2000, "Regulating Energy in Federal Transition Economies: the Case of China," in G. MacKerron, and P. Pearson, *The International Energy Experience: Markets, Regulation and the Environment*, London: Imperial College Press.

———, 2004, *Energy Policy and Regulation in the People's Republic of China*, The Hague/London/New York: Kluwer Law International.

Andrews-Speed, Philip, Xuanli Liao and Roland Dannreuther, 2002, *The Strategic Implications of China's Energy Needs*, New York and London: International Institute for Strategic Studies.

Ash, Robert, 2002, *China's Integration in Asia: Economic Security and Strategic Issues*. Richmond: Curzon.

Asia Research Center, 2001, *China: Energy Policy and Natural Gas Use*, Asia Research Center, Murdoch University, Western Australia.

Banaszak, Sara et al., 1999, *Promoting Energy Security in APEC Through Improved International Fuel Market Operations*, East-West Center.

Barry, Richard, 1993, *The Management of International Oil Operations*, Tulsa, Okla.: PennWell Books.

Beaubouef, Bruce Andre, 1997, *The Strategic Petroleum Reserve: U.S. Energy Security, Oil Politics, and Petroleum Reserves Policies in the Twentieth Century*, Ann Arbor, MI: University Microfilms International, 1997.

Beaudreau, Bernard C, 1999, *Energy and the Rise and Fall of Political Economy*, Westport, Conn.: Greenwood Press.

Bloomfield, Lincoln P. (ed.), 2001, *Global Markets and National Interests: The New Geopolitics of Energy, Capital, and Information*, Washington, DC: CSIS Press.

Bohi, Douglas R. and Michael A. Toman, 1996, *The Economics of Energy Security*, Boston: Kluwer Academic Publishers.

Bradbrook, Adrian J., et al., (eds.), 2005, *The Law of Energy for Sustainable Development*, Cambridge, UK; New York: Cambridge University Press.

Bugra, Ayse and Behlul Usdiken (ed.), 1997, *State, Market, and Organizational Form*, Berlin: Walter de Gruyter & Co.

Calder, Kent, Fereidun Fesharaki, Susan L. Shirk & Michael Stankiewicz, 1998, "Policy Paper 35: Energy and Security in Northeast Asia: Fueling Security," University of California at San Diego: Institution on Global Conflict and Cooperation, 1–12 September.

Carnoy, Martin et al., 1993, *The New Global Economy in the Information Age: Reflections on Our Changing World*, Pennsylvania: The Pennsylvania State University Press.

Cassedy, Edward S. and Peter Z. Grossman, 1998, *Introduction to Energy: Resources, Technology, and Society*, New York: Cambridge University Press.

Cawson, Alan (ed.), 1985, *Organized Interests and the State: Studies in Meso-Corporatism*, London, Beverly Hill and New Delhi: SAGE Publications.

Chan, Steve, Cal Clark, and Danny Lam (eds.), 1998, *Beyond the Developmental State: East Asia's Political Economies Reconsidered*, New York: St. Martin's & New York: St. Martin's Press.

Chase-Dunn, Christopher, 1989, *Global Formation: Structures of the World Economy*, Cambridge, MA: Basil Blackwell.

Cheng, Wei-qi and Philip Lawton, "SOEs Reform from a Governance Perspective and Its Relationship with the Privately Owned Publicly Listed Corporation in China," in David H. Brown and Alasdair Macbeen (eds.), 2005, *Challenge for China's Development: An Enterprise Perspective*, London and New York: Routledge.

Claes, Dag H., 2001, *The Politics of Oil-Producer Cooperation*, Boulder, CO: Westview Press.

Clawson, P., 1977, *Energy and National Security in the 21 Century*, Washington, DC: National Defense University Press.

Cordesman, Anthony H., and Khalid R. Al-Rodhan, 2006, *The Global Oil Market: Risks And Uncertainties*, Washington, DC: Center for Strategic and International Studies.

Dauvergene, Peter, 1998, *Weak and Strong States in Asia-Pacific Societies*, Australia: Allen & Unwin Australia Pty Ltd.

Derthick, Martha and Paul J. Quick, 1985, *The Politics of Deregulation*, Washington: Brookings.

Dittmer, Lowell and Samuel S. Kim, 1993, *China's Quest for National Identity*, Ithaca: Cornell University Press.

Dooley, Brendan (ed.), 2006, *Energy and Culture: Perspective on the Power to Work*, Hampshire, England: Ashgate.

Doug Guthrie, 1999, *Dragon in a Three-Piece Suit: The Emergence of Capitalism in China*, Princeton, NJ: Princeton University Press.

Downs, Eric S., 2004, China's *Energy Security*, PhD dissertation, Princeton University, Publication Number: AAT 3110228.

Dupont, Alan, 1998, *The Environment and Security in Pacific Asia*, New York: Oxford University Press Inc.

Edmonds, Jae and John M. Reilly, 1985, *Global Energy: Assessing the Future*, New York: Oxford University Press.

Elster, Jon, 1989, *Nuts and Bolts for the Social Sciences*, Cambridge: Cambridge University Press.

Evans, Peter, 1995, *Embedded Autonomy: States and Industrial Transformation*, Princeton, New Jersey: Princeton University Press.

Feng, Hui, 2005, *The Politics of China's Accession to the World Trade Organization: The Dragon Goes Global*, New York, NY: Routledge.

Fesharaki, Fereidun and David Fridley, 1986, *China's Petroleum Industry in the International Context*, Boulder, CO: Westview Press.

Fesharaki, Fereidun, et al., 1998, *Promoting Energy Security in APEC through Improved International Fuel Market Operations*, Honolulu, Hawaii: Program on Resources: Energy and Minerals, East-West Center, for the APEC Energy Working Group.

Fewsmith, Joseph, 2002, "Generational Transition in China," *The Washington Quarterly*, Vol. 25, No. 4, pp. 23–35.

Garg, Vibhuti, Balasubramanian Viswanathan, et al., 2020, *Mapping India's Energy Subsidies 2020—Fossil Fuels, Renewables and Electric Vehicles*, Winnipeg: International Institute for Sustainable Development, April. https://www.ceew.in/publications/mapping-indias-energy-subsidies-2020, accessed 2022 December 30.

Garnaut, Ross, and Huang Yiping (eds), 2000, *Growth without Miracles: Readings on the Chinese Economy in the Era of Reform*, New York: Oxford University Press.

Garrison, Jean A., 2009, *China and the Energy Equation in Asia*, Boulder and London: First Forum Press.

Geddes, Barbara, 2003, *Paradigms and Sand Castles: Theory Building and Research Design in Comparative Politics*, Ann Arbor: The University of Michigan Press.

Gilpin, Robert, 1975, *US Power and the Multinational Corporation*, New York: Basic Books.

———, 1987, *The Political Economy of International Relations*, Princeton, NJ: Princeton University Press.

Goldman, Merle and Roderick MacFarquhar, 1999, *The Paradox of China's Post-Mao Reforms*, Cambridge, MA: Harvard University Press.

Godement, François, François Nicolas and Taizo Yakushiji (eds), 2004, *Asia and Europe: Cooperating for Energy Security*, Paris: Institute Français des Relations Internationals.

Groombridge, Mark Allen, 1998, *The Politics of Industrial Bargaining: The Restructuring of State-Owned Enterprises in the People's Republic of China, 1978 to 1995*, Doctoral dissertation for Columbia University.

Guthrie, Doug, 1999, *Dragon in a Three-Piece Suit: The Emergence of Capitalism in China*, Princeton: Princeton University Press.

Haggard, Stephan, 1990, *Pathways from the Periphery*, Cornell University Press.

Hall, Peter, 1986, *Governing Economy: The Politics of State Intervention in Britain and France*, New York: Oxford University Press.

Hartwick, John M. and Nancy D. Olewiler, 1998, *The Economics of Natural Resource Use*, 2nd edition, Addison-Wesley.

Heal, Geoffrey and Graciela Chichilnisky, 1991, *Oil and the International Economy*, Oxford: Clarendon Press; New York: Oxford University Press.

Herberg, Mikkal E., "Energy: Asia's Energy Insecurity—Cooperation or Conflict?" in Ashley J. Tellis and Michael Willis (eds.), 2004, *Strategic Asia 2004–5: Confronting Terrorism in the Pursuit of Power*, Seattle, Washington: National Bureau of Asian Research.

Hirschman, Albert O., 1982, *Shifting Involvements: Private Interests and Public Action*, Princeton, NJ: Princeton University Press.

Hoopes, Stephanie M., 1997, *Oil Privatization, Public Choice and International Forces*, New York: St. Martin's Press.

Horsnell, Paul, 1997, *Oil in Asia: Markets, Trading, Refining and Deregulation*, Oxford and New York: Oxford University Press for the Oxford Institute for Energy Studies.

Hsiao, Russell, 2008, "Energy Security the Centerpiece of China's Foreign Policy," *China Brief*, Vol. 8, No. 16, August.

Hu, Angang, "Chinese Energy Strategy for the 21st Century: Production, Consumption, Trade and Security," in Kurt W. Radtke & Raymond Feddema (eds.), 2000, *Comprehensive Security in Asia: Views from Asia and the West on a Changing Security Environment*, Netherlands: Brill.

Huang, Jianrong, 1999, *The Applicability of Policy-Making Theories in Post-Mao China*, Aldershot, Brookfield USA, Singapore and Sydney: Ashgate.

Ikenberry, G. John, 1988, *Reasons of State: Oil Politics and the Capacities of American Government*, Ithaca: Cornell University Press.

Institute of Defense and Strategic Studies (IDSS), Nanyang Technological University, 2006, *Energy and Security: The Geopolitics of Energy in the Asia-Pacific*, Singapore: IDSS, October.

Johnson, Chalmers, 1982, *MITI and the Japanese Miracle*, Stanford University Press.

Katzenstein, Peter J. (ed), 1978, *Between Power and Plenty: Foreign Economic Policies of Advanced Industrial States*, Madison: University of Wisconsin Press.

Kennedy, Scott, 2005, *The Business of Lobbying in China*, Cambridge, MA: Harvard University Press.

Keohane, Robert, (ed.), 1984, *After Hegemony: Cooperation and Discord in the World Political Economy*, Princeton, NJ: Princeton University Press.

Keohane, Robert and Helen Milner, (eds.), 1996, *Internationalization and Domestic Politics*, New York: Cambridge University Press.

Keohane, Robert and Joseph Nye, 1977, *Power and Interdependence: World Politics in Transition.*

Klapp, Merrie Gilbert, 1987, *The Sovereignty Entrepreneur: Oil Politics in Advanced and Less Developed capitalist Countries.* Ithaca: Cornell University Press.

Klare, Michael T., 2001, *Resource Wars: The New Landscape of Global Conflict*, New York: Henry Holt.

———, 2004, *Blood and Oil: The Dangers and Consequences of America's Growing Petroleum Dependency*, New York: Metropolitan Books.

Kneese, A.V. and J.L. Sweeney, eds., 1993, *Handbook of Natural Resource and Energy Economics*, Vol. 3, Amsterdam: Elsevier B.V./North Holland.

Krapels, E. N., 1977, *Controlling Oil: British Oil Policy and the British National Oil Corporation*, Washington, DC: US Government Printing Office.

Krasner, Stephen D., 1978, *Defending the National Interest: Raw Materials Investments and U.S. Foreign Policy.* Princeton, NJ: Princeton University Press.

Labys, Walter C., 1999, *Modeling Mineral and Energy Markets*, Boston, MA: Kluwer Academic.

Laffont, Jean-Jacques with Claudia Senik-Leygonie, 1997, *Price Controls and the Economics of Institutions in China*, Paris: Development Center of the OECD.

Lam, Willy Wo-Lap, 1999, *The Era of Jiang Zemin*, Singapore: Prentice Hall.

———, 2006, *Chinese Politics in the Hu Jintao Era: New Leaders, New Challenges*, London and New York: M.E. Sharpe.

Landsberg, Hans H. (ed.), 1993, *Making National Energy Policy*, Washington, DC: Resources for the Future.

Lane, David, 1999, *The Political Economy of Russian Oil*, Lanham, MD: Rowman & Littlefield.

Lax, Howard L, 1988, *States and Companies: Political Risks in the International Oil Industry*, New York: Praeger.

Li, Jieping, 2002, "Urban Communication: Problems and Countermeasures—On the Function of TDM," Urban Transportation, Vol. 3.

Lieber, Robert J., 1983, *The Oil Decade: Conflict and Cooperation in the West*, New York, NY: Praeger.

Lieberthal, Kenneth and Michel Oksenberg, 1986, *Bureaucratic Politics and Chinese Energy Development*, Washington, DC: U.S. Department of Commerce, International Trade Administration.

———, 1988, *Policy Making in China: Leaders, Structures, and Processes*, Princeton, NJ: Princeton University Press.

Lieberthal, Kenneth G., and David M. Lampton., 1992, *Bureaucracy, Politics, and Decision Making in Post-Mao China*, Berkeley: University of California Press.

Lieberthal, Kenneth, 2004, *Governing China: From Revolution through Reform*, New York and London: W. W. Norton & Company, 2nd edition.

Lin, Kun-Chin, 2003, *Corporatizing China: Reinventing State Control for the Market*, PhD dissertation, University of California, Berkeley, Fall.

Lindblom, Charles E., 1977, *Politics and Markets: The World's Political Economic Systems*, New York: Basic.

Lindzey, Gardner and Elliot Aronson (eds.), 1968, *The Handbook of Social Psychology*, Reading, MA: Addison-Wesley Pub. Co.

Ling, H.C., 1975, *The Petroleum Industry of the People's Republic of China*, California: Hoover Institution Press.

Lodge, George Cabot, 1990, *Comparative Business-Government Relations*, New York: Prentice Hall.

Lu, Feng, 1999, *State, Market, and Enterprises: The Transformation of Chinese State Industry*, Doctoral dissertation, Columbia University, UMI No.: 9916899.

Madan, Tanvi, 2006, *The Brookings Foreign Policy Studies Energy Security Series: India*, Washington, DC.

Manning, Robert A, 2000, *The Asian Energy Factor: Myths and Dilemma of Energy Security, and the Pacific Future*. New York: Palgrave.

Marcusm Alfred A., 1992, *Controversial Issues in Energy Policy*, Newbury Park, CA: Sage Publications.

Maugeri, Leonardo, 2006, *The Age of Oil: The Mythology, History, and Future of the World's Most Controversial Resource*, Praeger Publishers, May 30.
Meidan, Michal (ed.), 2007, *Shaping China's Energy Security: The Inside Perspective*, Paris: Asia Centre/Centre etudes Asie.
Migdal, Joel S., 1988, *Strong Society and Weak State: State-Society Relations and State Capabilities in the Third World*, Princeton: Princeton University Press.
Milgate, Murray, John Eatwell, and Peter Newman (eds.), 1987, *The New Palgrave: A Dictionary of Economics*, London: Macmillan.
Mitchell, John, with Koji Morita, Norman Selley and Jonathan Stern, 2001, *The New Economy of Oil: Impacts on Business, Geopolitics and Society*, London: Earthscan.
Mommer, Bernard, 2002, *Global Oil and the Nation State*, Oxford and New York: Oxford University Press for the Oxford Institute for Energy Studies.
Monshipouri, Mahmood, Neil Englehart, Andrew J. Nathan and Kavita Philip (eds.), 2003, *Constructing Human Rights in the Age of Globalization*, New York: M.E. Sharpe.
Mtsiva, V.C. (ed.), 2003, *Oil and Natural Gas: Issues and Policies*, New York: Nova Science Publishers.
Müller-Kraenner, Sascha, 2008, *Energy Security*, London: Routledge.
Naughton, Barry J. and Dali L. Yang (eds.), 2004, *Holding China Together: Diversity and National Integration in the Post-Deng Era*, Cambridge: Cambridge University Press.
Naughton, Barry, 1999, "China's Transition in Economic Perspective," in Merle Goldman and Roderick MacFarquhar, *The Paradox of China's Post-Mao Reforms*, Cambridge, MA: Harvard University Press.
Nordhaus, William D., 1979, *The Efficient Use of Energy Resources*, Yale University Press.
Noreng, Oystein, 1997, *Oil and Islam: Social and Economic Issues*, New York, Singapore, etc.: Wiley.
North, Douglass C., 1990, *Institutions, Institutional Change and Economic Performance*, Cambridge: Cambridge University Press.
Okimoto, D. , 1989, *Between MITI and the Market*, Stanford University Press.
Olson, Mancur, 1971, *The Logic of Collective Action: Public Goods and the Theory of Groups*, Cambridge, MA: Harvard University Press, Revised edition.
Opsal, Ryan, *American and Chinese Energy Security: A Grand Strategic Approach*, Lexington Books, 2019.
Paik, Keun Wook, 1995, *Gas and Oil in Northeast Asia: Policies, Projects and Prospects*, London: Royal Institute of International Affairs, Energy and Environmental Programme.
Pardesi, Manjeet Singh (ed.), 2006, *Energy and Security: The Geopolitics of Energy in the Asia-Pacific*, Singapore: Institute of Defense and Strategic Studies, Nanyang Technological University.

Perry, Elizabeth J. and Christine Wong (eds.), 1985, *The Political Economy of Reform in Post-Mao China*, Cambridge, MA: Council on East Asian Studies/ Harvard University.

Peters, B. Guy, 1999, *Institutional Theory in Political Science*, London and New York: Pinter.

Pietz, David and Chris Ellsworth, 2000, *Fueling China: Oil and Gas Demand to 2010*, Wakefield, MA: Energy Security Analysis, Inc., January.

Polanyi, Karl, 1957, *The Great Transformation: The Political and Economic Origins of Our Time*, Boston: Beacon Press (originally published 1944).

Putterman, Louis and Dietrich Rueschemeyer (eds.), 1992, *State and Market in Development: Synergy or Rivalry?* Boulder: Lynne Rienner Publishers.

Reynolds, Bruce (ed.), 1987, *Reform in China: Challenges and Choices*, Armonk, NY: M. E. Sharpe.

Rock, Milton L., Robert H. Rock and Martin Sikra (eds.), 1994, *The Mergers & Acquisitions Handbook* (2nd ed.), New York: Mcgraw-Hill.

Romm, Joseph, 1993, *Defining National Security: The Nonmilitary Aspects*, Washington: Council on Foreign Relations.

Rosenbaum, Walter A., 1981, *Energy, Politics, and Public Policy*, Washington, DC: Congressional Quarterly Press.

Sachs, Jeffrey, 1993, *Poland's Jump to the Market Economy*, Cambridge, MA: Harvard University Press.

Sachs, Jeffrey D. and David Lipton, 1990, "Poland's Economic Reform," *Foreign Affairs*, Vol. 69.

Saint-Mézard, Isabelle (Asia Centre) and CSFRS (Conseil Supérieur de la Formation et de la Recherche Stratégiques), 2014, *The International Dimensions of India's Energy Security*, Note in the framework of the SECI project (Energy Security from China and India) in partnership with the CSFRS, February.

Sarbin, Theodore and L. Allen, "Role Theory," in Gardner Lindzey and Elliot Aronson (eds.), 1968, *The Handbook of Social Psychology*, Reading, MA: Addison-Wesley Pub. Co.

Saunders, Philip C., 2006, *China's Global Activism: Strategies, Drivers, and Tools*, Washington, DC: Institute for National Strategic Studies, National Defense University, October.

Segal, Adam, "Globalization Is a Double-Edged Sword: Globalization and Chinese National Security," in Jonathan Kirshner (ed.), 2006, *Globalization and National Security*, New York and Oxon: Routledge, pp. 293–320.

Shealy, Malcolm and James Dorian, 2007, "Growing Chinese Energy Demand: Is the World in Denial?" CSIS (Center for Strategic and International Studies) Report—A Report of the Energy & National Security Program, October.

Shirk, Susan L., 1993, *The Political Logic of Economic Reform in China*, Berkeley: University of California Press.

Smelser, Neil J. and Richard Swedberg (eds.), 1994, *The Handbook of Economic Sociology*, Princeton, NJ: Princeton University Press.

Solinger, Dorothy J., "Globalization and Human Rights for Workers in China: Convergence of Collision?" in Mahmood Manshipouri, Neil A. Englehart, et al., (eds.), 2003, *Constructing Human Rights in the Age of Globalizaation*, Armonk, NY: M.E.

Stares, Paul B., 2000, *Rethinking Energy Security in East Asia*, Tokyo: Japan Center for International Exchange.

Stephanie M. Hoopes, 1997, *Oil Privatization, Public Choice and International Forces*, New York: St. Martin's Press.

Stephen D. Krasner, 1978, *Defending the National Interest: Raw Materials Investments and U.S. Foreign Policy*. Princeton, NJ: Princeton University Press.

Stigliz, Joseph E., "Principal and Agent," in Murray Milgate, John Eatwell, and Peter Newman (eds.), 1987, *The New Palgrave: A Dictionary of Economics*, London: Macmillan.

Strange, Susan, 1996, *The Retreat of the State: The Diffusion of Power in the World Economy*, New York: Cambridge University Press.

Strares, Paul B., 2000, *Rethinking Energy Security in East Asia*, Tokyo: Japan Center for International Exchange.

Taylor, Monique, 2014, *The Chinese State, Oil and Energy Security*, Basingstoke: Palgrave Macmillan.

Tertzakian, Peter, 2006, *A Thousand Barrels a Second: The Coming Oil Break Point and the Challenges Facing an Energy Dependent World*, New York: McGraw-Hill.

The Center for Strategic and International Studies (CSIS), 2000, *The Geopolitics of Energy into the 21 Century*, Vol. 3: The Geopolitical Outlook, 2000–2020, A Report of the CSIS Strategic Energy Initiative, Washington.

Thelen, Kathleen, Sven Steinmo, and Frank Longstreth (eds.), 1992, *Structuring Politics: Historical Institutionalism in Comparative Analysis*, Cambridge and New York: Cambridge University Press.

Tunsjø, Øystein, 2013, *Security and Profit in China's Energy Policy: Hedging Against Risk* (Contemporary Asia in the World), Columbia University Press.

van der Linde, Coby, 1991, *Dynamic International Oil Markets: Oil Market Developments and Structure, 1860–1990*, Dordrecht, Netherlands; Boston: Kluwer Academic Publishers.

———, 2000, *The State and the International Oil Market: Competition and the Changing Ownership of Crude Oil Assets*, Boston: Kluwer Academic Publishers.

Venn, Fiona, 1986, *Oil Diplomacy in the Twentieth Century*, Basingstoke: Macmillan.

Vernon, Raymond and Yair Aharoni (eds.), 1981, *State-Owned Enterprise in the Western Economies*, London: Croom Helm.
Vivoda, Vlado, 2008, *The Return of the Obsolescing Bargain and the Decline of Big Oil: A Study of Bargaining in the Contemporary Oil Industry*, Saarbrücken, Germany: Vdm Verlag Dr. Müller.
Wade, Robert, 1990, *Governing the Market*, Princeton University Press.
Walker, Stephen G. (ed.), 1987, *Role Theory and Foreign Policy Analysis*, Durham, NC: Duke University Press.
Wang, Henry, 1999, *China's Oil Industry & Market*, New York: Elsevier.
Wang, Xiaoqiang, 1998, *China's Price and Enterprise Reform*, London and New York: St. Martin's Press.
Weiss, Linda, 1998, *The Myth of the Powerless State*, Ithaca, New York: Cornell University Press.
——— (ed.), 2003, *States in the Global Economy*, Cambridge University Press.
Weiss, Linda and John Hobson, 1995, *States and Economic Development*, Polity.
Wenger, Andreas, Robert W. Orttung & Jeronim Perovic (eds.), 2009, *Energy and the Transformation of International Relations: Toward a New Producer-Consumer Framework*, New York: Oxford University Press.
Whiting, Susan Hayes, 1995, *The Micro-Foundations of Institutional Change in Reform China: Property Rights and Revenue Extraction in the Rural Industrial Sector*, dissertation for PhD degree in the University of Michigan.
Williamson, Oliver E., 1975, *Markets and Hierarchies, Analysis and Antitrust Implications*, New York: Free Press.
Woodward, Kim, 1980, *The International Energy Relations of China*, Stanford: Stanford University Press.
Wu, Xinbo, "China: Security Practice of a Modernizing and Ascending Power," in Muthiah Alagappa (ed.), 1998, *Asian Security Practice: Material and Ideational Influences*, Stanford: Stanford University Press.
Wybrey-Bond, Ian and Jonathan Stern, 2002, *Natural Gas in Asia: The Challenges of Growth in China, India, Japan and Korea*, Oxford: Oxford University Press.
Yang, Dali L., "Economic Crisis and Market Transition in the 1990s," in Edwin A. Winckler (ed.), 1999, *Transition from Communism in China: Institutional and Comparative Analyses*, Boulder and London: Lynne Rienner Publishers, pp. 151–177.
———, "Taming the Market: China and the Forces of Globalization," in Aseem Parkash and Jeffrey A. Hart (eds.), 2000, *Responding to Globalization*, London and New York : Routledge.
———, 2004, *Remaking the Chinese Leviathan: Market Transition and the Politics of Governance in China*, Stanford, CA: Stanford University Press.
Yergin, Daniel, 1991, *The Prize: The Epic Quest for Oil, Money, and Power*, New York: Simon & Schuster.

Yusuf, Shahid, Kaoru Nabeshima, and Dwight H. Perkins, 2006, *Under New Leadership: Privatizing China's State-Owned Enterprises*, The World Bank and Stanford University Press.

Zhang, Jin, 2004, *Catch-up and Competitiveness in China: The Case of Large Firms in the Oil Industry*, London and New York, NY: Routledge Curzon.

Zhang, Wei-wei, 1999, *Transforming China: Economic Reform and Its Political Implications*, New York: St. Martin's Press.

Zhao, Hong, 2012, *China and India: The Quest for Energy Resources in the Twenty-first Century*, London and New York: Routledge.

Zhao, Jinping, 2021, *Reshaping the Economic Cooperation Pattern of the Belt and Road Initiative*, Singapore: Palgrave Macmillan.

Zhao, Suisheng, 2004, *Chinese Foreign Policy: Pragmatism and Strategic Behavior*, New York: M.E. Sharpe.

Zheng, Yongnian, 2004, *Globalization and State Transformation in China*, Cambridge: Cambridge: Cambridge University Press.

———, 2007, *De Facto Federalism in China: Reforms and Dynamics of Central-Local Relations*, Singapore and London: World Scientific Publishing.

Zheng, Yongnian and Minjia CHEN, 2006, "China Promotes Green GDP for More Balanced Development," Briefing Series—Issue 16, China Policy Institute, Nottingham University, December.

Zhu, Jieming, 1999, *The Transition of China's Urban Development: From Plan-Controlled to Market-Led*, Westport, CT and London: Praeger.

Secondary Sources—English Papers and Reports

Achakulwisut, Ploy, Peter Erickson, and Doug Koplow, 2021, "Effect of Subsidies and Regulatory Exemptions on 2020–2030 Oil and Gas Production and Profits in the United States," *Environmental Research Letters*, Vol. 16, No. 8.

Achen, Christopher H. and Duncan Snidal, 1989, "Rational Deterrence Theory and Comparative Case Studies," *World Politics*, Vol. 41, No. 2, January.

Adelman, M.A., 2002, "World Oil Production & Prices 1947–2000," *The Quarterly Review of Economics and Finance*, Vol. 42, pp. 169–191.

Alchian, A. and Harold Demsetz, 1972, "Production, Information Costs and Economic Organization," *American Economic Review*, Vol. 62, December, pp. 777–795.

Alden, Chris, 2005, "China in Africa," *Survival*, Vol. 47, No. 3, Autumn.

Amineh, Mehdi P. and Guang Yang, 2018, "China's Geopolitical Economy of Energy Security: A Theoretical and Conceptual Exploration," *African and Asian Studies*, Vol. 17, No. 1–2, February, pp. 9–39.

Andrews-Speed, Philip, et al., 2000, "The Ongoing Reforms to China's Government and State Sector: The Case of the Energy Sector," *Journal of Contemporary China*, Vol. 23, No. 9.

An, Qi, 2012, "Guoji huashi ranliao butie xianzhuang pingshu" (Review of the Status Quo of International Subsidies to Fossil Fuels), *Zhongguo Nengyuan* (China Energy), No. 4, June.

Areddy, James T., 2006, "China Turns on Green Light for Domestic Firms' Large-Scale Overseas Investment," *Washington Street Journal*, 9 June.

Arruda, Michael E. and Ka-Yin Li, 2004, "Legal Reforms Opening Doors to Foreign Investment in China's Oil, Gas Sector," *Oil & Gas Journal*, 13 September.

Asif, Muhammad and T. Muneer, 2006, "Energy Supply, Its Demand and Security Issues for Developed and Emerging Economies," *Renewable and Sustainable Energy Reviews*. Available online 30 January.

Backman, Carl W., 1970, "Role Theory and International Relations: A Commentary and Extension," *International Studies Quarterly*, Vol. 14, No. 3, September, pp. 310–319.

Bajpaee, Chietgj, 2005, "Sino-U.S. Energy Competition in Africa," *The Power and Interest News Report*, 7 October. http://www.pinr.com.

Baldwin, David A., 1996, "Security Studies and the End of the Cold War," *World Politics*, Vol. 48, No. 1.

Barta, Patrick, 2004, "China Is Joining Global Hunt for Oil and Coming up Dry," *Wall Street Journal*, Eastern edition, 23 September.

Beng, Phar Kim and Vic Y.W. Li, 2005, "China's Energy Dependence on the Middle East: Boon or Bane for Asian Security?" *The China and Eurasia Forum Quarterly*, Vol. 3, No. 3, November.

Bentley, R.W., 2002, "Global Oil & Gas Depletion: An Overview," *Energy Policy*, Vol. 30.

Bielecki, J., 2002, "Energy Security: Is the Wolf at the Door?" *Quarterly Review of Economics and Finance*, Vol. 42, No. 2, pp. 235–250.

Bissell, Richard E., 1978, "The Role of the International Oil Companies," *Current History*, Vol. 74, No. 437, May–June.

Bremmer, Ian, 2005, "Are the U.S. and China on a Collision Course?" *Fortune (Europe)*, Vol. 151, No. 1, 24 January.

Cauley, Jon and Todd Sandler, 1992, "Agency Theory and the Chinese Enterprise Under Reform," *China Economic Review*, Vol. 3, pp. 39–56

Chafetz, Glenn, Hillel Abramson and Suzette Grillot, 1996, "Role Theory and Foreign Policy: Belarussian and Ukrainian Compliance with the Nuclear Nonproliferation Regime," *Political Psychology*, Vol. 17, No. 4, December, pp. 727–757.

Chassin, Laurie, Antonette Zeiss, et al., 1985, "Role Perceptions, Self-Role Congruence and Marital Satisfaction in Dual-Worker Couples with Prescholl Children," *Social Psychology Quarterly*, Vol. 48, No. 4.

Chen, Matthew E., 2007, "Chinese National Oil Companies and Human Rights," *Orbis*, Vol. 1, Winter.

Chen, Shaofeng, 2006, "East Asia Energy Community: A Fantasy or Not?" Conference paper, at the 7th Doctoral Students Conference of Association of Pacific Rim University, Singapore, 17–21 July.

———, 2008, "Motivations Behind China's Foreign Oil Quest: A Perspective from the Chinese Government and the Oil Companies," *Journal of Chinese Political Science*, Vol. 13, No. 1, Spring, pp. 79–103.

———, 2009, "Marketization and China's Energy Security," *Policy and Society*, Vol. 27.

———, 2011, "Has China's Foreign Energy Quest Enhanced Its Energy Security?" *The China Quarterly*, Vol. 207, September, pp. 600–625.

———, 2012, "State-Managed Marketization: The Role of the Chinese State in the Petroleum Industry," *The Copenhagen Journal of Asian Studies*, Vol. 30, No. 2, pp. 29–60.

Cheung, Kui-yin and Elspeth Thomson, 2004, "The Demand for Gasoline in China: A Cointegration Analysis," *Journal of Applied Statistics*, Vol. 31, No. 5, June, pp. 533–544.

Chhibber, Pradeep and Sumit K. Majumdar, 1998, "State as Investor and State as Owner: Consequences for Firm Performance in India," *Economic Development and Cultural Change*, Vol. 46, No. 3, April.

Christofersen, Gaye, 2005, "The Dilemmas of China's Energy Governance: Recentralization and Regional Cooperation," *The China and Eurasia Forum Quarterly*, Vol. 3, No. 3, November.

Christopher, Mark, 2005, "In Need of a China Energy Strategy," *The Asian Wall Street Journal*, 27 June.

Chung, Chien-peng, 2002, "China's 'War on Terror'," *Foreign Affairs*, Vol. 81, No. 4, July/August.

———, 2004, "The Shanghai Co-operation Organization: China's Changing Influence in Central Asia," *The China Quarterly*, Vol. 180, pp. 989–1009.

Clarke, Kieran, Shruti Sharma and Damon Vis-Dunbar, 2004, *India Energy Subsidy Review*, Vol. 1, No. 1, February. https://www.iisd.org/gsi/sites/default/files/ffs_india_review_february2014.pdf.

Collins, Gabe, 2006, "China Seeks Oil Security with New Tanker Fleet," *Oil & Gas Journal*, 9 October.

Congress of the United States, Congressional Budget Office, 2012, "Energy Security in the United States," *Congressional Budget Office (CBO) Report*, May.

Constantin, Christian, 2005, "China's Conception of Energy Security: Sources and International Impacts," *Working Paper* of the Centre of International Relations, University of British Columbia, No. 43, March. http://www.iir.ubc.ca/Papers/Constantin-WP43.pdf.

Cornelius, Peter and Jonathan Story, 2007, "China and Global Energy Market," *Orbis*, Vol. 51, No. 1, Winter. Available online 20 November 2006.

Dannreuther, Roland, 2003, "Asian Security and China's Energy Needs," *International Relations of the Asia-Pacific*, Vol. 3.

Dansie, Grant, Marc Lanteigne and Indra Overland, 2010, "Reducing Energy Subsidies in China, India and Russia: Dilemmas for Decision Makers," *Sustainability*, No. 2.

DeCanio, Stephen J., 1979, "Rational Expectations and Learning from Experience," *The Quarterly Journal of Economics*, Vol. 93, No. 1, February.

Deese, David A., 1979-1980, "Energy: Economics, Politics, and Security," *International Security*, Vol. 4, No. 3, Winter, pp. 140–153.

Ding, X.L., 2000, "The Illicit Asset Stripping of Chinese State Firms," *The China Journal*, No. 43, January, pp. 1–28.

Dion, Douglas, 1998, "Evidence and Inference in the Comparative Case Study," *Comparative Politics*, Vol. 30, No. 2, January, pp. 127–145.

Doner, R., 1992, 'Limits of State Strength', *World Politics*, Vol. 44, No. 3, pp. 398–431

Downs, Erica S., 2000, *China's Quest for Energy Security*, RAND Document No.: MR-1244-AF, p. 12. http://www.rand.org/publications/MR/MR1244/.

———, 2004, "The Chinese Energy Security Debate," *The China Quarterly*, Vol. 177, March.

———, 2006, "National Energy Security Depends on International Energy Security," *The Brookings Institution*, March 17. http://www.brookings.edu/views/op-ed/fellows/downs20060317.htm.

Dwyer, F. Robert, and Orville C. Walker, Jr., 1981, "Bargaining in an Asymmetrical Power Structure," *Journal of Marketing*, Vol. 45, No. 1, Winter, pp. 104–115.

Eisenman, Joshua, and Joshua Kurlantzick, 2006, "China's Africa Strategy," *Current History*, May. http://www.afpc.org/china-africa.shtml.

Fan, Ying, Hua Liao and Yi-Ming Wei, 2006, "Can Market Oriented Economic Reforms Contribute to Energy Efficiency Improvement? Evidence from China," *Energy Policy*. Available online 25 September.

Feng, Xunan, Anders C. Johansson, 2013, "CEO Incentives in Chinese State-Controlled Firms," Stockholm School of Economics Asia Working Paper, No. 27, September.

Fishelson, James, 2007, "From the Silk Road to Chevron: The Geopolitics of Oil Pipelines in Central Asia," *Vestnik*, No. 7, Winter.

Fisher-Vanden, Karen, et al., 2004, "What Is Driving China's Decline in Energy Intensity?" *Resource and Energy Economics*, No. 26, pp. 77–97.

———, 2013, "Factors Influencing Energy Intensity in Four Chinese Industries," Policy Research Working Paper 6551, The World Bank, July.

Garbaccio, R.F., M.S. Ho, and D.W. Jorgenson, 1999, "Why Has the Energy-Output Ratio Fallen in China?" *Energy* Journal, Vol. 20, No. 3, pp. 63–91.

Garbaccio, Richard F., 1994, "Price Reform and Structural Change in the Chinese Economy: Policy Simulations Using a CGE Model," *China Economic Review*, Vol. 6, No. 1.

Geddes, Barbara, 1990, "How the Cases You Choose Affect the Answers You Get: Selection Bias in Comparative Politics," *Political Analysis*, Vol. 2.

Gennady Chufrin, 2003, "Russia's Economic and Strategic Interests in North-East Asia," *Asia Europe Journal*, Vol. 1, pp. 251–262.

Goldstein, Avery, 1994, "Trends in the Study of Political Elites and Institutions in the PRC," *The China Quarterly*, No. 139, September, pp. 714–730.

Goldstein, Carl, 1992, "China's Oil Shock," *Far Eastern Economic Review*, Vol. 155, No. 45, November 12.

———, 1993, "Energy: Lost Privileges," *Far Eastern Economic Review*, Vol. 156, No. 30, 29 July.

———, 1994, "No So Slick," *Far Eastern Economic Review*, Vol. 157, No. 14, 7 April.

Goldstein, Steven M., 1995, "China in Transition: The Political Foundations of Incremental Reform," *The China Quarterly*, No. 144, Special Issue: China's Transitional Economy, December.

Gourevitch, Peter, 1978, "The Second Image Reversed: The International Sources of Domestic Politics," *International Organization*, Vol. 32, No. 4, pp. 881–911.

Grantham Institute for Climate Change Report GR4, 2012, "An Assessment of India's 2020 Carbon Intensity Target," Imperial College, London, April.

Greene, D.L., J.L. Hopson and J. Li, 2005, "Running Out of and into Oil: Analyzing Global Oil Depletion and Transition through 2050," *Transportation Research Record 1880*, pp. 1–9, Transportation Research Board, Washington, DC.

Gu, Mengdi, 2005, "China Wants More Pipelines for Improved Oil Import Security," *Tulsa: Oil & Gas Journal*, Vol. 3, No. 1, 3 January.

Guo, Sujian, 2003, "The Ownership Reform in China: What Direction and How Far?" *Journal of Contemporary China*, Vol. 12, No. 36, August, pp. 553–573.

Guthrie, D., 1998, "The Declining Significance of *guanxi* in China's Economic Transition," *The China Quarterly*, Vol. 154, pp. 254–282.

Hamel, G., 1980, "The Multinational Corporation and Home Country Foreign Policy: A Research Agenda," Working Paper No. 229, Graduate School of Business Administration, The University of Michigan, August.

Hamilton, James D., 2003, "What Is an Oil Shock?" *Journal of Econometrics*, Vol. 113.

Handke, Sansann, 2006, *Securing and Fueling China's Ascent to Power: The Geopolitics of the Chinese-Kazakh Oil Pipeline*, The Hague: Clingendael International Energy Programme, http://www.clingendael.nl/publications/2006/20060900_ciep_paper_handke.pdf.

Hayashi, Yuka, 2005, "China Studies Japan's Mistakes as the Pursuit for Oil Continues," *Wall Street Journal*, 3 August.

Hayes, Peter and David von Hippel, 2006, "Energy Security in Northeast Asia," *Global Asia*, Vol. 1, No. 1, September.

Herring, Horace, 1999, "Does Energy Efficiency Save Energy? The Debate and Its Consequences," *Applied Energy*, Vol. 63, pp. 209–226.

Houthakker, Hendrik S., 2002, "Are Minerals Exhaustible," *The Quarterly Review of Economics and Finance*, Vol. 42, pp. 417–421.

Hu, Xiaobo, 2000, "The State, Enterprises, and Society in Post-Deng China: Impact of the New Round of SOE Reform," *Asian Survey*, Vol. 40, No. 4, July–August, pp. 641–657.

IEA, 2004, "Analysis of the Impact of High Oil Prices on the Global Economy," May. www.iea.org.

———, 2012, "Oil and Gas Security-Emergency Response of IEA Countries—PR China".

Jakobson, Linda and Dean Knox, 2010, "New Foreign Policy Actors in China," SIPRI (Stockholm International Peace Research Institute) Policy Paper 26, September. http://books.sipri.org/files/PP/SIPRIPP26.pdf.

Jaffe, Amy Myers and Steven W. Lewis, 2002, "Beijing's Oil Diplomacy," *Survival*, Vol. 44, No. 1, Spring.

Jaffe, Amy Myers, and Ronald Soligo, 2002, "The Role of Inventories in Oil Market Stability," *The Quarterly Review of Economics and Finance*, Vol. 42, pp. 401–415.

———, 2007, "The International Oil Companies," Policy Report Prepared in Conjunction with an Energy Study Sponsored by the James A. Baker III Institute for Public Policy and Japan Petroleum Energy Center, November.

Jakobson, Linda and Daojiong Zha, 2006, "China and the Worldwide Search for Oil Security," *Asia-Pacific Review*, Vol. 13, No. 2.

Jiang, Julie and Jonathan Sinton, 2011, "Overseas Investments by Chinese National Oil Companies: Assessing the Drivers and Impacts," *International Energy Agency Information Paper*, February.

Jiang, Wenran, 2006, "China's Booming Energy Relations with Africa," *Association for Asian Research Journal*, 3 August. http://www.asianresearch.org/articles/2911.html.

Kane, Thomas and Lawrence Serewicz, 2001, "China's Hunger: The Consequences of Rising Demand for Food and Energy," Parameters, Vol. 31, Autumn.

Kanekiyo, Kensuke, 2005, "Siberian Oil Pipeline and Its Implication for Northeast Asia," Institute of Energy Economics, Japan. https://eneken.ieej.or.jp/en/data/pdf/290.pdf.

Kennedy, Scott, 1997, "The Stone Group: State Client or Market Pathbreaker?" *The China Quarterly*, Vol. 152, December.

———, 2003, "The Price of Competition: Pricing Policies and the Struggle to Define China's Economic System," *China Quarterly*, No. 49, January.

Kilian, Lutz, 2008, "The Economic Effects of Energy Price Shocks," *Journal of Economic Literature*, Vol. 46, No. 4, December, pp. 871–909

Kim, E. Y., 1993, 'The Developmental State and the Politics of Business Interest Associations', *Pacific Focus*, Vol. 8, No. 2, pp. 31–60.

Klare, Michael, 2006, "Fueling the Dragon: China's Strategic Energy Dilemma," *Current History*, April.

Kong, Bo, 2005, "An Anatomy of China's Energy Insecurity and Strategies," in the Conference of *China's Search for Energy Security and Implications for the U.S.*, co-sponsored by National Bureau of Asian Research (NBR), U.S. Department of Energy, etc, 27–28 September, Washington, DC. http://pnwcgs.pnl.gov/Newsletter/otherdocs/anatchinaenergy.pdf.

Kornai, Janos, 1986, "The Soft Budget Constraint," *Kyklos*, Vol. 39, pp. 3–30.

———, 1990, "The Affinity Between Ownership Forms and Coordination Mechanisms," *Journal of Economic Perspectives*, Vol. 4, No. 3, pp. 131–147.

Krasner, Stephen, 1984, "Approach to the State: Alternative Conceptions and Historical Dynamics," *Comparative Politics*, Vol. 16, pp. 223–246.

Lai, Hongyi, 2005, "China's Oil Diplomacy Going Global: Reducing Reliance on the Middle East and the Malacca Strait," *East Asian Institute (EAI) Background Brief No. 246*, 6 June.

Lee, Hong Yung, 1994, "Book Review: Political Reform in Post-Mao China: Democracy and Bureaucracy in a Leninist State," *The Journal of Asian Studies*, Vol. 53, No. 3.

Lee, Pak K., 2005, "China's Quest for Oil Security: Oil (Wars) in the Pipeline?" *The Pacific Review*, Vol. 18, No. 2, June.

Lesbirel, S. Hayden, 2004, "Diversification and Energy Security Risks: The Japanese Case," *Japanese Journal of Political Science*, Vol. 5, No. 1, pp. 1–22.

Leverett, Flynt and Jeffrey Bader, 2005–2006, "Managing China-U.S. Energy Competition in the Middle East," *The Washington Quarterly*, Vol. 29, No. 1, Winter.

Levy, Marg A., 1995, "Is the Environment a National Security Issue?" *International Security*, No. 20, pp. 35–62.

Lieber, Robert J., 1992, "Oil and Power After the Gulf War," *International Security*, Vol. 17, No. 1, Summer.

Lieberthal, Kenneth and Mikkal Herberg, 2006, "China's Search for Energy Security: Implications for U.S. Policy," *NBR Analysis*, Vol. 17, No. 1, April.

Lin, Chen & Dongwei Su, 2009, "Does State Control Affect Managerial Incentives? Evidence from China's Publicly Listed Firms," *Journal of Business Economics and Management*, Vol. 10, No. 4.

Lin, Justin Yifu, Fang Cai, and Zhou Li, 1998, "Competition, Policy Burdens, and State-Owned Enterprise Reform, " *The American Economic Review*, Vol. 88, No. 2, May, pp. 422–427.

Lin, Kun-Chin, 2003, "The State as Market Surrogate: Pricing Goods and Services for Oil and Petrochemical Industries in China," Paper presented at the Annual Meeting of the Association for Asian Studies, New York, 28 March.

———, 2006, "Disembedding Socialist Firms as a Statist Project: Restructuring the Chinese Oil Industry, 1997–2002," *Enterprise & Society*, Vol. 7, No. 1, pp. 59–97.

———, 2006, "Explaining Evolving Wage Structures in State-Owned Enterprises in China: Evidence from the Oil Industry," paper presented at the Workshop "Globalization and the Workplace" at ST. Anthony's College, University of Oxford, 27–28 October.

Lin, Kun-Chin and Chen Shaofeng, "The Local Government in Corporate Restructuring: Case Studies in Fractured Bargaining Relations," *Journal of Current Chinese Affairs*, Vol. 42, No. 4, pp. 171–198.

Lin, X., K.R. Polenske, 1995, "Input-Output Anatomy of China's Energy Use Changes in the 1980s," *Economic Systems Research*, Vol. 7, No. 1.

Luft, Gal, 2008, "Fueling the Dragon: China's Race into the Oil Market," Institute for the Analysis of Global Security. www.iags.org/china.htm.

Ma, Chunbo and David I. Stern, 2006, "China's Changing Energy Intensity Trend: A Decomposition Analysis," Rensselaer Working Papers in Economics No. 0615, December.

Mabro, Robert, 2005, "The International Oil Price Regime: Origins, Rationale and Assessment," *The Journal of Energy Literature*, Vol. XI, No. 1, June.

Magid, Alvin, 1980, "'Role Theory,' Political Science, and African Studies," *World Politics*, Vol. 32, No. 2, January, pp. 311–330.

Mai, Yinhua, 2001, "Can the New Chinese Oil Giants Compete After China's WTO Entry?" Singapore: National University of Singapore, East Asia Institute (EAI), EAI Working Paper No. 74, 8 May.

March, James G., 1962, "The Business firm as a Political Coalition," *The Journal of Politics*, Vol. 24, No. 4, November, pp. 662–678.

McNamara, Dennis L., 1993, "Associations and Adjustment in Japan's Textile Industry," *Pacific Affairs*, Vol. 66, No. 2, Summer, pp. 206–218.

Meidan, Michal, Philip Andrews-Speed & Ma Xin, 2009, "Shaping China's Energy Policy: Actors and Processes," *Journal of Contemporary China*, Vol. 18, No. 61.

Meyer, Marshall W., 2005, "Is CNOOC's Bid for Unocal a Threat to America?" *Knowledge at Wharton*, 21 November, https://knowledge.wharton.upenn.edu/article/is-cnoocs-bid-for-unocal-a-threat-to-america/.

Mi, Zhou and Xiaoming Wang, 2000, "Agency Cost and the Crisis of China's SOE," *China Economic Review*, Vol. 11, pp. 297–317.

Mitchell, John V., 2002, "A New Political Economy of Oil," *The Quarterly Review of Economics and Finance*, Vol. 42.

Morse, Edward L., 1999, "A New Political Economy of Oil?" *Journal of International Affairs*, Vol. 53, No. 1, Fall.

Müller-Kraenner, Sascha, 2008, "China's and India's Emerging Energy Foreign Policy", (Discussion Paper, Deutsches Institut für Entwicklungspolitik <German Development Institute>), Bonn.

Myszewski, David, 2001, "News: Stanford Scholars Host Energy Conference," *The Stanford Review*, Vol. XXVII, No. 2, 24 October.

Naughton, Barry, 2002, "China's Economic Think Tanks: Their Changing Role in the 1990s." *China Quarterly*, Vol. 33.

Newton, David, 2003, "Securing a Bridge Loan," *Entrepreneur*, 28 April. http://www.entrepreneur.com/article/0,4621,308255,00.html.

Noguera, Jose and Rowena A. Pecchecnino, 2007, "OPEC and the International Oil Market: Can a Cartel Fuel the Engine of Economic Development?" *International Journal of Industrial Organization*, Vol. 25, No. 1, February, pp. 187–199.

Nolan, Peter and Zhang, Jin, 2003, "Globalization Challenge for Large Firms from Developing Countries: China's Oil and Aerospace Industries," *European Management Journal*, Vol. 21, No. 3.

O'Brien, Kevin J., 1992, "Bargaining Success of Chinese Factories," *China Quarterly*, No. 132, December, pp. 1086–1100.

———, 1994, "Agents and Remonstrators: Role Accumulation by Chinese People's Congress Deputies," *The China Quarterly*, No. 138, June, pp. 359–380.

OECD & IEA, "OECD Green Growth Studies: Energy," 2011. http://www.oecd.org/greengrowth/greening-energy/49157219.pdf.

Oil & Gas Journal, 1998, "China's Oil Price Reforms a Major Step in Deregulating Its Petroleum Sector," Vol. 96, No. 32, 10 August.

———, 1999, "China's Oil Imports Rise Possible Boon for U.S.," Vol. 97, No. 23, 7 June.

———, 1999, "CNPC Shelves China-Kazakhstan Oil Pipeline," Vol. 97, No. 35, 30 August.

Onis, Ziya, 1991, "The Logic of the Developmental State," *Comparative Politics*, Vol. 24, No. 1, October, pp. 109–126.

Pei, Minxin, 2005, "Dangerous Denials: China's Economy of Blinding the World to Its Political Risks," *Foreign Policy*, February.

Pierson, Paul, 2000, "Path Dependence, Increasing Returns, and the Study of Politics," *American Political Science Review*, Vol. 94, No. 2, pp. 251–267.

Pottinger, Matt , 2005, "Behind the CNOOC Deal: Cnooc's Fu Shows Complex Trends In Chinese Firms," *Wall Street Journal* (Eastern edition), New York, NY, 24 June.

Putnam, Robert, 1988, "Diplomacy and Domestic Politics: The Logic of Two Level Games," *International Organization*, Vo. 42, No. 3, Summer, pp. 427–460.

Putterman, Louis and Xiao-Yuan Dong, 2000, "China's State-Owned Enterprises: Their Role, Job Creation, and Efficiency in Long-Term Perspective," *Modern China*, Vol. 26, No. 4, October, pp. 403–447.

Qian, Yingyi, 1996, "Enterprise Reform in China: Agency Problems and Political Control," *Economics of Transition*, Vol. 4, No. 2, October, pp. 427–447.

Qian, Yingyi and Gérard Roland, 1998, "Federalism and the Soft Budget Constraint," *American Economic Review*, Vol. 88, No. 5, December, pp. 1143–1162.

Qian, Yingyi and Xu Chenggang, 1993, "Why China's Economic Reforms Differ: The M-Form Hierarchy and Entry/Expansion of the Non-state Sector," *Economic of Transition*, Vol. 1, No. 2.

Radtke, Kurt W. and Raymond Feddema, 2000, *Comprehensive Security in Asia: Views from Asia and the West on a Changing Security Environment*, Netherlands: Brill.

Rasmussen Reports, 2006, "71% Say Finding New Energy Sources More Important Than Conservation."

Rauch, Jason N. and Ying F. Chi, 2010, "The Plight of Green GDP in China," *Consilience: The Journal of Sustainable Development*, Vol. 3, No. 1, pp. 102–116.

Resources Quarterly, 2013, "China, and Its Rush for Foreign Oil," Vol. 1, No. 1, Summer.

Riain, Sean O., 2000, "States and Markets in an Era of Globalization," *Annual Review of Sociology*, Vol. 26, pp. 187–213.

Sachs, Jeffrey D., Andrew Warner, Anders Aslund, Stanley Fischer, 1995, "Economic Reform and the Process of Global Integration," *Brookings Papers on Economic Activity*, Vol. 1.

Salameh, Mamdouh, 1995–1996, "China, Oil and the Risk of Regional Conflict," *Survival*, Vol. 37, No. 4, Winter, pp. 133–146.

———, 2003, "The New Frontiers for the United States Energy Security in the 21st Century," *Applied Energy*, Vol. 76, No. 1, September–November 2003, pp. 135–144.

Salisbury, Robert H., John P. Heinz, et al., 1987, "Who Works with Whom? Interest Group Alliances and Opposition," *The American Political Science Review*, Vo. 81, No. 4. December.

Sappington, D., 1991, "Incentives in Principal Agent Relationships," *Journal of Economic Perspectives*, Vol. 3, No. 2, pp. 45–66.

Shambaugh, David, 2001, "China's Ambivalent Diplomacy," *Far Eastern Economic Review*, 15 November.

Sinton, Jonathan E., 2001, "Accuracy and Reliability of China's Energy Statistics," *China Economic Review*, Vol. 12, pp. 373–383.

Sinton, Jonathan E., Mark D. Levine, et al., 1998, "Energy Efficiency in China: Accomplishments and Challenges," *Energy Policy*, Vol. 26, No. 11.

Soligo, Ronald and Amy Jaffe, 2004, "China's Growing Energy Dependence: The Costs and Policy Implications of Supply Alternatives," http://bakerinstitute.org/Pubs/workingpapers/claes/cpis/cpis.html.

Spinetta, Major Lawrence, 2006, "'The Malacca Dilemma'—Countering China's "String of Pearls" with Land-Based Airpower," A Thesis Presented to the Faculty of the School of Advanced Air and Space for Completion of Graduation Requirements, Air University, Maxwell Air Force Base, Alabama, June. https://research.au.af.mil/papers/ay2006/saas/spinetta.pdf.

Su, Fubing and Dali L. Yang, 2000, "Political Institutions, Provincial Interests, and Resource Allocation in Reformist China," *Journal of Contemporary China*, Vol. 9, No. 24, pp. 215–230.

Taylor, Monique, 2018, "Fuelling China's Rise: Building Oil State Capacity," *China: An International Journal*, Vol. 16, No, 1, February.

Texas Comptroller of Public Accounts, 2008, *The Energy Report*, 6 May.

The Stanley Foundation, 2006, "China's Energy Security and Its Grand Strategy," Policy Analysis Brief, September.

Thelen, Kathleen, 1999, "Historical Institutionalism in Comparative Politics," *Annual Review of Political Science*, Vol. 2, pp. 369–404.

Thomson, Elspeth, 2001, "China's Growing Dependence on Oil Imports," *EAI Background Brief No. 87*, 11 May.

———, 2005, "Power Shortages in China: Why?" *China: An International Journal*, Vol. 3, No. 1, March.

Tunsjø, Øystein, 2010, "Hedging Against Oil Dependency: New Perspectives on China's Energy Security Policy," *International Relations*, Vol. 24, No. 1, pp. 25–45.

Underhill, Geoffrey R.D., 2000, "State, Market, and Global Political Economy," *International Affairs*, Vol. 76, No. 4, October, pp. 805–824.

———, 2007, "Markets, Institutions, and Transaction Costs: The Endogeneity of Governance," Working paper in the World Economy & Finance Research Programme, WEF0025, June.

Underhill, Geoffrey R.D. & Xiaoke Zhang, 2005, "The Changing State-Market Condominium in East Asia: Rethinking the Political Underpinnings of Development," *New Political Economy*, Vol. 10, No. 1, March, pp. 1–24

Vanden, Karen Fisher et al., 2004, "What Is Driving China's Decline in Energy Intensity?" *Resource and Energy Economics*, No. 26, pp. 77–97.

Victor, David G. and Nadejda M. Victor, 2003, "Axis of Oil?" *Foreign Affairs*, Vol. 82, No. 2. March/April.

Vivoda, Vlado, 2010, "International Oil Companies, US Government and Energy Security Policy: An Interest-Based Analysis," *International Journal of Global Energy Issues*, Vol. 33, No. 1–2, pp. 73–88.

Wader, Robert Hunter, 2005, "Beyond Asian Horizon: Neoliberalism and the Emergence of a Hereditary World Oligarchy," Workshop in the First Congress of Asian Political & International Studies Association—Asia in the New Millennium, Singapore, 27–30 November.

Walder, Andrew G., 1995, "Local Governments as Industrial Firms: An Organizational Analysis of China's Transitional Economy," *American Journal of Sociology*, Vol. 101, pp. 263–301.

Wang, Qiang, 2003, "Disencumber Accepting Passively World Oil Prices, China Expects to Participate in Oil Price Formulation", *Business Weekly*, 31 December.

Watkins, Eric, 2005, "A Pipeline Stage Issue," *Oil & Gas Journal*, Vol. 103, No. 22, 13 June.

Westwell, Steve, 2010, "Key Roles and Responsibilities of IOCs in an Age of Uncertainty," speech at the World National Oil Companies Congress, London, 22 June, http://www.bp.com/en/global/corporate/press/speeches/key-roles-responsibilities-iocs.html.

Williams, Paul A., 2006, "Projections for the Geopolitical Economy of Oil After War in Iraq," *Futures*, Vol. 38, No. 9, November, pp. 1074–1088.

Williamson, Oliver E., 1979, "Transaction Cost Economics: The Governance of Contractual Relations," *Journal of Law and Economics*, Vol. 22, No. 2, October 1, pp. 233–261.

World Economic Forum, 2006, "The New Energy Security Paradigm," *Energy Vision Update*, Spring.

Wu, Kang and S. L. Han, 2005, "Chinese Companies Pursue Overseas Oil and Gas Assets," *Oil and Gas Journal*, Vol. 103, No. 15, 18 April.

Wu, Yanrui, 2003, "Deregulation and Growth in China's Energy Sector: A Review of Recent Development," *Energy Policy*, Vol. 31, pp. 1417–1425.

Xia, Yishan, 2000, "China-Russia Energy Cooperation: Impetus, Prospects and Impacts," The James A. Baker III Institute for Public Policy of Rice University, May.

Xu, Xiaojie, 1999, "The Oil and Gas Links Between Central Asia and China: A Geopolitical Perspective," *OPEC Review*, March.

Yang, Dali L., 1996, "Governing China's Transformation to the Market," *World Politics*, Vol. 48, April, pp. 424–452.

Yergin, Daniel, 2006, "Ensuring Energy Security," *Foreign Affairs*, Vol. 85, No. 2, March/April.

———, 2006, "What Does 'Energy Security' Really Mean?" *Wall Street Journal*, 11 July.

Yergin, Las, et al., 1998, "Fueling Asia's Recovery," *Foreign Affairs*, March/April.

Zhang, Jun, 2006, "Market Transition, State Connections and Internet Geography in China," *The China Review*, Vol. 6, No. 1, Spring.

Zhao, Hong, 2009, "China and India: The Energy Policies," *EAI* (East Asian Institute, Singapore) *Background Brief*, No. 462, 2 July.

Zou, Gaolu and K.W. Chau, 2006, "Short- and Long-run Effects Between Oil Consumption and Economic Growth in China," *Energy Policy,* Vol. 34, No. 18, December.

Zou, Keyan, 2004, "China's Governance over Offshore Oil and Gas Development and Management," *Ocean Development & International Law*, Vol. 35, pp. 339–364.

Zweig, David and Bi Jianhai, 2005, "China's Global Hunt for Energy," *Foreign Affairs*, September/October.

Secondary Sources—Chinese Books and Articles

An, Fengquan, Jun'an Liu, Peng Hai, "Shiyou anquan weixi guomai" (Oil Security Maintains the Nation's Pulse), *Zhongguo shihua* (China Petrochemicals), Vol. 7, 2003;

Andrews-Speed, Philip, 2006, "Nengyuan Jianguan de Tiaozhan" (Challenges for Energy Regulation), Huangqiu Qiyejia (Global Entrepreneur), No. 4.

Bi, Jinquan, 1994, "Gaige shiyou jiage guanli tizhi, cujin shiyou gongye fazhan" (Reform Oil Price Management Regime and Promote the Development of the Petroleum Industry), *Jiage Lilun yu Shijian* (Price Theory and Practice), Vol. 7.

Chu Juehai and Li Hui, 2004, *Shiyou qihuo jiaoyi* (*Oil Futures Trading*), Beijing: Zhongguo jinrong chubangshe (China Financial Press).

Cui, Junping, 2001, "Eight Cliffhangers Associated with the 'West-East Gas Pipeline'," *Fazhan (Development)*, No. 11.

Dai, Jinping, Meng Xia, and Wan Zhihong, 2004, *WTO yu Zhongguo Changye Fazhan* (WTO and Chinese Industry Development), Tianjin: Tianjin University Press.

Department of Petroleum and Natural Gas, National Energy Administration, el al, 2021, *Zhongguo Tianranqi Fazhan Baogao* (2021) (China Natural Gas Development Report <2021>), Beijing: Shiyou Gongye Chubanshe (Petroleum Industry Press), 2021.

Dizhi Zhuangbei (Equipment for Geotechnical Engineering), 2009, "Xiqidongshu sanxian gongcheng qudong neibu lunzheng" (Internal Demonstration for WEGP-3 Project Was Started), No. 4.

Diao, Xiuhua, 2005, "Xin shiji Zhong E nengyuan hezuo" (Sino-Russia Energy Cooperation in the New Century), *Xiboliya yanjiu* (Siberia Studies), No. 1.

Du, Liang and Wang Zhiqiang, 2005, "Zhonghaiyou shougou an shimo" "Case of CNOOC Acquisition over Unocal: From the Beginning to the End," *Zhongguo Qiyuejia* (China Entrepreneur), Vol. 17, 12 September. www.cnemag.com.cn/magazine_view.asp?a_id=1457.

———, "Liu wen Fu Chengyu – Younike shougou an fangsi" (Six Questions to Fu Chengyu—Reflections on the Case of Unocal Acquisition), Beijing: *Zhongguo Qiyejia* (*China Entrepreneur*), Vol. 17, 12 September 2005, http://www.cnemag.com.cn/magazine_view.asp?a_id=1456.

Fang, Qiufang, 1999, "Jinyibu wanshan shiyou jiage xingcheng jizhi de gouxiang" (Some Thoughts About Further Perfecting Oil Pricing Shaping Mechanisms), *Jiage Lilun yu Shijian* (Price Theory and Practice), Vol. 12.

Feng, Yuewei, 2012, "2011, Anquan shigu weihe biaosheng" (Why Incidents skyrocketed in 2011?), Zhongguo Shiyou Shihua (China Petroleum and Petrochemical), No. 3.

Gao, Peng, 2022, "2021 Nian Zhongguo Youqi Guandao Jianshe Xin Jinzhan" (New Progress in China's Oil and Gas Pipeline Construction in 2021), *Guoji Shiyou Jingji* (International Petroleum Economics), No. 3.

Gong, Zhongming and Jiayu Cheng, 2004, "Cong shijie nengyuan fazhan qushi tansuo weilai Zhongguo nengyuan zhanlue" (To Probe into China's Future Energy Strategy in Light of World Energy Developing Trends), *Keji bu Diao yan baogao* (Research Report by Ministry of Science and Technology), Vol. 38. 8 June.

Guo, Kesha, 2002, *Jiaru WTO hou de Zhongguo Gongye* (Chinese Industries After China's Entry into WTO), Beijing: Jingji Guanli chubanshe.

Guo, T., 2001, "Discussion on the Optimization of China's Energy Structure in the Tenth Five-Year Plan," *China Energy*, No. 1.

Guowuyuan Fazhan Yanjiu Zhongxin Ziyuan yu Huanjing Zhengce Yanjiusuo (Institute of Resources and Environmental Policy, Development Research Center of the State Council) (ed.), 2020, *Zhongguo Nengyuan Geming Jinzhan Baogao* (Progress Report of China Energy Revolution (2020)), Beijing: Shiyou Gongye Chubanshe (Petroleum Industry Press).

Hu, Jiayuan, 2005, "Shiyou butie 'youling'" (The "Specter" of Oil Subsidies), *Nanfengchuang*, First Half of October.

Huagong Wenzhai (China Chemicals), 2000, "Xiqidongshu gongcheng jiang quanmian duiwai kaifang" (The WEGP Project Would Be Fully Opened to Foreign Investors), No. 8.

Jiage Lilun yu Shijian (*Price: Theory & Practice*), 2000 "Jianli yu guoji shichang jiage bianhua xiang shiying de shiyou jiage jizhi" (Establish the Oil Pricing Mechanisms Adaptive to the Price Changes in the International Market), Vol. 7.

Jia, Wenrui, Qing Xu, Yanling Wang, et al., 2002, *21 Shiji Zhongguo Nengyuan, Huanjing yu Shiyou Gongye Fazhan* (China Energy, Environment and the Development of Oil Industry in the 21st Century), Beijing: Shiyou Gongye Chubanshe (Petroleum Industry Press).

Jiang, Jianhua, 2001, *Zhonguo Shiyou Gongye – Quanqiu Kaifang Shichang Tiaojian xia de Zhanlue Yanjiu* (Chinese Petrochemical Industry—Studies on the Strategies in Open Global Market), Doctoral dissertation of Graduate School, The Chinese Academy of Social Sciences.

Lee, Winnie, 2004, "China Launches Complete West-East Gas Pipeline," *Platts Oilgram News*, Vol. 82, No. 191, 5 October.

Li, Lianghui, 1997 "Jiaqiang bianfang budui zhiliang jianshe yu jianshe qiangda de bianfang" (Beef Up Quality Building of the Frontier Troops and Construct a Powerful Frontier Defense), *Zhongguo junshi kexue* (China Military Science), No. 4.

Li, Ruansheng, Liu Yan and Liu Keyu, 2002, *Shiyou yu Jianguan* (Oil and Supervision), Beijing: Shiyou Gongye Chubanshe (Petroleum Industry Press).

Li, Shuqing, 1996, "Shiyou gongji yu shiyou jiage" (Oil Supply and Oil Price), *Shiyou huagong jishu jingji* (Petrochemical Technological Economy), Vol. 12, No. 3.

Li, Wei, 2003, "Zhongguo Shiyou Anquan de Dongnanya Yinsu" (The Southeast Asia Factor in China's Oil Security), *Dongnanya Zongheng* (Around Southeast Asia), Vol. 10.

Li, Xinxin, 2003, "Zhongguo Nengyuan Anquan de Bage Shijiao" (China's Energy Security as Viewed from Eight Perspectives) *Liaowang* (Outlook), No.13, 31 March.

Liu, Jianping and Zhu He, 2003, "Characteristics and Trend of Investment in China by Multinational Petroleum and Petrochemical Companies in Recent Years," *International Petroleum Economics*, Vol. 11, No. 9.

———, 2005, "New Characteristics Analysis of Multinational Petroleum and Petrochemical Companies' Investment in China since Its WTO Entry," *International Petroleum Economics*, Vol. 13, No. 5, May.

Liu, Wengang, 2003, *Jingji Quanqiuhua yu Zhongguo Qiye "Zouchuqu" Zhanlue* (Economic Globalization and the "Go out" Strategy of Chinese Firms), Beijing: Press of Economic Science.

National Energy Strategy Project Group Headed by Chen, Qingtai, 2003, *Guojia Nengyuan Zhanlue de Jiben Gouxiang* (Basic Plans for China's Energy Strategies), 10 November. http://www.china.org.cn//chinese/OP-c/438517.htm.

Pan, Zhijian, et al., 2002, "Guo neiwai youqi ziyuan xingshi fenxi" (Analysis of Domestic and Foreign Oil and Gas Resources Situation). *Guoji shiyou jingji* (International Petroleum Economics), Vol. 10, No. 11.

Pu, Shi, 2005, "Three New Trends of the MOCs' Businesses in China," *Sinopec Monthly*, June.

Qin, Xuanren, 2004, "Guoji da huanjing ji daguo nengyuan waijiao yunchou" (The International Environment and the Energy Diplomatic Strategies of the Big Powers), *Guoji shiyou jingji* (International Petroleum Economics), Vol. 12, No. 1.

Research Group on *New Oil Price Mechanisms* headed by Lu Nan, "Shenhua shiyou jiage gaige silu de xuanze" (Options for the Plan of Deepening Oil Price Reform), *Zhongguo Wujia* (China Price), February 1995.

San Lian Shenghuo Zhoukan (*Life Week*), 2005, "Zhongguo de haiwai luxian tu, jike caiyao zouchuqu" (China Oil's Overseas Route Map, Going Out Because of Energy Hunger), 16 December. http://www.oilnews.cn/gb/zhuanti/2005-12/16/content_646011.htm.

Smith, Christopher E., 2012, "China Starts Construction on Third West-East Gas Pipeline," *Oil & Gas Journal*, 23 October.

Song, Hai, 2007, "2007 nian guoneiwai shiyou jingji redian zhanwang zhi: guonei chengpinyou shichang de kaifang, zhunru ji jianguan" (Prospects of Hot Issues Concerning Petroleum Economy at Home and Abroad in 2007: Openness, Entry and Monitoring of Domestic Refined Oil Market), *Guoji Shiyou jingji* (International Petroleum Economy), Vol. 2.

Sun, Qirui, and Xusheng Huang, 1999, "Shiyou Jiage jiegui dui shiyou gongye de yingxiang" (Impact of Oil Price Integration on the Petroleum Industry), *Zhongguo Nengyuan* (China Energy), Vol. 1.

Tan, Jun, *Da Bosha: Shiji Shiyou zhi zheng* (Struggle for Oil for Centuries), Beijing: World Knowledge Press, 2004.

Tong, Xiaoguang, 2002, "Zhongguo zai eluosi dong Xiboliya diqu de youqi hezuo ruhe qibu?" (How Should China Start the Oil and Gas Cooperation in the Eastern Siberia?). *Shijie shiyou gongye* (World Petroleum Industry), Vol. 9, No. 5.

Wang, Yichao, 2004, "Xiqi dongshu houyizheng" (The Sequela of the WEGP), Beijing: *Caijing* (*Finance*), Vol. 21, 1 November.

Wei, Yimin, 2006, *Zhonguo Nengyuan Baogao: Zhanlue yu Zhengce Yanjiu* (China Energy Report: Studies on its Strategies and Policies), Beijing: Kexue Chubanshe (Scientific Press).

———, 2012, *Zhongguo Nengyuan Baogao: Nengyuan anquan yanjiu* (China Energy Report <2012>: Energy Security Research), Beijing: Kexue Chubanshe (Scientific Press).

Wei, Yiming, Zhiyong Han and Gang Wu, 2006, *Zhongguo Nengyuan Baogao (2006): Zhanlue yu Zhengce Yanjiu* (China Energy Report (2006): Strategy and Policy Research), Beijing: Kexue chubanshe (Science Press).

Wen, Houwen et al., 2002, *Bainian Shiyou: 1878-2000 (Hundred Year's Oil: 1878–2000)*, Beijing: Dangdai Zhongguo chubanshe (Contemporary China Press).

Wu, Lei, 2003, *ZhongGuo Shiyou Anquan* (China's Oil Security), Beijing: China Social Sciences Press.

Wu, Shiqing and Chen, Siyang, 2002, "2001 nian Zhongguo tianranqi gongye zongshu" ("Summarization of China's Natural Gas Industry in 2001"). *Guoji shiyou jingji* (International Petroleum Economics), Vol. 10, No. 6. pp. 17–19.

Xi qi dong shu jiage yanjiu ketizu (West-East Gas Price Study Group), 2003, *Tianranqi Gongye Dingjia* (Natural gas industry pricing), Beijing: Shiyou Gongye Chubanshe.

Xiao, Huijun and Fenghua Qing, 2003, "Xiqidongshu teda gongcheng xiangmu duiwai kaifang de lichengbei" (WEGP: A Milestone for Mega Projects Opening to the Outside World—Interview with Zhang Guobao), *Zhongguo Touzi* (China Investment), No. 1.

Xin de shiyou jiage jizhi ketizu (Project Group on New Oil Pricing Mechanisms), 1995, "Shenhua shiyou jiage gaige silu de xuanze" (The Option for Furthering Oil Price Reform), *Zhongguo Wujia* (China Price), Vol. 2 and Vol. 3.

Yan, Arthur, 2005, "China's Local Governments, State Energy Companies, and the Development of the West-East Gas Pipeline," presentation in the Northeast Asia Energy Cooperation Workshop Program, "*Investment in China's Local Energy Infrastructure*," workshop sponsored by James A. Baker III Institute for Public Policy, 11 April, Houston, TX. http://www.rice.edu/energy/research/asiaenergy/docs/ArthuYan_041105.pdf.

Yan, Xuzhao and Huang Wangping, 1995, "Jiakuai Jianli Woguo heli de shiyou jiage xingcheng jizhi" (Step Up to Establish Reasonable Petroleum Price Framing Mechanisms in China), *Guoji Shiyou Jingji* (International Petroleum Economics), Vol. 3, No. 1, January.

Yan, Xuzhao and Yang, Jingmin, 1999, *Wei 21 Shiji Zhongguo Jiayou: Zhongguo Shiyou Gongye Tisheng Guoji Jingzhengli Baogao* (Cheer up for China in the 21st Century: China's Oil Industry Has Improved Its International Competitiveness), Beijing: Qiye Guanli Chubanshe.

Yang, Qing, 2002, "Zhongguo shiyou wenti de zhanlue diwei fenxi" (Analysis of China's Oil Problem and Strategic Position), *Zhongguo shiyou* (China Oil), 1 January.

Yang, Xingbing, 1995, "Jianli yu shiyou jiage moshi xiang shiying de shiyou hagye qiye moshi" (Establish Firm Models of Oil Industry Which Are in Accord with Oil Price Models), *Zhongguo Wujiai* (China Price), Vol. 3.

Yu, Min, 1999, "Shichang cengfou shui zhuzhai: Guoji shiyou jiage 12 nian zoushi fenxi" (Who Decides Market Winners and Losers: Analysis of the

12-Year Trend of Global Oil prices), *Zhongguo Shiyou he Huagong* (China Petroleum and Chemicals), No. 6 and No. 7.

Zeng, Peiyan (former vice premier), 2010, "Xiqidongshu: zhujiu nengyuan da dongmai" (WEGP: Being Casted as an Energy Aorta), *Zhongguo Shichang* (China Market), No. 37.

Zhang, Guobao, 2018, "Zhong E Yuanyou Guandao Shiwunian Tanpan Jishi: Riben Jiaoju hou, Putin Zuizhong Paibang" (A Record of 15 Years of Negotiations on the Sino-Russian Crude Oil Pipeline: After Japan Disrupted It, Putin Finally Made the Decision), *Zhongguo Jingji Zhoukan* (China Economic Weekly), No. 2.

Zhang, Haiyun (eds), 1998, *Da Jubian: 1998 Zhongguo Shiyou Shihua Da Chongzu Jishi* (Large Battle: Report on China's Oil Restructuring in 1998), Beijing: Jingji Ribao Chubanshe (Economic Daily Press).

Zhang, Jinglian and Xiangbo Li, 2003, "'Xiqi dongshu' yu woguo shiyou anquan" (WEGP and China's Oil Security). *Tianranqi diqiu kexue* (Natural Gas Geoscience), Vol. 14, No. 1, February.

Zhang, Lantao, 2002, "Lun shiyou liyi yu rushihou woguo de shiyou anquan," (On Oil Interest and China's Oil Security after the Entry into WTO), *Guojiguangxi xueyuan xuebao* (Journal of University of International Relations), No. 5.

Zhang, Lei, 2001, "Lun Zhongguo nengyuan anquan" (On China's Energy Security), *Zhongguo Shiyou Jingji* (International Petroleum Economics), Vol. 9, No. 3.

Zhang, Liang, 2002, *Zhongguo Jiage Gaige de Huigu yu Sikao* (Retrospect and Reflections on China's Oil Price Reform), *Journal of Ningxia Communist Party Institute*, Vol. 4, No. 1, January.

Zhang, Yuqing, 2000, "Shishi 'Zouchuqu' fazhan zhanlue" (Implement the 'Go Abroad' Development Strategy), *Hongguan Jingji Guanli* (Macroeconomic Management), No. 10.

Zhao, Hongtu, 2002, "Huanjing baohu xia de nengyuan anquan" ("Energy Security Under Environmental Protection", *Zhongguo shiyou shihua* (China Petroleum and Petrochemics), No. 10.

Zheng, Ming and Fujun Chu, 2005, "Nengyuanbu huzhiyuchu?" (The MoE Was Ready to Come Out?), *Zhongguo Shiyou Shihua* (China Petroleum and Petrochemical), No. 1, January.

Zheng, Zuoshi, 2005, "Shiyou liruan de jixing liuxiang" (Freakish Flow of Oil Profits), *Nanfengchuang*, First Half of September.

Zhong, Yanyang, 1998, "Shiyou jiage xingcheng jizhi gaige yiyi shenyuan: Fang CNPC xiaoshou gongsi zong jingjishi Yaohua Chen" (The Reform of Oil Shaping Mechanisms Has Far-Reaching Meanings: An Interview with Marketing Economist-in-General of CNPC, Yaohua Chen), *Shiyou Qiye Guanli* (Oil Firms Management), Vol. 7.

Zhongguo Guojia dili (*China National Geography*), Beijing, December 2004.
Zhongguo Nengyuan Fazhan Zhanlue yu Zhengce Yanjiu ketizu (Project Group of China energy development strategy and policy) headed by Chen, Qingtai, 2004, *Zhongguo Nengyuan Fazhan Zhanlue yu Zhengce Yanjiu* (Studies on China Energy Development Strategy and Policy), Beijing: Economic Science Press.
Zhongguo shehui kexueyuan gongye jingji yanjiusuo (Institute of Industrial Economics of Chinese Academy of Social Sciences), 2000, *Zhongguo gongye fazhan baogao (2000)* [*Report on the Development of Chinese Industries (2000)*], Beijing: Jingji guanli chubanshe (Economic Management Press).
Zhongguo Ti Gai Yanjiuhui Ketizu (Project Team of China Society of Economic Reform), "Tuijin Yaosu shichanghua" (Push Forward Marketization over Factors of Production), in *Zhongguo Gaige Luntan yu Zhongguo ti gai yanjiuhui 2005 nian Beijing nianhui lunwen ji* (Collections of Paper of China Economic Reform Forum and Annual Meeting of China Society of Economic Reform), Beijing: China Society of Economic Reform, 2005.
Zhou, Dadi and Zhu Xingshan, 2002, "Zhongguo shiyou gongying xingshi he ziyuan ji anquan zhanlue" (China's Oil Supply Situation, Resources and Security Strategy), *Guoji shiyou jingji* (International Petroleum Economics), No. 10.
Zhou, Fengqi and Zhou, Dadi, 1999, *Zhongguo Zhongchangqi Nengyuan Zhanlue* (China's Mid- to Long-term Energy Strategy), Beijing: Zhongguo Jihua Chubanshe (China Planning Press).
Zhu, Runmin, 2022, "Jin'e guo Qianyi, Zhong E Hezuo zai Jiama" (The Amount of Money Exceeds 100 Billion Yuan, and the Cooperation Between China and Russia Will Be Increased), *Zhongguo Shiyou Shihua* (China Petrochem), 22 Feburary, http://www.chinacpc.com.cn/info/2022-02-22/news_6150.html.
Zhu, Tong, 2019, "Woguo Kezaisheng Nengyuan de Fazhan Jieduan yu Mianlin Tiaozhan" (The Development Stage and Challenges of Renewable Energy in China), *Zhongguo Guoqing Guoli* (China's National Conditions and National Strength), No. 7.
Zhu, Xingshan and Zhou Dadi, 2002, "Ruhe sikao Zhongguo de nengyuan anquan wenti" (How to Think about China's Energy Security Problem) *Guoji Shiyou Jingjixue* (International Petroleum Economics), No. 10.

Newspaper and Website Reports and Commentaries

Pointers, 2022, "Energy Security: India's Perspective," 12 March, https://www.10pointer.com/current-affairs/energy-security-indias-perspective.
shiji jingji baodao (21 Century Economic Report), 2004, "Dapo E, Mei, Ri, Yin de baoweiquan, Zhongguo nengyuan de wuhuan waijiao" (Breaking Through

the Besiege of Russia, US, Japan and India, the Five-Circle Diplomacy of China Energy), 2 April.

ANI, 2013, "India Pursuing All Options to Achieve Energy Security: Manmohan Singh," 3 December, http://www.dnaindia.com/india/report-india-pursuing-all-options-to-achieve-energy-security-manmohan-singh-1928968.

Areddy, James T., 2006, "China Turns on Green Light for Domestic Firms' Large-Scale Overseas Investment," *Washington Street Journal*, 9 June.

———, 2013, "Data Illustrate Poor State of China's Soil," *The Wall Street Journal*, 30 December.

Australian Trade Commission, 2014, "China's Landbridge Makes a Strategic A$200m Investment in Australian Gas," 4 November.

Bai, Jim and Tom Miles, 2009, "PetroChina Pumps Coal Seam Gas in West-East Pipeline," Reuters, 16 September. http://uk.reuters.com/article/2009/09/16/petrochina-gas-methane-idUKPEK27598720090916.

Banerjee, Neela, 2003, "Arabs Have a Litmus Test for US Handling of Iraqi Oil," *New York Times*, 6 April.

Barboza, David and Andrew Ross Sorkin, 2005, "Chinese Oil Giant in Takeover Bid for U.S. Corporation," *New York Times*, 23 June.

BBC Monitoring Asia Pacific, 2004, "Russia to Keep Promises to China, Others on Energy Programs," London, 14 April.

———, 2004, "China, Kazakhstan Move to Build Oil Pipeline," London, 29 July.

———, 2005, "Hong Kong Paper Reviews Importance of China-Kazakhstan Oil Pipeline Project," London, 4 July 2005.

BBC Monitoring Former Soviet Union, 2004, "Russia's New Far Eastern Oil Pipeline to Skirt Chinese Border," London, 31 December.

———, 2005, "Russia Takes Decision on Building First Stage of Siberia-Pacific Oil Pipeline," 27 April.

Beijing Chenbao (Beijing Morning Post), "Fagaiwei nengyuanju juzhang toulu: shiyou chanye jiang xiang minqi kaifang" (Director of Energy Bureau of NDRC Disclose: Oil Industry to Be Open to Private Firms), 29 November 2004. http://www.china.org.cn/chinese/EC-c/715979.htm.

Beijing Daily, 2007, "Gaoe lirun cong he er lai? Shiyou san jutou shoudu huiying gongzong zhiyi" (Where Did the Huge Profits Come from? The Three Oil Giants Responded to the Public Skepticism), 6 January.

Blas, Javier, 2012, "China Stops Filling Strategic Oil Reserve," *Financial Times*, 23 November.

Bao, Dan, 2012, "Xiqidongshu sanxian gongcheng kaigong, minzi shouci jinru youqi guandao lingyu" (WEGP-3 Was Kicked Off, Private Capitals Were First Allowed to Enter the Oil and Gas Pipeline Area), *Renmin Ribao* (People's Daily), 17 October.

Buckley, Chris, 2010, "China Says Is World's Top Greenhouse Gas Emitter," Reuters, 23 November. http://www.reuters.com/article/2010/11/23/climate-cancun-china-idAFTOE6AM02N20101123.

Cai, Peter Yuan, 2010, "China's New National Energy Commission," *East Asia Forum*, 12 March, https://www.eastasiaforum.org/2010/03/12/chinas-new-national-energy-commission/.

Cai, Wei, 2003, "Zhong Ri E Guanxian zhi zheng de beihou" (Behind the Pipeline Strife Among China, Japan and Russia), *Sanlian Shenghuo Zhoukan* (Life Week) 22 September, http://old.lifeweek.com.cn//2003/1015/6735.shtml.

Cao, Xiuying, 2022,"2021 nian yuanyou chanliang chao 3000 wandun, Bohai youtian chengwei woguo diyida yuanyou shengchan jidi" (Crude Oil Production Exceeded 30 Mt in 2021, Bohai Oilfield Has Become China's Largest Crude Oil Production Base), *Keji Ribao* (Science and Technology Daily), 9 January. https://www.china-journal.net/news/9785.html.

"Carbon conundrum: a look at China's targets," 2011, *China Dialogue*, 3 November, https://www.chinadialogue.net/blog/4156-Carbon-conundrum-a-look-at-China-s-targets/en.

Cary, Eve, 2013, "The Curious Case of China's GDP Figures," *The Diplomat*, 5 March, http://thediplomat.com/2013/03/the-curious-case-of-chinas-gd-figures/.

CCTV, 2005, "Xiqi dongshu dui dongxibu shehui jingji fazhan de shenyuan yingxiang" (The Profound Influence of the WEGP on the Social and Economic Development in East and West Regions), 10 January.

———, 2005, former vice premier Zeng Peiyan's speech at global forum Fortune, "Zou kechixu fazhan zhi lu, cujin jingji gongtong fanrong" (Taking a Sustainable Development Way, Promote Joint Economic Prosprity), 17 May, http://www.cctv.com/news/financial/inland/20050517/101207.shtml.

Chang, Zhipeng and Shuyun Liu, 2004, "Xiqi dongshu jiang dailai shenme?" (What Will the WEGP Bring?). *Xinhuanet*. 29 December, http://news.xinhuanet.com/newscenter/2004-12/29/content_2392131.htm.

Chen, Dai, 2008, "Bu chenli Nengyuanbu de daoli: zhege hangye feichang fuza" (The Reason Why Not Establish a MoE: The Energy Industry Is Extremely Complex), Diyi Caijing Ribao (China Business News), 13 March.

Chen, Huai, 2002, "Jiage reng shi Zhongguo shiyou anquan zuida fengxian" (Price Risk Is the Central Risk of China's Oil Security), *Beijing Chenbao* (Beijing Morning), 12 October. http://finance.sina.com.cn/g/20021012/0918265321.html.

Chen, Jibao, 2004, "Zhongguo nengyuan 'wuji' waijiao" (China's 'Five-pole' Energy Diplomacy), *21 Shiji Jingji Baodao* (Nanfangdaily) 17 March, http://www.nanfangdaily.com.cn/jj/20040318/chj/200403170017.asp.

Chen, Jinguo, 2004, "Chongwen Deng Xiaoping tongzhi dui shiyou gongye fazhan de qinqie guanhuai he zhongyao zhishi" (Reviewing Deng Xiaoping's Cordial Concern About and Important Instructions on the Petroleum Industry), *Zhongguo Shiyou Bao* (China Petroleum), 20 August. http://www.oilnews.com.cn/GB/misc/2004-08/20/content_583529.htm.

Chen, Junfeng, 2005, "Jiemi Zhong Ha shiyou guandao, chenggong tupo junshi jingqu" (Decipher Sino-Kazakhstan Oil Pipeline, Successfully Broke the Military Forbidden Areas), *Guoji Xianqu Daobao* (International Herald Leader), 23 December. http://news.xinhuanet.com/world/2005-12/23/content_3960592.htm.

Chen, Mo, 2005, "Zhongwai qiye guomin daiyu chabie jiujing zai nali" (What Is on earth the Difference of the National Treatment Between Domestic and Foreign Firms), *Zhongguo jingji shibao* (China Economic Times), 26 January. http://www.ce.cn/new_hgjj/hgplun/more/200501/26/t20050126_2948665.shtml.

Chen, Qingtai, 2006, "zhongguo guojia nengyuan zhanglue he zhengce" (China National Energy Strategy and Policy), *Xin Nengyuan Wang* (New Energy), 12 July, http://newenergy.giec.cas.cn/zcfg/200607/t20060712_184070.html.

Chen, Ting and Chen Jibao, 2003, "Shui lai jianguan san da shiyou guatou" (Who Can Regulate the Three Petroleum Monopolies?), *21 Shiji Jingji Baodao* (21 Century Economic Report), 30 December, http://www.nanfangdaily.com.cn/southnews/zt/jjtk/xlzg/200312300114.asp.

China Business Information Network, 1997, "China Cracks Down on Oil Smuggling," 28 July.

———, 1998, "China Pegs Crude Oil Prices to International Market Rates," 8 June.

China Daily, 1998, "Xinjiang Oilfields Increase Production," 22 January.

———, 2002, "World Giants Get Foot in Door to Oil, Gas Reserves," 5 July, http://www.chinadaily.com.cn/en/doc/2002-07/05/content_126692.htm.

———, 2004, "PetroChina Drops Foreign Partners on Pipeline," 4 August. http://www.chinadaily.com.cn/english/doc/2004-08/04/content_357832.htm.

———, 2005, "Rosy Future for West-East Pipeline", 6 January.

China Daily (HK Edition), 2004, "West-East Gas Pipeline JV Collapses," 4 August, http://www.chinadaily.com.cn/english/doc/2004-08/04/content_357425.htm.

China Economic Review, 2003, "China—Pipeline Operator to Charge Different Rates," 1 May 2003. *Dow Jones Factiva*.

———, 2009, "Green GDP Project Cancelled," 4 March, http://www.chinaeconomicreview.com/dailybriefing/2009_03_04/green_gdp_project_cancelled.html.

"China Exploring Oversea Petroleum Business," www.chinaeco.com, 8 September 1997.

China Knowledge, 2009, "Xinjiang Guanghui to Acquire Kazakhstan TBM Oil Assets," 24 August. http://news.alibaba.com/article/detail/energy/100161228-1-xinjiang-guanghui-acquire-kazakhstan-tbm.html.

"China Willing to Promote Energy Cooperation with Russia," Lanham: *World-Sources Online*, 21 September 2004.

Chufrin, Gennady, 2003, "Russia's Economic and Strategic Interests in North-East Asia," *Asia Europe Journal*, Vol. 1, pp. 251–262.

CNN, 2005, "Fortune Global 500," http://money.cnn.com/magazines/fortune/global500/2005/index.html.

"CNOOC ltd. Ensures China's Energy Security Through Foreign Acquisition," *Shijie Jingliren Zhoukang* (World Entrepreneur Weekly), 26 February 2004, http://www1.cei.gov.cn/energy/doc/NYgsml/200409022438.htm.

CNOOC, 2004, "China's Increment of Crude Oil Mainly Comes from Offshore," 31 March, www.cnooc.com.cn.

———, 2004, "Fu Chengyi: Energy Use Cannot Over-Depend on Oil," 26 April 2004. www.cnooc.com.cn.

———, 2005, "Offshore Contracts Under Execution," September 2005, http://www.cnooc.com.cn/defaulten.asp.

———, 2013, "What We Do—Upstream," http://en.cnooc.com.cn/data/html/english/channel_118.html.

CNPC, 2004, "Xingjiang Is Being Molded into China's Largest Gas Producing Region," 8 December. http://www.cnpc.com.cn/xwygg/1200412080041.htm.

———, 2005, "Zhengxie weiyuan qiwang Zhongguo shiyou gongsi jiakuai zouchuqu bufa" (CPPCC Member Expects China Oil Companies Can Speed Up the 'Going Abroad' Step), 16 March. http://www.cnpc.com.cn/xwygg/1200503180025.htm.

———, 2013, "Brief Introduction of Zhongguo Shiyou Tarim Oilfields Company," April, http://www.cnpc.com.cn/tlmyt/gsgk/tlmjj/.

Collier, Robert, 2005, "Backlash to Chinese Bid for Unocal," *The San Francisco Chronicle*, 24 June.

Crabtree, James, 2014, "The Threat of Energy Dependency in India," *ABO* (About Oil), 26 August, https://www.abo.net/oilportal/topic/view.do?contentId=2291217.

Davenportsept, Coral, 2014, "Emissions from India Will Increase, Official Says," *The New York Times*, 24 September.

Deloitte, 2013, "Energy Access for the Poor," Background Paper of India Energy Congress 2013, "Securing Tomorrow's Energy Today: Policy & Regulations", New Delhi, 7–8 February. http://www.indiaenergycongress.in/iec/Energy%20access%20for%20the%20poor%20-%20020213.pdf.

Development Research Center of the State Council of P. R. China, 2003, "Zhongguo shihua hangye jidu fenxi baogao" (Quarterly Analysis Report on Chinese Petrochemical Industry), 3 March, http://www.drcnet.com.cn.

Diyi Caijing Shibao (First Financial Times), 2004, "Zhongguo Bushu Yaou Dalu Shiyou Anquan Zhanlue" (China Laid out Eurasian Continent Oil Security Strategy), 16 December. http://finance.sina.com.cn/g/20041216/01351227888.shtml.

Diyi Caijing (Yicai), 2013, "Guotubu Guanyuan: Zhongguo Tianranqi kaifa chuyu zaoqi jieduan, liyong chengdu jin 5%" (MLR Official: China's Natural Gas Development Is in the Early Stages, and the Utilization Rate Is Only 5%), 19 June, https://www.yicai.com/news/2792792.html.

Diyi Caijing ribao (*First Finance Daily*), 2004, "Guojia guli minqi haiwai youyuan kaicai, zijin he zhengce cheng zhang'ai" (The State Encourage Private Firms to Exploit Oversees Oil, Capital and Policy Be the Obstacles), 14 December, http://www.china.org.cn/chinese/jingji/728087.htm.

Dong, Lara and Xiaonan Feng, 2021, "China's 'Dual-Control' Implementation: A Tight Balancing Act Amid the Energy Transition," IHS Markit 26 October, https://ihsmarkit.com/research-analysis/chinas-dualcontrol-implementation-a-tight-balancing-act-amid-t.html.

Dow Jones News, 1997, "Resourceful Competitors," *The Wall Street Journal*, 28 July.

Du, Juan, 2012, "Third Line to Boost Gas Supply," China Daily, 17 October. http://www.chinadaily.com.cn/bizchina/2012-10/17/content_15823188.htmn.

Du, Yanfei, 2022, "'Santongyou' 2021nian chengjidan: jiada youqi kangtan kaifa, tuijin lvse ditang zhuanxing" ("Three Barrels of Oil" 2021 Report Card: Increase Oil and Gas Exploration and Development to Promote Green and Low-Carbon Transformation), Renmin Wang, 1 April, http://finance.people.com.cn/n1/2022/0401/c1004-32390117.html.

Economist Intelligence Unit—Executive Briefing, "China Energy: Mix Motives Behind CNOOC's Bid," 27 June 2005.

———, 2005, "China Energy: Mixed Motives Behind CNOOC's Bid," 27 June.

Economist Intelligence Unit—Viewswire, 1999, "China Finance—Buyers Beware of Upcoming Oil Listings," 29 September 1999, *Dow Jones Factiva*.

Editorial of New York Times, 2005, "Chinese Strength, U.S. Weakness," 26 June.

EIA, "Country Analysis—China," http://www.eia.gov/countries/cab.cfm?fips=CH.

Ellichipuram, Umesh, 2021, "India to Build Nuclear Plants to Increase Generation Capacity," *Power Technology*, 30 July, https://www.power-technology.com/news/india-nuclear-power/.

Engdahl, F. William, 2005, "China Lays Down Gauntlet in Energy War: The Geopolitics of oil, Central Asia and the United States," *Asian Times*, 22 December.

Erickson, Peter, Adrian Down, Michael Lazarus and Doug Koplow, 2017, "Effect of Subsidies to Fossil Fuel Companies on United States Crude Oil Production," *Nature Energy*, Vol. 2, pp. 891–898.

Fei, Yu and Meng Na, 2003, "Meiyi zhanzheng yinyun yinfa Zhongguo shiyou anquan huati" [US-Iraq War Eliciting the Topic of China's Oil Security], Xinhua, 7 March, http://news.xinhuanet.com/fortune/2003-03/07/content_764778.htm.

Feng, Qiyu, 2021, "Woguo yi Qianshu Gongjian 'Yidaiyilu' Hezuo Wenjian 205 fen" (China Has Signed 205 Cooperation Documents for the Joint Construction of the "Belt and Road Initiative"), *Jingji Ribao* (Economic Daily), 1 February. http://ydyl.china.com.cn/2021-02/01/content_77175407.htm.

Fitch Ratings, 2014, "India's Diesel Deregulation Positive for Oil Companies," 21 October.

Golubkova, Katya and Vladimir Soldatkin, 2014, "Russia Says Long-Sought China Gas Supply Deal Is Close," *Reuters*, 9 April, http://www.reuters.com/article/2014/04/09/russia-china-gas-idUSL6N0N11XM20140409.

Gulf Oil and Gas, 2006, "Sinochem Signed Contract to Explore UAQ Gas Field," 31 March. http://www.gulfoilandgas.com/webpro1/MAIN/Mainnews.asp?id=2773.

Guo, Haiyan, 2000, "Zhongguo zhuanjia jianyi guojia qixinxieli zhichi shiyou qiye" (Chinese Experts Recommend That the State Make a Concerted Effort to Support the Participation of Oil Enterprises in Overseas Competitions), *Zhongguo Gongshang Shibao* (China Industry and Commerce Times), 20 November.

Guo, Liangping, 2005, "What 'Green Storm?'—The Politics of 'Green GDP' in China," East Asia Institute Seminar, National University of Singapore, 24 June.

Guo, Si Zhi (Kaku Shi Shi), 2003, "Trends of Petroleum Distribution Business in China," The Institute of Energy Economics, Japan (IEEJ), May, http://eneken.ieej.or.jp/en/data/pdf/195.pdf.

Heilongjiang Ribao (Heilongjiang Daily), 2022,"Daqing Youtian 2021 nian wancheng youqi changliang dangliang 4322.6069 wandun" (Daqing Oilfield Completed 43.226069 Million Tons of Oil and Gas Equivalent in 2021), 3 January.

He, Qing, 2013, "Disanqi shiyou chubei kaijian, xuanzhi Heilongjiang Daqing he Shangdong Rizhao" (The Third Phase of SPR Has Started, with Sites in Daqing and Rizhao), *21 Shiji Jingji Baodao* (21 Century Business Herald), 26 February.

Hexun, 2014, "Li Daokui: sanda liyi jituan chezhou jingji zhidu bianqian" (Daokui Li: Three Interest Groups Encumbered China's Economic System Reform), 11 January, http://news.hexun.com/2014-01-11/161348300.html.

"India's Energy Plan Aims to Ensure Energy Justice: PM Modi," Modi's speech at the Fourth edition of India Energy Forum CERA Week, 26 October 2020, https://www.narendramodi.in/prime-minister-narendra-modis-address-at-the-inauguration-of-india-energy-forum-552078.

Infraline Energy, 2011, "Marketing and Distribution of Petroleum Products in India," Updated in July 2011, http://www.infraline.com/ong/petroproducts/MandD.aspx.

Jiang, Jieming (the then vice President of CNPC), 2005, "CNPC Has Fulfilled Three Obligations to Ensure Energy Security," Xinhua, 1 March, http://www.oilnews.com.cn/GB/misc/2005-03/11/content_607576.htm.

Jingji Cankao Bao (Economic Information Daily), 2004, "Shiyou Shihua: Rushi sannian touzi zhuti duoyuanhua chubu xingcheng" (Petroleum and Petrochemical: Diversified Investing Actors Initially Taken Shape After Three Years' WTO Entry), 7 December. http://www.china.org.cn/chinese/EC-c/722950.htm.

Jingji Ribao (*Economic Daily Online*), 2005, "Shiyou san jutou shuo you dao qi" (The Three Oil Giants Talking About Oil and Gas), 19 May. http://www.cnooc.com.cn/.

Jing, Shuiyu, 2019, "BRI Energy Investment to Hit $27 Trillion by 2050," *China Daily*, 27 April, http://www.chinadaily.com.cn/a/201904/27/WS5cc3ef61a3104842260b8bba.html.

Kahn, Joseph, 2005, "China's Costly Quest for Energy Control," *New York Times*, 27 June.

———, 2005, "A Deft Balance in Orchestrating China's Oil Offer," *New York Times*, 7 July.

Kaktiya, Rakteen, 2010, "ONGC, Oil India Ordered to Buy 'Big' Assets Overseas," *Bloomberg*, 18 March.

Kalyanarama, Anand, 2020, "All You Wanted to Know About Fuel Pricing," *The Hindu Business Line*, 14 December, https://www.thehindubusinessline.com/opinion/columns/slate/all-you-wanted-to-know-about/article33330388.ece.

Kohl, Keith, 2012, "India's Solution to an Oil Crisis," *Energy & Capital*, 25 September.

Lan, Xinzhen, "2006 nian waizi neng zhan Zhongguo chengpinyou shichan duoda fen'e" (What Proportion Will Foreign Investment Occupy in China's Refined Oil Market After 2006?) *Beijing Zhoubao* (Beijing Weekly), 27 April 2005. http://www.china.org.cn/chinese/zhuanti/qkjc/849078.htm.

Leslie Hook, "China Set to Miss Targets for Shale Gasfield Development," *Financial Times*, 2 July 2013.

Li, Chunlian, 2012, "Chao jiucheng shiyou jinkou yunshu yilai guowai, Zhongshiyou zi jian daxing youlun pouju" (Over 90% Oil Imports Transportation Needs to Rely on Foreign Oil Cargos, CNPC Builds Large Tankers to Address the Issue), *Zhengquan Ribao* (Securities Daily), 23 October.

Liding chanye yanjiu wang (Leading Industry Research), 2021, "Zai 'tang da feng' 'tang zhonghe' de mubiao xia, meitang xiaofei bizhong 2030 nian jiangzhi 45% zuoyou" (Under the Goals of "Carbon Peak" and "Carbon Neutrality", the Proportion of Coal Consumption Will Drop to About 45% in 2030), 30 August, http://www.leadingir.com/hotspot/view/3206.html.

Li, Xinmin and Li Wang, 2008, "Zujian nengyuanbu tiaojian yijing jiben chenshu" (The Conditions for Setting up a MoE are Basically Available), Jingji Cankao Bao (Economic Information Daily), 29 January. http://jjckb.xinhuanet.com/cjxw/2008-01/29/content_83612.htm.

Li, Yanzheng, 2006, "Zhongguo qidong zhanlue shiyou chubei buhui yinfa youjia julue bodong" (Chinese Start of It SPR Will Not Incur Drastic Oil Prices Fluctuation), *Shanghai Zhengquan Bao* (Shanghai Stock), 11 October, http://cn.chinagate.cn/economics/2006-10/11/content_2357403.htm.

Li, Yusi, 2011, "Shengli Youtian 50 nian chanyou zhan quanguo 1/5, 'shierwu' wen chan 2700 wandun" (Crude Oil Output from Shengli Oilfield Accounted for 1/5 in China for 50 Years, Maintaining an Output of 27 Mt During the Twelfth Periods), *Zhongguo Jingji wang* (China Economic Net), 16 June, http://www.ce.cn/cysc/ny/shiyou/201106/10/t20110610_20989809.shtml.

Li, Yuyang, 2007, "Three Oil Companies Promised to Take Social Responsibilities," *Jingji Ribao* (Economic Daily), 10 January. http://www.sasac.gov.cn/2007rdzt/2007rdzt_0001/200701100142.htm.

Liao, Liang and Haihong Chu, 2004, "DangZhongyang yingming juece, shiji gongcheng angran shangma – xiqi dongshu gongcheng huozhun lixiang jishi" (Wise Decision of the CCP Central Commission, Centenary Project Being Started—Report of the Approval Process of WEGP), *Shiyou shang bao* (Oil China), 1 October, www.oilchina.com/xxzx/sysb_xl.jsp?bsm=041662650.00002AD9.59E2.

Liaowang (Outlook), 1997, "Li Peng Zongli Lun Zhongguo Shiyou Gongye Fazhan" (Premier Li Peng Talks About the Development of China's Oil Industry), No. 41, 13 October.

Liu, Changjie and Xinyu Gou, 2006, "Daqing zhaodao xin youtian" (New Oilfields Have Been Found in Daqing), *Jingji guancha* (Economic Observer), 27 October, http://www.eobserver.com.cn/jjgcb/yaowen/2006/10/27/24115.html.

Liu, Kunzhe, 2006, "Zhongguo waijiaobuzhang zhuli tan jiu da ZhongFei guanxi wenti" (China's Foreign Minister Assistant Talked About Nine Issues

Regarding China-Africa Relations), *China Youth Daily*, 30 October. Also available at: http://world.people.com.cn/GB/14549/4971637.html.

Lu, Huaibin, 1999, "China's Oil Market in 1998: A Market in Transition, But to Where?" *CERA Decision Brief*, April.

Lu, Wenjun, 2011, "WEGP Will Add a 10Bcm Increase of Gas Transmission within This Year," Xinhua Net, 15 July, http://news.xinhuanet.com/fortune/2011-07/15/c_121673550.htm.

Ma, Yunfei, 2014, "Zhongguo nengyuan qiye haiwai touzi 'tu' shenme" (What Do the Energy Companies Want to 'Gain' from Foreign Investments?) *Zhongguo Jingji Daobao* (China Economic Herald), 22 July.

Mallet, Victor, 2013, "India's Reliance on Imported Energy Threatens Long-term Recovery," *Financial Times*, 12 September.

Mao, Xiaomei and Xiaofang Feng, 2004, "China Released the First National Compulsory Criterion to Control Vehicles' Oil Consumption," *Xinhua News Agency*, 28 October. http://www.people.com.cn/GB/shehui/1060/2950752.html.

Mosnews Information Service, "Russia Not to Build an Oil Pipeline to China," 2004, Moscow, 1 March. http://www.mosnews.com/money/2004/03/01/chinapipe.shtml.

Nakamura David and Steven Mufson, 2014, "China, U.S. Agree to Limit Greenhouse Gases," *The Washington Post*, 12 November.

National Audubon Society, 2014, "Curbing Global Warming: Fact Sheets," http://policy.audubon.org/sites/default/files/documents/curbingglobalwa rming.pdf.

National Economic Department, SDPC, 2002, "Zhongguo shiyou de jiben shexiang" (Basic Plans for China's Oil Reserve), *Jingji Yanjiu cankao* (Economic Research Reference), 9 January.

New York Times, 2009, "Hu Jintao's Speech on Climate Change," 22 September.

Nezavisimaya Gazeta, 6 September 2001.

Ottaway, David B. and Dan Morgan, 1997, "China Pursues Ambitious Role in Oil Market," *Washington Post*, 26 December.

Pan, Jiaoming, 2005, "Li Deshui Strongly Questioned, Green GDP Had Been Utopiaed in the Dispute Between Ministries," *Shangwu Zhoukang* (Business Weekly), 20 May.

Petroleum Intelligence Weekly, 1997, "China's CNPC Leaps on to Global Oil Production Stage," 9 June.

Pottinger, Matt, 2005, "Behind the Cnooc Deal: Cnooc's Fu Shows Complex Trends in Chinese Firms," *Wall Street Journal* (Eastern edition), New York, NY, 24 June.

Pfund, Nancy and Ben Healey, 2011, "What Would Jefferson Do? The Historical Role of Federal Subsidies in Shaping America's Energy Future," San Francisco,

CA: DBL Investors, September, https://www.dbl.vc/wp-content/uploads/2012/09/What-Would-Jefferson-Do-2.4.pdf.
Pu, Shi, 2005, "Three New Trends of the MOCs' Businesses in China," Sinopec Monthly, June.
Qi, Hui, 2019, "Daqing Youtian: Tingqi Gongheguo Youmian Jiliang" (Daqing Oilfield: Standing Up the Backbone of the Oil Vein of the Republic), *Jingji Ribao* (Economic Daily), 20 September.
Qiu, Xiangde, 2009, "Nengyuan Gaige Bianzouqu" (Energy Reform Variations), *Huanqiu Qiyejia* (Global Entrepreneurs), 22 April.
Qu, Yuanyuan, 2012, "'Xiqidongshu' wu tiao xian zhicheng yizhang yongqi wang, rang rizi biande gengmei" (Five Lines of the WEGP Were Woven into a Gas Network, Making Our Life More Beautiful), Xinjiang Nengyuan wang (Xinjiang Energy Net), 8 February. http://xjny.ts.cn/content/2012-02/08/content_6824569.htm.
Ran, Yongping, et al., 2022, "Quanchang yue 3340 Gongli! Xiqidongshu Sixian Gongcheng Quanxian Kaigong" (The Total Length Is About 3340 Kilometers! Construction of the Fourth Line of West-to-East Gas Transmission Project Started), *Renmin Ribao* (People's Daily), 28 September.
Rashid, Ahmed, 2000, "China Forced to Expand Role in Central Asia," *Central Asia-Caucasus Analyst*, 19 July.
Ray, Raj Kumar, 2014, "India's Energy Intensity Rises 10.5% Since FY06," *The Financial Express*, 1 April.
Raznick, Jason, 2011, "Should the Government Really End Oil Subsidies?" *Forbes*, 1 February, http://www.forbes.com/sites/benzingainsights/2011/02/01/should-the-government-really-end-oil-subsidies/.
Rediff Business, 2013, "How India Can Ensure Fuel Security," 1 April, http://www.rediff.com/money/slide-show/slide-show-1-column-how-india-can-ensure-fuel-security/20130401.htm#4.
Renmin Wang (People Daily Online), "Zhengfu jigou gaige: huantang you huanyao" (Governmental Organization Reform: Change Both Format and Substance), 18 March 2003. http://www.people.com.cn/GB/guandian/183/6103/6104/20030318/946373.html.
———, 2004, "Youhuang bian 'you huang': ziyuan quekou chu xian, tizhi pingjing you zai" (Oil Shortage Turns into 'Oil Flurry': Resource Gap Appears, But System Bottleneck Still Exists), 22 July, http://www.china.org.cn/chinese/EC-c/616541.htm.
———, 2004, "Promoting Plural Energy Supply," 29 September.
Reuters, 2011, "China Tried to Close Local Small Refineries," 2 May. http://cn.reuters.com/article/wtNews/idCNCHINA-4229120110502.
RGGI Inc., "Regional Greenhouse Gas Initiative," http://www.rggi.org/.
"Rich Mineral Resources," 11 January 2008. http://www.aboutxinjiang.com/topic/content/2008-01/11/content_2389669.htm.

Riley, Charles, 2013, "Air Pollution Cuts Life Expectancy by 5.5 Years in China—Study," CNN, 9 July, http://money.cnn.com/2013/07/09/news/china-air-pollution/index.html.

Rocha, Euan, 2013, "CNOOC Closes $15.1 Billion Acquisition of Canada's Nexen," *Reuters*, 25 February.

Settle, Kristopher, 2013, "India Combats Energy Poverty Through Natural Resources," *Energy Biz*, 8 August, http://www.energybiz.com/article/13/08/india-combats-energy-poverty-through-natural-resources.

Sevast'ianov, Sergei, 2005,"The Russian Far East's Security Perspective: Interplay of Internal and External Challenges and Opportunities," in *Siberia and the Russian Far East in the 21st Century: Partners in the "Community of Asia"*, Vol. 1, Crossroads in Northeast Asia, edited by Iwashita Akihiro, the Slavic Research Center.

Shambaugh, David, 2001, "China's Ambivalent Diplomacy," *Far Eastern Economic Review*, 15 November.

Shi, Xia, 2022, "Geguo Shiyou Chubeiliang" (Oil Reserves of Various Countries), *Shang Meiti* (Business Media), 23 June.

Shiyou Xinxi wang (*Petroleum Information Net*), 2005, "Youqi chuyun: xunsu jueqi de 'guandao jingji'" (Oil and Gas Storage and Transport: Rapidly Rising Pipeline Economy), 1 July. http://www.infopetro.com.cn/Dissertation/ShowDissertation.aspx?cid=6&id=5579.

Song, Futian, 2000, "Jiakuai xinjiang weiwu'er zizhiqu fazhan jige wenti" ("Several Issues on Stepping Up the Development of the Xinjiang Uighur Autonomous Region), *Jingji yanjiu cankao* (Economic Research Reference), 10 April.

South China Morning Post, 2002, "Jiang Says Helping Poor Key to Stability," 5 February.

Strategic Forecasting, 2007, "China, Kazakhstan: Pipelines and the Balance of Power," *Strategic Forecasting*, 11 December. http://www.stratfor.com/analysis/china_kazakhstan_pipelines_and_balance_power.

Su, Miaohan, 2009, "Nengyuan jianguan jigou de quanli bianjie wenti yanjiu" (Studies on the Power Boundaries of Energy Regulatory Bodies), Ecological Civilization and Environmental Resource Law—Collection of Papers of the Annual Meeting of the Environmental Resource Law, 2009. http://cpfd.cnki.com.cn/Article/CPFDTOTAL-FXHJ200908001233.htm.

Tang, Yongbing, 2003, "shiyou qihuo – shichanghua bixian de biran xuanze" (Petroleum Futures—The Necessary Choice of Avoiding Risks for Marketization), *Jingji Ribao* (Economic Daily), 14 November.

"Temporary Measures on the Administration over the Refined Oil Market," MC Mandate No. 23 in 2004, 2 December 2004. Available at: http://news.xinhuanet.com/zhengfu/2004-12/10/content_2316763.htm.

The Economist, 2013, "The Future of Cars: Gloom and Boom", 20 April.

The Guardian, 2009, "India to Reduce Carbon Intensity by 24% by 2020," 2 December.

The Reuters, 2013, "Guanghui Energy Co Ltd Announces Acquisition of Stake in Tarbagatay Munay LLP by Sub-subsidiary; Announces Acquisition of Stake in Xinjiang-based Company by Subsidiary," 13 September.

Tong,Yin, 2005, "Oil Resource Tax Reform Takes Preliminary Shape, Use Both Hands of Raising Price and Tax Levying," *Shanghai Zhengquan Xinwen* (Shanghai Securities News), 23 May, http://www.oilnews.com.cn/gb/misc/2005-05/23/content_616650.htm.

US Environmental Protection Agency, http://www.epa.gov/statelocalclimate/state/topics/renewable.html.

US Energy Information Administration, "Country Analysis: China," http://www.eia.gov/countries/cab.cfm?fips=CH.

Walk Through India, 2023, "Top 10 Largest Oil and Gas Companies in India," 9 January, http://www.walkthroughindia.com/industry/top-10-largest-oil-and-gas-companies-in-india/.

Wall Street Journal, 2014, "There Is No Global Energy Solution, Only Local Ones: Noted Scholar Vaclav Smil Says What We Produce and Use Depends on Where We Are," 8 April.

Wall Street Journal (Eastern edition), 2005, "China's Oil Thirst," 24 June, p. A.12.

Wang, Hongjiang, 2001, "Zhongguo guanzhu shiyou anquan" (China Pays Attention to Oil Security), Beijing: Zhongguo Hongguan Jingji Xinxi wang (China Macroeconomic Information Web), 26 April, http://www.macrochina.com.cn/zhzt/000044/002/20010426002822.shtml.

Wang, Mengkui (President of the DRCSC), 2005, "Growth Model Needs Modification," *China Daily*, 11 May, http://www.chinadaily.com.cn/english/doc/2005-05/11/content_440884.htm.

Wang, Tao, 2012, "Yingnan'ershang zhengzhan siwang zhi hai – Talimu shiyou kantan kaifa chuqi huiyi" (Meet the Difficulties to Fight with the Death Sea—Memory of the Initial Stage of Oil E&P in Tarim Oilfield), *Renmin wang* (People's Daily Online), 3 December 2012. http://gx.people.com.cn/cpc/n/2012/1203/c339646-17807300-10.html.

Wang, Xiaozong, 2009, "09 Nian Zhongguo youqitian yuanyou changliang shi qiang gongbu, Zhongshiyou zhan liuxi" (The Ten Largest Oil & Gasfields in Terms of Crude Oil Output in 2009 Have Been Publized, CNPC Snatched Six), *Zhongguo JIngji Zhoukan* (China Economic Weekly), 10 September.

Webpage of Guanghui Energy, "Jimunai Gas Pipeline," http://www.xjguanghui.com/Typ.aspx?id=040303&Type=NYKF_SYTRQKTKF_ZHSLBLKJMNTRQGD&nid=187.

Webpage of the Consulate General of the People's Republic of China in Houston, 2004, "Oil Reserve Key to Energy Security," 11 August, http://houston.china-consulate.org/eng/nv/t147043.htm.

Wen, Jing, "Gao Shixian: jianli shiyou chubei tixi bushi wei pingyi youjia" (Gao Shixian: the Establishment of Oil Stock System Is Not for the Purpose of Curbing Oil Prices), *Jingji cankao bao* (Economic Information Daily), 2 September 2004. http://www.china.org.cn/chinese/OP-c/651226.htm.

"Wen Sees Rise in Russian Energy Links Ahead of a Moscow Visit, the Premier Pushes for an Increase in Oil Imports," Hong Kong: *South China Morning Post*, 22 September 2004.

Western Australia Trade Office—India, "An Overview of India's Oil and Gas Market," April 2011.

WindPowerIndia: www.windpowerindia.com.

World Energy Council, 2006, "Global Energy Issues," Speech by Chairmen of the e8, Evian, France, May 30 and 31.

Wu, Xuean, 2004, "Lüse GDP jichu zhengji shuifen" (Green GDP Squeeze Out False Performance), *Zhongguo gongshang shibao* (China Business Times), 18 March. http://www.cbt.com.cn/cbtnews/frontend/news.asp?ID=59104.

Xi qi dong shu wang (west gas transported to the east webpage), 2005, "Xiqi dongshu: wei Zhongguo nengyuan shichang dailai xin keti" (WEGP: Bring New Topic for China's Energy Market), 10 January, www.westgas.com.

Xie Xiyao & Yilin Yan, 2022, "Woguo yi yu 147 ge Guojia, 32 ge Guojizuzhi Qianshu 200 duo fen Gongjian 'Yidaiyilu' Hezuo Wenjian" (China Has Signed More Than 200 Cooperation Documents on Jointly Building "Belt and Road Initiative" with 147 Countries and 32 International Organizations), *Xinhua*, 19 January, http://www.gov.cn/xinwen/2022-01/19/content_5669215.htm.

Xie, Ye, 2001, "World Top 3 Look at US$18b Gas Plan," *China Daily*, 6 June, www.chinadaily.com.cn/en/doc/2001-06/06/content_61963.htm.

———, 2004, "PetroChina Goes Solo on Gas Line," *China Daily*, 5 August, http://www.chinadaily.com.cn/english/doc/2004-08/05/content_359058.htm.

Xie, Ye and Jing Fu, 2004, "Gas Pipeline May Be Profitable Next Year," *China Daily*, 30 December.

Xinhua ribao (Xinhua Daily), 2003, "Zhong shiyou zhuanjia xi shi 'xiqi' redian wenti" (CNPC Experts Explain the Hot Issues on West Gas in Length), 18 December.

Xinhuashe (Xinhua News Agency), 2000, "West Faces Challenges, Opportunities," 6 March, http://www.chinadaily.com.cn/chinagate/doc/2000-03/06/content_248035.htm.

———, 2001, "Shell, Exxon in US$5.6b Gas Plan," 19 December, http://www.chinadaily.com.cn/en/doc/2001-12/19/content_98670.htm.

———, 2002, "President Jiang Zemin and President Putin Sign the Full Text of the Sino-Russian Joint Statement," 3 December, http://m.law-lib.com/law/law_view.asp?id=74890&page=1.

———, 2005, "Fagaiwei silu gaibian, guonei chengpinyou dingjia jiasu yu guoji jiegui" (NDRC Changed Thinking, Domestic Refined Oil Pricing Is Accelerating to Integrate with International Market), 27 June.

———, 2005, "Oil, Gas Supply Line Built Along Silk Road," 17 September, http://china.org.cn/english/BAT/142534.htm.

———, 2005, "Oil Pipeline Links China, Kazakhstan," 15 November.

———, 2006, "An Interpretation of China's First Green GDP Report: What Do 3.05 % and 1.8 % Mean?" http://news.xinhuanet.com/fortune/2006-09/07/content_5063137.htm.

———, 2006, "China Embraces New Scientific Development Concept: Hu," 22 April.

——— 2006, "Focusing on 'Green GDP': Optimising Economic Development Through Environmental Protection," 7 September, http://news.xinhuanet.com/environment/2006-09/07/content_5066043.htm.

———, 2007, "Guanzhu 'Jieyue Nengyuan Fa': Jiang Jieyue Ziyuan Queding wei Jiben Guoce" (Pay Attention to the Energy Conservation Law: Defining Resource Conservation as a Basic National Policy), 28 October, http://www.gov.cn/jrzg/2007-10/28/content_788510.htm.

———, 2010, "China's 'Eleventh Five-Year' Emission Reduction Targets Have Been Completed Ahead of Schedule," 30 November. http://news.xinhuanet.com/2010-11/30/c_13628755.htm.

———, 2013, "China Reveals Multi-Pronged Air Pollution Battle Plan," 12 September, http://news.xinhuanet.com/english/china/2013-09/12/c_132715799.htm.

———, 2013, "Organization Department of the CCP Central Committee Issued Circular on Improving Evaluation of Local Authorities," 9 December, http://news.xinhuanet.com/2013-12/09/c_118484309.htm.

———, 2013, "Zhongjin shangtiao wo zhanlue shiyou chubei guimo yuqi zhi 6.2 yi tong" (CICC Raised the Scale of China's SPR and Expected to Reach 620m Barrels), 22 May, http://info.glinfo.com/13/0522/09/86CD0D0F9A0D38F2.html.

———, 2021, "Xinhua Headlines: China on Fast Track to Cut Energy Consumption Intensity," 2 November, http://www.news.cn/english/2021-11/02/c_1310286250.htm.

Xinwen Chenbao (*Shanghai Morning Post*), 2006, "Chinese Premier Wen Jiabao Wins Civilian Hearts, Applauded for Eight Times in His Half-Hour Speech," 5 April.

Xinxi Shibao (*Information Times*), 2005, "Guangzhou Youzhan gaoji" (Guangzhou Petroleum Stations in an Emergency), 4 August.

Xiao, Yan, 2005, "Coal Resources Tax Raised in 8 Provinces, Limited Influence on the Performances of Coal Industry," Shanghai Zhengquan Xinwen

(Shanghai Securities News), 2 June. http://sms.cnstock.com/ssnews/2005-6-2/jryw/t20050602_810780.htm.

Xiu, Wen, 2004, "Experts Talk About China's Inflation Alert Line, Prices First Rise then Decline in the Next Half Year," *China Economy*, http://www.ce.cn/new_hgjj/hgplun/more/200409/04/t20040904_1670718.shtml.

Xu, Hang, 2020, "Yi fa wei 'duo': Zhutui kezaisheng nengyuan fazhan" (Taking Law as the "Rudder": Boosting the Development of Renewable Energy), Zhongguo Renda (China National People's Congress), 21 January. http://www.npc.gov.cn/npc/c30834/202001/e8675d245bae45ada6cdcd10db9f9b89.shtml.

Ye, Xie, 2004, "Energy-Saving a Pressing Issue," *China Daily*, 9 December, http://www.chinadaily.com.cn/english/doc/2004-12/09/content_398542.htm.

Yergin, Daniel, 2012, "Innovation, Diversification, Cooperation Vital to Energy Security," *The Asahi Shimbun AJW* (Asia and Japan Watch), 12 August, http://ajw.asahi.com/article/globe/economy/AJ201208120013.

Yoder, Sheldon, "Energy Intensity of Global Economy Rises, Reversing Long-time Trend," World Watch Institute, http://www.worldwatch.org/energy-intensity-energy-efficiency-gross-world-product-emerging-economies-infrastructure-development.

Yu, Liang, 2001, "Gas Pipeline Project Delayed." Beijing: *China Daily*. 9 October, http://www.chinadaily.com.cn/en/doc/2001-10/09/content_87458.htm.

Yuki, 2020, "China's Energy Belt & Road Initiative: Priorities Are Shifting," *Energy Iceberg Analysis*, 16 December, https://energyiceberg.com/chinese-energy-belt-and-road-initiative/.

Zaobao, 2004, "Global Oil Production Peaks, Oil Will Dry Up Soon?" Singapore, 1 July, http://www.zaobao.com/special/newspapers/2004/07/nanyang010704.html.

———, 2006, "China Will Remove the Restriction of Foreign Exchange for Chinese Firms' Foreign Investment," 18 February. Available at: http://www.zaobao.com/stock/pages14/china060218a.html.

———, 2006, "Zhongguo jiang quxiao qiye haiwai touzi yonghui xianzhi" (China Will Remove Foreign Exchange Use Limitations for Chinese Enterprises Foreign Investments), 18 February 2006.

Zeng Pengyan (Deputy Secretary General of the Central Economic and Financial Leading Group and Minister of the State Development Planning Commission at that Time), 2000, "Zhongguo jiang jiakuai shishi xibu da kaifa zhanlüe" (China Will Speed Up the Implementation of the Western Development Strategy), *Zhongguo jingji baodao* (China Economic Herald), 1 March.

Zhang, Xiaoli, 2004, "Shiyou zhanlue chubei li duo haishi bi da" (Does the SPR Have More Advantages or Disadvantages), *Guanzhou jingmaowang*

(Guanzhou Economic and Trade Net), 12 July, http://www.gzii.gov.cn/middle2/jjrd/07/72002.htm.

Zhang, Yumin, 2013, "Daqing Youtian shixian yuanyou siqian wandun shinian wenchan" (Daqing Oilfield Produced 40 Mt with Ten-Year Stabilized Production), Heilongjiang Daily, 5 January.

Zhongguo Binggou Jiaoyi wang (*Mergers-China*), 2005, "Dangdai Kuaguo binggou langchao yu Zhongguo qiye 'zouchuqu'" (Contemporary Transnational M&A Wave and Chinese Firms' 'Go Out'), 27 December. Available at http://www.mergers-china.com/guwen/zjzxdetail.asp?id=1811.

Zhongguo Dianli (*China Electricity*), 2020, "2020 Nian Quanqiu ji Zhongguo Nengyuan Jiegou\Nengyuan Qiangdu Xianzhuang Fenxi ji Yuce" (Analysis and Forecast of Global and Chinese Energy Structure and Energy Intensity in 2020), 26 August, http://www.chinapower.com.cn/zx/jzqb/20200826/28667.html.

Zhongguo Gongshang Shibao (China Business Times), 2004, "Minying you qi qidai 'huayuquan', zongli pishi maotou zhi zhi shiyou jutou" (Private Oil Firms Expect Having a Say, Premier's Verdict Points to Oil Giant), 15 December. http://www.china.org.cn/chinese/2004/Dec/729617.htm.

———, 2014, *Zhonghua Gongshang Shibao* (China Business Times), "Mei you qi duiwai yicundu gaoqi, qunian meitan jinkouliang chuang xin gao" (Dependence on Foreign Coal, Oil and Gas Heightened, Import of Coal Broke New Record Last Year), 24 January, http://energy.people.com.cn/n/2014/0124/c71890-24212885.html.

Zhongguo Gongye Bao (*China Industry News*), 2004, "Zhonghaiyou: haiwai shougou bao Guojia nengyuan anquan" (CNOOC: Overseas Takeover Ensures National Energy Security), 19 February.

Zhongguo Haiyou Xinwen Zhongxin (CNOOC News Center), 2012, "Nengyuan gongying: Youqi gongying zongliang fanbei" (Energy Supply: Total Oil and Gas Supplies Doubled), 10 May, http://www.cnooc.com.cn/data/html/news/2012-05-10/chinese/308129.html.

Zhongguo Jingji Zhoukan (China Economic Weekly), 2011, "Jiemi Zhongguo zhanlue shiyou chubei: 2020 nian ti zhi 8500 wandun" (Decipher China's SPR: To Be Increased to 85 Mt), 18 January.

Zhongguo Qiyejia (*China Entrepreneur*), 2005, "Shougou Younike, Zhonghaiyou zai Fu Chengyu shidai de maoxian zhi lu" (Acquiring Unocal, CNOOC's Risky Tour Under the Leadership of Fu Chengyu), 22 July.

Zhongguo shiyou shangwu (Oil China), 2005, "Zhongguo jian zhanlue shiyou chubei, yiqi gongcheng yi zhankai" (China Will Establish Strategic Petroleum Reserve, the Initial Project Has Been Unfolded), 9 June, http://www.oilchina.com/xxzx/xl.jsp?bsm=042A4FC9F.000151F9.751F&db=yw.

Zhongguo Xinwen wang (China News Net), 2006, "Behind the Curtain of Publishing China's Green GDP: Some Localities Requested Not to

Publish the Results," 11 September, http://www.chinanews.com/other/news/2006/09-11/787916.shtml.
Zhongguo Wang (China.org.cn), 2004, "Zhongguo jianli zhanlue shiyou chubei tixi weihu guojia shiyou anquan" (China Constructs SPR to Preserve National Oil Security), September, http://www.china.org.cn/chinese/2004/Sep/668361.htm.
Zhou, Ting, 2010, "Nengyuan Jingji guize sheng bian, 'shi'erwu' tianranqi xiaofei bili jiang fanfang" (Energy Economic Rules Changed, the Proportion of Natural Gas Consumption Will Be Doubled During "the Twelfth Five-Year" Periods), *Zhongguo Zhengquan Bao* (China Securities Times), 3 July.

Websites for Energy News, Data, & Papers

Alexander's Gas & Oil Connections: http://www.gasandoil.com/
Cambridge Energy Research Associates: http://www.cera.com/aspx/cda/publicl/home/home.aspx
Center for the Advancement of Energy Markets: http://www.caem.org/
Energy Efficiency and Renewable Energy Network, DOE, USA: http://www.eren.doe.gov/
EAI (Official Energy Statistics from the US Government): www.eia.doe.gov
Institute of Energy Economics of Japan: www.eneken.ieej.or.jp/en
International Association for Energy Economics: http://www.iaee.org/en/index.aspx
IEA: http://www.iea.org
Platts: http://www.platts.com/
Resources For the Future: http://www.rff.org/
The Baker Institute Energy Forum: http://www.rice.edu/energy/
The Energy Institute: http://www.energyinst.org.uk/
The Oxford Institute for Energy Studies: http://www.oxfordenergy.org/
United Nations Environment Programme: http://www.unep.org
WEC, http://www.worldenergy.org/wec-geis/publications/reports/ser/coal/coal.asp
World Energy Council: www.worldenergy.org
World Energy News: http://www.worldenergynews.com/
World Resources Institute: http://www.wri.org/

Chinese Newspaper

Beijing Chenbao: Beijing Morning Post
Beijing Qingnian Bao: Beijing Youth Daily
Beijing Ribao: Beijing Daily

Beijing zhoubao: Beijing Weekly
Caijing Jie: Money China
Caijing Shibao: Business Post
Caijing: Finance
China Economic Daily
China Industry Daily News
China Oil & Gas
China Securities Bulletin
Diyi Caijing Ribao: First Finance Daily
Dongfang Xinbang
Guoji Jingrong Bao: International Finance News
Guoji Shangbao: International Business
Hong Kong AFP
Huanqiu Caijing: Global Finance and Economics
Jiefangjun Bao: Liberation Army Daily
Jingji Cankao Bao: Economic Reference News
Jingji Guancha Bao: Economic Observer
Jingji Ribao: Economic Daily
Jingji yanjiu cankao: Economic Research Reference
Keji Shibao: Science and Technology Times
Nanfang Zhoumo: Southern Weekend
Renmin Ribao: People's Daily
Shanghai Zhengquan Bao: Shanghai Securities News
Shenghuo Zhoukang: Life Weekly
Shenzhen Ribao: Shenzhen Economic Daily
Shijie Zhishi: World Knowledge
Shiji Jingji Baodao: 21st Century Economic Report
Shiji Jingji Daobao: 21st Century Economic Herald
Shiyou Shangbao: Oil Business News
South China Morning Post
Ta Kung Pao
Wenhuibao
Xinhua Daily Telegraph
Xinhua News Agency
Xinwen Chenbao: Shanghai Morning Post
Xinxi Shibao: Information Times
Zhongguo Gaige Bao: China Reform News
Zhongguo Gongshang Bao: China Industry and Commerce Times
Zhongguo Gongshang Shibao: China Business Times
Zhongguo Gongye Bao: China Industry News
Zhongguo Jingji Daobao: China Economic Herald
Zhongguo Jingji Shibao: China Economic Times

Zhongguo Jingyin Bao: China Business
Zhongguo Kuangye Bao: China Mining News
Zhongguo Maoyi Bao: China Trade News
Zhongguo Meitan Bao: China Coal News
Zhongguo Qingnian Bao: China Youth Daily
Zhongguo QiYe Bao: China Enterprise News
Zhongguo Qiyejia: China Entrepreneur
Zhongguo Ribao: China Daily
Zhongguo Shiyou Bao: China Oil News
Zhongguo Shiyou he Huagong: China Petroleum and Chemical Industries
Zhongguo Shiyou Shangye Wang: China Oil Business Network
Zhongguo Shiyou: China Oil
Zhongguo Xinwen Zhoukang: China News Weekly
Zhongguo Zhengquan Bao: China Securities News
Zhong Xinwen she: China News Agency

Chinese Major Oil and Gas Companies

China National Petroleum Corporation: www.cnpc.com.cn
China Petrochemical Corporation: www.sinopecgroup.com.cn
China Petroleum & Chemical Corporation: www.sinopec.com.cn
China National Offshore Oil Corporation: www.cnooc.com.cn
China National Chemicals Import and Export Corporation: www.sinochem.com
PetroChina Company Limited: www.petrochina.com.cn

Major Websites for Chinese Energy News

China Coal Information Network: www.coalinfo.net.cn
China Economy: http://www.ce.cn
Phoenixtv: http://www.phoenixtv.com
Shiyou Shangbao: http://www.pbnews.com.cn/
Shiyou Xinxi (*Petro Information*): http://www.infopetro.com.cn
Xiqi dong shu wang: www.westgas.com
Zhongguo Shiyou he Huaxue Gongye Xiehui: www.cpcia.org.cn
Zhongguo shiyou shangwu (Oil China), http://www.oilchina.com
Zhongguo Xin Nengyuan Wang: www.newenergy.org.cn
Zhongguo Xin Nengyuan yu Kezaisheng Nengyuan: www.crein.org.cn
Zhongguo zaixian: www.cn1n.com
Zhonggup Nengyuan Wang: www.china5e.com
Zhongyou wang: www.oilnews.com.cn

Foreign Newspaper

APS Review Oil Market Trends
Asia Times
Asian Wall Street Journal
Asiaweek
BBC Monitoring Asia Pacific
BBC Monitoring Former Soviet Union
China Economic Review
China Business Information Network
Financial Times
Business Week
Business Weekly
International Herald
New York Times
Washington Post
Dow Jones Energy Sevice
Economist
Economist Intelligence Unit—Executive Briefing
Economist Intelligence Unit—Viewswire
Energy Compass
Energy Economist
Far Eastern Economic Review
FinanceAsia
Fortune
Interfax China Business News
International Herald Tribune
Jane's Intelligence Review
Jiji Press English News Service
Hart's Asian Petroleum News
Hart's Asian Petroleum Monitor
Lianhe Zaobao
Los Angeles Times
Middle East Economic Survey
Mosnews Information Service
Newsweek International
Offshore
Oil & Gas Investor
Oil & Gas Journal
Oil Daily
OPECNA News Service
Petroleum Economist
Petroleum Intelligence Weekly

Reuters
Straits Times
The Guardian
The San Francisco Chronicle
Time Asia
The Washington Post
Time Europe
Wall Street Journal
Weekly Gas Intelligence
World Sources Online
World Gas Intelligence

Index

S. Chen, *China's Approach to Energy Security*,
https://doi.org/10.1007/978-981-99-3573-4

Kolibri 360 GmbH
Ferdinand-Jühlke-Straße 7
99095 Erfurt, Deutschland
produktsicherheit@kolibri360.de